DAY HIKING

Eastern
Washington

Placid Swan Lake in the Okanogan Highlands

Previous Page: White Bluffs, Hanford Reach National Monument

Looking toward the Pend Oreille River valley from Sherlock Peak ridge

Big Rock is prominent in the Dishman Hills Conservation Area.

Tall pines and firs silhouetted in evening light on the Shedroof Divide

*Fawn hunkered
in meadows
on Clackamas
Mountain*

*Opposite:
Palouse River
careening through
a basalt canyon*

Blue Mountain's forest fires scorched the edges of Middle Point Ridge.

Sunset at the Crowell Ridge trailhead below Sullivan Mountain Lookout

There's gold in them thar hills (in October) in the Kettles.

DAY HIKING

Eastern Washington

Kettles–Selkirks/Columbia Plateau/Blue Mountains

**by Rich Landers
& Craig Romano**

THE MOUNTAINEERS BOOKS

THE MOUNTAINEERS BOOKS
*is the nonprofit publishing arm of The Mountaineers, an
organization founded in 1906 and dedicated to the exploration,
preservation, and enjoyment of outdoor and wilderness areas.*

1001 SW Klickitat Way, Suite 201, Seattle, WA 98134

© 2013 by Rich Landers and Craig Romano

First edition, 2013

Distributed in the United Kingdom by Cordee, www.cordee.co.uk

Manufactured in the United States of America

Copy Editor: Julie Van Pelt
Book Design: The Mountaineers Books
Cover design and layout: Jennifer Shontz, www.redshoedesign.com
Cartographer: Pease Press Cartography
All photographs by authors unless otherwise noted.

Cover photograph: *Gypsy Peak, Eastern Washington's highest summit, as seen from the Salmo Divide Trail*
    (Photo by Craig Romano)
Frontispiece: *Copper Butte carpeted with wildflowers* (Photo by Craig Romano)

Library of Congress Cataloging-in-Publication Data
Landers, Rich, 1953–
    Day hiking Eastern Washington : Kettles–Selkirks, Columbia Plateau,
Blue Mountains / by Rich Landers and Craig Romano.
        p.   cm.
    Includes index.
    ISBN 978-1-59485-494-1 (pbk)—ISBN 978-1-59485-495-8 (ebook)
1. Hiking—Washington (State), Eastern—Guidebooks. 2. Washington
(State), Eastern—Guidebooks. I. Romano, Craig. II. Title.
    GV199.42.W2L36 2013
    796.51097971—dc23   2012042303

Maps shown in this book were produced using National Geographic's TOPO!
software. For more information, go to www.nationalgeographic.com/topo.

ISBN (paperback): 978-1-59485-494-1
ISBN (ebook): 978-1-59485-495-8

Certified Chain of Custody
Promoting Sustainable Forestry
www.sfiprogram.org
SFI-01268

SFI label applies to text stock

Table of Contents

Around Spokane

Columbia Plateau

BUT WAIT! THERE'S MORE!
Still need more hikes? Find information about access to twenty-five additional hikes on
The Mountaineers Books' website (www.mountaineersbooks.org/DHEWBonus), including:

In the Okanogan Highlands:
- McLoughlin Canyon
- Island Park
- Fourth of July Ridge
- Ten Mile Trail
- Long Lake

In the Kettle River Range:
- Profanity Trail

In the Selkirk Mountains:
- Pierre Lake Trail
- Newport Wolf Trails
- Halliday Trail
- Silver Creek Trails

In the Columbia Plateau:
- Umatilla Rock
- Blythe and Chukar Lake
- Saddle Mountain

Around Spokane:
- McKenzie Conservation Area
- Glenrose Conservation Area
- Dwight Merkel Trail
- Spokane River Centennial Trail
- West Branch Little Spokane River
  Wildlife Area
- Medical and West Medical Lakes
- Columbia Plateau Trail
- Sacajawea State Park
- Badger Mountain (Waterville
  Plateau)
- Odessa Craters

In the Palouse:
- Lyons Ferry
- Bill Chipman Palouse Trail

LEGEND

==84==	Interstate Highway	**P**	Parking
=197=	US Highway	▲	Campground/Campsite
=14=	State Highway	■	Building/Landmark
———	Secondary Road	开	Picnic Area
=======	Unpaved Road	▲	Summit
==24==	Forest Road	)(	Pass
---------	Hiking Route	～	River/Stream
••••••••	Off-Trail Route	～#～	Falls
- - - - -	Other Trail	▰	Lake
•••••••••	Other Off-Trail	⚓	Wetland/Marsh
—•—•—	Wilderness Boundary	)(	Bridge
1	Hike Number	⊶	Gate
T	Trailhead	且	Lookout
Ⓣ	Alternate Trailhead	◤	Ranger Station/Entrance Station

Hikes at a Glance

HIKE	DISTANCE (ROUND-TRIP)	DIFFICULTY	HIKABLE EARLY SEASON	KID-FRIENDLY	DOG-FRIENDLY
COLUMBIA HIGHLANDS: OKANOGAN HIGHLANDS					
1. Similkameen Trail	7.2 miles	1	•	•	•
2. Whistler Canyon and Frog Pond	5.1 miles	2	•	•	
3. Mount Bonaparte via Antoine Trail	15.2 miles	5			•
4. Mount Bonaparte via South Side Trail	10.8 miles	3			•
5. Strawberry Mountain	3.4 miles	2		•	•
6. Big Tree Botanical Area	2.8 miles	1		•	•
7. Beth and Beaver Lakes	3.8 miles	2		•	•
8. Virginia Lilly Trail	3.5 miles	2		•	•
9. Pipsissewa Trail	4.2 miles	3		•	•
10. Clackamas Mountain	9.4 miles	3		•	•
11. Maple Mountain	5.2 miles	3			•
12. Fir Mountain	5.2 miles	4			•
13. Swan Lake and Swan Butte	3.1 miles	2		•	•
14. Golden Tiger Pathway	4.6 miles	1	•	•	•
15. Curlew Lake Nature Trail	1.6 miles	1	•	•	•
KETTLE RIVER RANGE					
16. Gibraltar Trail	3.2 miles	2		•	•
17. Thirteenmile Canyon	9 miles	3			•
18. Thirteenmile Mountain	9.2 miles	3			•
19. Edds and Bald Mountains	10.6 miles	4			•
20. Snow Peak Cabin	6.4 miles	3		•	•
21. Sherman Peak	6 miles	3		•	•
22. Barnaby Buttes	7.4 miles	3		•	•
23. White Mountain	6.8 miles	3		•	•
24. Columbia Mountain	8 miles	3		•	•
25. Jungle Hill	8 miles	4		•	•
26. Wapaloosie Mountain	6 miles	3		•	•
27. Copper Butte via Marcus Trail	9.6 miles	4			•
28. Copper Butte via Old Stage Trail	6 miles	3		•	•
29. Midnight Mountain	10.6 miles	3			•
30. Mount Leona	6 miles	3			•
31. Ryan Cabin–Stickpin Loop	6.4 miles	3			•
32. Sentinel Butte	7 miles	2			•

WILD-FLOWERS	OLD GROWTH	FISHING	BIRD-WATCH-ING	WILDERNESS	HISTORICAL	WHEEL-CHAIR-ACCESS	BIKES OK	CAR CAMP NEAR	BACK-PACKING
•		•	•		•	•	•		
•			•						•
	•				•		•		•
•					•		•	•	•
					•		•	•	
	•					partial		•	
		•	•				•	•	
•			•					•	
•							•	•	
•	•								•
•	•								•
•					•				
•			•		•			•	
•					•	•	•		
•			•	•				•	
•							•		
•	•				•		•	•	•
•	•				•		•	•	•
•							•		•
•							•		•
•							•	•	•
•					•		•		•
•					•		•		
•					•		•	•	•
•							•	•	•
•							•	•	
•					•		•		•
•					•		•	•	
•	•				•		•	•	•
•							•		
•	•				•		•	•	•
	•						•	•	

HIKE	DISTANCE (ROUND-TRIP)	DIFFICULTY	HIKABLE EARLY SEASON	KID-FRIENDLY	DOG-FRIENDLY
33. Taylor Ridge	5.8 miles	2		•	•
34. US Mountain	5.8 miles	3			•
35. King Mountain	7.4 miles	3			•
36. Sherman Creek and Log Flume Heritage Site	1.6 miles	1	•	•	•
37. Emerald Lake and Hoodoo Canyon	6.2 miles	2		•	•
38. Old Kettle Falls Trail	2.6 miles	1	•	•	•
SELKIRK MOUNTAINS					
39. Frater Lake	1.8 miles	1		•	•
40. Big Meadow Lake	2.8 miles	2		•	•
41. Rogers Mountain and Gillette Ridge	5 miles	3			•
42. Sherlock Peak	8.2 miles	3			
43. Abercrombie Mountain	7.3 miles	3			•
44. Mill Butte	4.2 miles	2	•	•	•
45. McDowell Lake	1.3 miles	1	•	•	
46. Sullivan Mill Pond	2 miles	2		•	•
47. Elk Creek Falls	2.1 miles	2		•	•
48. Red Bluff	9 miles	3			•
49. Sullivan Lake Shoreline	4.6 miles	3		•	•
50. Hall Mountain	14 miles	4			•
51. Crowell Ridge	8.4 miles	3			
52. Gypsy Peak	6.5 miles	5			
53. Salmo River	6 miles	3			•
54. Shedroof Mountain (Shedroof Divide)	8.8 miles	4			
55. Thunder Creek and Mountain (Shedroof Divide)	14.4 miles	5			•
56. Mankato Mountain (Shedroof Divide)	7 miles	3			
57. Grassy Top Mountain	7.8 miles	3			
58. Roosevelt Grove of Ancient Cedars	2.5 miles	2		•	•
59. Little Grass Mountain	10.5 miles	5			•
60. Kalispell Rock	5.6 miles	3			•
61. Hungry Mountain	8.4 miles	3			
62. Bead Lake	11.2 miles	3	•	•	•
63. Pend Oreille County Park	4.1 miles	3	•	•	•
64. Mount Spokane Summit	2.4 miles	3		•	•
65. Day Mountain	6 miles	2		•	•
66. Burping Brook Basin	6.2 miles	3		•	•
67. Quartz Mountain	5.5 miles	2		•	•

WILD-FLOWERS	OLD GROWTH	FISHING	BIRD-WATCH-ING	WILDERNESS	HISTORICAL	WHEEL-CHAIR-ACCESS	BIKES OK	CAR CAMP NEAR	BACK-PACKING
•					•		•	•	
•							•	•	
							•	•	
•		•	•		•	•		•	
•	•	•	•				•	•	
•		•	•		•	•		•	
		•	•				•	•	
		•	•		•	partial		•	
•					•		•		
•							•	•	•
•			•		•			•	
•			•					•	
•		•	•			partial		•	
		•			•	partial		•	
•			•					•	
•	•						•	•	•
		•						•	•
•		•			•		•	•	•
				•	•			•	•
•			•					•	•
•	•			•	•			•	•
				•	•			•	•
	•			•	•			•	•
•				•				•	•
					•		•	•	
	•				•			•	
•	•				•			•	•
		•			•		•	•	
							•		
	•	•							•
•			•				•	•	
		•			•		•	•	
•		•			•		•	•	
•							•	•	
•					•		•	•	

HIKE	DISTANCE (ROUND-TRIP)	DIFFICULTY	HIKABLE EARLY SEASON	KID-FRIENDLY	DOG-FRIENDLY
AROUND SPOKANE					
68. Antoine Peak	6.8 miles	3			•
69. Liberty Lake	9 miles	3		•	•
70. Saltese Uplands	7.3 miles	3	•	•	•
71. Iller Creek and Rocks of Sharon	5.5 miles	3		•	•
72. Eagle Peak	4 miles	3	•	•	•
73. Beacon Hill	4.2 miles	3	•	•	•
74. Downtown Spokane Bridges	7.7 miles	2	•	•	
75. South Hill Bluff	3 miles	1	•	•	•
76. Fish Lake Trail	15 miles	1	•	•	•
77. James T. Slavin Conservation Area	5.5 miles	2	•	•	•
78. Palisades Park	4.2 miles	3	•	•	•
79. T.J. Meenach Bridge–Fort George Wright (Spokane River)	4.3 miles	2	•	•	•
80. Fort George Wright–Bowl and Pitcher (Spokane River)	6.8 miles	3	•	•	•
81. Bowl and Pitcher (Spokane River)	5.1 miles	3	•	•	•
82. Deep Creek Canyon	4.6 miles	4			•
83. Indian Painted Rocks–Saint George's School (Little Spokane River)	4.7 miles	3	•	•	
84. Little Spokane River Overlook	6.4 miles	3		•	
85. McLellan Conservation Area	3.8 miles	3	•		•
COLUMBIA PLATEAU					
86. Turnbull National Wildlife Refuge Auto Tour Trails	3 miles	1	•	•	•
87. Pine Lakes	6 miles	3	•	•	
88. Frenchman Coulee	4 miles	2	•	•	•
89. Quincy Lakes	4.4/6 miles	2/3	•	•	•
90. Beezley Hills	2.2 miles	2	•	•	
91. Steamboat Rock	3.2 miles	2	•		
92. Northrup Canyon	6.2 miles	2	•	•	•
93. Fort Spokane	2.5 miles	1	•	•	
94. Crab Creek (Columbia National Wildlife Refuge)	2.6 miles	1	•	•	
95. Frog Lake	3 miles	2	•	•	
96. Hanford Reach North	7 miles	3	•		
97. Hanford Reach South	5.4 miles	3	•		
98. Badger Mountain	4.4 miles	2	•	•	•

WILD-FLOWERS	OLD GROWTH	FISHING	BIRD-WATCH-ING	WILDERNESS	HISTORICAL	WHEEL-CHAIR-ACCESS	BIKES OK	CAR CAMP NEAR	BACK-PACKING
•			•				•		
	•	•	•				•	•	
•			•				•		
•			•				•		
•			•						
•							•		
		•			•	partial	•		
•			•				•		
			•		•	•	•		
•			•						
•					•	partial	•		
		•				partial	•		
•		•			•	partial	•	•	
		•				partial	•	•	
•			•		•	partial	•		
•			•						
•			•						
•			•						
•			•			partial			
•			•			partial			
•			•						
•		•	•						•
•			•						
•		•	•		•			•	
•		•	•		•	partial		•	
		•	•		•	partial		•	
•			•					•	
•			•					•	
•		•	•		•				
•		•	•		•				
•							•		

HIKE	DISTANCE (ROUND-TRIP)	DIFFICULTY	HIKABLE EARLY SEASON	KID-FRIENDLY	DOG-FRIENDLY
99. Chamna Natural Preserve	3.6 miles	1	•	•	•
100. Amon Basin	2.3 miles	1	•	•	•
101. Bateman Island	2.4 miles	1	•	•	•
102. Burbank Slough Wildlife Trail	2.8 miles	1	•	•	
103. Juniper Dunes Wilderness	2 miles	2	•		
104. Z Lake	3.5 miles	3	•		•
105. Twin Lakes	10 miles	3	•		•
106. Lakeview Ranch	13 miles	3	•	•	•
107. Crab Creek	6 miles	3	•		•
108. Hog Canyon	5.4 miles	4	•		•
109. Fishtrap Lake	6.4 miles	2	•	•	•
110. Escure Ranch–Towell Falls	6.4 miles	2	•		•
PALOUSE HILLS					
111. Kamiak Butte	2.9 miles	2	•	•	
112. Palouse Falls	1.3 miles	2	•		
BLUE MOUNTAINS					
113. Lewis and Clark Trail State Park	0.8 mile	1	•	•	•
114. Mill Creek	5.2 miles	1	•	•	•
115. Deadman Peak	6 miles	3			
116. Middle Point Ridge	5.5 miles	3			•
117. Sawtooth Ridge	5.8 miles	3		•	•
118. Twin Buttes	3.8 miles	3		•	•
119. Grizzly Bear Ridge	8.2 miles	3			•
120. Oregon and West Buttes	6.1 miles	2		•	•
121. Panjab Loop	13.3 miles	4			•
122. Tucannon River	8 miles	2		•	•
123. Diamond Peak and Sheephead Corral	5.8 miles	3		•	•
124. North Fork Asotin Creek	20 miles	2	•	•	•
125. Puffer Butte	2.5 miles	2		•	•

WILD-FLOWERS	OLD GROWTH	FISHING	BIRD-WATCH-ING	WILDERNESS	HISTORICAL	WHEEL-CHAIR-ACCESS	BIKES OK	CAR CAMP NEAR	BACK-PACKING
		•	•						
•			•						
		•	•		•				
•		•	•			partial			
•			•	•					
		•	•						
•		•	•				•	•	
•			•			partial	•	•	•
•		•	•					•	
•		•	•				•	•	
•		•	•				•	•	
•		•	•				•	•	
•			•					•	
•			•					•	
		•	•		•			•	
		•	•		•	partial	partial		
•	•				•		•	•	
								•	
•	•			•				•	•
	•				•			•	•
	•				•			•	•
•				•	•			•	•
•	•			•				•	•
	•	•						•	•
•				•	•			•	
			•				•	•	•
•			•		•			•	

Acknowledgments

Working on *Day Hiking Eastern Washington* was fun, exciting, and a lot of hard work. I couldn't have finished this project without the help and support of the following people. A big thanks to my co-author Rich Landers for bringing me onboard. It has been an honor working with you. A big thanks too to all the great people at Mountaineers Books; especially publisher Helen Cherullo, editor in chief Kate Rogers, and project manager Mary Metz for allowing us to hike all over Eastern Washington!

I want to especially acknowledge once again, my editor, Julie Van Pelt. I have worked with her on all my Day Hiking books and I feel that we have hiked the state together. Your professionalism and attention to detail has greatly contributed to making this book a finer volume.

While I spent a lot of time in my tent and the back of my pickup researching this book, it was nice to know that in Republic, I had a "second home." A big thanks to Kathy Ciais of the Northern Inn for setting me up with a comfortable base camp in town!

I want to thank the folks that accompanied me on the trail while researching this book: Alicia Glass, Ellen Picken, Joe Theisen, and especially Aaron Theisen. Aaron, you have been a vast source of knowledge on Eastern Washington and your love of the Kettles rivals mine! I look forward to working with you on an upcoming book!

I want to thank God for once again watching over me while on the trail. And lastly, but most importantly, I want to thank my loving wife, Heather, for supporting me while I worked on yet another guidebook. Thanks for hiking with me too, to some of the special places in this book. The Kettles are our mountains!

—*Craig Romano*

In the Spokane area, special thanks for help from the Spokane Mountaineers, Inland Northwest Hikers, and fire lookout historian Ray Kresek.

—*Rich Landers*

Preface

Day hiking is the root of all outdoor exploration. Before humans backpacked, rode bikes, toured on skis, launched ships, and took off in airplanes, they day hiked. Craig Romano and I explored all those modes of travel before joining to research and write this guidebook involving our most basic travel instinct. When we first met over coffee to chart a collaboration, we discovered we had similar passions for muscle-powered exploration. We're veterans of backpacking adventures in the Northwest, North America, and beyond. Both of us have ridden our bicycles across the United States, climbed the region's tallest mountains, and paddled extensively. We've done as much dirtbagging and sleeping on the ground as some critters that live in the forest.

Most important, both of us settled in the Northwest with an obsession for exploring outback trails—and taking notes along the way. Writing is our profession. Our craft is the vehicle for sharing the sweat equity we've invested in researching worthwhile routes and encouraging conservation of the land and water around them. We consider those our major qualifications, aside from being on our wives' top ten list for handsome men. Promoting day hiking is our way of exposing Eastern Washington's outdoor treasures to the widest base of people, young and old, whether they're trail veterans or taking their first steps out of town. We have enjoyed working together to share this with you.

—*Rich Landers*

It was Rich Landers' *100 Hikes in the Inland Northwest* that first lured me east of the Cascades in search of trails in 1989 (a mere four months after settling in Washington)—and I've been an Eastern Washington disciple ever since! The Salmo-Priest Wilderness, Hanford Reach, Kettle River Range, and Blue Mountains rank right up there in my all-time hiking greats list with Mount Rainier, the Olympic Peninsula, and the Columbia River Gorge.

Northeastern Washington in particular is a very special place to me. Curlew Lake State Park in Ferry County was the first place I went camping with a young woman I had met at the University of Washington (sorry Cougs). The Kettles became our mountains and that woman became my wife ten years later at Curlew Lake State Park.

The Pacific Northwest is blessed with an abundance of natural areas rife with excellent hiking trails—the regions of Eastern Washington among them. But Eastern Washington often delivers more of a wilderness experience than the national parks and wilderness areas of the Cascades. In Eastern Washington, grizzlies, wolves, caribou, wolverines, and lynx still roam the backcountry. Just knowing these majestic megafauna are out there with me is one of the best attributes of hiking this area.

Rich and I are excited to share these trails with you. I am honored to be working with the person who first introduced me to the region. Now, with Rich's help, I'm paying it forward.

—*Craig Romano*

Wetlands have been restored at the James T. Slavin Conservation Area near Spokane.

Introduction

Day hiking has an attractive cost-benefit ratio compared with other means of venturing outdoors. It requires a minimal investment in equipment for traveling the widest variety of routes. Since day hikers often need little time for packing and planning, they have more time and incentive to discover new places. Carrying less weight, you can cover more ground and tackle more elevation than you could carrying a heavy backpack—with a lower toll on your knees and other body parts. Day hikers are more likely than bikers, paddlers, and backpackers to "stop and smell the roses" or snap photos, identify a new bird species through binoculars, investigate a track or scat, take a side trail, or pause to harvest a quart of huckleberries.

Bottom line: Day hiking is so cheap and uncomplicated, even doubters are left with few excuses to stay inside. A gray sky and drizzle don't have to be deterrents, since a day hiker can enjoy the vibrant colors of a wet landscape with the promise of heading back to the comfort of a car camp, restaurant, or home. For many people—perhaps all of us at one time or another—this is the way to go.

Day hiking is genuinely good low-impact exercise for the body and soul. It's equally rewarding solo or with a group; a chance to lighten up for a few hours or reflect on what's truly important. As America grows more urban and attached to electronics, day hiking is an attractive antidote to the temptation of being sedentary. Families in particular can take advantage of day hiking within limited budgets and busy schedules while still confronting the "nature deficit syndrome" afflicting our nation's youth.

This book is written to help you discover good walking routes that are virtually under your nose as well as those in choice places you may not have considered. For example, the route connecting eighteen bridges over the Spokane River in downtown Spokane (Hike 74) is so inspirational and handy for Spokane residents, coauthor Rich Landers and his wife annually invite friends to join them on this hike to celebrate their wedding anniversary. Badger Mountain, Chamna Natural Preserve, Amon Basin, and Bateman Island (Hikes 98–101) are located within the Tri-Cities—a place many hikers wouldn't immediately consider for day hiking.

On the other hand, serious backcountry isn't far away from anyone on the east side of the state. Day hikers with a yen to get away from it all will find fascinating one-day routes in the 7140-acre Juniper Dunes Wilderness just outside of Pasco (Hike 103). Or head to the remote, extreme northeast corner of the state into the 41,335-acre Salmo-Priest Wilderness. One highly rated route leads to a challenging scramble to the top of Gypsy Peak (Hike 52), the highest point in Eastern Washington.

This book also zeroes in on the best day hikes into more than 200,000 acres of roadless areas proposed for wilderness designation in the Okanogan-Wenatchee and Colville National Forests. Check out the Twin Sisters, Profanity, Snow-Bald, and Thirteenmile Canyon roadless areas of the Kettle River Range (Hikes 17–35) and see why proponents consider them wilderness-worthy.

We have hiked these regions for years and still discovered new, exciting routes while researching this book. Eastern Washington is big on remote places.

The hikes in this guidebook are those you can do in a day. The hikes can be shortened or extended, and many can be converted into overnighters and explored as introductions to longer trips. Be our guests! Let these featured trips be your springboard to the best day hikes in the wide-ranging landscape of Eastern Washington, from the sagebrush-steppe flats and canyons of the Columbia Plateau to lush forests and fire lookout sites of past and present. You'll find something for every season of the year. Some of the hikes are in or near towns such as the Tri-Cities, Walla Walla, Lewiston-Clarkston, Republic, and Colville. One group of treks (Hikes 68–85) highlights the natural areas being protected in and near Spokane—Washington's second-largest city.

Choose from hikes that are perfect for children, ideal for old friends, welcoming to dogs, or notably splendid with birds or wildflowers. Explore trails of historical relevance or those of special interest to waterfall connoisseurs. Many hikes are likely places for observing wildlife. In time, these experiences will connect you with trails that lead to where you've never been before—to the top of a mountain or another sort of high point in your life. Ultimately, we hope you find a connection with the land surrounding these routes too.

USING THIS BOOK

The Day Hiking guidebooks were developed to be easy to use while still providing enough detail to help you explore a region. They include all the information you need to find and enjoy the hikes but leave enough room for you to make your own discoveries. We

have hiked every mile of trail described in *Day Hiking Eastern Washington* so you can follow the directions and advice with confidence. However, conditions can change. More on that later in this introduction.

What the Ratings Mean

Each hike starts with two subjective ratings: a rating of 1 to 5 stars for overall appeal, and a numerical score of 1 to 5 for a route's difficulty. This is purely subjective and based on our impressions of each route, though the assessments do follow a formula of sorts.

The overall **rating** is based on scenic beauty, natural wonder, and other unique qualities, such as solitude potential and wildlife-viewing opportunities.

***** Unmatched hiking adventure, great scenic beauty, and wonderful trail experience

**** Excellent experience, sure to please all

*** A great hike, with one or more fabulous features to enjoy

** May lack the "killer view" but offers lots of little moments to enjoy

* Worth doing as a refreshing walk, especially if you're in the neighborhood

The **difficulty** score is based on trail length, overall elevation gain, steepness, and trail conditions. Generally, trails that are rated more difficult (4 or 5) are longer and steeper than average. But it's not a simple equation. A short, steep trail over talus slopes may be rated 5 while a long, smooth trail with little elevation gain may be rated 2.

5 Extremely difficult: Excessive elevation gain and/or more than 5 miles one-way

4 Difficult: Some steep sections, possibly rough or poorly maintained trail

3 Moderate: A good workout but no real problems

2 Moderately easy: Relatively flat or short route with good trail

1 Easy: A relaxing stroll in the woods

To help explain the difficulty scores, you'll also find **round-trip mileage** (unless otherwise noted as one-way), total **elevation gain**, and **high point**. While we have measured the hikes using GPS and have consulted maps, a trip's distance can vary depending on how you customize the route. The elevation gain measures the *cumulative* gain and loss you'll encounter on a trip, accounting for all significant changes in elevation along the way. As for the trip's high point, it's worth noting that not all high points are at the end of the trail—a route may run over a high ridge before dropping to a lake basin, for instance.

The recommended **season** is a tool to help you choose a hike. Many trails can be enjoyed from the time they lose their winter snowpack right up until they're buried in fresh snow the following fall. But snowpacks vary from year to year, so a trail that's open in May one year may be snow-covered until July the next. The hiking season for each trail is an estimate. Contact land managers for current conditions.

The **maps** noted for each hike are usually 7.5-minute USGS topographical maps. However, we also list maps available from local groups, agencies, or national forests. USGS topo maps—highly recommended for hikes in remote areas—are available online and from some retail stores. The **contact** listed for each hike should have information about localized maps. Each hike lists the area's governing agency, along with website and/or phone number, so you can get current access and trail conditions. **Notes** for each

trip detail things like permits required, road conditions, possible hazards, and seasonal closures. Trailhead **GPS coordinates** are provided to help get you to the trail—and back to the car should you wander off-trail.

Finally, **icons** at the start of each hike give a quick overview of what each trail has to offer:

 Kid-friendly

 Dog-friendly

 Exceptional wildflowers in season

 Exceptional waterfalls

 Exceptional old growth

 Fishing options

 Bird-watching

🏠 Historical relevance

❌ Endangered trail (threatened with loss or closure)

⭐ Saved trail (rescued from permanent loss)

The route descriptions tell you what might be found on the hike, including geographic features, scenic potential, flora and fauna, and more. Thorough driving directions from the nearest large town or geographic feature will get you to the trailhead. Options for extending your trip round out many hikes.

PERMITS, REGULATIONS, AND FEES

Hikers have a responsibility to know and abide by regulations governing the areas they explore. As our public lands have

Beargrass blooms along Eagle Crest Trail in the Mount Spokane Nordic skiing area.

become increasingly popular, and as both state and federal funding have declined, regulations and permits have become components in managing our natural heritage. The US Forest Service, National Park Service, Washington State Parks, and other land managers have set sometimes complex regulations governing the use of these lands.

Federal lands: National forests in Eastern Washington may or may not charge parking fees at trailheads. Most Umatilla and Okanogan-Wenatchee National Forest parking areas require that vehicles display a Northwest Forest Pass or federal equivalent (like the America the Beautiful Pass described below). The Colville National Forest does not require the Northwest Forest Pass, except at one site. The Northwest Forest Pass sells for $5 a day or $30 for an annual pass that's good throughout Washington and Oregon.

Hikers who frequent national parks and forests should consider buying the annual America the Beautiful Pass (http://store.usgs .gov/pass) for $80. This pass grants the driver and three other adults in a vehicle access to all federal recreation sites that charge a day-use fee (children under sixteen are admitted free). These include national parks, national forests, national wildlife refuges, and Bureau of Land Management areas throughout the country. For example, without the American the Beautiful pass (or a federal Duck Stamp), visitors have to pay a $3 day-use vehicle entry fee to Turnbull National Wildlife Refuge (Hikes 86 and 87).

State lands: Washington State Parks and other state lands adopted the Discover Pass (www.discoverpass.wa.gov) for vehicle access in 2011. This is a political solution to keep the underfunded state parks system alive. Until lawmakers find another solution, a Discover Pass costs $10 per vehicle per day or $30 for up to two vehicles annually. Purchase the pass online or at many retail outlets or, better yet, from a state park office to avoid a $5 handling fee.

Local areas: Local parks, such as Liberty Lake County Park (Hike 69), may charge an entrance fee at certain times of year.

All required fees and permits (subject to change) are listed for each hike.

WHOSE LAND IS THIS?

Almost all of the hikes in this book are on public land. That is, they belong to you and the rest of the citizenry. What's confusing, however, is who exactly is in charge of this public trust. More than half a dozen different governing agencies manage lands described in this guide.

Most of the hikes are on land administered by the **US Forest Service**. A division of the Department of Agriculture, the Forest Service strives to "sustain the health, diversity, and productivity of the nation's forests and grasslands to meet the needs of present and future generations." The agency purports to do this under the notion of "multiple-use." However, supplying timber products, providing grazing allotments, managing wildlife habitat, and developing motorized and nonmotorized recreation options have a tendency to conflict with each other. Some of these uses may not exactly sustain the health of the forest either. Several areas within the forests featured in this book have been afforded stringent protections as federal wilderness (see "Untrammeled Eastern Washington" sidebar in the Blue Mountains section), barring development, roads, and motorized recreation.

The **US Bureau of Land Management** manages 245 million acres across the country, more than any other agency. Uses on these lands include development for energy, grazing, recreation, wildlife, and conservation. BLM areas featured in this book are off-limits to motorized recreation but open to limited livestock grazing.

The **National Wildlife Refuge System** is a network of lands and waters for the conservation, management, and, where appropriate, restoration of the fish, wildlife, and plant resources and their habitats. Recreation also is encouraged on most refuges, as well as limited hunting and fishing in some areas.

State and county park lands are managed primarily for recreation and preservation.

State Department of Natural Resources lands are managed primarily for timber harvest, with pockets of natural-area preserves.

State wildlife areas, overseen by the Department of Fish and Wildlife, are managed primarily for protecting habitat while providing access to wildlife-related recreation, including hunting and fishing.

Be aware of the agency that manages the land you'll be hiking on, for each agency has its own rules and fees. And remember, we have a say in how public lands are managed. Agencies have planning periods during which public participation can have a big impact.

—C. R.

WEATHER

Eastern Washington ranges from low elevations along the Snake and Columbia Rivers, through the open scablands, to high elevations in the Selkirk Mountains. You could experience the gamut, from T-shirt weather to a snow blizzard in a day's drive. The Juniper Dunes area near Pasco receives about 8 inches of rainfall a year, while the wet cedar forests in the Salmo-Priest Wilderness average around 50 inches of annual precipitation.

Summer storms build over Abercrombie and Hooknose Mountains.

Late February into June are premier times to find the Columbia Plateau snow-free, welcoming spring migrant birds, and blooming with wildflowers. The heat that bears down on the Channeled Scablands of the plateau starting in late June through August spurs on the wildflower bloom and huckleberry crop in the mountains. Trails in the higher elevations of the Columbia and Okanogan Highlands, the Selkirks, and the Blue Mountains aren't snow-free until June or early July. September and October are the months when all of Eastern Washington is accessible and weather conditions are generally most inviting across the board.

Generalities aside, short-term forecasts are key to planning the safest and most enjoyable trip. A high-pressure system could offer a week of premier weather in May, while a low-pressure system could present a week of wetness in June. We have experienced snow in the high country in August two days after the temperatures soared into the 90s.

Plan your hike according to your weather preference. But no matter where you hike in the region, the following should be standard procedure:

- Check the National Weather Service forecast for the region before you go, and plan accordingly.
- Pack raingear. Even in arid areas, being caught in a sudden rain and windstorm without adequate clothing can lead to hypothermia (loss of body temperature), which is deadly if not immediately treated. Most hiking fatalities related to hypothermia (exposure) occur during the milder months when hikers get caught in a sudden change of temperature accompanied by winds. Always carry extra clothing layers, including rain and wind protection.

BEFORE LIGHTNING STRIKES

Thunderstorms are common throughout Eastern Washington, especially during the summer. The lightning produced by these powerful storms poses a threat worth taking seriously. If you hear thunder, you're within striking distance.

Waste no time getting off summits or exposed ridges and away from water. Take shelter, but not under big trees or rock ledges. The taller an object is relative to its immediate surroundings, the more likely it is to be struck by lightning. Any tree can be a conductor, although hunkering in a grove of small trees or under a blowdown is a bit safer than being around an area's taller trees.

Afternoon is prime time for thunderstorms during summer, especially in higher elevations. Savvy hikers and climbers time ascents to the high country for early morning so they can retreat before noon from open alpine areas where lightning is more likely to pound. The safest place to be in a lightning storm is sitting in your vehicle.

If you're caught in an electrical storm, seek the lowest point in the area; crouch down, making minimal contact with the ground; and wait for the boomer to pass. Remove metal-framed packs and ditch the trekking poles! Wrap yourself in raingear or a tarp for protection from the wind and rain. No, a foam sleeping pad will not insulate you from lightning that strikes the ground.   —R. L.

Episodes of rain and snow also create conditions and hazards to consider. River and creek crossings can be extremely dangerous after periods of heavy rain or snowmelt. Always use caution and sound judgment when fording.

Snowfields left over from the previous winter's snowpack can be hazardous, especially for hikers who head into steep high-country slopes early in the hiking season. Depending on the severity of the past winter, and the weather conditions of the spring and early summer, some trails may not melt out until well into summer. In addition to treacherous footing and difficulties in routefinding, lingering snowfields can be prone to avalanches or slides. Use caution crossing them. You may need to review techniques for self-arrest.

Strong winds can be a concern anywhere in the region. Avoid hiking during high winds, which carry with them the hazards of falling trees and branches.

ROAD AND TRAIL CONDITIONS

Trails generally vary little year to year, but change can occur. A heavy storm can cause a river to jump its channel, washing out sections of a trail or access road in moments. Windstorms can blow down trees across trails by the hundreds, making paths unhikable. And snow can bury trails well into the summer. Avalanches, landslides, and forest fires can damage or obliterate trails. Lack of funding is also responsible for trail neglect and degradation.

On the other hand, some trails are created, improved or rerouted over the course of time. Groups such as the Washington Trails Association, Kettle Range Conservation Group, the Spokane Mountaineers, and friends groups for state parks and federal

Cedars border the gently graded trail into the Salmo River Basin.

refuges have been sources of countless hours of volunteer labor, helping local, state, and federal crews build and maintain trails in this book. These groups and more are listed at the end of the book to help you connect with them—and perhaps add some muscle power or other expertise to the cause.

Management decisions can have greater impacts than floods and fires. For example, as national forests have cut back on timber production for reasons ranging from watershed damage to political and market forces, many forest roads have been closed and some have been decommissioned (see Hike 59, Little Grass Mountain). This can be good—as in providing more solitude for a person willing to walk away from motor vehicles. In many cases, closed forest roads can become excellent hiking routes. In other cases, a closed road can be an inconvenience, adding distance to the approach. In the worst cases, abandoned roads wash out or grow over, cutting off access entirely.

Some trails are being neglected or abandoned because of budget shortfalls. In other cases, the usage of a trail might change from hiking to allowing motorized vehicles such as dirt bikes and ATVs. Only a few trails in this book are open to motorized vehicles, sometimes for short periods, such as at Towell Falls at Escure Ranch (Hike 110) or the Clackamas Mountain area (Hikes 10 and 11), where motorbikes are allowed but rarely encountered. The value of the routes override the possible disruption. Where motorized vehicles are prohibited, hikers still might share the route with mountain bikers and/or equestrians. Occasional conflicts are possible, but it's more productive for hikers to think of these other trail users as allies in the cause for more and better trails.

This guide includes several trails that are in danger of becoming unhikable because of threats from motorized use, access, or other issues. These Endangered Trails are marked with a special icon in this book. On the other side of the coin, we've had some great trail successes in recent years, thanks in large part to a massive volunteer movement spearheaded by statewide and local organizations. These Saved Trails are marked too, to help show that individual efforts do make a difference. As you enjoy these Saved Trails, stop to consider the contributions made by fellow hikers. And consider getting involved.

Each hike in this book lists the land manager's contact information so you can find out about current road and trail conditions prior to your trip.

WILDERNESS ETHICS

Ensuring the long-term survival of our trails and the wildlands they cross requires a group effort. To avoid fouling our own nest, hikers have nourished a "wilderness ethic" to leave the land as good as or better than we found it.

Instead of merely complying with no-litter rules, bring a bag and carve out time to pick up after others. Avoid creating unauthorized trails. Rest on rock and camp on bare ground when possible to avoid tramping down and killing vegetation in fragile dryland or alpine areas. Don't pollute streams or lakes with soaps or chemicals In the words of others who've boiled the ethic down: Take only pictures, leave only footprints.

Wilderness ethics, most of which apply to visiting all public open-space lands, rise from attitude and awareness rather than rules and regulations. The following are the accepted principles of the Leave No Trace concept:

Plan ahead and prepare: Know the regulations of the area you plan to visit. Call ahead for current conditions. Check the weather forecast. Bring proper gear. Plan for emergencies. Consider the abilities of your group. Assure that the group understands wilderness ethics. Protect food from bears and other critters to avoid turning them into nuisance—or dangerous—beggars.

Travel and camp on durable surfaces: Stay on the trail. Avoid tramping parallel trails to talk with a companion or avoid mud. Don't cut switchbacks. Picnic and camp on hard, dry surfaces such as rock, sand, gravel, or pine-needle duff rather than on vegetation or meadows. Take special care to avoid tramping or camping within 100 feet of backcountry stream or lake shorelines.

Dispose of waste properly: Pack out everything you pack in. Human food and trash is unhealthy for animals and leads to harmful habituation by animals to human presence and food. Bury human waste at least 100 feet from water sources, trails, or campsites. Use toilet paper sparingly and pack it out. A plastic bag confines odors effectively and double bagging it prevents any accidental contamination.

Leave what you find: Wildflowers, fossils, and other natural objects of beauty or interest should be left for others to discover and enjoy.

Minimize campfire impacts: Where fires are permitted, use existing fire rings if possible. Never cut live trees or branches for firewood. Most fires are not necessary, but if you must build one, be sure it's dead out when you leave. A small, thoughtfully built fire can be completely extinguished and the ashes removed or buried to leave no trace.

Respect wildlife: Never feed wild animals or leave food available to them. This is for your own good and the protection of those who follow, regardless of the size of the critter. Observe from a distance, for your safety as well as to prevent the animal from unnecessary exertion or danger. Keep pets under control so they don't disturb wildlife.

Be considerate of other visitors: Read on to find out how.

TRAIL ETIQUETTE

While wilderness ethics hone our respect for the land, trail etiquette steers us into balance with others we might see along the way. Common sense and courtesy will smooth out the possible bumps in any encounter. Beyond that, here are a few guidelines:

- **Right-of-way:** When meeting other hikers, the uphill group has the right-of-way. There are two general reasons for this. First, on steep ascents, hikers may be watching the trail and might not notice the approach of descending hikers until they're face-to-face. More importantly, it's easier for descending hikers to break their stride and step off the trail than it is for those who have gotten into a good, climbing rhythm. But by all means, if you're the uphill trekker and you wish to grant passage to oncoming hikers, go right ahead with this act of trail kindness.
- **Moving off-trail:** When meeting other user groups (like bicyclists and horseback riders), the hiker should yield. This is because hikers are more mobile and flexible than other users.
- **Encountering horses:** When meeting horseback riders, the hiker should step off the downhill side of the trail unless the terrain makes this difficult or dangerous. All hikers in a group should move to the same side of the trail. Remain visible and talk in a normal voice to the riders. This calms the horses. If hiking with a dog, keep your buddy very close and under control.
- **Hiking with dogs:** Hikers should have their dog on a leash or under very strict voice command at all times while on the trail. Some areas require dogs to be on-leash, such as state and local parks, national wildlife refuges, and Spokane County Conservation Areas. One of the most contentious issues in hiking circles is whether dogs should be allowed on trails. Some people are uncomfortable with loose dogs that rush toward them—and they may have had a bad experience to justify that. Respect their right to a

Rich Landers' English setter detects a dusky grouse on Crowell Ridge in the Salmo-Priest Wilderness.

dog-free space. On the other hand, a well-behaved leashed dog can help warm up these hikers to canine companions.

- **Never roll rocks off trails or cliffs:** You risk injuring someone or something below.

WATER

As a general rule, treat all backcountry water sources to avoid Giardia, waterborne parasites, and other aquatic nasties. Assume that all water is contaminated. Treating water can be as simple as boiling it, using an ultraviolet light purifier, chemically purifying it with iodine tablets, or pumping it through a water filter and purifier. Note: Pump units labeled as filters generally remove everything but viruses, which are too small to be filtered out. Pumps labeled as purifiers use a chemical element—usually iodine—to render viruses inactive after filtering out all the other bugs.

FISHING

Some hikers consider a fishing rod essential gear in their daypacks. A fishing icon at the start of a hike in this book indicates the trip will bring you into the realm of angling opportunity. However, fishing is a highly regulated sport, with seasons, gear restrictions, and catch limits that can vary by fish species as well as by stream or lake. Anglers age fifteen and older must have a Washington State fishing license. Regulations and requirements are spelled out in the Sport Fishing Rules pamphlet available at the Washington Department of Fish and Wildlife website (www.wdfw.wa.gov).

HIKING AMONG HUNTERS

Many public lands are opened to hunting. The season dates vary, but generally big-game hunting begins in early August and ends in December. While hiking in areas frequented by hunters, it's best to make

SAFETY AMONG PREDATORS: TOP FIVE TIPS

Several notable "hunters" roam Eastern Washington, including bears, cougars, and wolves. Like their human counterparts, they rarely pose a threat to hikers. Keep it that way by following the top five tips experts suggest:

1. **Bear spray** can be an effective deterrent in many tense wildlife encounters.
2. **Store food and garbage** in vehicles or other places where wildlife won't be attracted to it.
3. **Don't run** when confronted by bears, cougars, or wolves. This can trigger the predator's instinct to chase prey.
4. **Keep dogs leashed** and under control.
5. **Closely spaced groups** of four or more hikers are an effective deterrent in confrontations with bears, cougars, and wolves. A lone person far ahead or behind a group is at higher risk.

—R. L.

yourself visible by donning an orange cap and vest. If hiking with a dog, your buddy should wear an orange vest, too. The majority of hunters are responsible, decent folks (and conservationists who provide significant support for public lands), and you should have little concern when encountering them in the backcountry. Still, if being around outdoors-people schlepping rifles is unnerving to you, stick to hiking where hunting is prohibited, such as in national and state parks and county conservation areas.

WILDLIFE
The Bear Essentials

Eastern Washington's forested areas harbor a healthy population of black bears, especially the Columbia Highlands and Selkirk Mountains in the northeast and the Blue Mountains in the south. The Selkirks have the bonus of being home to some grizzly bears.

Most hikers consider themselves lucky to catch a glimpse of a bear's bottom as it reacts normally to human scent—by running away. But occasionally a bruin may want to get a look at you. In very rare cases, a bear may act aggressively. To avoid an un-bearable encounter, heed the following advice compiled from bear experts:

- **Respect a bear's need for space.** If you see a bear in the distance, make a wide detour around it. If that's not possible, leave the area.
- **Avoid direct eye contact** if you encounter a bear at close range, and, most important, **do not run.**
- **Talk in a low, calm manner** to the bear to help identify yourself as a human.
- **Wave your arms slowly** above your head to make yourself look taller.
- **Slowly move upwind** of the bear if you can do so without crowding the bear. The bear's strongest sense is its sense of smell, and if it can sniff you and identify you as human, it may retreat.
- **Know how to interpret bear actions.** A nervous bear will often rumble in its chest, clack its teeth, and "pop" its jaw. It may paw the ground and swing its head violently side to side. If the bear does this, watch it closely (without staring directly

at it). Continue to speak low and calmly.

- **If you cannot safely move away from the bear, and the animal does not flee,** try to scare it away by clapping your hands or yelling .

- **A bear may bluff-charge**—run at you but stop well before reaching you—to try and intimidate you. Resist the urge to run, as that would turn the bluff into a real charge and you will not be able to outrun the bear.

- **In the case of a bear attack**, a human without the benefit of bear spray should react differently depending on whether the bear is being predatory or defensive. **In the case of a predatory confron-tation** (more typical of the rare black bear that's stalking you), fight back aggressively. **In the case of a defensive confrontation** (more typical of grizzly encounters, especially sows with cubs or food caches), drop to the ground and play dead if contact is about to be made. Lie on your stomach, clasp hands behind your neck, and use your elbows and toes to avoid being rolled over. If the bear succeeds in rolling you over, keep rolling until you're on your stomach. Remain still and try not to struggle or scream. A defensive bear will stop attacking once it feels it has stopped the threat. Do not move until you're sure the bear has left the area.

THE BENEFITS OF BEAR SPRAY

Bear spray is highly recommended for people who hike in bear country, especially grizzly bear country. It's far more effective than a firearm, according to surveys conducted in Alaska. It's easier to hit the target, and both the humans and the bear have a good chance of coming out of an encounter alive. Win-win. Wildlife biologists also say it can be effective in the rare encounter with gray wolves, which are expanding in Washington.

Buy cans labeled "bear spray," not "pepper spray." There can be a difference in the active ingredients as well as in the nozzle. Buy cans 12 ounces or larger that indicate they will spray for at least 9 seconds. Bear spray should be used in bursts. A bear that's deterred by the first burst could advance again, and you want to have more spray left in the can.

Carry bear spray in a holster readily accessible on a pack strap or belt.

If bear spray must be deployed, use two hands and shoot a burst on the ground directly in front of the bear to form a cloud-like barrier that may deter the bear from advancing. Montana bear-spray experts who studied how people perform using bear spray found the force of the propellant usually pivoted the can in a user's hand so the spray was going into the air above the target. While they were shooting into the sky, disabling birds and butterflies, a bear would advance directly under the cloud, unaffected. The spray should be aimed down in front of the bear. When the spray hits the ground, it billows up and creates a barrier most bears will not want to penetrate. Stand your ground and continue shooting bursts of spray just ahead of the bear or into its face as needed.

Online information sources include the Washington Department of Fish and Wildlife (http://wdfw.wa.gov/living) and the Center for Wildlife Information (www.centerforwild lifeinformation.org).
—R. L.

WHERE COUGARS ROAM

Cougars, also called mountain lions, are among the most secretive of the apex predators lurking in the wilds of Eastern Washington. They're linked to virtually anywhere deer are found in good numbers. Even though it's extremely rare even for avid outdoor folks to see a cougar, they're around. Therefore, it's wise to know a bit about *Felix concolor*.

Cougars are curious critters (after all, they're cats). They will follow hikers simply to see what kind of beasts we are, but they rarely (almost never) attack adult humans. Heed the following recommendations of the Washington Department of Fish and Wildlife:

While recreating in cougar habitat:

- Keep small children close to the group, preferably in plain sight just ahead of you.
- Don't approach dead animals, especially deer or elk; they could have been cougar prey left for a later meal.

The Roosevelt Grove of Ancient Cedars protects 2000-year-old specimens.

If you encounter a cougar:

- **Stop, stand tall, and don't run.** A cougar's instinct is to chase. Pick up small children.
- **Don't approach the animal,** especially if it's near a kill or with kittens.
- **Try to appear larger than the cougar.** Don't crouch down or try to hide.
- **Never take your eyes off the animal or turn your back.**
- **If the animal displays aggressive behavior, shout, wave your arms, and throw rocks.** The idea is to convince the cougar that you are not prey, but a potential danger.

THE WOLF IS BACK

After humans used guns, traps, and poison to extirpate the gray wolf from Washington and the rest of the West by the 1940s, endangered species legislation, followed by reintroductions in Yellowstone Park and Idaho wilderness areas in the mid-1990s, paved the way for a wolf comeback.

Wolves have not been released in Washington, but they are naturally moving in and staking out territories. Washington's first recovery-era breeding pack was documented in the Okanogan-Chelan County region in 2008. In 2012, wildlife biologists confirmed nine breeding packs and suspected other packs had been formed.

Wolf-country hikes in this book include those in the Columbia and Okanogan Highlands, the Selkirk Mountains—which has the highest known concentrations—and the Blue Mountains. Hikers who frequent these areas have a decent chance of hearing wolves howl. That said, resist the temptation to approach wolves, their kills, or dens.

Should you have a close encounter with wolves while hiking, Washington Fish and

Wildlife experts recommend the following:

- **Stand tall** and make yourself look larger.
- **Act aggressively,** making noise, throwing objects, waving clothing.
- **Slowly back away.**
- **Maintain eye contact**—this is different than the recommendation for confrontations with bears.
- **Don't run** or turn your back to a wolf.
- **Keep dogs on-leash and under control.** This is critical in wolf country. Wolves view dogs as competitors or territorial intruders and have attacked and killed them, especially in remote areas.

GIVE MOOSE THEIR SPACE

Washington's entire population of about a thousand moose lives in Eastern Washington, mostly in the northeast quarter. They can be found on many of the trails in this book, including those near Spokane. Despite their docile demeanor, moose can be aggressive, especially:

- In late spring and early summer, when a cow feels her very young calf is in danger
- In fall, when a breeding bull is competitive and agitated
- In winter, when moose are hungry and tired from walking in deep snow
- Anytime dogs chase or bark at them
- Anytime people approach them too closely

If you encounter a moose, don't approach it. A moose that sees you and walks slowly toward you is not trying to be your friend. It's probably warning you to keep away (or looking for a handout if someone has been foolish enough to give it food). A moose can easily weigh more than 600 pounds and it's as unpredictable as a bison. Give it lots of space. Back off; change direction; look for the nearest tree, fence, building, or other

Hiking to the summit of Mount Kit Carson in Mount Spokane State Park

obstruction to hide behind if the moose is becoming aggressive. Enjoy the animal from a distance.

If you're charged by a moose, don't fall to the ground and play dead—you'll get pummeled by hooves. If a moose knocks you down, it may continue running, or it could start stomping and kicking. Curl up in a ball, protect your head with your arms and hands, and hold still. Don't move or try to get up until the moose moves a safe distance away, or it may renew its attack.

PLANTS AND CRITTERS WITH A BITE

Poison oak and poison ivy are found along hiking routes in Eastern Washington, as are ticks (especially in early season) and rattlesnakes (in certain areas during warm months). Don't be alarmed—just be aware.

Rattlesnakes: Rattlesnakes generally keep to themselves. If you get too close, they'll usually let you know by rattling their tails. Fair enough! Simply move away slowly and go widely around the snake. Problem solved.

Rattlesnake bites are very rare. The two most common scenarios in which a hiker might get bit are:

- Climbing through rock outcroppings and accidentally stepping or reaching a hand to a ledge where a snake is resting.
- Messing with a snake intentionally. Never try to catch, provoke, or pursue a rattlesnake.

Should you be bitten by a rattlesnake, regardless of its size, remain calm. Wash the bite. Immobilize the limb. Apply a wet wrap. Seek medical attention immediately.

Ticks: Ticks want blood. These hard-shelled arachnids wait in grass and on shrubs or leaves for the chance to cling onto any warm-blooded critter, including you. If they go unnoticed, they'll eventually attach and engorge themselves as they feed on the blood of their host. The main concern in Eastern Washington is their role as a vector for disease, such as relapsing fever and Rocky Mountain spotted fever.

Ticks are found throughout Eastern Washington. They become active as early as late February in the grass and sage of Columbia Basin's Channeled Scablands. From April well into June, they're notably active up into the low forest areas.

During tick season, take precautions to keep ticks from gaining contact with your skin. Wear long sleeves, tuck pant legs into socks, and check yourself and your companions regularly (and your dog too). If you wear convertible hiking pants, check the flap of material that covers the zipper of the removable pant legs. Ticks will crawl up and snuggle under that flap.

Before going hiking, consider using permethrin to treat the lower leg and waist of your pants and the collar and sleeve cuffs of your shirt. Treated hats are helpful too. DEET repellent is effective.

If one of the little buggers has fastened himself to you, gently squeeze its head right next to the skin with your fingers or tweezers. Pull slowly and steadily and the tick will come free, mouth parts and all. Wash and disinfect the bite area. Monitor the bite. If a rash develops, see a doctor.

Poison oak and poison ivy: Poison ivy, and poison oak to a lesser extent, is found in the lower elevations of Eastern Washington. The adage we all heard as kids still works: Leaves of three, let them be.

Both can grow as a vine, shrub, or brush, although poison ivy in this region tends to

Female Rocky Mountain wood tick (Photo by James Gathany, Center for Disease Control)

Summer wildflowers on the Snow Peak Trail

grow mostly along the ground. The leaves and twigs of these plants contain urushiol, a surface oil that causes an allergic reaction in most people who contact it with their skin. Symptoms range from mild itching to blistering, and the reaction can last up to two weeks, inflicting discomfort. Wearing long pants and long-sleeve shirts can help you avoid contact, but it's important to be able to identify the plants. Leaves of three is your first clue, but even the leafless, hairy stems contain the irritant oils.

If your skin contacts poison ivy or poison oak, immediately wash the area with a high volume of water. Go into a stream or lake if possible so you can dilute the oil and get it off rather than just spread it around on your skin. By 30 minutes after contact, most of the oil has been absorbed into your skin and can't be washed off. Urushiol can also remain active on clothing and your dog. Both should be thoroughly washed if they come in contact with these plants.

DAY HIKING GEAR

While gear is beyond the scope of this book (which is about where to hike, not how to hike) it's worth noting a few points. No hiker should venture up a trail without being properly equipped. Starting with the feet, a good pair of boots—and good socks—can make all the difference between a wonderful hike and a blistering affair. Keep your feet happy and you'll be happy.

For clothing, wear whatever is most comfortable unless it's cotton. Cotton is a wonderful fabric, but not the best for hiking. When it gets wet, it stays wet and lacks insulation value. In fact, wet cotton sucks away body heat, leaving you susceptible to hypothermia. Think synthetics and layering.

While your gear list will vary from another hiker's, a few items should be universal in every daypack. Every hiker who ventures deep into the woods should be prepared to spend the night out, with emergency food and shelter. Mountain storms or whiteouts can whip up in a hurry, catching fair-weather hikers by surprise. And there's always the chance of an illness or injury that could prevent you from getting back to the trailhead immediately. Be prepared with the Ten Essentials.

The Ten Essentials

1. **Navigation (map and compass):** Carry a topographic map of the area you plan to be in and knowledge of how to read it. Take a compass, too, and know how to use it.
2. **Sun protection (sunglasses and sunscreen):** Even on gray days, carry sunscreen and sunglasses. The burning rays of the sun penetrate the clouds. At higher elevations your exposure to UV rays is much more intense than at

sea level. Burning is significantly enhanced by the reflectiveness of snow and water.

3. **Insulation (extra clothing):** It may be 70 degrees at the trailhead, but at the summit it can be 45 and windy. Even a summer thunderstorm can cool the air temperature by 40 degrees in minutes. Snow is possible any time at high elevations. Carry raingear, wind protection, and extra layers.

4. **Illumination (flashlight/headlamp):** If caught after dark, you'll need a headlamp or flashlight to follow the trail. If forced to spend the night, you'll need it to set up emergency camp and gather wood. Carry extra batteries too.

5. **First-aid supplies:** At a minimum, your kit should include bandages, moleskin, gauze, scissors, tape, tweezers, pain relievers, antiseptics, and perhaps a small first-aid manual. Consider first-aid training.

6. **Fire (firestarter and matches):** If you're forced to spend the night, an emergency campfire will provide warmth and light. Be sure you keep matches dry. Resealable plastic bags do the trick, but a hard plastic container is better. Firestarter can be purchased commercially. One homemade version is cotton balls swabbed in petroleum jelly and stored in a container. Tip: The Vaseline-coated cotton ball will glow with a better, longer-lasting fire-starting flame if you pull tufts of greased fibers out in every direction before lighting. A candle can come in handy too.

7. **Repair kit and tools (including a knife):** A knife is helpful; a compact multitool is better, adding lightweight pliers and scissors to your options. A basic repair kit should include nylon cord, a small roll of duct tape, and a small tube of superglue. A few safety pins can work wonders too.

8. **Nutrition (extra food):** Always pack more food than what you need for your hike. Energy bars are easy options for a pick-me-up or emergency rations.

9. **Hydration (extra water):** Carry two full water bottles, unless you're hiking entirely along a water source. You'll need to carry iodine tablets or a purifying device on longer or remote hikes.

10. **Emergency shelter:** This can be as simple as a large garbage bag, or something more useful and efficient such as a reflective space blanket. A poncho can double as an emergency tarp.

BEFORE YOU GO

Always tell somebody reliable—best to write it down—where you're going, what you're doing, and when you plan to be home. Also include which land manager, agency, or emergency operator to contact should you not return in a reasonable time.

TRAILHEAD CONCERNS

Sadly, crime occasionally occurs at trailheads. The most common issue is vehicle break-ins. Never leave anything valuable in a vehicle left at a trailhead. Avoid leaving anything, such as bags or even empty coolers, in sight that might tempt a vandal to break a window or punch a lock just to see if there's something valuable inside.

Violence at trailheads in Eastern Washington is exceedingly rare, but not out of the question. Be aware of your surroundings. If something doesn't feel right, it probably isn't. If someone looks suspicious, take action by leaving the place or situation immediately. Record descriptions and license plate numbers and report them to authorities if necessary, but avoid confronting questionable situations in remote areas.

ENJOY THE TRAILS

Most importantly, be safe and enjoy the thrill of discovery and exercise on the trails in this book. They exist for our enjoyment and for the enjoyment of future generations of hikers.

If you enjoy these trails, consider stepping up to be one of their advocates. Your involve-

ment can be as simple as picking up trash, signing up for a volunteer work party, joining a trail advocacy group, educating fellow citizens, or writing a letter to Congress or your state representatives. Introduce children to our trails. We need to continue a legacy of good trail stewards. All of these seemingly small acts can make a big difference. At the end of this book is a list of organizations working on behalf of trails and wildlands in Eastern Washington. Many of them organize great group hikes into the areas covered by this book and beyond. Check them out.

Happy hiking!

A NOTE ABOUT SAFETY

Safety is an important concern in all outdoor activities. No guidebook can alert you to every hazard or anticipate the limitations of every reader. Therefore, the descriptions of roads, trails, routes, and natural features in this book are not representations that a particular place or excursion will be safe for your party. When you follow any of the routes described in this book, you assume responsibility for your own safety. Under normal conditions, such excursions require the usual attention to traffic, road and trail conditions, weather, terrain, the capabilities of your party, and other factors. Because many of the lands in this book are subject to development and/or change of ownership, conditions may have changed since this book was written that make your use of some of these routes unwise. Always check for current conditions, obey posted private property signs, and avoid confrontations with property owners or managers. Keeping informed on current conditions and exercising common sense are the keys to a safe, enjoyable outing.

— *The Mountaineers Books*

Opposite: Curlew Lake State Park

columbia highlands:
okanogan highlands

Reaching from the Okanogan River to Idaho, from the Canadian border to the Columbia Plateau, the Columbia Highlands are a sprawling region in the northeast corner of Washington. Part of the geological province known as the Okanogan Highlands, the Columbia Highlands consist primarily of two mountain ranges lining the Columbia River as it enters Washington from British Columbia.

West of the Columbia, the Kettle River Range runs north–south for approximately 75 miles. East of the Columbia, the Selkirk Mountains also run north–south, but unlike the Kettles, which consist of a single high crest with radiating ridges, the Selkirks are composed of parallel subranges. Both the Kettle and Selkirk Ranges are part of the Rocky Mountains. They form a transitional zone, rich in biological diversity, between interior ranges and the coastal Cascades.

While the Okanogan Highlands generally refers to the geological province ranging from the Okanogan River to the Idaho border and north into British Columbia, in this book it describes the region between the Okanogan and Sanpoil Rivers. A sparsely populated region of isolated mountains, deep valleys, and open rolling hills, the Okanogan Highlands contain great mineral wealth and is dotted with mines (old and still active) and ghost towns. This region contains some of the least-known trails in the state, rewarding intrepid hikers who discover them with solitude, scenic splendors, and a few surprises.

1 Similkameen Trail

RATING/ DIFFICULTY	ROUND-TRIP	ELEV GAIN/ HIGH POINT	SEASON
***/1	7.2 miles	245 feet/ 1060 feet	Year-round

Map: USGS Oroville; **Contact:** BLM Spokane District, (509) 536-1200, www.blm.gov/or/districts/spokane; **Notes:** Wheelchair-accessible. Open to mountain bikes, horses; **GPS:** N 48 56.302 W 119 26.647

 *Walk down a sage- and pine-scented canyon cut by the Similkameen River, along an old rail line that once transported ore from the mines of Hedley, British Columbia, to the now ghost town of Nighthawk. Pass frothy rapids and sunny ledges where lizards and snakes bask in the warm Okanogan sun. Reflect on the past with the help of interpretive displays—and admire the power and beauty of the river from a gorge-spanning bridge.*

GETTING THERE
From Tonasket, follow US Highway 97 north for 16.8 miles to Oroville, turning left onto 12th Avenue (near Frontier Foods grocery store). Proceed one block west and turn right onto Ironwood Street. Proceed one block north (passing Old Oroville Depot Museum and Visitors Center) and turn left onto Kernan Road. Continue 0.3 mile, passing soccer fields, to the trailhead (elev. 935 ft) located on your right.

ON THE TRAIL
Opened in 2009 and slated to be part of the Pacific Northwest Trail (see "North by Northwest" sidebar), the Similkameen Trail is shaping up to be a recreational gem in the growing trail system near Oroville. Thanks to government agencies, local businesses, and dedicated volunteers, including local students, this trail is well maintained and lined with benches and interpretive signs. This route overflows with historical interest, and

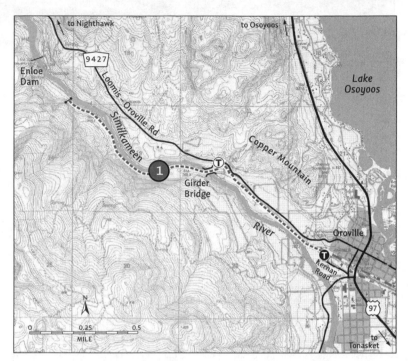

the bird-watching and spring flower gazing are pretty good too.

From the trailhead walk a couple of hundred feet north to the old rail line. The Great Northern began construction on this line in 1909 and it remained In use until 1972. Now heading west, pass some apple warehouses and a couple of pines and cottonwoods. There isn't too much shade on this trail, so hike early or late in the day.

At about 0.3 mile, the Similkameen River comes into view. Starting in British Columbia's Manning Provincial Park, the river is named for a band of Okanogan First Peoples and means "treacherous waters." It flows more than 120 miles into the Okanogan River at Oroville.

After crossing a dirt road, the trail climbs a little, leaving its original right-of-way to bypass a vineyard. At 1.4 miles, come to the Taber trailhead (elev. 1025 ft) on Loomis–Oroville Road—an alternative start. Continue west, and then switchback east and wind down to the Girder Bridge (elev. 980 ft), which replaced the original trestle in 1952. The 375-foot span hovers 86 feet above the churning river in a tight chasm.

Continue west, leaving crushed gravel tread for double-track, and start traversing open range (close gate after you). Pass through a cut where quails and the occasional rattler may be startled (or may startle you) and continue upstream, passing rapids

The Girder Bridge spanning the Similkameen River

NORTH BY NORTHWEST: THE PACIFIC NORTHWEST TRAIL

During the backpacking boom of the 1970s, transplanted New Englander Ron Strickland was struck with a novel idea. How about adding another classic long-distance hiking trail to our country's trail inventory? One that would accompany and rival the likes of the Appalachian, Pacific Crest, and Colorado Divide Trails. Such began his quest to build the Pacific Northwest Trail (PNT), a 1200 mile path from Cape Alava on the Olympic Peninsula to Montana's Glacier National Park.

Soon forming the Pacific Northwest Trail Association, Strickland and a good number of tireless volunteers set out to promote, construct, and maintain the new trail. Utilizing existing trails along with new tread, the PNT traverses a good chunk of northeastern Washington. And while parts of the trail still exist only on paper (following roadway where no tread yet exists), much of the Pacific Northwest Trail is currently hikable; and more than a handful of backpackers have already through-hiked it. The trail has been receiving more attention as the result of President Obama signing a bill in 2009 designating the Pacific Northwest Trail as our newest national scenic trail—a status the PCT and the AT hold.

Many hikes in this book follow portions of the Pacific Northwest Trail. They are a diverse lot and offer some of the best hiking in Eastern Washington. Among them: Similkameen Trail (Hike 1), Whistler Canyon (Hike 2), Antoine Trail (Hike 3), South Side Trail (Hike 4), Clackamas Mountain (Hike 10), Thirteenmile Canyon (Hike 17), Thirteenmile Mountain (Hike 18), Edds and Bald Mountains (Hike 19), Sherman Peak (Hike 21), Columbia Mountain (Hike 24), Copper Butte (Hikes 27 and 28), Ryan Cabin Loop (Hike 31), Sentinel Butte (Hike 32), Abercrombie Mountain (Hike 43), Crowell Ridge (Hike 51), Gypsy Peak (Hike 52), and Shedroof Divide (Hike 54).

Visit the Pacific Northwest Trail Association online (www.pnt.org) for more information.

—C. R.

and good views of Kruger Mountain across the river.

Old mines litter the surrounding hillsides. Pines and firs shroud the north-facing slopes to your left, contrasting with the sagebrush-steppe ridges to your right. At 2.8 miles, cross a side creek in a lush draw. Good bird observing here. At 3.2 miles, pass through a cut with glacial till left behind from the Ice Age.

At 3.6 miles, come to a gate (elev. 1060 ft) and the end (for now) of the line. Look northwest to the 1907-built Enloe Dam, with the river thundering over it. Once the dam is relicensed and the area surrounding it improved, trail advocates hope to open the second phase of this great trail, to Nighthawk and including a tunnel.

gan Valley also abound along this recently opened section of the Pacific Northwest Trail. And miles of connector trails entice you to explore farther.

GETTING THERE

From Tonasket, follow US Highway 97 north for 14.5 miles to the trailhead turnoff, signed and upgraded in 2012. The trailhead turnoff is about 0.3 mile north of the gravel pit at milepost 329. (From Oroville, the turnoff is 2.4 miles south of city center.) Continue 0.2 mile to trailhead (elev. 1000 ft) located in a field below some impressive ledges.

② Whistler Canyon and Frog Pond

RATING/ DIFFICULTY	ROUND-TRIP	ELEV GAIN/ HIGH POINT	SEASON
***/2	5.1 miles	1250 feet/ 1950 feet	Mar–Dec

Maps: USGS Oroville, USGS Mount Hull; **Contact:** Okanogan-Wenatchee National Forest, Tonasket Ranger District, (509) 486-2186, www.fs.fed.us/r6/okawen; **Notes:** Open to horses. Keep dogs under strict control so as to not disturb bighorn sheep; **GPS:** N 48 54.300 W 119 25.335

Whistlers? Yes—and ground squirrels too! But the biggest animal attraction is California bighorn sheep. The largest band in the state roams Whistler Canyon, and it's not unusual to see more than fifty at a time. Wildflowers and views of the Okano-

The trail to Whistler Canyon climbs out of the Okanogan River valley.

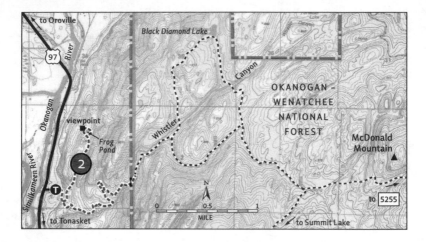

ON THE TRAIL

Colonies of ground squirrels greet you at the trailhead. And colonies of marmots—aka whistlers—greet you as the trail angles beneath rocky ledges. Thank the Back Country Horsemen, Pacific Northwest Trail Association, and other volunteers for the recently constructed, well-built trail. A private-property owner had closed the previous access point, putting this mostly public-lands trail off-limits. But that's all in the past—so keep hiking.

After winding along ledges and through a small pine grove, reach a junction (elev. 1200 ft) at 0.3 mile with the Frog Pond Trail. This is a mandatory side trip. Follow this rose-lined trail left, beneath a canopy of ponderosas and up through a rocky cleft. At 1 mile from the trailhead, reach a junction (elev. 1500 ft) with the 0.3-mile loop circling Frog Pond. More of a mosquito incubator (and therefore a frog feeder), the pond isn't much to look at. The real treat is the ledgy lookout on the west side of the loop: peer out at Oroville, Osoyoos Lake,

and into British Columbia; and straight down at the oxbowing confluence of the Similkameen and Okanogan Rivers. Consider a trip at sunset.

Retrace your steps to the junction and continue left, shortly intersecting an old road. Turn left and after a few steps follow a bypass around private property, returning to the old road at 0.5 mile from the trailhead. Now within BLM land, follow the road into Whistler Canyon. Whistler Creek tumbles below. Watch above for the bighorns and if you spot them (better chances early and late in the day), tread quietly in their presence. Look for deer, turkeys, cedar waxwings, and whistlers—and rubber boas, a docile constrictor fairly common to these parts.

At 0.9 mile from the trailhead, pass a campsite (elev. 1600 ft) in a grove of pines and cottonwoods. Then leave the creek and angle left, traversing ledges with excellent viewing out over the Okanogan Valley, before switchbacking right and returning above the creek. Look for a semihidden waterfall below. The trail eventually enters a forest of pine and fir, reaching a gate (elev. 1950 ft) and national forest boundary at 1.7 miles from the trailhead. Just beyond, the trail—now an old woods road—crosses the creek. This is a good spot to turn around, savoring good valley views and perhaps catching sight of that band of bighorns.

EXTENDING YOUR TRIP

The Whistler Canyon Trail continues in thick forest along Whistler Creek for 0.6 mile, before leaving the canyon, reaching FR 3525 more than 10 miles later near Summit Lake at 4200 feet. The trail is primarily used by equestrians and Pacific Northwest Trail through-hikers. Several side trails diverge, but routefinding can be tricky. Skip the steep McDonald Trail, which climbs in forest to a draw beneath McDonald Mountain before climbing a ridge to meet FR 5255. But consider the 2.5-mile Black Diamond Lake loop, which takes off left 0.6 mile from the suggested turnaround. The upper part of the loop—after crossing and climbing out of the canyon—traverses open slopes with nice views west to the Loomis State Forest high country and snowy North Cascades.

3 Mount Bonaparte via Antoine Trail

RATING/ DIFFICULTY	ROUND-TRIP	ELEV GAIN/ HIGH POINT	SEASON
****/5	15.2 miles	3360 feet/ 7257 feet	mid-June– Nov

Maps: USGS Mount Bonaparte, USGS Havillah; **Contact:** Okanogan-Wenatchee National Forest, Tonasket Ranger District, (509) 486-2186, www.fs.fed.us/r6/okawen; **Notes:** Open to horses, mountain bikes; **GPS:** N 48 48.115 W 119 11.882

It's a long way to the top of Eastern Washington's third-highest summit via the Antoine Trail. Why go this way when there's a much shorter route? For one thing, you'll follow a quiet trail carpeted in soft larch and fir needles instead of a rutted, dusty ATV track. And you'll see an old trapper's cabin, a couple of cool dark ravines fed by crashing creeks, groves of big firs, and miles of excellent furry-and-feathered-critter habitat. It's a good workout rewarded with extensive views from Bonaparte, or a pleasant walk in the woods if you just want to sample this quiet path in the Okanogan Highlands.

GETTING THERE

From the junction of State Route 20 and US Highway 97 in Tonasket, head north on US 97 for 0.4 mile, turning right onto Whitcomb Avenue (signed "Havillah 17" and "Sitzmark Ski Area"). Immediately bear right onto Jonathan Avenue, which soon becomes Havillah Road (County Road 9467). Follow this good road for 15.4 miles, turning right (before reaching the hamlet of Havillah) onto Mill Creek Road (Forest Road 3230 and signed "Highlands Sno-Park"). At 1.3 miles, pass the Sno-Park and continue on FR 3230 for another 0.4 mile, coming to gated FR Spur 150 on your left. Park here; this is the trailhead (elev. 3900 ft).

ON THE TRAIL

The most direct way to Mount Bonaparte, Mount Bonaparte Trail No. 306, can no longer be recommended. Back in the early 1990s, the Forest Service converted this once-pleasant path into an ATV track for transporting supplies to the fire lookout. What followed was unregulated motorized

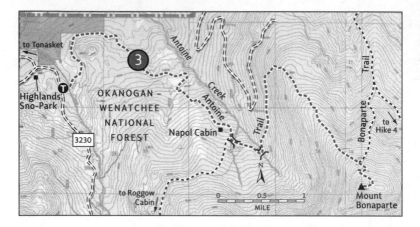

use that pulverized this path to dust. What a shame. In 2007, the Forest Service closed the trail to public motorized use, but a lack of rehabilitation and the occasional illegal motorized user still render it unacceptable. Except as a winter route, skip it and opt for the three other longer but appealing trails traversing this 9500-acre wilderness study area.

The way via Antoine Creek starts by following gated FR Spur 150. A logging operation several years past obstructed the lower part of the Antoine Trail, so it's wiser to walk the pleasant road instead of the original tread. Traversing an area selectively cut and grazed by cattle, the way winds around a small knob. The rolling terrain and territorial views warrant a return visit with skis in winter. At 2.6 miles, turn left and leave the road at an old logging landing (elev. 4400 ft).

Follow an old jeep track, first through an old cut, then through old-growth western larch that are stunning come October. Admire new tread compliments of volunteers who welcomed the Antoine Trail as part of the newly designated Pacific Northwest

Trail. At 3.3 miles, reach the dilapidated Napol Cabin, an old trapper's domicile. The Roggow Cabin on the Fourth of July Ridge Trail on Bonaparte's southwest slopes is in much better condition and is occasionally used by outdoors folks.

Just beyond the cabin, at 3.5 miles, reach a junction (elev. 4850 ft) with the Napol Cabin Trail. This trail connects with the Fourth of July Ridge Trail in about 2.5 miles near the Roggow Cabin. It is used primarily by equestrians. For Bonaparte, continue left into a thick lodgepole pine forest, soon coming to a bridged crossing of a tributary of Antoine Creek. Now on bona fide trail, reach another tributary crossing (last reliable water) at 4 miles.

The way transitions into a Douglas-fir forest interspersed with big larches as you traverse a slope on good trail. At 5.1 miles, bear right at an unmarked junction (elev. 5400 ft) and begin steadily climbing to attain the ridge crest. Now through a forest of lodgepole pine, snag teaser views through the trees.

Continue upward, and eventually the

The 1914 lookout cabin still graces Bonaparte's summit.

alpine-suited whitebark pines indicate you're getting close. At 7.1 miles, reach the Bonaparte Trail (elev. 6890 ft) just shy of the summit. Turn right and follow this dusty track (or pick up pieces of the old trail) for 0.5 mile to the broad 7257-foot summit. This stand-alone peak commands far-reaching views, but you'll need to climb the "new" fire lookout, built in 1961, to get

them. Admire the Kettle Crest (east), Moses Mountain and the Columbia Plateau (south), the Okanogan Valley and North Cascades (west), and British Columbia's Baldy and Big White Mountains (north). When you're finished, marvel over the "old" fire lookout, built in 1914 from hand-hewn logs. It's on the National Register of Historic Places and one of our oldest lookouts still standing.

4 Mount Bonaparte via South Side Trail

RATING/ DIFFICULTY	ROUND-TRIP	ELEV GAIN/ HIGH POINT	SEASON
****/3	10.8 miles	2730 feet/ 7257 feet	June–Nov

Map: USGS Mount Bonaparte; **Contact:** Okanogan-Wenatchee National Forest, Tonasket Ranger District, (509) 486-2186, www.fs.fed.us/r6/okawen; **Notes:** Open to mountain bikes, horses. Watch for ticks; **GPS:** N 48 47.913 W 119 04.175

Horizon-spanning 360-degree views await you from Eastern Washington's third-highest summit. A granite dome rising well above the surrounding ridges, 7257-foot Mount Bonaparte stands all alone. It's graced by two fire lookouts—one built in 1914, a testament to the early days of the Forest Service, and one built in 1961, still staffed in the summer. This is not the shortest way to the Bonaparte's summit, but it's one of the nicer routes, complete with views, flowers, old forest, and solitude.

GETTING THERE

From Tonasket follow State Route 20 east for 20 miles, turning left onto Bonaparte Lake Road (County Road 4953, signed "Bonaparte Recreation Area"). (From Republic, follow SR 20 west for 20 miles, turning right onto CR 4953.) Proceed on Bonaparte Lake Road (which eventually becomes Forest Road 32), bearing left at 8.5 miles onto FR 33. Continue 5.3 miles to a four-way junction (FR 34 and Lost Lake access). Proceed straight on FR 33 for another 0.4 mile, turning left onto FR Spur 100. (Alternatively, approach via Hike 3 directions, continuing 0.6 mile to Havillah instead of turning onto Mill Creek Road. Then turn right onto Lost Lake Road/CR 4850, which becomes

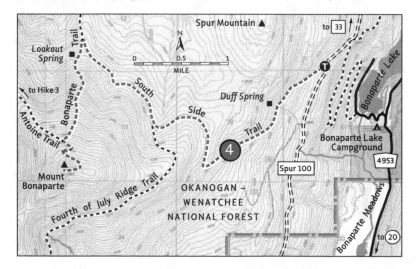

FR 33, driving 10.3 miles to FR Spur 100.) Follow FR Spur 100 for 4.7 miles (passing the upper trailhead for the Pipsissewa Trail at 4.3 miles) to the trailhead (elev. 4600 ft). Parking is tight; there is better parking at the Pipsissewa trailhead (Hike 9).

ON THE TRAIL

The shortest way to Mount Bonaparte, Mount Bonaparte Trail No. 306, is an unappealing mess from years of motorized use, even though the Forest Service closed it to public motorized access in 2007. Fortunately, other trail options exist within this 9500-acre wilderness study area. Unfortunately, accessing Bonaparte's summit from the south side still requires some hiking on the dusty north trail. But the views are well worth it.

The trip up Bonaparte from the south side was once much longer, having started from Bonaparte Lake. But FR Spur 100 severed the trail, knocking considerable distance and elevation off the hike. The lower trail still exists and has since been renamed the Pipsissewa Trail (Hike 9). With this in mind, ignore the trailhead sign that says the lookout is 8 miles away: The Forest Service moved this sign from the lower trailhead and never adjusted the mileage.

The way starts in a selectively cut forest, providing lots of warming sun. The grass-lined trail (be tick aware) steadily ascends. Mount Bonaparte is a *monadnock*, an Abenaki word that means "mountain standing alone" (and the name of southern New Hampshire's historically prominent and well-loved Mount Monadnock). Geologists have since used the term in place of another, *inselberg*, meaning "isolated mountain"— which Mount Bonaparte is indeed!

At 0.6 mile, come to a spring (elev. 5000 ft) and an eroded section of trail. Tread improves as the way traverses first parkland forest, then dark forest of spruce and fir, then lodgepole pines punctuated with granite ledges and boulders. Steadily climbing, the way switches east to round a small ridge before resuming a westward direction. At 2.2 miles, cross Myers Creek (elev. 5750 ft) flowing through patches of huckleberry.

Reach a junction with the Fourth of July Ridge Trail (elev. 5825 ft) at 2.6 miles. Continue right, over big granite ledges. Slightly

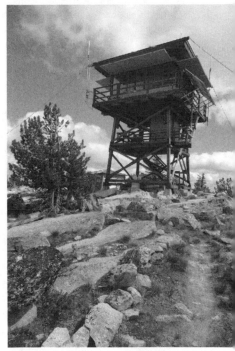

The "new" fire lookout is still seasonally staffed.

drop into a small gulch and reach the Mount Bonaparte Trail (elev. 5750 ft) at 3.4 miles. Now turn left on radically different tread—wide and trenched and covered in dust. Just beyond the junction, a spur leads right 0.1 mile to a spring, the last reliable water.

Slogging upward, the path cuts through dense stands of lodgepole pine. Some sections of the old trail along the way offer some relief from the dust. At 4.9 miles, come to a junction with the Antoine Trail (elev. 6890 ft). Continue left 0.5 mile through groves of whitebark pine (and look for Clark's nutcrackers fond of pine nuts), before approaching Bonaparte's broad granite summit from the east.

Admire the historic 1914 fire lookout and then head up the "new" lookout to take in the views. They're exceptional and reach as far as Mount Rainier on a clear day: Bonaparte Meadows and the monadnocks Mount Annie and Moses Mountain are closer to the south. Loomis country is to the west, with Chopaka Mountain's 6000-foot prominence above the Similkameen Valley. Lake Osoyoos and British Columbia's 7558-foot Mount Baldy are to the north. And to the east trace the entire Kettle Crest into Canada's Granby country.

5 Strawberry Mountain

RATING/ DIFFICULTY	ROUND-TRIP	ELEV GAIN/ HIGH POINT	SEASON
**/2	3.4 miles	890 feet/ 4742 feet	May–Nov

Map: USGS Mount Bonaparte; **Contact:** Okanogan-Wenatchee National Forest, Tonasket Ranger District, (509) 486-2186, www .fs.fed.us/r6/okawen; **Notes:** Open to mountain bikers; **GPS:** N 48 51.135 W 119 02.959

This is a sweet hike to the top of Strawberry Mountain, where you'll find Lost Lake twinkling below and bulky Mount Bonaparte rising above. Through pine and larch groves, wind up gentle slopes to this old fire lookout site. It's easy enough for young children and neophyte hikers and satisfying enough for hikers who want to stretch their legs more by combining it with the nearby Big Tree Trail (Hike 6).

Stands of western larch add a golden hue to Strawberry Mountain in the autumn.

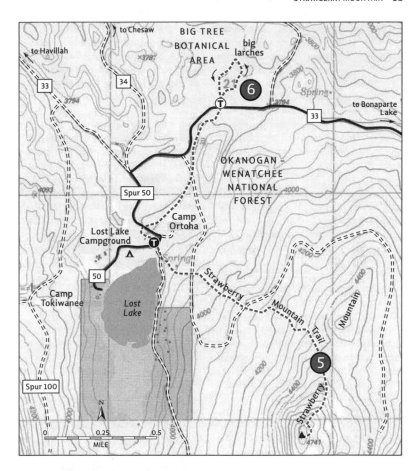

GETTING THERE

From Tonasket, follow State Route 20 east for 20 miles, turning left onto Bonaparte Lake Road (County Road 4953, signed "Bonaparte Recreation Area"). (From Republic, follow SR 20 west for 20 miles, turning right onto CR 4953.) Proceed on Bonaparte Lake Road (which eventually becomes FR 32), bearing left at 8.5 miles onto FR 33. Continue 5.3 miles to a four-way junction. Turn left onto FR Spur 50 and drive 0.4 mile, turning right into the Lost Lake Campground. Park at the historic Civilian Conservation Corps guard station (elev. 3850 ft). Privy available.

ON THE TRAIL

After admiring the simple elegance of the old guard house, walk 0.1 mile south on

FR Spur 50, along lovely Lost Lake, to the Strawberry Mountain trailhead. Begin gently climbing through open forest that was selectively cut. Deer are profuse. Pass an electric line and at 0.3 mile cross a logging road.

Continue through larch, Doug-fir, and aspen groves. In autumn the forest is streaked yellow, while the trail is carpeted with soft golden needles. Gently ascending the broad forested peak, cross another road (elev. 4150 ft) at 0.6 mile; then return to open forest.

After skirting an old selective cut, the way levels off before making a steep final pitch. Cross yet another road (this one old and making for some good wandering) and soon afterward emerge on the broad grassy summit (elev. 4742 ft).

All that remains of the fire lookout that stood here from 1934 to 1963 are four concrete foundation blocks, but you won't need a tower to enjoy the views. Lost Lake ripples directly below, with Mount Bonaparte's broad forested ridges providing an emerald backdrop. To the north, British Columbia's Mount Baldy hovers above golden hills. South you can catch a glimpse of Mount Annie and rows of rolling ridges.

On an evening hike in the summer, you might hear the eerie call of the loon echoing below. And yes, there are strawberries here, but just the small wild type (*Fragaria virginiana*), favored more by woodland critters and birds than hungry hikers.

6 Big Tree Botanical Area

RATING/ DIFFICULTY	ROUND-TRIP	ELEV GAIN/ HIGH POINT	SEASON
**/1	2.8 miles	100 feet/ 3850 feet	Apr–Nov

Map: USGS Mount Bonaparte; **Contact:** Okanogan-Wenatchee National Forest, Tonasket Ranger District, (509) 486-2186, www.fs.fed.us/r6/okawen; **Notes:** Partly wheelchair-accessible; **GPS:** N 48 51.135 W 119 02.959

 Hike to a pair of towering larches more than 900 years old. Saunter beneath ancient ponderosa pines. While the botanical preserve is more readily accessed from Forest Road 33, take the longer route from Lost Lake via the Big Tree Trail and enjoy one of the region's more peaceful walks. Well-graded and nearly level, it's ideal for all ages and perfect for an evening stroll if you're camped at Lost Lake.

GETTING THERE

From Tonasket, follow State Route 20 east for 20 miles, turning left onto Bonaparte Lake Road (County Road 4953, signed "Bonaparte Recreation Area"). (From Republic, follow SR 20 west for 20 miles, turning right onto CR 4953.) Proceed on Bonaparte Lake Road (which eventually becomes FR 32), bearing left at 8.5 miles onto FR 33. Continue 5.3 miles to a four-way junction. Turn left onto FR Spur 50 and drive 0.4 mile, turning right into the Lost Lake Campground. Park at the historic Civilian Conservation Corps guard station (elev. 3850 ft). Privy available.

ON THE TRAIL

Begin directly across the campground road from the Lost Lake Guard Station. Called both the Big Tree Trail and the Lost Lake Trail, the trail connects these two popular and lovely attractions. Start with a short descent and soon afterward cross FR Spur 50.

The Big Tree Trail weaves through towering larches, pines, and firs.

Continue under a cool canopy supported by giant pillars of western larch. Pass (or sit and contemplate) the first of several inviting benches along the trail. At about 0.25 mile, a spur trail leads right, to a church camp. Continue left through a swinging gate, entering open range. Then continue through open larch and fir forest carpeted with pipsissewa.

After crossing a forest road at 0.5 mile, the trail meanders through some impressive boulders and granite slabs. At 1 mile, reach FR 33 and the main trailhead (start here if you're short on time), complete with privy (elev. 3800 ft). Continue on a wheelchair-accessible trail, soon coming to a junction. The way loops from here. Continue right, dropping into a draw (elev. 3775 ft) and then out of it, reaching a junction at 1.3 miles. Absolutely head right on the 0.1-mile spur, dropping to a pair of giant ancient western larches more than 900 years old. Retrace your steps back to the loop and continue right. At 1.7 miles, close the loop. You know the way back to the trailhead from here.

7 Beth and Beaver Lakes

RATING/ DIFFICULTY	ROUND-TRIP	ELEV GAIN/ HIGH POINT	SEASON
**/2	3.8 miles	190 feet/ 2850 feet	Apr–Nov

Map: USGS Bodie; **Contact:** Okanogan-Wenatchee National Forest, Tonasket Ranger District, (509) 486-2186, www.fs.fed.us/r6/okawen; **Notes:** Open to mountain bikes; **GPS:** N 48 51.893 W 118 59.896

Evening reflections on Beaver Lake

Hike through a cool narrow canyon along two slender lakes teeming with fish and anglers intent on luring them. Beth and Beaver Lakes are two of the popular high-country gems of the Tonasket Ranger District's Five Lakes Area. Each season offers its own delights, with fall being exceptionally nice, when western larches cast golden reflections across placid waters.

GETTING THERE

From Tonasket follow State Route 20 east for 20 miles, turning left onto Bonaparte Lake Road (County Road 4953, signed "Bonaparte Recreation Area"). Proceed on Bonaparte Lake Road (which eventually becomes FR 32) for 11.7 miles to Beaver Lake Campground (alternate trailhead), at the junction with CR 9480. Turn left and drive 1.8 miles, passing Beth Lake Campground (another alternate trailhead), to the trailhead (elev. 2800 ft). (From Republic, follow SR 20 west for 16.5 miles, turning right onto Toroda Creek Road/CR 9495. Continue 13.5 miles, turn left onto CR 9480, and follow it 5.9 miles to the trailhead.)

ON THE TRAIL

This is a nice little trail along two little, quiet lakes connecting two little, quiet campgrounds. While you can easily access this trail from the campgrounds, day-use parking is limited. It's best to begin at the northern trailhead if you're just out for the day.

Start by crossing North Fork Beaver Creek on a small bridge and enter a forest of big larches and firs. The trail bends south to hug the western shore of Beth Lake. The road hugs the eastern shore of both lakes, but traffic is light, so frog and bird song,

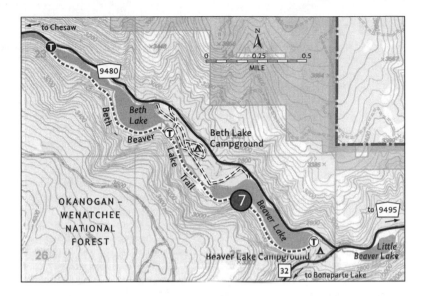

along with happy campers, are the sounds you'll likely hear. Travel through forest, occasionally crossing small scree slopes, nearly always within sight of water. Keep an eye out for handsome wood ducks.

At about 0.4 mile, the way climbs about 50 feet over a ledge and then drops back down to round the wider eastern half of the lake. Cross an earthen dam and reach Beth Lake Campground at 0.8 mile. Turn right on the campground road, and pick up the trail near campsite number 7.

Skirt a wetland cove and arrive at Beaver Lake. Climb about 50 feet over a ledge, where the lake bends, and then drop closer to the water, resuming your shoreline strolling. The lake is murky, but it reflects the surrounding mature trees nicely. Scan for roosting eagles, and watch the lake surface for dippers.

Pass by an odd structure before cross-

ing a small scree slope. Then climb 40 feet around a small rib near Beaver Lake's outlet. The trail winds down off it and crosses a little creek before terminating near campsite number 5 (elev. 2700 ft). Consider spending the night at one of the campgrounds and taking a moonlit stroll along this pleasant trail.

8 Virginia Lilly Trail

RATING/ DIFFICULTY	LOOP	ELEV GAIN/ HIGH POINT	SEASON
***/2	3.5 miles	900 feet/ 4270 feet	Apr–Nov

Map: USGS Bodie; **Contact:** Okanogan-Wenatchee National Forest, Tonasket Ranger District, (509) 486-2186, www.fs.fed.us /r6/okawen; **Notes:** Range area; **GPS:** N 48 49.392 W 118 55.772

 *Named not for a southern flower but for an Okanogan Highlands resident who cherished the region's threatened old growth and ecologically diverse landscapes, this delightful loop through parkland forest, wildflower meadows, and sun-kissed ridges is dedicated in her memory. Solitude is almost guaranteed here, on one of the least-hiked trails in the Mount Bonaparte area.*

GETTING THERE

From Tonasket, follow State Route 20 east for 20 miles, turning left onto Bonaparte Lake Road (County Road 4953, signed "Bonaparte Recreation Area"). (From Republic, follow SR 20 west for 20, miles turning right onto CR 4953.) Proceed on Bonaparte Lake Road (which eventually becomes FR 32) for 7.1 miles, turning right onto FR 3240 (1.3 miles beyond Bonaparte Lake Campground). At 1 mile, bear left and continue on FR 3240 for

another 5.7 miles to the trailhead on your left (elev. 4050 ft).

ON THE TRAIL

After languishing for a few years, the Virginia Lilly Trail is finally getting a little upkeep. The new trailhead avoids driving a rough road, though you can still walk up the road to access the trail. And the Forest Service, in cooperation with several groups and individuals, put together a booklet to go along with the hike (more literary than field guide; download it from www.fs.fed.us /outdoors/naturewatch/resources/virginia -lilly-old-growth-trail.pdf). But don't believe the Forest Service's description of this trail as 2 miles long. It's nearly twice that length.

Hike counterclockwise to end going downhill. Head southwest across a selectively cut area, soon coming to a junction on an open hillside in about 0.25 mile. Now on the main loop, continue straight, across grassy slopes and through groves of big

Virginia Lilly Trail offers good views of the golden hills of the Okanogan Highlands.

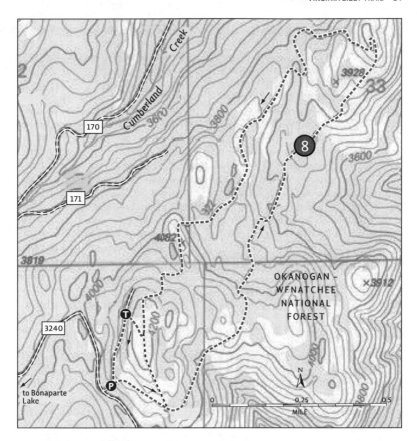

ponderosa pines. Watch for cows as you plod through this open range country.

The way turns north, makes a short climb, and then drops into a grove of firs. Make a short steep climb up an open knoll (elev. 4075 ft) with excellent views east to Bodie and Clackamas Mountains. Reenter forest and steeply descend 300 feet into a damp draw. With numerous cattle paths diverging from and intersecting the trail, it's easy to go astray here. Note trail markers.

Now climbing again, the way cuts through meadows accented with stately pines and splotched gold in spring by arrowleaf balsamroot. Deer are profuse, and your approach will send them scampering. At 1.6 miles, top a grassy rocky knoll (elev. 4025 ft) with good views of the Toroda Creek valley east, Mount Bonaparte west, and the old mining town of Chesaw and new mining area of Buckhorn Mountain north.

The trail then loops back south, dropping back into forest to a cool draw (elev. 3800 ft), before once again climbing. At 2.5 miles, reach a cow-trampled, larch-encircled, cattail-sporting wetland. Then continue climbing to a 4100-foot bump. Turn right, following cairns through a lovely aspen grove before making a steep ascent up an open grassy knoll (elev. 4270 ft). Kick back and walk along the open hillock, coming to a post at 3.2 miles. To complete the loop, either continue straight across meadows, reaching the spur back to the lower trailhead, or turn right to reach the upper trailhead and walk a short distance on the spur road back to your car.

⑨ Pipsissewa Trail

RATING/ DIFFICULTY	ROUND-TRIP	ELEV GAIN/ HIGH POINT	SEASON
***/3	4.2 miles	860 feet/ 4420 feet	May–Nov

Map: USGS Mount Bonaparte; **Contact:** Okanogan-Wenatchee National Forest, Tonasket Ranger District, (509) 486-2186, www.fs.fed.us/r6/okawen; **Notes:** Open to mountain bikes; **GPS:** N 48 47.570 W 119 03.786

From the inviting shoreline of Bonaparte Lake to sunny ledges high above it, the delightful Pipsissewa Trail takes in stately pines, showy rock gardens, and breathtaking views of the Bonaparte Meadows. And pipsissewa? Also known as prince's pine, this small member of the heath family brightens the dry, cool woodlands in the summer with its pink and white flowers.

GETTING THERE

From Tonasket, follow State Route 20 east for 20 miles, turning left onto Bonaparte Lake Road (County Road 4953, signed "Bonaparte Recreation Area"). (From Republic, follow SR 20 west for 20 miles, turning right onto CR 4953.) Proceed on Bonaparte Lake Road for 5.8 miles, turning left into the Bonaparte Lake Campground. Continue 0.1 mile, passing the boat launch, to a small parking area near campsite number 27 and the hike's start (elev. 3560 ft). Privy available.

ON THE TRAIL

From the campground loop, locate a sign indicating the trailhead is 500 feet away. Walk north on a quiet dirt road that leads to seasonal cabins. Soon after crossing the lake's outlet stream, come to the trail as it veers left into the forest. Bypass a row of cabins and moderately ascend above Bonaparte Lake.

Under a cool canopy of large ponderosa pines and western larches, the good trail continues to gain elevation along a couple of sweeping switchbacks. Cross several grassy openings, which in spring and summer display pretty floral arrangements. In fall, western larches and aspens add soothing touches of gold.

Throughout most of the summer, the small delicate flowers of pipsissewa (incorrectly spelled on the trail signs) add touches of pink and white to the dry forest floor. This relative of the wintergreen family thrives across the northern states and southern Canada. Numerous First Peoples used it for medicinal purposes.

Continue gaining elevation, traversing a few seeps and maneuvering around a couple of granite slabs. At 2.1 miles, the trail comes to its end at FR 33-100 (elev. 4420 ft). Yes,

Pipsissewa Trail ends at an excellent viewpoint of Bonaparte Lake.

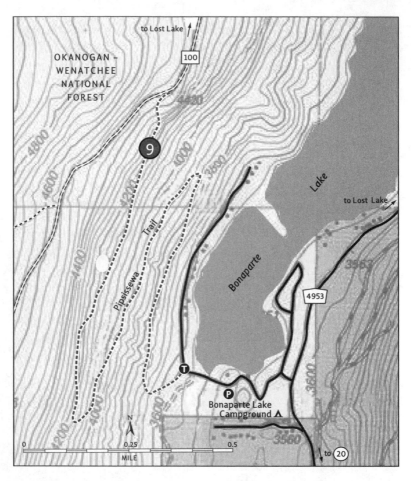

you could have driven here—but why? You've instead earned the fantastic views from the sunny ledges here at trail's end: Bonaparte Lake twinkling below, piney hills and Bodie Mountain to the east, and the lush Bonaparte Meadows west to Mount Annie. On the return, consider sampling the waters of Bonaparte Lake by submersion!

EXTENDING YOUR TRIP

The Pipsissewa Trail was part of the South Side Trail (Hike 4) until FR Spur 100 severed it. Challenge yourself with a 15-plus mile hike by subduing Mount Bonaparte from Bonaparte Lake. Consider spending a night in the family-friendly lakeside campground afterward.

Clackamas Mountain

RATING/ DIFFICULTY	LOOP	ELEV GAIN/ HIGH POINT	SEASON
****/3	9.4 miles	2400 feet/ 5450 feet	May–Nov

Map: USGS Wauconda Summit; **Contact:** Okanogan-Wenatchee National Forest, Tonasket Ranger District, (509) 486-2186, www.fs.fed.us/r6/okawen; **Notes:** Open to horses. Range area; **GPS:** N 48 40.827 W 118 54.284

    One of the finest ridgeline, wildflower, and larch hikes in the Okanogan Highlands—and a loop too. Enjoy far-reaching views from this little-known peak. Centerpiece of a wilderness study area, Clackamas Mountain is excellent habitat for rare and threatened fauna and flora, including lynx and the Okanogan fameflower. This hike ascends via two long ridges, circling the Sweat Creek basin without making you expend too much sweat.

GETTING THERE

From Tonasket, follow State Route 20 east for 31 miles. (From Republic, travel 8.5 miles west on SR 20.) Turn left into the Sweat Creek Picnic Area and trailhead (elev. 3550 ft). Privy available.

ON THE TRAIL

Starting from a former car campground, now a picnic area, hike north along Sweat Creek into a cool forest, coming to a junction at a stile at 0.1 mile. You'll be returning on the left-hand trail, so head right on the Sweat Creek Basin Trail, briefly following a power-line swath and fence line before turn-

ing northward. Start climbing an at-times open, at-times steep ridge that's cloaked in wildflowers in spring. Balsamroot, lupine, cinquefoil, daisy, arnica, desert parsley, larkspur, shooting star—the list goes on!

When your nose isn't to the ground, look up and out to Fir Mountain to the south. At about 1.8 miles, ascend a knoll and descend slightly as you walk along a ridgeline through parkland forest of old larches and Douglas-fir. At about 2.5 miles, a short spur leads left to an outcropping (elev. 4850 ft) with views over the Sweat Creek basin.

A hiker heading through flowered parkland meadows on Clackamas Mountain

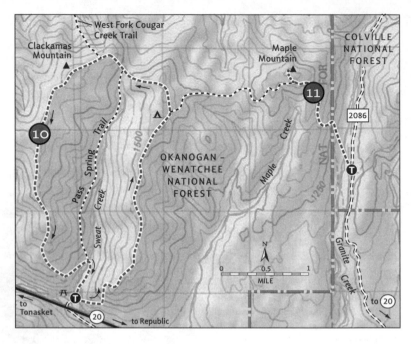

Pass an old mileage post. This trail was one of many that once traversed the surrounding ridges and peaks straddling the Okanogan-Ferry County border. Most of them have faded into memory, but this trail is now part of the Pacific Northwest Trail.

At 3.5 miles, come to Hunter Spring and Camp (elev. 5000 ft) and the unmarked junction with the Maple Mountain Trail (Hike 11) just beyond it. Continue north through larches, cresting a rocky knoll (elev. 5200 ft) before descending slightly and passing a small wetland and open ledges with good views south and glimpses north.

After a short steep drop into a 4800-foot saddle, start climbing again, to a junction (elev. 4850 ft) at 4.5 miles. The Pass Spring Trail heads left into the basin, following Sweat Creek for about 3 miles back to the trailhead. Keep hiking right, coming to another junction (elev. 5200 ft) at 4.8 miles. The trail right is the old West Fork Cougar Creek Trail, now part of the Pacific Northwest Trail. Continue left instead on the Clackamas Mountain Trail, reaching the forested 5450-foot summit at 5.3 miles.

Pass above a small frog pond, and after a few ups and downs start descending through open forest and on ledges. At 6.7 miles, emerge onto an open ridgeline (elev. 5250 ft) with excellent views south to Fir and Annie, west to Bonaparte, and east to the Kettle Crest. Savor the wildflowers too, perhaps spotting the indigenous Okanogan fameflower among the sedums. Be careful not to go astray on one of the many cattle paths here. Look across the Sweat Creek drainage to the ridge you hiked up—Clackamas Mountain's southern ridges form a huge horseshoe.

At about 7.5 miles, the way crests a 4900-foot knoll, enters forest, and steeply drops. The tread is now sketchy in places, crying out for a maintenance party to pay a visit. The trail bends eastward, passing a spring (elev. 4200 ft) as it descends into the Sweat Creek basin. Pass big ponderosa pines, and at 8.9 miles come to the Pass Spring Trail at Sweat Creek among a confusion of windfall. Cross the creek (may be tricky early in the season) and soon afterward cross it again. Don't put dry socks on just yet, because you need to cross the creek one more time before coming back to the junction at the stile and closing your loop at 9.3 miles. Your vehicle awaits 0.1 mile to the right.

⑪ Maple Mountain

RATING/ DIFFICULTY	ROUND-TRIP	ELEV GAIN/ HIGH POINT	SEASON
***/3	5.2 miles	1750 feet/ 5299 feet	May–Nov

Maps: USGS Storm King Mountain, USGS Wauconda Summit; **Contact:** Okanogan-Wenatchee National Forest, Tonasket Ranger District, (509) 486-2186, www.fs.fed.us/r6/okawen; **Notes:** Open to horses; **GPS:** N 48 41.888 W 118 49.948

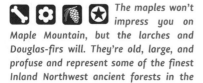 *The maples won't impress you on Maple Mountain, but the larches and Douglas-firs will. They're old, large, and profuse and represent some of the finest Inland Northwest ancient forests in the*

state. The views across the golden hills of the Okanogan Highlands aren't too bad either. Like its neighbors on Clackamas Mountain, this lonely but much admired trail has been saved from obscurity thanks to the Ferry County chapter of the Back Country Horsemen.

GETTING THERE
From Republic, travel 2.5 miles west on State Route 20, turning right onto Trout Creek Road (County Road 257). (From Tonasket, follow SR 20 east for 37 miles, turning left onto Trout Creek Road/CR 257.) Drive north 0.7 mile, bearing left onto Sheridan Road (CR 253). Continue 4.1 miles (road becomes rough at about 2 miles; later becomes FR 2086) to the trailhead (located about 0.1 mile north of national forest boundary), on your left (elev. 3900 ft). Limited parking.

ON THE TRAIL
The trail starts in a forest of big firs and larches, slowly descending to a narrow valley cut by Granite Creek (elev. 3725 ft). At 0.5 mile, cross the creek on a fairly new and rather sturdy boardwalk (thanks volunteers!); then begin a steep climb.

No silly switchbacks here—it's get down to business and scale that summit. Ascend grassy slopes shaded by a canopy of massive western larches (consider this hike in October). Pocket meadows with views east to Storm King Mountain (a name shared by countless summits from the Olympics to the Appalachians) give reason to pause and catch your breath.

At about 1.4 miles, cross a fence line (elev. 4500 ft), leaving Ferry County and Colville National Forest for Okanogan County and the Okanogan-Wenatchee National Forest. After traversing glades of mature fir, the

Hikers pause to admire a towering western larch.

grade eases a little, now following along a ridgeline. Forest cover thins and views expand, especially east to Storm King and the Kettles, while stately Douglas-firs and western larches in this parkland forest hold up the sky.

At 2.2 miles, the trail cuts across a steep open slope (elev. 4900 ft) beneath the 5299-foot summit of Maple Mountain. Take in good views down Maple Creek and out to Fir Mountain. In summer, this south-facing slope sports showy blossoms. Look for bitterroot, biscuitroot (a parsley), and the rare and endemic Okanogan fameflower (in the miner's lettuce family).

The trail continues across the open slope

for about another 0.25 mile before descending. Continue, or consider summiting Maple Mountain, an easy 0.4-mile off-trail hike from this point. Just turn north and pick a route across the grassy ledges, climbing about 350 feet for good views and even better flower gazing.

EXTENDING YOUR TRIP

Adventurous hikers can continue on the Maple Mountain Trail all the way to Clackamas Mountain. From the flowered slopes, reach Maple Spring in about 0.4 mile, where the trail is easy to lose among cow paths. Angle above the spring and across a meadow to pick up tread again, and round a ridge (elev. 5000 ft) before dropping to a 4650 foot saddle. Then it's about 2.1 miles through larches and over and around open knolls to the Sweat Creek Basin Trail (elev. 5100 ft). Arrange a car shuttle and exit via one of the three trails down Clackamas to the Sweat Creek trailhead.

12 Fir Mountain

RATING/ DIFFICULTY	ROUND-TRIP	ELEV GAIN/ HIGH POINT	SEASON
***/4	5.2 miles	2200 feet/ 5687 feet	June–Nov

Map: USGS Wauconda Summit; **Contact:** Okanogan-Wenatchee National Forest, Tonasket Ranger District, (509) 486-2186, www.fs.fed.us/r6/okawen; **Notes:** Open to horses. Range area. Watch for ticks; **GPS:** N 48 40.567 W 118 53.911

It's a stiff climb to this lonely peak in the heart of the Okanogan Highlands. Long gone is the fire lookout, but views from *the rocky open summit remain in all directions. This short trail, though close to Republic, hasn't netted many visitors. Expect solitude, except for the deer— they're prolific here. In summer, woodland wildflowers are abundant, and in autumn, larches brush the slopes gold.*

GETTING THERE

From Republic, travel west on State Route 20 for 8.5 miles, turning left onto Forest Road 31 (directly across from Sweat Creek Picnic Area). (From Tonasket, head east on SR 20 for 31.5 miles, turning right onto FR 31.) Continue 0.5 mile to the trailhead (elev. 3500 ft) located on your right.

Clackamas Mountain, Maple Mountain, and Storm King Mountain viewed from Fir's open summit

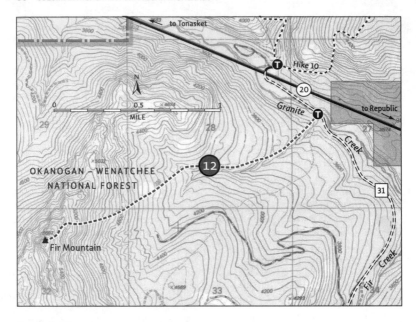

ON THE TRAIL

Start by passing through a gate (and be sure to close it after you). Fir Mountain, like most of the Okanogan and Columbia Highlands, is open range country. After a short initial climb, the way gradually ascends through open forest that has been selectively logged. Plenty of big pines, firs, and larches remain. High grasses line the tread, so be tick wary early in the season. Abundant snags make this a good trip for spotting woodpeckers.

At 1.2 miles, cross a creekbed (elev. 4175 ft) that is usually dry by late summer. Next come some brushy sections, and the grade gets serious. Climb steadily and steeply to reach an open grassy area at about 2 miles. Teaser views east hint at what lies ahead. The trail works its way up, over, and around Fir's granite and gneiss ledges. Admire some unusual rock formations and use caution along the ledges, especially if they're wet, icy, or snowy.

After traversing some open ledges and negotiating a small cleft that warrants a handhold or two, emerge just below the broad open summit. Head right, through a clump of evergreens hiding a privy long out of operation. Then pop back out onto open rock and make the final short ascent to Fir's 5687-foot summit at 2.6 miles.

Some debris remains of the fire lookout last used in the 1950s. Mount Bonaparte dominates the view north, while British Columbia's Baldy and Midway Mountains can be spotted beyond. Just across SR 20, admire Clackamas, Maple, and Storm King Mountains, which share Fir's geological features. The jagged North Cascades line the western horizon, foregrounded by the rounded and gentler Mount Annie and

Moses Mountain. South is Swan Butte, east the Kettle Crest. Lookout worthy to say the least.

13 Swan Lake and Swan Butte

RATING/ DIFFICULTY	LOOP	ELEV GAIN/ HIGH POINT	SEASON
***/2	3.1 miles	360 feet/ 3960 feet	mid-Apr– Nov

Map: USGS Swan Lake; **Contact:** Colville National Forest, Republic Ranger District, (509) 775-7400, www.fs.usda.gov/main /colville; **Notes:** Dogs permitted on-leash except on beach; **GPS:** N 48 30.932 W 118 50.138

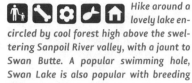

Hike around a lovely lake encircled by cool forest high above the sweltering Sanpoil River valley, with a jaunt to Swan Butte. A popular swimming hole, Swan Lake is also popular with breeding loons. Wander along the tranquil shoreline in early evening or morning to hear this threatened bird's primeval calls.

GETTING THERE
From Republic, follow State Route 21 south for 6.7 miles, turning right onto Scatter Creek Road (Forest Road 53). Follow it for 7.3 miles to Swan Lake Campground and another 0.3 mile to the day-use area and trailhead (elev. 3720 ft). Privy and camping available.

Loon cries can often be heard from Swan Lake's placid waters.

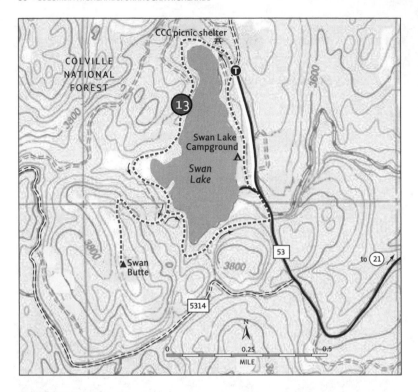

ON THE TRAIL

From the day-use area, head down a stairway to the lakeshore (elev. 3660 ft) to pick up the trail, and start hiking right. Pass a swimming area and a rustic but charming kitchen shelter constructed by the Depression-era Civilian Conservation Corps. Then continue on the trail, rounding a boggy area.

Free of gas-powered boats, the lake is serene, as is the surrounding forest. But the air is filled with the chatter of ground and Douglas squirrels and a cacophony of birdsong from nuthatches, chickadees, and warblers. The buzz of mosquitoes is also frequent in early season.

Trace Swan's shoreline up and over ledges, through pine and fir groves, beneath big cottonwoods and larches, and across huckleberry patches. In late spring, arnica, lupine, penstemon, and wild strawberries brighten the way.

At about 0.6 mile, come to an area prone to early season flooding. Shortly afterward, come to some shoreline ledges perfect for lunching, sunning, and napping. Then round a cove, scamper across a floating bridge, and pass by another marshy area. Look for moose and beaver.

At 1.3 miles, after rounding a ledge providing excellent lake views, reach a junction. The trail right leads to Swan Butte in 0.5 mile—take the flower-lined trail to the 3960-foot butte, with its tattered flag and decent views of the Kettle Crest.

Retrace your steps to the junction and resume looping around the lake. The way passes by yet another quiet cove before utilizing an old road lined with cedars. At 2.7 miles (including the 1-mile butte round-trip), come to FR 53. Turn left. Pass the boat launch and find the trail once more as it travels 0.4 mile through the campground, back to the spur leading to the day-use area.

EXTENDING YOUR TRIP
Spend the night at the inviting Swan Lake Campground and check out the nearby short trails along Fish and Long Lakes.

14 Golden Tiger Pathway

RATING/ DIFFICULTY	ROUND-TRIP	ELEV GAIN/ HIGH POINT	SEASON
**/1	4.6 miles	80 feet/ 2435 feet	Mar–Dec

Map: USGS Republic; **Contact:** Ferry County Trails Association, http://fctrails.com; **Notes:** Wheelchair-accessible. Dogs permitted on-leash. ATVs, motorcycles permitted parallel to paved trail; **GPS:** N 48 38.744 W 118 43.281

 *Located on the eastern edge of the little gold-mining city of Republic, this short paved path is one of the most scenic rail trails in the state. Traversing sunny slopes, stately pine groves, and deep notches blasted into stubborn ledges, the Golden Tiger Pathway chugs along on a route once used for transporting ore to Canadian*

smelters. The path makes for a nice run or a leisurely hike with pauses at scenic overlooks of the pastoral Sanpoil River valley and the imposing Kettle River Range.

GETTING THERE
From the junction of State Routes 20 and 21-south in Republic, head east on SR 20 for 0.6 mile (just past the high school) to the western trailhead (elev. 2425 ft) located on your right. Access for wheelchair users is on the left, 0.2 mile west of the main parking area. (From Kettle Falls, the eastern trailhead is 0.2 mile west of the SR 20/21-north junction, on SR 20 at milepost 305.)

ON THE TRAIL
This trail was named for Republic High School's mascot, and plenty of golden tigers and alumni use this trail that connects the high school to the Ferry County Fairgrounds. The trail uses just a couple of the 28 miles of a former Great Northern Railroad trunk line (built in 1902) that extended from Republic to Danville on the Canadian border. A coalition of trail users and citizens are working hard to keep the section beyond the Golden Tiger nonmotorized (see "On Track with the Ferry County Rail Trail" sidebar). The Golden Tiger is unique in that it has a nonpaved motorized section running beside it. Motorized use is light and should not dissuade you from enjoying this wonderful trail.

Carefully cross the highway and come to a junction. The trail left leads to the wheelchair-accessible parking lot. Turn right and enjoy the old rail grade as it runs along sun-soaked south-facing slopes, home to ground squirrels, yellow-bellied marmots, lizards, and the occasional snake.

Pass groves of big ponderosas, through

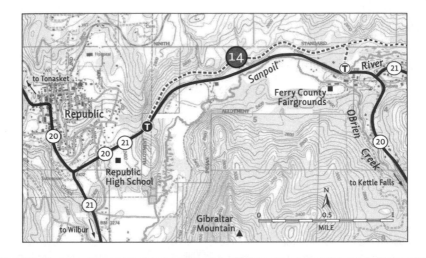

ON TRACK WITH THE FERRY COUNTY RAIL TRAIL

In the golden hills and emerald mountains of Ferry County, a broad coalition of folks called the Ferry County Rail Trail Partners (FCRTP) are moving full-steam ahead trying to create the state's next great rail trail. Realizing the potential this trail has for four-season muscle-powered recreation (and other benefits, including as a safe nonmotorized route for schoolchildren and an economic driver spurring tourism) the partners have their hands full trying to convince critics of the plan and interests that would rather see the corridor opened to motorized recreation.

The partners see the former 28-mile rail line that once serviced timber and mining lands as ideal for hikers, cyclists, and cross-country skiers, taking them along a corridor from the historic gold-mining city of Republic to Danville on the Canadian border. They're also hoping to tie in to British Columbia's Kettle Valley Rail Trail, making the Ferry County Rail Trail the first international rail trail in the western United States.

With stunning views of the Kettle River and the lofty and wild Kettle River Range, the new trail has great potential to lure visitors and promote an economy based on sustainable ecotourism. A major highlight along the trail, Curlew Lake (Hike 15), is home to one of Washington's loveliest state parks, with lakeshore camping and wonderful swimming, fishing, and paddling opportunities. At the north end of the 7-mile-long lake is a historic trestle, destined to be a popular feature along the trail.

For more information, visit the FCRTP online (www.ferrycountyrailtrail.com).

—C. R.

The Golden Tiger pathway makes a good running route as well as a fine hiking path.

cuts below cliffs, and above creek-cradling ravines. Stop to read interpretive signs (the work of Eagle Scout Austin Thompson in 2008) and gaze out from numerous overlooks at the Sanpoil Valley below, and Gibraltar Mountain hovering above it (from this angle, resembling the big European rock of the same name). Enjoy, too, views of the rooftop of Ferry County—the Kettle River Range—off in the east.

At 1.3 miles, reach what we like to call Privy Depot, which aside from its obvious function as a pit stop also offers an excellent valley and mountains view. At 2.2 miles, the paved path bends right to leave the railroad grade, descending a little to reach the eastern trailhead (elev. 2355 ft) near the fairgrounds. It's worth it to walk the last 0.1 mile or so, as it skirts wildlife-rich wetlands fed by the Sanpoil River.

EXTENDING YOUR TRIP

While most of the Ferry County Rail Trail is currently better suited for mountain biking and cross-country skiing than hiking, the section on the north end of Curlew Lake sports a classic trestle spanning a cove on the lake. Access the trail from Kiwanis Road off of SR 21.

15 Curlew Lake Nature Trail

RATING/ DIFFICULTY	LOOP	ELEV GAIN/ HIGH POINT	SEASON
**/1	1.6 miles	160 feet/ 2500 feet	Mar–Nov

Maps: USGS Republic, state park map online (not accurate); **Contact:** Curlew Lake State Park, (509) 775-3592, www.parks.wa.gov /parks; **Notes:** Discover Pass required. Dogs permitted on-leash; **GPS:** N 48 43.069 W 118 39.847

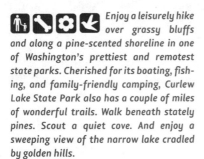 *Enjoy a leisurely hike over grassy bluffs and along a pine-scented shoreline in one of Washington's prettiest and remotest state parks. Cherished for its boating, fishing, and family-friendly camping, Curlew Lake State Park also has a couple of miles of wonderful trails. Walk beneath stately pines. Scout a quiet cove. And enjoy a sweeping view of the narrow lake cradled by golden hills.*

GETTING THERE

From Republic, head east on State Route 20 for 2.9 miles to a junction with SR 21 (just past the county fairgrounds). (From Kettle Falls, follow SR 20 west for 40 miles to the junction.) Follow SR 21 north for 6 miles, turning left onto the state park road. Pass the ranger

residence and bear left to reach a day-use parking area near a beach in 0.8 mile. The trailhead (elev. 2340 ft) is located just south of the restrooms in the campground loop.

ON THE TRAIL

Pick up the trail in the small campground. Within a few steps, the way splits. The trail left was once the main route—now offering a shortcut. Veer right on newer tread cushioned with soft needles from the impressive ponderosa pines overhead.

The trail hugs the shore of the long, slender lake, coming to a nice point at 0.2 mile, complete with a bench for contemplation. When boats aren't present, this is a truly peaceful spot—and a great vantage for birdwatching. Eagles, geese, osprey, and ducks can often be observed, and dragonflies usually flit about. Then hike alongside a quiet cove frequented by docile deer. The rockysandy soil of the hillside is moraine left from the great glaciers of the Ice Age.

At 0.4 mile, come to a junction. The trail left heads back to the trailhead. Continue right, soon coming to an observation deck. Come in the evening and sit still for the bird-watching. The largest North American shorebird, long-billed curlews favor dry grasslands like the ones found in this valley, but they're not common here despite the place name (try the Columbia Basin instead).

Continue past the observation deck and follow a service road a short distance before picking up trail once more. At 0.6 mile, come to another junction (elev. 2400 ft). The loop continues left, but first go right for 0.2 mile—an absolute-must side trip to a viewpoint (elev. 2500 ft) at the edge of an airstrip. Don't venture onto the runway, but do enjoy the sweeping view of Curlew Lake from this vantage.

Towering ponderosa pines grace Curlew's shoreline.

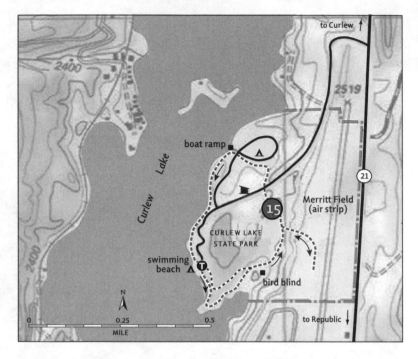

Retrace your steps to the junction and continue straight, soon coming out to the park entrance road. Cross it and find the trail just to the right of the ranger residence. After 0.1 mile, you'll reach the main campground loop. Head left on the campground road to the boat launch. Pick up the trail for a final time and continue 0.3 mile along the lakeshore beneath a canopy of pines, returning to the beach and your vehicle.

EXTENDING YOUR TRIP

Venture by car to the north end of Curlew Lake for a short hike along the old railbed to an intact, historic, and highly scenic trestle. Park where the Ferry County Rail Trail crosses Kiwanis Road (1.7 miles from the junction with SR 21), and walk a short distance west.

Opposite: Barnaby Buttes and White Mountain from alpine meadows on Bald Mountain

kettle river range

Corralled by the Kettle River in the north and northeast, the Columbia River in the east and south, and the Sanpoil River in the west, the Kettle River Range forms an imposing wall across the western Columbia Highlands, with several peaks exceeding 7000 feet. It's an impressive range, yet these peaks—among the oldest in Washington— are gentle giants. Their smooth contours and rounded ridges make them more like the Smoky Mountains of North Carolina than the North Cascades. The surrounding countryside resembles Montana, with its big-sky valleys, parkland pine forests, and golden grassy hillsides. Deer are profuse and other wildlife abundant too. The Kettles contain some of the largest roadless tracts of national forest lands in Eastern Washington. To the Colville First Peoples, these mountains were sacred—a sanctuary for young warriors to engage in vision quests. With miles of excellent trails traversing them, including a 43-mile route across the range's rooftop crest, the Kettles offer some of the finest hiking in the state.

16 Gibraltar Trail

RATING/ DIFFICULTY	ROUND-TRIP	ELEV GAIN/ HIGH POINT	SEASON
***/2	3.2 miles	550 feet/ 4200 feet	May–Nov

Map: USGS Bear Mountain; **Contact:** Colville National Forest, Republic Ranger District, (509) 775-7400, www.fs.usda.gov /main/colville; **Notes:** Open to mountain bikes, horses. Trail is under construction. Call ahead for updates, closures. Completed trail will be 12+-mile loop connecting to Ferry County Fairgrounds; **GPS:** N 48 35.856 W 118 41.478

Locally known as Old Gib, 3782-foot Gibraltar Mountain rises 1200 feet above the quaint mining town of Republic. Long admired from the valley, now thanks to a consortium of recreationists this beloved local landmark is sprouting a network of scenic trails. The first few miles are in place, and you can amble along a rolling ridge bursting with wildflowers and sweeping views, from Republic nestled below to the nearby lofty Kettle Crest.

GETTING THERE
From Republic, head east on State Route 20 for 7.3 miles, turning right onto Hall Creek Road (Forest Road 99) (4.3 miles beyond the junction with SR 21). (From Kettle Falls, head west on SR 20 for 36 miles, turning left onto FR 99.) Continue 0.3 mile and turn right onto FR 2053. Follow this good dirt road 5 miles to the trailhead (elev. 3675 ft) located on your left. Privy available.

ON THE TRAIL
Not since the 1930s, when the Civilian Conservations Corps was in full swing, has there been any major trail building in the hills above Republic. But all that changed in 2010 when recreation and conservation groups, in cooperation with the Forest Service, broke ground on a new trail network. Hard-working volunteers from Conservation Northwest, the Ferry County Trails Association, the Kettle Range Conservation Group, the Spokane Mountaineers, and the Washington Trails Association, along with trail crews from the Forest Service and the Curlew Job Corps (for disadvantaged youth), have constructed the first few miles of trail in what will eventually become a 12-mile loop with a connecting 6-mile spur to the Ferry County Fairgrounds.

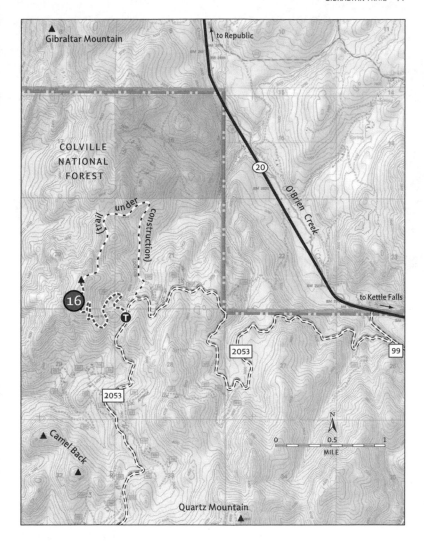

Close to town and open to hikers, equestrians, and mountain bikers, and with an elevation low enough to allow for early and late-season rambling, the Gibraltar Trail is sure to become a popular destination for locals and visitors alike. As of this book's publication, a short but highly scenic section has been constructed to a 4200-foot knoll.

While the Kettles are shrouded in clouds, balsamroot embraces spring sunshine.

In the summer of 2012, there was no tread taking off from the trailhead—just flagging denoting where the route would run. To reach the section of trail currently built, walk a short distance left on FR 2053 and then turn right onto a secondary dirt road. Yes, you could drive this road, but it makes for nice walking and gives you a little more exercise.

Follow this road 0.7 mile to an old gravel quarry (elev. 3825 ft). Look just to the west and notice new tread. Heading north, the way immediately leaves the forest for flowered slopes. Wind up balds and ridges bursting with blossoms, and enjoy emerging views along with the floral show. Locate Brown Mountain's open pyramidal summit to the south. Just in front of it, notice the open slopes of the Camel Back. The trail is slated to wrap around that enticing ridge!

Continue on newly constructed tread, gently climbing and wrapping around a 4200-foot knoll at 1.4 miles. Views are excellent—especially southwest down the Sanpoil River valley and southeast over the Thirteen-mile Canyon region. The Kettle Crest rises prominently to the east, but that view gets better, so keep hiking along the ridge, with flowers like shooting stars, balsamroot, and phlox at your feet, to name just a few.

As of 2012, the tread ended at 1.6 miles in a small saddle (elev. 4175 ft). Continue left a short distance to a 4200-foot open knoll for a sweeping view that encompasses Mount Bonaparte and the Okanogan Highlands and the Kettle Crest from Mount Leona to White Mountain. Republic sits snuggly below, between hills that once yielded gold and that turn gold each fall thanks to larches. The peak just to your north is Old Gib, where a spur trail will eventually lead and then continue on to the fairgrounds. Anticipate more great hiking in the near future.

EXTENDING YOUR TRIP

The completed trail will drop down from this knoll into groves of larches and impressive ponderosas, passing a few small ponds along the way. It will then angle back via an old woods road, returning to the trailhead at about 4.3 miles. The southern loop will traverse more open ridges, with a spur to 4784-foot Quartz Mountain, before dropping into a drainage, wrapping around the Camel Back, and crossing Camel Creek to meet up with the present tread. It will be glorious!

17 Thirteenmile Canyon

RATING/ DIFFICULTY	ROUND-TRIP	ELEV GAIN/ HIGH POINT	SEASON
****/3	9 miles	1700 feet/ 3750 feet	Apr–Nov

Maps: USGS Thirteenmile Creek, USGS Bear Mountain; **Contact:** Colville National Forest, Republic Ranger District, (509) 775-7400, www.fs.usda.gov/main/colville; **Notes:** Open to mountain bikes, horses. Watch for rattlesnakes, ticks; **GPS:** N 48 28.904 W 118 43.643

    *Venture through some of the most lonely, rugged, and spectacular backcountry in all of northeastern Washington. Traverse a deep and narrow canyon flanked by towering granite walls, before emerging onto its lofty rim graced with groves of stately old-growth ponderosa pine and sprawling meadows awash with wildflowers. Bears, deer, and cougars prowl this wild corridor, while eagles and hawks ride thermals above looking for bounty.*

GETTING THERE
From Republic, follow State Route 21 south for 12.3 miles to the trailhead (elev. 2050 ft), located just within the Colville Indian Reservation at milepost 148. (From Wilbur, follow SR 21 north for 56 miles to the trailhead.) Privy and primitive camping available.

ON THE TRAIL
The Thirteenmile Trail leads 18 miles from the cottonwood-lined Sanpoil River to Hall Creek Road near the pine and larch–shrouded Kettle Crest. An old sheep and cattle drive, this trail travels through the 4700-acre Cougar Mountain and 12,700-acre Thirteenmile Roadless Areas. Both parcels are rich in wildlife and old growth

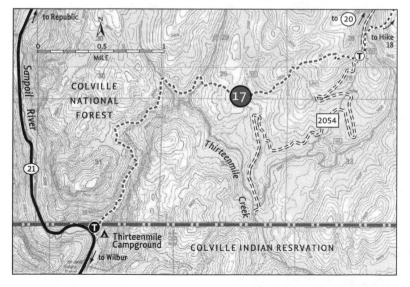

and have long been sought by area conservation groups for inclusion in the national wilderness preservation system.

These lands are also historically significant and were once part of the Colville Confederated Tribes' reservation. But by the late 1800s, settlement in this region had accelerated, as miners, ranchers, and squatters trespassed onto these Native lands. Bowing to pressure, Congress withdrew the northern half of the Colville Reservation in 1892, reducing the reservation by 1.5 million acres. The influx of homesteaders brought an increase in ranching, logging, sheep grazing, and mining. Remnants and relics of these early pursuits can be seen along this trail.

Some of the biggest and oldest ponderosa pines in the state grow in the Thirteenmile Canyon.

The way immediately enters the impressive canyon of Thirteenmile Creek. Extreme heat is common in the summer, but big pines provide some shade relief. Spring is lovely, with agreeable temperatures and carpets of wildflowers that brighten the canyon floor. Look for larkspur, calypso orchid, and arnica. And keep an eye out for rattlesnakes—the canyon harbors a healthy population.

At about 1 mile, cross a scree slope and begin working your way up out of the canyon. The tread can be rocky at times. When not watching your footing, stare up at the impressive sheer canyon walls surrounding you. At about 1.8 miles, reach an overlook (elev. 3000 ft) of the canyon and the terrain you just traversed. Then enjoy easy going along the rim through pine groves and thickets of Douglas maple that add golden streaks to the forest come autumn.

At about 2.2 miles, reach a draw that usually harbors a flowing creek. Just shy of 3 miles, come to another creek-flowing draw (elev. 2900 ft). Continue through open forest and grassy areas (watch for ticks), coming to a small wetland and the remains of an old herder camp at about 3.4 miles. A quarter mile beyond, reach an old road (elev. 3050 ft). Carry on if curiosity and wanderlust persist.

At 4.5 miles, crest a small ridge (elev. 3750 ft) that grants views of the surrounding wild and lonely hills and meadowy Thirteenmile Mountain to the east. This is a good spot to call it a day. From here the trail switchbacks downward, reaching the Cougar trailhead (elev. 3550 ft) on FR 2054 in about 0.8 mile.

EXTENDING YOUR TRIP

Continue beyond the Cougar trailhead for 3.2 miles to Thirteenmile Mountain (Hike 18), traversing impressive old-growth groves of ponderosa pines and some of the wildest and prettiest country in northeastern Washington. Or, arrange a car shuttle for a one-way trip from the Bear Pot or Cougar trailheads down to the Sanpoil River trailhead.

⑱ Thirteenmile Mountain

RATING/ DIFFICULTY	ROUND-TRIP	ELEV GAIN/ HIGH POINT	SEASON
*****/3	9.2 miles	1800 feet/ 4885 feet	May–Nov

Maps: USGS Bear Mountain, USGS Edds Mountain; **Contact:** Colville National Forest, Republic Ranger District, (509) 775-7400, www.fs.usda.gov/main/colville; **Notes:** Open to mountain bikes, horses. Watch for ticks. FR 2053 is rough in spots, requires high-clearance; **GPS:** N 48 30.998 W 118 36.069

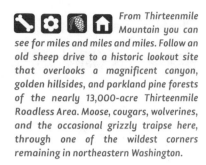 From Thirteenmile Mountain you can see for miles and miles and miles. Follow an old sheep drive to a historic lookout site that overlooks a magnificent canyon, golden hillsides, and parkland pine forests of the nearly 13,000-acre Thirteenmile Roadless Area. Moose, cougars, wolverines, and the occasional grizzly traipse here, through one of the wildest corners remaining in northeastern Washington.

GETTING THERE
From Republic, head east on State Route 20 for 7.3 miles, turning right onto Hall Creek Road (Forest Road 99) (4.3 miles beyond the junction with SR 21). (From Kettle Falls, head west on SR 20 for 36 miles, turning left onto FR 99.) Follow this at-first good gravel road 5.2 miles to where FR 600 bears left.

An endless landscape of rolling hills and grassy slopes can be viewed from the old lookout site.

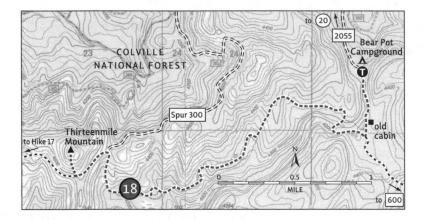

(Note: County Road 233 through Refrigerator Canyon is washed out, hence this longer approach.) Continue right, now on Nine Mile Road (FR 2053), and come to a junction in 2.7 miles. Bear left onto FR 2054, passing the Nine Mile Falls trailhead (an excellent 0.3-mile trail to the falls), and after 0.6 mile bear left onto FR 2055. Follow it for 3.4 miles to a primitive campground and the trailhead at road's end (elev. 4200 ft).

ON THE TRAIL

The hike begins on the Bear Pot Trail near a seasonal wetland. Follow the good trail through boggy forest and at 0.5 mile reach an old trapper's cabin. Then continue through a stand of lodgepole pine, and after a brief climb reach a junction (elev. 4400 ft) with the Thirteenmile Trail at 0.8 mile.

An old sheep drive, the Thirteenmile Trail travels nearly 18 miles from the Sanpoil River to Hall Creek Road near the Kettle Crest. Except for a handful of intrepid Pacific Northwest Trail through-hikers and a few deer hunters in the fall, expect to be alone. Chances are better of meeting up with

four-legged trail users—deer, moose, bear, coyotes, and cougars. Moose tracks and droppings attest to the frequency of at least these visitors.

Turn right, heading west through parkland ponderosa pine forest, with its carpet of golden grasses (watch for ticks in spring) and clusters of shrubby Douglas maples (admire colors in fall) that provide excellent forage for woodland critters. After ascending a small knoll (elev. 4575 ft) and passing an old mine bore, the way drops into a small lush ravine. At 1.9 miles, cross Thirteenmile Creek (elev. 4150 ft), a mere trickle at this point; then begin climbing 125 feet or so out of the canyon.

Now traversing south-facing slopes, wander by some pines impressive in age and stature. Pass meadows and an old burn rife with big snags that harbor all types of insects, birds, and small mammals. At 3.4 miles, skirt a large grassy wetland lined with aspen (elev. 4175 ft). Then begin climbing again, weaving through more ancient groves of giant ponderosas. The way rounds some knolls and makes a few dips, crossing meadows and forest of spruce and larch. The habitat diversity is rich.

At 4.1 miles, reach an old jeep track (elev. 4500 ft) once used to access the fire tower on Thirteenmile Mountain. Known as FR Spur 300, it can still be driven by high-clearance vehicles and offers a much shorter (and less interesting) approach to this hike. Walk left along the track a short way, and then turn left back onto the trail.

Climb across open grassy slopes, skirting just below the summit of Thirteenmile Mountain. At about 4.4 miles (elev. 4650 ft), where the trail begins to curve west, leave the tread and head directly north for 0.2 mile off-trail, up to the 4885-foot summit. All that remains of the fire lookout are concrete blocks, some well-weathered timbers—and spellbinding views in every direction: North along the Kettle Crest to British Columbia's Midway Mountains. West to Mount Bonaparte and the rolling Okanogan Highlands. South, trace Thirteenmile Creek through its magnificent canyon. And east, admire the well-rounded lofty summits of Granite, Fire, and Seventeenmile Mountains. Resembling Appalachian peaks with their well-worn façades, these mountains are among the oldest in Washington.

EXTENDING YOUR TRIP
For a truly lonesome journey, follow the Thirteenmile Trail east from the Bear Pot Trail junction. The way climbs to a 5150-foot gap between Fire and Seventeenmile Mountains (both nice off-trail scrambles) before descending 800 feet through ancient ponderosas to reach FR 600 at 4.9 miles.

19 Edds and Bald Mountains

RATING/ DIFFICULTY	ROUND-TRIP	ELEV GAIN/ HIGH POINT	SEASON
*****/4	10.6 miles	2450 feet/ 6300 feet	June–Nov

Map: USGS Edds Mountain; **Contact:** Colville National Forest, Republic Ranger District, (509) 775-7400, www.fs.usda.gov /main/colville; **Notes:** Open to mountain bikes, horses. Watch for ticks. FR 99 is rough in spots, requires high-clearance; **GPS:** N 48 33.999 W 118 33.642

Hike one of the Kettle River Range's loneliest trails to one of its most beautiful alpine meadows set beneath one of its most distinguished summits. It's a stiff climb with many

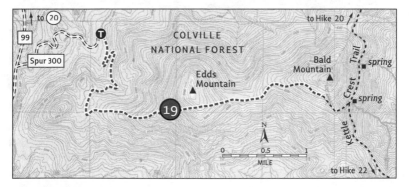

A "holy" snag among the sprawling meadows of Bald Mountain.

rewards: solitude, stunning scenery, and the opportunity to scramble a couple of soaring summits. The wildflower displays along this trail rank among the finest in Eastern Washington, and the habitat traversed is some of the best in the state for elusive megafauna.

GETTING THERE

From Republic, head east on State Route 20 for 7.3 miles, turning right onto Hall Creek Road (Forest Road 99) (4.3 miles beyond the junction with SR 21). (From Kettle Falls, head west on SR 20 for 36 miles, turning left onto FR 99.) Follow this at-first good gravel road 4.4 miles and turn left onto FR Spur 300. Continue 1.5 miles to the trailhead (elev. 4350 ft). Privy and primitive campsites available.

ON THE TRAIL

The way starts by following an old logging road. The grade is gentle and the walking pleasurable, but the roadway is covered in tall grasses, so be tick aware early in the season. At 1.9 miles, come to the old trailhead (elev. 4880 ft). Turn left and follow cairns to begin climbing—steeply at times—up a ridge and through the 1988 White Mountain burn zone (hot and dry; carry lots of water). Clumps of willows and hardy evergreens that survived the fire dot the hillside, and wildflowers paint the open hillsides.

Savor the sweet smell of juniper and sage and admire lichen-blotched granite ledges along the way. Survey the countryside too. The views west and south are expansive. Look south at Granite, Fire, and Seventeenmile Mountains—they look like they belong in the Appalachians. The last Ice Age did a nice job wearing down these peaks, among the oldest in Washington.

Climbing higher, the way steepens and the tread gets sketchy across grassy slopes. Watch for cairns. The trail skirts below Edds's 6550-foot summit, topping out at about 6300 feet at 3.6 miles. It's an easy scramble to the mountain's high point if you're so inclined. Otherwise, continue on what soon becomes one of the prettiest sections of trail in the entire Kettle River Range.

Across sprawling meadows bursting with blossoms, slowly descend to a saddle. Only the views can rival the wildflowers: Look south to the Barnaby Buttes, Grizzly Mountain, and White Mountain along the Kettle Crest. Locate the Hall Ponds, a research area with rare flora, straddling the high divide between Hall and Ninemile Creeks. And stare east at pyramidal Bald Mountain, the rockiest and craggiest of all the Kettles. When viewed from the north Bald looks forbidding, but from the south the summit appears more subdued, wrapped in inviting alpine meadows.

After passing through a patch of pines that escaped the big fire of 1988, reach the saddle (elev. 6050 ft) between Edds and Bald Mountains at 4.1 miles. Then gently ascend and traverse sublime meadows, high across Bald's southern slopes, to crest a ridge (elev. 6300 ft) at 5.3 miles. This is a good turnaround point. From here the trail drops 300 feet in 0.5 mile, reaching the Kettle Crest Trail at a spring.

In the past few years, there have been a few confirmed grizzly sightings in this lonely and wild country. Whether this monarch of the mountains will survive in Washington is a matter of public policy. Groups like Conservation Northwest advocate and educate about the importance of retaining and recovering grizzly populations in the Northwest.

EXTENDING YOUR TRIP

Bald Mountain's 6940-foot summit makes a nice scramble. Head up open slopes to the summit block, and then carefully pick your way up through jumbled talus to the pointy peak for one of the best 360-degree views in the Kettles.

20 Snow Peak Cabin

RATING/ DIFFICULTY	ROUND-TRIP	ELEV GAIN/ HIGH POINT	SEASON
****/3	6.4 miles	1275 feet/ 6350 feet	June–Nov

Map: USGS Sherman Peak; **Contact:** Colville National Forest, Republic Ranger District, (509) 775-7400, www.fs.usda.gov/main /colville; **Notes:** Open to mountain bikes, horses. Watch for ticks. Reserve the cabin at www.recreation.gov; **GPS:** N 48 35.058 W 118 31.916

  Hike across an eerily beautiful landscape of silver snags left behind from the 1988 White Mountain Burn. It's been over a quarter century since much of Snow Peak went up in flames, but a new and regenerating forest is busy reclaiming the mountain. Enjoy prolific wildflowers and sweeping views en route to a charming mountain cabin set high along the Kettle Crest.

GETTING THERE

From Republic, head east on State Route 20 for 7.3 miles, turning right onto Hall Creek Road (Forest Road 99) (4.3 miles beyond the

The Snow Peak Cabin sits on a high gap beneath the summit of Snow Peak.

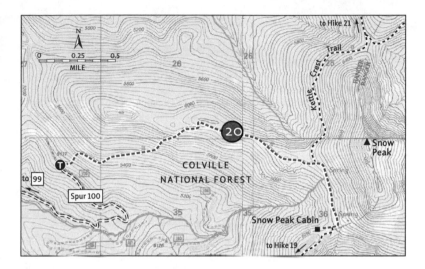

junction with SR 21). (From Kettle Falls, head west on SR 20 for 36 miles, turning left onto FR 99.) Follow this at-first good gravel road for 3.3 miles, turning left just beyond a cattle guard onto FR Spur 100. Reach the trailhead (elev. 5250 ft) in 4.7 miles.

ON THE TRAIL

Immediately starting in the old burn zone, the trail wastes no time climbing. A few surviving big firs provide some shade among the many snags. The understory is grassy here (planted after the fire to prevent erosion), so watch for ticks early in the season. The open forest and plentiful forage favors deer. You should see plenty. Lots of flowers too—asters and lupine paint the hillsides purple.

Continue ascending. At times the trail is lined with walls of willows and 15- to 20-foot pines—nature in action regenerating the mountain. At 2.3 miles, crest a 6325-foot knoll. Then descend slightly, coming to a junction with the Kettle Crest Trail (elev.

6300 ft) at 2.5 miles. Turn right and traverse the high open slopes of Snow Peak. At 7103 feet, Snow is the second highest of the Kettle peaks and, as its name suggests, often harbors snow into the summer months. A popular backcountry skiing destination, the cabin you are heading to is well used and appreciated by winter recreationists.

After a little more climbing, reach a spring (elev. 6350 ft); then begin descending across open slopes. Lupine, paintbrush, fireweed, and pearly everlastings contrast with the silver snags and blackened logs left behind by the fire. Views are excellent to pointy Bald Mountain (south) and across the Okanogan Highlands to Mount Bonaparte, Clackamas Mountain, and Bodie Mountain.

At 3.1 miles, come to a junction near a spring. Take the trail right for a short distance to the Snow Peak Cabin (elev. 6200 ft). Resembling a pioneer cabin (with solar panels!), it has space for six people (dogs allowed). It was built by the Snow

Peak Shelter Alliance (consisting of various recreation groups) and the Colville National Forest, and it opened to the public in 1996. If it's unoccupied, check it out. Otherwise, please respect the privacy of any groups staying at the facility. Stargazing is amazing from the cabin site—and morning coffee on the porch looking out at Snow Peak is divine.

EXTENDING YOUR TRIP
The Kettle Crest Trail south to the Edds Mountain Trail offers lonely rambling and nice views east. And the 7103-foot summit of Snow Peak makes for a good cross-country ramble. Although steep, it's fairly straightforward, across alpine meadows. The views are amazing, from British Columbia's Rossland Range to Lake Roosevelt.

21 Sherman Peak

RATING/ DIFFICULTY	LOOP	ELEV GAIN/ HIGH POINT	SEASON
*****/3	6 miles	1200 feet/ 6400 feet	mid-June– Nov

Maps: USGS Sherman Peak, USGS Copper Butte; **Contact:** Colville National Forest, Republic Ranger District, (509) 775-7400, www.fs.usda.gov/main/colville; **Notes:** Open to mountain bikes, horses; **GPS:** N 48 36.514 W 118 28.605

Enjoy striking views of the forces of nature. This full circle around 6998-foot Sherman Peak passes through two radically different landscapes: a lush, green old-growth forest and one that was scorched by wildfire, leaving surreal silver snags behind. But nature has come full circle too, as the fire-consumed forest is nicely regenerating.

And with these diverse forest communities, wildlife is prolific. Don't forget the binoculars.

GETTING THERE
From Republic, head east on State Route 20 for 16.8 miles to Sherman Pass. (From Kettle Falls, follow SR 20 west for 26 miles to Sherman Pass.) Turn left (north) and follow the access road 0.1 mile to the trailhead (elev. 5500 ft). Privy available.

ON THE TRAIL
Easy access, being a loop, and having plenty of views make this hike one of the more popular in the Kettles. From the trailhead, head left (south) on the Kettle Crest Trail, quickly coming to a junction with the Sherman Pass Trail (which travels 4 miles to the Jungle Hill Trail) and the Sherman Pass Tie Trail (which heads 0.7 mile to the Sherman Overlook Campground). For Sherman Peak, continue right, dropping steeply into a cool, wet, tight ravine (elev. 5360 ft). Climb out of it and come to SR 20 at 0.4 mile. The trail resumes on the other side of the highway; be careful crossing the road.

In cool larch and lodgepole pine forest, gently climb, winding around granite ledges and passing window views east. At 1 mile, come to a junction (elev. 5800 ft) by a creek and winter emergency cache. You'll be returning from the right on the Sherman Peak Loop Trail, so continue left on the Kettle Crest Trail. At 1.4 miles, after skirting beneath a large talus slope, reach the edge of the 1988 White Mountain burn zone (elev. 5900 ft). This lightning-caused fire burned more than 20,000 acres, but more than twenty-five years later, new green growth has crowded out the silver snags and blackened logs.

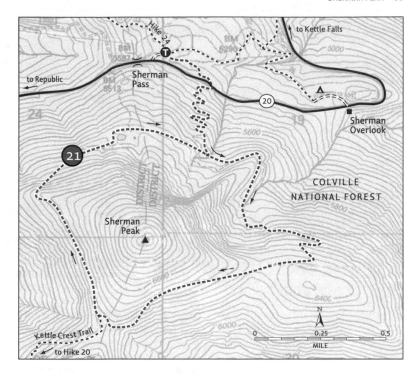

Begin a long sweeping traverse of Sherman's eastern ridge. Rows of 10+-foot-tall pines and fragrant lupines line the way. Pause to take in excellent views north of Columbia, Wapaloosie, King, and Mack Mountains. At 2.4 miles, crest the ridge in a small saddle (elev. 6300 ft). Then traverse Sherman's southern slopes, with views of Snow Peak, the Barnaby Buttes, and White Mountain.

Aster and lupine paint Sherman a purple mountain majesty. Woodpeckers and nuthatches flit upon the snags. The mountain is vibrant and alive. The trail climbs higher but doesn't go to the top of Sherman. It's an easy scramble to the 6998-foot pyramidal summit if you feel like peak bagging.

At 3.2 miles, just beyond a faint trail leading down to a campsite, come to a junction (elev. 6400 ft). The Kettle Crest Trail continues south to the Snow Peak Cabin (Hike 20). Head right instead, onto the Sherman Peak Loop Trail, crossing gorgeous meadows and savoring sweeping views west across snaking Highway 20 to the Okanogan Highlands and North Cascades.

The way then descends at a good clip to reenter forest before wrapping around the north side of Sherman Peak. At 4.1 miles, take a break at a ledge that grants a superb view of Columbia Peak and Sherman Pass. Then leave the burn zone at 4.4 miles, entering cool stands of pine and larch. Skirt

Silver snags punctuate grassy slopes on Sherman Peak.

beneath a scree slope and by little Sherman Pond, one of the few ponds located within this mountain range. Cross its outlet and shortly afterward, at 5 miles, reach a familiar junction and turn left to close the loop in 1 mile.

22 Barnaby Buttes

RATING/ DIFFICULTY	ROUND-TRIP	ELEV GAIN/ HIGH POINT	SEASON
***/3	7.4 miles	1975 feet/ 6534 feet	June–early Nov

Map: USGS Sherman Pass; **Contact:** Colville National Forest, Three Rivers Ranger District, Kettle Falls, (509) 738-7700, www.fs.usda .gov/main/colville; **Notes:** Open to mountain bikes, horses. Last 1.5 miles of FR 2014-500 are rough, requires high-clearance; **GPS:** N 48 32.274 W 118 26.741

 Follow an old fire road, first through thick timber, then through silver forest to an old fire lookout site propped above meadows flush with flowers and fauna. Only four pillars and a concrete staircase remain of the Barnaby Buttes lookout tower. But the views from this lonely post across this wild corner of the Kettles are still grand. This is moose, bear, coyote, and cougar habitat, so you might luck into seeing them on this seldom-hiked route.

GETTING THERE

From Kettle Falls, drive west on State Route 20/US Highway 395 for 3.6 miles to where the routes split. Continue west on SR 20 (Sherman Pass National Scenic Byway) for 10.3 miles, turning left onto South Fork Sherman Creek Road (FR 2020). Follow this good gravel road for 6.5 miles to a junction.

(From Republic, follow SR 20 east for 20.5 miles, turning right onto FR 2020—3.6 miles east of Sherman Pass. Continue south for 5.9 miles to the junction with FR 2014.) Bear left onto Barnaby Creek Road (FR 2014), and after 0.3 mile turn right onto FR 2014-500. Follow this road for 2.4 miles (bear left at 0.9 mile) to the trailhead (elev. 4600 ft).

ON THE TRAIL

Beginning on an old, well-graded fire road, immediately start climbing through a thick stand of pine and larch. Skirt a creek (the only water along the way) and an old cut, and continue beneath a cool forest canopy. The way may be littered with moose and deer droppings and plenty of tracks from the predators that pursue them, particularly cougars and coyotes.

At 2.1 miles, after making a couple of sweeping switchbacks, enter the 1988 White Mountain burn zone. The forest is recovering well, but plenty of snags and blackened logs still provide excellent habitat for insects and birds. White Mountain, where the fire began, can be seen to the south. Its northern slopes of granitic talus fields put the "white" into the mountain.

At 2.6 miles, come to a junction with the Kettle Crest Trail, atop the crest itself (elev. 6060 ft). Left leads to White Mountain (Hike 23). Right meanders toward the Barnaby Buttes—your objective. Cutting a path through 5- to 8-foot-tall lodgepole pines, the trail soon leaves the old fire road to march up a knob cloaked in golden grasses. Enjoy excellent views down into the wild Hall and Thirteenmile Creek drainages.

Slightly descend into a pocket of greenery spared from the conflagration of 1988, and once again follow the old woods road. At 3.4 miles (elev. 6300 ft), come to a signed junc-tion with the spur leading to the old lookout site. The spur exists only in memory. Numerous blowdowns obfuscate the way, which completely disappears in the grassy slopes below the summit. Don't let that hinder your exploration. Just make your way north across the open slope, aiming for a small knob graced with aspen and juniper. After about 0.3 mile, reach the 6534-foot summit with its staircase to heaven.

Views are grand across Barnaby's lofty lawns to Huckleberry Mountain and Calispell Peak to the east; White Mountain and Grizzly Mountain to the south; Thirteenmile, Fire, Granite, and Moses Mountains to the west;

White Mountain from Kettle Crest Trail on the way to Barnaby Buttes

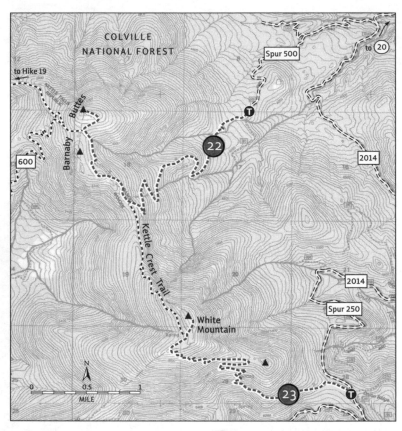

and Edds and Bald Mountains to the north. A sliver of Lake Roosevelt can often be seen shimmering in the late-afternoon sun. Consider staying on the summit late into the day, for it abounds with wildlife.

EXTENDING YOUR TRIP

Hike to White Mountain (Hike 23) from the Barnaby Buttes and Kettle Crest Trail junction. It's about 1.5 miles to the summit spur trail and another 0.3 mile to the top.

23 White Mountain

RATING/ DIFFICULTY	ROUND-TRIP	ELEV GAIN/ HIGH POINT	SEASON
****/3	6.8 miles	1725 feet/ 6923 feet	mid-June– Nov

Map: USGS Sherman Pass; **Contact:** Colville National Forest, Three Rivers Ranger District, Kettle Falls, (509) 738-7700, www.fs.usda .gov/main/colville; **Notes:** Open to mountain bikes, horses. Respect this sacred site of the Colville Confederated Tribes. Do not disturb artifacts or rock pits; **GPS:** N 48 30.092 W 118 25.312

 *A broad, lofty summit along the Kettle Crest, White Mountain provides stunning views down to Lake Roosevelt and across the vast ridges and valleys of northeastern Washington. Sacred site to Native peoples for vision questing, and home to moose, wolverine, and the occasional grizzly, White will instill a sense of reverence for nature in all who hike its wildflower-carpeted slopes.*

GETTING THERE
From Kettle Falls, drive west on State Route 20/US Highway 395 for 3.6 miles to where the routes split. Continue west on SR 20 (Sherman Pass National Scenic Byway) for 10.3 miles, turning left onto South Fork Sherman Creek Road (FR 2020). Follow this good gravel road for 6.5 miles to a junction, and bear left onto Barnaby Creek Road (FR 2014). (From Republic, follow SR 20 east for 20.5 miles, turning right onto FR 2020—the junction is 3.6 miles east of Sherman Pass. Continue south for 5.9 miles to the junction with FR 2014.) Continue on FR 2014 for 4.1 miles, turning right onto FR Spur 250. Follow this rough road 4.4 miles to the trailhead (elev. 5225 ft).

ON THE TRAIL
The epicenter of a 1988 wildfire that scorched more than 20,000 acres along the Kettle Crest, White Mountain's natural communities were radically altered—but not destroyed. Nature is resilient and always in flux. It didn't take long for feisty pine

Sunny flowered slopes on White Mountain

saplings to burst from the blackened soil. Grasses and a profusion of wildflowers now carpet the once scorched forest floor. And the now-more-diverse floral cover favors a wider variety of wild critters. Moose, deer, bear, coyote, and cougar are abundant, woodpeckers and raptors profuse.

While patches of mature fir and larch survived the fire, shade is at a premium. Start early, don't forget the sunscreen, and carry plenty of water. Start in the burn zone and weave through a few lone larches and thickets of willows. After about 0.4 mile, start to climb. After about another 0.4 mile, skirt a talus slope of the shiny white granite that gives the mountain its name.

At 1.2 miles, begin to switchback near a spring and stock trough (elev. 5600 ft). Steadily ascend nicely graded switchbacks through patches of mature forest. At 1.8 miles, emerge in sprawling meadows bursting with summer wildflowers. Views are excellent south into the Colville Indian Reservation, of Grizzly Peak and the Hall Creek drainage.

At 3 miles, crest the mountain's southwestern shoulder (elev. 6770 ft). Enter forest and slightly descend, coming to a small meadow at about 3.1 miles. The unmaintained trail to the summit heads to the right (look for a weathered sign on a snag) and may be hard to follow in spots, but the route is pretty straightforward. After about 0.3 mile, reach White's 6923-foot summit and its extensive views: from the Columbia Plateau south to all along the Kettle Crest north, and from the Selkirks east to the North Cascades west. Just below the old lookout site are talus slopes dotted with rock pits built by young tribal members for vision quests. Close your eyes. Listen to the winds. Feel the sun's rays. A powerful place indeed.

EXTENDING YOUR TRIP

The Kettle Crest Trail begins here and travels more than 43 miles along some of the highest summits in Eastern Washington, making it a fine backpacking route. And Barnaby Buttes (Hike 22) is just a few miles north along the trail.

24 Columbia Mountain

RATING/ DIFFICULTY	ROUND-TRIP	ELEV GAIN/ HIGH POINT	SEASON
****/3	8 miles	1360 feet/ 6782 feet	June–Nov

Maps: USGS Sherman Peak, USGS Copper Butte; **Contact:** Colville National Forest, Republic Ranger District, (509) 775-7400, www.fs.usda.gov/main/colville; **Notes:** Open to mountain bikes, horses. Range area; **GPS:** N 48 36.519 W 118 28.609

You'll find excellent views of Wapaloosie and King Mountains from Columbia's summit loop trail.

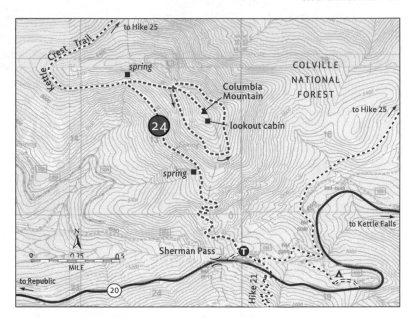

Roam high-country meadows carpeted with dazzling wildflowers. Enjoy sweeping views south to the lofty, lumpy Kettle Crest and east to the unbroken swaths of forest cloaking the Sherman Creek valley, King Mountain, and the Twin Sisters. Flush clutches of grouse and greet herds of deer while ambling to a historic fire lookout cabin that has graced this summit since 1914. These are some of the charms awaiting you on this easily accessible hike.

GETTING THERE
From Republic, head east on State Route 20 for 16.8 miles to Sherman Pass. (From Kettle Falls, follow SR 20 west for 26 miles to Sherman Pass.) Turn left (north) and follow the access road 0.1 mile to the trailhead (elev. 5500 ft). Privy available.

ON THE TRAIL
Sherman Pass offers the easiest access to the 43+-mile Kettle Crest Trail. A national recreation trail, lucky Trail No. 13 (the trail's official number) winds along the soaring spine of the Kettle River Range. Heart of the Columbia Highlands and transition zone between the coastal Cascades and interior Rockies, the Kettles are rich in biological diversity and act as an ecological bridge between those two other ranges.

Follow the Kettle Crest Trail north through cool groves of pine and fir and carpets of lupine, arnica, and other showy flowers. At 0.2 mile, cross a power-line swath and then enter the 29,000-acre Profanity Roadless Area, the largest unprotected roadless tract remaining in Eastern Washington (see "Untrammeled Eastern Washington" sidebar in the Blue Mountains section). This

WILDERNESS, JOBS, AND A WAY OF LIFE IN THE BALANCE

Northeast Washington's Columbia Highlands is the Evergreen State's final frontier. It's a land of wide-open spaces still harboring some of the West's wildest and most threatened species—grizzly, caribou, wolverine, and lynx. It's sparsely populated by folks who still make a living working off the land.

While large portions of the Columbia Highlands consist of public lands, just less than 3 percent of it is protected as wilderness. Conservationists would like to see more wilderness established to protect habitat for endangered and threatened species; preserve the area's old-growth forests; and provide unparalleled opportunities for hiking, horseback riding, skiing, hunting, and other sustainable forms of recreation. And while mining, ranching, and forestry still make up a large percentage of the economy here, economic forces are threatening to change that, affecting the livelihoods of thousands of residents in this remote corner of the state. Sounds like all of the makings for a jobs versus wilderness scenario, doesn't it?

Not this time around. Conservation groups have been seeking cooperative and collaborative solutions rather than combative ones. An effort called the Columbia Highlands Initiative has been seeking to restore forests, promote working ranches, and join with the New Forestry Coalition (formerly the Northeast Washington Forestry Coalition), a diverse group of forest products manufacturers, conservation leaders, government officials, business owners, educators, loggers, hikers, and citizens at large. The goal is to help ensure that the Colville National Forest is managed in a balance that preserves wilderness, guarantees outdoor recreation opportunities, and sustains jobs in the region.

The initiative calls for creating up to 350,000 acres of new wilderness from existing roadless areas as well as providing for enough timber from managed areas to sustain local forestry jobs. The initiative and even the Forestry Coalition have detractors. But US Department of Agriculture officials have pegged the effort as a model for finding common ground on land-use issues.

For more information, visit the Northeast Washington Forestry Coalition online (www .newforestrycoalition.org).   —C. R.

and other nearby roadless areas were left out of the 1984 Washington Wilderness Act, and conservationists—most notably the Kettle Range Conservation Group—continue to advocate that these areas receive federal wilderness protection.

A pure delight to hike, the trail climbs gently, weaving around granite ledges. Soon you'll meander through sage-scented pocket meadows flanked by patches of aspen that glow golden in autumn. At 1.6 miles, come to a small ledge granting good views west. Then enter mature forest, including groves of Engelmann spruce.

Pass a spur that leads left to a cattle trough. Cattle paths throughout the Kettles have caused more than a few hikers to go astray. At 2.4 miles, reach a junction (elev. 6130 ft). Turn right, immediately coming to a fence-enclosed spring. Then steadily gain elevation, passing big mossy-trunked Douglas-firs. At 3 miles, come to another junction (elev. 6425 ft).

If your sole objective is to Columbia's summit, head left. But you'll miss a scenic loop around the mountain, so reconsider and head right instead; first across sun-kissed meadows bursting with wildflowers, then through cool larch and fir forests teeming with huckleberries. After dropping about 75 feet, gain it back and then some, working your way over north-facing ledges with breathtaking views of Wapaloosie, King, and Mack Mountains. In October stare out across waves of gold, compliments of the Kettle's profusion of larches.

At 4.1 miles, just after cresting a small gap, reach yet another junction (elev. 6500 ft). The loop trail continues right 0.3 mile, bringing you back to familiar territory. But first, turn left and steadily climb 0.3 mile through rows of lodgepoles to reach the 6782-foot summit of Columbia Mountain. Immediately be wooed by a fire lookout cabin, built in 1914. Gracing this peak since the Woodrow Wilson administration, this structure is on the National Historic Register and was lovingly restored by the Forest Service through their Passport in Time program, which connects volunteers with professionals for archeological and historical preservation projects. The lookout cabin on Mount Bonaparte (Hikes 3 and 4), also built in 1914 (and still standing), is nearly identical.

Be sure to wander around the broad summit for excellent views south of Sherman and Snow Peaks, pointy Bald Mountain and Granite, Fire, and Seventeenmile Mountains. Moses Mountain can be seen to the southwest, and Mount Bonaparte dominates the northwest horizon.

EXTENDING YOUR TRIP

From the Columbia Mountain trail junction, the Kettle Crest Trail continues north through big firs and western larches that set the range aglow in yellow come October. At 1.2 miles from the junction is a piped spring and good camp.

25 Jungle Hill

RATING/ DIFFICULTY	ROUND-TRIP	ELEV GAIN/ HIGH POINT	SEASON
****/4	8 miles	2250 feet/ 6550 feet	late May–Nov

Map: USGS Copper Butte; **Contact:** Colville National Forest, Three Rivers Ranger District, Kettle Falls, (509) 775-3305, www.fs.fed.us /r6/colville; **Notes:** Open to mountain bikes, horses; **GPS:** N 48 38.085 W 118 27.062

 Few people venture onto this obscure peak in the Kettle River Range. That's because Jungle Hill's 6544-foot summit is forested and no trail leads to it. The little-used Jungle Hill Trail, however, will lead you close, delivering you high on the lonesome Kettle Crest, where an abundance of deer track and paw prints prove that this wilderness path is far from lightly traveled.

GETTING THERE

From Republic, head east on State Route 20 for 21 miles, turning left onto Albian Hill Road (FR 2030) (4.2 miles beyond Sherman Pass). (From Kettle Falls, head west on SR 20 for 22 miles, turning right onto FR 2030.) Follow FR 2030 for 0.5 mile, turning left onto a spur. Continue 0.25 mile to the trailhead (elev. 4350 ft) at a small campground. Privy available.

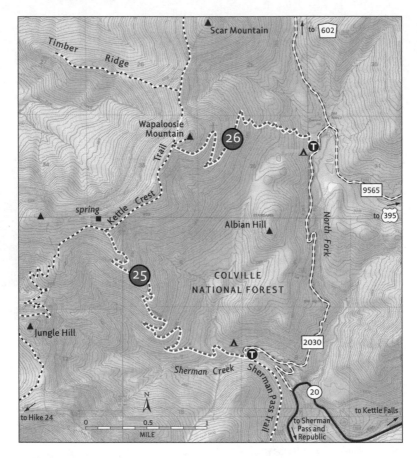

ON THE TRAIL

The trail starts with a short descent to Sherman Creek (elev. 4300 ft), reaching a junction at 0.1 mile with the Sherman Pass Trail. Continue straight on the Jungle Hill Trail, crossing the creek and beginning to climb. The trail parallels Sherman Creek for a short distance and eventually pulls away from it, although you'll hear its tumbling waters for most of the hike.

Winding through giant larches and clusters of aspens, this path is quite colorful come late September. But owing to its southern exposure, the Jungle Hill Trail is a good choice for spring hiking too, often snow-free by late spring. Along a sun-kissed ridge, the way steadily gains elevation, steeply at times and occasionally via short switchbacks.

At about 1.5 miles, come to a ledge (elev. 5100 ft) with views of nearby Columbia

The views east are extensive from Jungle Hill.

Mountain and the basin cradling the headwaters of Sherman Creek. About 0.5 mile farther, Jungle Hill comes into view. The trail continues upward, now traversing lodgepole pine forest punctuated with pocket meadows. At about 2.5 miles, reach alpine meadows that bake in the afternoon sun.

Cool forest soon offers relief, and an easier grade some respite. Walking along the meadow edge fragranced with sage is pure delight, with more excellent views eastward over the Sherman Creek valley and out to Huckleberry Mountain and Calispell Peak; westward through a gap in the Kettle Crest out to Moses Mountain and the North Cascades; and south along the crest itself. At 4 miles, near a campsite and spring, reach the Kettle Crest Trail (elev. 6550 ft). Call it a hike, or consider rambling farther.

EXTENDING YOUR TRIP
Wapaloosie Mountain (Hike 26) is an easy 1.2 miles north along the Kettle Crest Trail, primarily through open meadow. Or, if you're up for a big adventure, make a loop by following the Kettle Crest Trail south for 7 miles to Sherman Pass, and then take the Sherman Creek Trail 4 miles back to the trailhead.

26 Wapaloosie Mountain

RATING/ DIFFICULTY	ROUND-TRIP	ELEV GAIN/ HIGH POINT	SEASON
*****/3	6 miles	2000 feet/ 7018 feet	late May– Nov

Map: USGS Copper Butte; **Contact:** Colville National Forest, Three Rivers Ranger District, Kettle Falls, (509) 775-3305, www.fs.fed.us

/r6/colville; **Notes:** Open to mountain bikes, horses; **GPS:** N 48 39.828 W 118 26.402

One of the highest summits on the Kettle Crest, 7018-foot Wapaloosie Mountain offers extensive views and some of the finest alpine meadows in the Columbia Highlands. The trail traverses slopes of sagebrush interspersed with pine and fir groves. And thanks to a southeastern exposure, the trail usually melts out by midspring, when arrowleaf balsamroot speckles the mountainside bright yellow. Later, lupines add shades of violet to the soft greens of the summit's sedges and grasses before western larches give a golden performance and finally winter's white blanket descends.

GETTING THERE
From Republic, head east on State Route 20 for 21 miles, turning left onto Albian Hill Road (FR 2030) (4.2 miles beyond Sherman Pass). (From Kettle Falls, head west on SR 20 for 22 miles, turning right onto FR 2030.) Follow FR 2030 for 3.3 miles to the trailhead (elev. 5025 ft) at a small campground. Privy available.

ON THE TRAIL
Maintained by the Ferry County Back Country Horsemen, this popular trail is in excellent shape. Beginning in a thick forest of lodgepole pine, follow the trail as it crosses a tributary of the North Fork Sherman Creek—the only reliable water on this hike. Then get down to business climbing and after about 1.2 miles, break out from under the forest canopy to begin traversing Wapaloosie's sprawling meadows.

The climb eventually eases as the trail takes to a series of long, sweeping switchbacks. The eastern side of the Kettle Crest sees less range activity than the western slopes, allowing native fescue to proliferate. By late spring, wildflowers brush pastels and bright colors across the meadows, and sunbaked sage permeates the air.

Views grow with elevation gained. Look northwest to British Columbia's Rossland Range and the Abercrombie-Hooknose Highlands. The Twin Sisters, Mack Mountain, and King Mountain are emerald sentinels guarding the eastern flank of the Kettle Crest. Flickering birds, scurrying ground squirrels, and flitting butterflies will keep your eyes focused nearby too.

A pair of hikers admire the extensive view south across the Kettle Crest.

At 2.7 miles, amid glorious alpine meadows, reach the Kettle Crest Trail (elev. 6850 ft). From this junction it's a short and easy off-trail ramble to Wapaloosie's 7018-foot summit. Head northeast through meadows and open forest of Engelmann spruce and whitebark pine for about 0.25 mile. A large cairn marks the broad summit's high point.

EXTENDING YOUR TRIP

Continue south along the Kettle Crest Trail for about 1.2 miles to the Jungle Hill Trail for (Hike 25)—more delightful meadows and views. You can make a 12-mile loop by returning via the Jungle Hill Trail and walking 3 miles on FR 2030 back to the trailhead.

27 Copper Butte via Marcus Trail

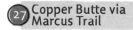

RATING/ DIFFICULTY	ROUND-TRIP	ELEV GAIN/ HIGH POINT	SEASON
*****/4	9.6 miles	2340 feet/ 7140 feet	June–Nov

Map: USGS Copper Butte; **Contact:** Colville National Forest, Republic Ranger District, (509) 775-7400, www.fs.usda.gov/main /colville; **Notes:** Open to mountain bikes, horses. Range area; **GPS:** N 48 41.884 W 118 30.715

At 7140 feet, Copper Butte is the highest summit in the Kettle River Range and the sixth-highest mountain in Eastern Washington. Of the several ways to reach this lofty peak, none is more beautiful than the Marcus Trail. On this lightly traveled trail, you'll pass through old-growth, fire-succession, and subalpine forests; and traverse prolific alpine meadows. The views

The trail traverses sprawling meadows with far reaching views west.

from this old lookout site, down the Kettle spine and out to the Selkirks and a myriad of Canadian peaks, are just as dazzling.

GETTING THERE

From Republic, head east on State Route 20 for 2.8 miles to the junction with SR 21 (just past the county fairgrounds). (From Kettle Falls, follow SR 20 west for 40 miles to the junction.) Head north on SR 21 for 0.8 mile, turning right at the Ferry County PUD onto Old Kettle Falls Road (County Road 280). After 2.4 miles, turn left onto CR 287 (access for Kinross Mine). Continue 0.8 mile, bearing right onto Hatchery Road (CR 284). Then continue east (past mining operations) 0.6 mile and bear right onto FR 2152. Proceed (staying right at 0.7 mile) for 3.3 miles, bearing left onto FR 2040. Follow FR 2040 for

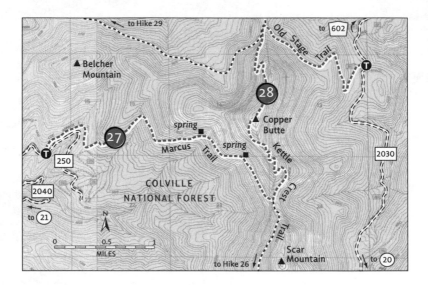

5.2 miles to a junction with FR Spur 250 (signed Marcus Trail No. 8). Turn right and come to the trailhead (elev. 4800 ft) in a small clearing at 1.5 miles.

ON THE TRAIL

If you want to reach the king of the Kettles by the fastest route possible, don't hike this trail. Head on over to the Old Stage Trail (Hike 28) instead. But if you want to wander through the most supreme wildflower meadows in these parts, this is your trail! The route once extended to the small town of Marcus on the confluence of the Kettle and Columbia Rivers. It's much shorter now, but just as wild as it was in the late 1800s.

From an old logging yard, the trail starts by following an old road through tall timber. Despite selective logging over the years, you'll pass lots of big old ponderosa pines, western larches, and Douglas-firs. Soon afterward, enter a large area that succumbed

to fire in the early 1990s. At 0.6 mile, cross a creek (elev. 5025 ft) that has been heavily trampled by cattle. This is active range area, so beware of confusing cow paths. At 0.9 mile, be sure to stay left as one of those cow paths veers right.

As you climb the at-times dusty path, the surrounding countryside slowly begins to reveal itself as views emerge. Head back into mature forest and then back into the burn zone. After passing a spring (elev. 5550 ft) at 1.5 miles, the climb eases. Then round a ridge, staying uphill of more confusing cow paths. Forest soon yields to meadows.

At 2.2 miles, reach Copper Butte Spring (elev. 5925 foot), a popular watering hole for the resident bovines. Paths diverge everywhere. The trail you want heads left uphill and away from the spring. It soon reenters forest for a short ways. Come to Copper Butte Spring 2 (elev. 6075 ft), and then break back out into meadows.

For over a mile, traverse the sun-kissed southwestern slopes of Copper Butte, delighting in westward views and outstanding floral shows that include bistorts, lupines, yarrows, roses, golden peas, asters, buttercups, buckwheat, harebells, locoweed, bluebells, paintbrush, and more.

At 3 miles, pass another spring. The grade eases as you reenter forest and come to an intersection with the Kettle Crest Trail in a saddle (elev. 6400 ft) at 3.4 miles. Turn left and head north 1.4 easy miles through cool lodgepole pine forest, pocket meadows, and corridors of wildflowers to the broad 7140-foot summit of Copper Butte. Once home to a fire lookout, all that remains is a rusty bed frame. Wander around the butte for horizon-spanning views to the Cascades west, Idaho's Selkirks east, Mount Spokane south, and British Columbia's Rossland Range north.

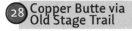

28 Copper Butte via Old Stage Trail

RATING/ DIFFICULTY	ROUND-TRIP	ELEV GAIN/ HIGH POINT	SEASON
****/3	6 miles	1615 feet/ 7140 feet	mid-June– Nov

Map: USGS Copper Butte; **Contact:** Colville National Forest, Three Rivers Ranger District, Kettle Falls, (509) 775-3305, www.fs.fed.us /r6/colville; **Notes:** Open to mountain bikes, horses; **GPS:** N48 42.595 W 118 26.579

Follow an old wagon road to a gap high on the Kettle Crest. Then climb steeply through silver forests adorned with showy wildflowers to the highest point in the Kettle River Range. From this lofty perch, a mile above the surrounding golden valleys, survey the wild and expansive Columbia Highlands. The views are breathtaking from this former fire lookout site, from Idaho to the North Cascades and all along the imposing wall of the Kettle Crest, from the Colville nation to the nation of Canada.

GETTING THERE
From Republic, head east on State Route 20 for 21 miles, turning left onto FR 2030 (Albian Hill Road) (4.2 miles beyond Sherman Pass). (From Kettle Falls, head west on SR 20 for 22 miles, turning right onto FR 2030.) Follow FR 2030 for 7.1 miles, turning left onto the spur to the Old Stage Trail. Reach the trailhead (elev. 5525 ft) in 0.2 mile. Privy available.

ON THE TRAIL
Of the several routes to Copper Butte, this is the shortest to this highest point in the Kettles. And thanks to a starting elevation of more than 5500 feet, it's short on elevation gain too. The hike starts on the Old Stage Trail, a restored section of a wagon road constructed in 1892. An early attempt by legislators to construct a northern east–west route across the state, the Old Stage route was short lived, replaced in 1898 by one over Sherman Pass.

Beginning by a creek (the only water on this hike) in cool forest, the way gradually climbs on a gentle grade. After rounding a ridge, the trail breaks out into a recovering burn zone. More than 10,000 acres on Copper Butte and adjacent Midnight Mountain went up in flames following a 1995 lightning strike. The forest is recovering, but with much of the canopy gone this can be a hot hike in July and August.

Copper Butte offers good views of the lofty lumpy Kettle Crest.

After 1.6 miles of enjoyable strolling, reach a junction with the Kettle Crest Trail at a high windblown saddle (elev. 6050 ft). A nice albeit waterless campsite invites hikers interested in experiencing sunrises and sunsets from the lofty crest. For Copper Butte, turn left (south) and very soon afterward, turn left again. The Old Stage route continues straight to Lambert Creek (Hike 29), but you're now following the 43+-mile Kettle Crest Trail. Up the steep northern slopes of Copper Butte, steadily climb through snags and rejuvenating greenery. Blueberry bushes provide forage for grouse and create a crimson carpet come October. Views can be had west and north, but they pale in comparison to what awaits.

A couple of switchbacks ease the climb, and then it's one final push to the top. At 3 miles, crest the broad butte. A big cairn marks the mountain's 7140-foot high point. The site of a fire lookout from 1921 until the 1950s, all that remains is a rusted bed frame and some scattered debris. But the views haven't changed: Look south along the rounded Kettle Crest to bulky peaks cloaked in golden lawns and emerald canopies. Peer northward and trace the lumpy spine of the crest into British Columbia. Gaze west over sprawling rangelands in spacious valleys carved by retreating glaciers from another era. Then cast your eyes east to a sea of peaks rising progressively higher on the horizon. Not a bad visual payoff for such a nontaxing hike!

29 Midnight Mountain

RATING/ DIFFICULTY	LOOP	ELEV GAIN/ HIGH POINT	SEASON
****/3	10.6 miles	2250 feet/ 6150 feet	June–Nov

Maps: USGS Cooke Mountain, USGS Copper Butte; **Contact:** Colville National Forest, Republic Ranger District, (509) 775-7400, www.fs.usda.gov/main/colville; **Notes:** Open to mountain bikers, popular with equestrians. Range area; **GPS:** N 48 43.711 W 118 31.297

This trip takes you through recovering fire-scorched hillsides, fragrant alpine meadows, and parkland forests of towering western larch. Follow a historic wagon road up to a lofty pass in the shadow of Copper Butte, highest summit in the Kettles. Then traverse sage-scented flowering meadows high upon Midnight Mountain before slowly descending along a ridge through forest and field. Come in summer for the blossoms, fall for the colors, anytime for sweeping sublime views of the Okanogan Highlands.

GETTING THERE

From Republic, head east on State Route 20 for 2.8 miles to the junction with SR 21 (just past the county fairgrounds). (From Kettle Falls, follow SR 20 west for 40 miles to the junction.) Head north on SR 21 for 9 miles, turning right onto Lambert Creek Road (CR 540). At 6 miles, bear right onto FR 2156 and continue for another 1.2 miles to the

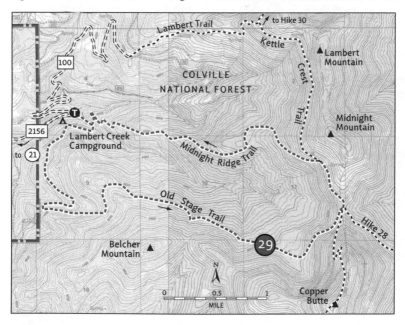

trailhead at Lambert Creek Campground (elev. 3900 ft). Privy available.

ON THE TRAIL

The trail begins next to a beautiful wooden sign depicting the route, compliments of the Ferry County chapter of the Back Country Horsemen. Rock-hop across Lambert Creek and reach a junction in 0.3 mile. You'll be returning left, so continue right on the Old Stage Trail. Constructed in 1892, just three years after statehood, this old wagon road was an early attempt by legislators to construct a northern east–west route across the state. It was short lived, replaced in 1898 by a route over Sherman Pass that proved more favorable for hauling freight.

Copper Butte from Midnight Mountain

In the 1990s much of the surrounding forest burned. Lack of shade warrants postponing this hike on the hottest of summer days, but spring and fall are lovely and surprisingly colorful. New greenery continues to colonize the scorched slopes. Flowers are dazzling in spring, and autumn colors are brilliant thanks to the blueberry bushes, cascaras, and currants. Look for woodpeckers among the snags and spruce grouse feasting on the buds of new plants.

The grade is gentle, with wide sweeping switchbacks. At 1.8 miles, bear left at a junction. The trail right connects to an old forest road. At 2.7 miles, come to a spring (elev. 4700 ft), which like most in the Kettles should be treated because of contamination by cattle.

After passing a grove of large fire-spared larches, the trail rounds a ridge to grant viewing of Midnight Mountain and then advances through a thicket of lodgepole pine. At 4.5 miles, cross a small creek. At 5 miles, skirt a small wetland. Alpine breezes high on the slopes of Copper Butte often leave more than a few downed snags across the trail here for you to hone your hurdling skills.

At 5.8 miles, intersect the Kettle Crest Trail (elev. 6000 ft) at a high pass just north of the blocky butte. Continue left a few steps to a high and dry campsite and another junction. The old wagon road continues east to Albian Hill Road (see Hike 28). Your route carries on north along the crest, ascending a little more to top out at about 6150 feet. Enjoy a good view south to Copper Butte with its dog-hair stands of silver snags and west across the Curlew Valley to Bodie Mountain and the Bonaparte Highlands. Views are even better from the 6660-foot summit of Midnight Mountain, which can easily be attained by leaving the trail and angling northeast across sage-dotted meadows.

Otherwise, keep hiking north and reach a junction with the Midnight Ridge Trail at 6.1 miles. Bear left onto the heavily cow- and horse-hoofed trail and begin descending across meadows and through patches of aspen. At 6.7 miles, pass a spring (elev. 5800 ft). Continue losing elevation, traversing young pine forest, before coming to groves of impressive old Doug-firs, ponderosa pines, and western larches. The larches in particular are quite grand.

Winding farther down Midnight Ridge, the trail drops more rapidly. At 10.3 miles, come to a familiar junction with the Old Stage Trail. Turn right and reach the trailhead in 0.3 mile.

EXTENDING YOUR TRIP

Consider side trips along the Kettle Crest, south to Copper Butte or north to meadows high on Lambert Mountain.

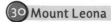

30 Mount Leona

RATING/ DIFFICULTY	ROUND-TRIP	ELEV GAIN/ HIGH POINT	SEASON
***/3	6 miles	1500 feet/ 6474 feet	June–late Oct

Map: USGS Mount Leona; **Contact:** Colville National Forest, Republic Ranger District, (509) 775-7400, www.fs.fed.us/r6/colville; **Notes:** Open to mountain bikes, horses. Range area. Last few miles of road are rough, requires high-clearance; **GPS:** N 48 45.922 W 118 29.278

 An easy climb to a prominent Kettle Crest summit, Mount Leona offers far-reaching views across the Okanogan Highlands and into the Boundary Country of British Columbia. A lonely peak except for the cows, chances

Profanity Peak from Mount Leona's summit

are good of seeing wilder ungulates—and perhaps a carnivore as well. Wildfires have scorched the mountain in the last two decades, but each year the peak gets a little greener and arrangements of sun-loving wildflowers soften the fires' impact.

GETTING THERE

From Republic, head east on State Route 20 for 2.8 miles to the junction with SR 21 (just past the county fairgrounds). (From Kettle Falls, follow SR 20 west for 40 miles to the junction.) Head north on SR 21 for 12.4 miles, turning right onto Saint Peters Creek Road (County Road 584) at Malo Store (milepost 175). At 1.1 miles, the pavement ends. At 1.7 miles, bear right. At 5.7 miles, bear left onto FR 2157 and follow it for 3.9 miles to the trailhead (elev. 5000 ft) in a large clearing on the left.

ON THE TRAIL

From the trailhead clearing, look up at Leona, straight ahead and straight up. But your route is much gentler. First follow a cow-pied cow path to an old road. This is open range, and the views west across the golden Curlew Creek valley look like they're right out of Montana.

Leona's open southern slopes rise above as you skirt east around the mountain. Raptors catch thermals while busy nuthatches

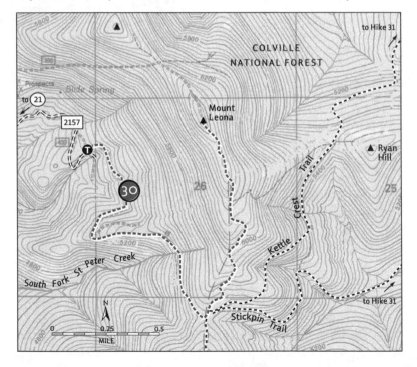

work the trees lining the way. Stay on the main path, avoiding cattle trails and spurs to nowhere. At 0.8 mile, the trail swings left, steepens, and then soon eases. Come to a spring and stock trough (elev. 5375 ft) at 1.2 miles. Water sources beyond are less reliable. At 1.7 miles, at the edge of a burn zone, reach a saddle on the Kettle Crest (elev. 5600 ft) and a junction with the Kettle Crest Trail and Leona Loop Trail.

Views from this gap east are excellent to Clackamas Mountain, Bodie Mountain, and Mount Bonaparte. Winds whistle through the snags, and lupines paint the forest floor purple. To summit Mount Leona, take the trail to your left. It receives minimum maintenance, so expect to be hopping over some windfall as you work your way—steeply at times—up Leona's south shoulder.

At 2.1 miles, bear left at a sign (elev. 5975 ft), crawling over a big blowdown. The tread gets a little tricky to follow—angle to the northwest. At 2.3 miles, reach an unmarked junction (elev. 6100 ft) at the edge of a small meadow. The trail right is a continuation of the Leona Loop Trail, leading back to the Kettle Crest Trail. Unless you're a pine marten, you'll want to avoid this trail, as it is covered with blowdown and is a nightmare to travel.

Head left up an old jeep track. Numerous cow paths make it easy to get lost. Stay along the ridge and head up, eventually emerging in a trampled meadow. Pick your way up through sage and juniper, looking for cairns and a resumption of trail. The route once again becomes clear as you travel up the increasingly open ridge crest. At 3 miles, reach the 6474-foot rocky summit, with its sedums and gilia and a communications tower.

Look northwest to British Columbia's Mount Baldy; northeast to Profanity Peak and Taylor Ridge; east to the Twin Sisters Roadless Area and the Selkirks beyond; west across the Okanogan Highlands to the North Cascades; and south along the Kettle Crest to Lambert Mountain, Midnight Mountain, and Copper Butte, granddaddy of the crest.

EXTENDING YOUR TRIP
Follow a jeep track off the summit northwest to Leona's western summit. Or, from the junction with the Kettle Crest Trail, travel south along the crest to Lambert's sprawling meadows.

31 Ryan Cabin–Stickpin Loop

RATING/ DIFFICULTY	LOOP	ELEV GAIN/ HIGH POINT	SEASON
***/3	6.4 miles	1365 feet/ 5600 feet	mid-June– Nov

Map: USGS Mount Leona; **Contact:** Colville National Forest, Three Rivers Ranger District, Kettle Falls, (509) 775-3305, www.fs.fed.us /r6/colville; **Notes:** Open to mountain bikes, horses. Range area. Last 4 miles of approach road can be rough; **GPS:** N 48 45.671 W 118 26.093

 This easy loop hike in the northern Kettles follows two lightly traveled trails and a section of the Kettle Crest Trail that sees nary a soul. Human souls that is. Moose, deer, and other large mammals are another story. Stroll through sunny wildflower patches and cool streamside forest. Take in a few nice views along the way too as you try to locate Ryan's dilapidated cabin.

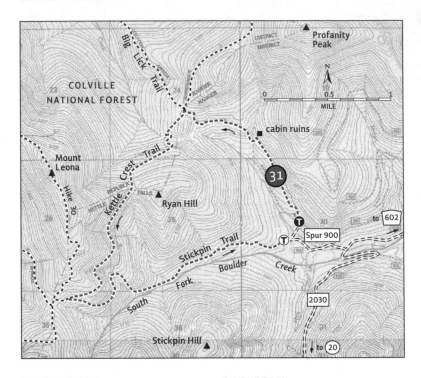

GETTING THERE

From Republic, head east on State Route 20 for 21 miles, turning left onto Albian Hill Road (FR 2030) (4.2 miles beyond Sherman Pass). (From Kettle Falls, head west on SR 20 for 22 miles, turning right onto FR 2030.) Follow FR 2030 for 11.8 miles (the last 4 miles can be rough) to a junction with FR Spur 900 (signed Stickpin Trail No. 71, Ryan Cabin Trail No. 30 Trailhead). Turn left and proceed on rough road, bearing left at 0.2 mile, left again immediately afterward, and right in another 0.1 mile. Reach the Stickpin trailhead in 0.3 mile and Ryan Cabin trailhead (elev. 4450 ft) 0.1 mile beyond on the right. Park here.

ON THE TRAIL

On good tread, start climbing through a windblown forest of lodgepole pine. Visible north through gaps in the forest is Profanity Peak with its inviting meadows. But the bushwhacking involved in getting to that trail-less summit may provoke its namesake from your lips. Stay on the blueberry- and pipsissewa-lined trail instead and enjoy the hike.

At 1.2 miles, after entering mature forest, reach a small spring (elev. 4825 ft). See if you can locate the Ryan Cabin nearby, an old trapper's cabin rapidly being recalled by nature. Beyond the cabin site, switchback up a sunny slope speckled with granite ledges and glacial erratics, reaching the Kettle Crest Trail (elev. 5150 ft) at 1.7 miles.

Head south on the Kettle Crest Trail, dropping into a cool notch (elev. 5025 ft) before beginning a steep climb through cool forest. At 2.8 miles, reach a 5500-foot gap between Mount Leona and Ryan Hill and a junction with the Leona Loop Trail. Unmaintained, only a fisher or pine marten will appreciate this littered-with-blowdown trail. Best to continue on the Kettle Crest Trail, traversing the east slopes of Mount Leona. Soon enter a 1990s burn zone that is rapidly reforesting. The way can be brushy at times but also abundant with wildflowers.

Cross two small creeks (elev. 5435 ft) that occasionally run dry late in the season, and then round a ridge with an excellent view of Profanity Peak. Continue across a meadow, passing a cow-trampled spring and some good views east along the way. At 4.2 miles, come to a junction (elev. 5600 ft) with the Stickpin Trail.

Turn left and begin descending, soon coming to a big wildflower-filled meadow. Across an herbaceous hillside, continue losing elevation, eventually reentering forest. At 4.8 miles, reach a bridge across the South Fork Boulder Creek, a mere trickle here. The trail then follows the creek into a lush valley, one of the few creek-hugging trails in the Kettles.

Traverse cool spruce and cedar groves, muddy seeps, and thimbleberry patches—this is one of the wetter areas in the Kettles. A few boardwalks help keep your boots dry. At 6.3 miles, reach the Stickpin trailhead (elev. 4425 ft). Turn left and walk the road 0.1 mile back to your vehicle to complete the loop.

Stickpin Trail traverses boggy forest.

EXTENDING YOUR TRIP

You can easily hike to Mount Leona's summit from this loop. Before turning off on the Stickpin Trail, head south on the Kettle Crest Trail for a little over 0.1 mile to the trail to Leona, taking off right (see Hike 30).

32 Sentinel Butte

RATING/ DIFFICULTY	LOOP	ELEV GAIN/ HIGH POINT	SEASON
**/2	7 miles	1025 feet/ 5625 feet	May–Nov

Map: USGS Mount Leona; **Contact:** Colville National Forest, Republic Ranger District, (509) 775-7400, www.fs.fed.us/r6/colville; **Notes:** Open to mountain bikes, horses. Popular cross-country ski route, winter Sno-Park Pass required; **GPS:** N 48 51.823 W 118 23.721

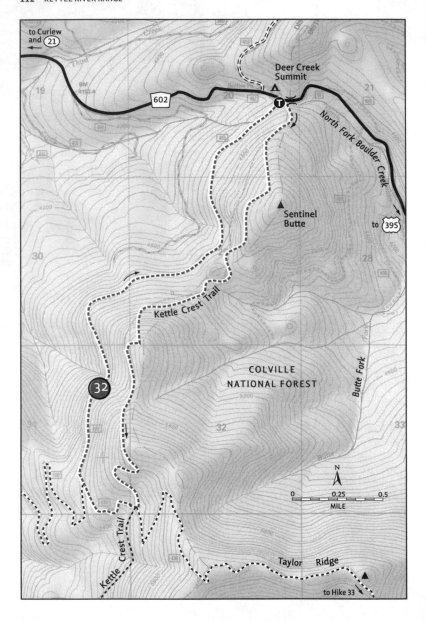

A popular winter skiing destination, this forested loop at the northern terminus of the 43+-mile Kettle Crest Trail is pretty quiet the rest of the year. It's an excellent area for seeing moose and other large mammals, but the best features are the trees—particularly the larches. Majestic western larches line the way and by October streak the slopes gold and brighten the trail with a carpet of flaxen needles.

GETTING THERE

From Republic, drive 2.8 miles east on State Route 20, turning left onto SR 21. Continue for 18.4 miles to Curlew and turn right onto Boulder Creek Road (County Road 602). Proceed 11.2 miles to the trailhead at Deer Creek Summit (elev. 4600 ft). Privy available. (From the junction of US Highway 395 with SR 20 west of Kettle Falls, follow US 395 north for 16 miles and turn left onto CR 602, continuing 11.8 miles to trailhead.)

ON THE TRAIL

Start by taking the Kettle Crest Trail—you'll be returning on the road just to the west of it. Beginning its 43-mile journey southward across the spine of the Kettle River Range, the excellent trail moderately ascends, traversing groves of larch, fir, and pine. Occasional openings offer good viewing west across the Kettle River valley to the Bonaparte Highlands and north to Mount Baldy in British Columbia.

Rounding Sentinel Butte, the trail takes a break from climbing at about 1.5 miles. After dipping about 50 feet, it resumes the ascent. Make a couple of switchbacks, skirt a couple of knolls. The walking is peaceful and delightful through grassy openings and by granite outcroppings.

After reaching a high point of 5625 feet, the trail descends. At 3.5 miles, before Long Alec Creek, come to a junction with an old road (elev. 5400 ft). The way left ascends and travels along Taylor Ridge. Head right, following grassy tread for about 0.4 mile to another old road. Turn right again and follow this old ski path, which eventually becomes FR 455 (and an excellent ski run in winter), for 3.1 miles back to the trailhead.

EXTENDING YOUR TRIP

Venture out on the Taylor Ridge Trail (Hike 33), or saunter on more ski trails that take off north from the campground at Deer Creek Summit.

Moose are frequent travelers along the Kettle Crest Trail.

33 Taylor Ridge

RATING/ DIFFICULTY	ROUND-TRIP	ELEV GAIN/ HIGH POINT	SEASON
***/2	5.8 miles	1200 feet/ 6190 feet	mid-June– Nov

Maps: USGS Mount Leona, USGS Bulldog Mountain; **Contact:** Colville National Forest, Three Rivers Ranger District, Kettle Falls, (509) 775-3305, www.fs.fed.us/r6/colville; **Notes:** Open to mountain bikes, horses. Range area; **GPS:** N 48 47.557 W 118 20.362

👫 🔧 ⚙️ 🏠 *A lonely hike in the northern reaches of the Kettles, Taylor Ridge lacks a "wow" factor but is packed with little surprises. There are good views to colorfully named and little-known peaks—like Profanity Peak, Alligator Ridge, Togo Mountain, and Stickpin Hill. There are a few historical relics from the Colville National Forest's early days and the Civilian Conservation Corps. And there's always a good chance of hiking into a bear, deer, or moose. In autumn, larches streak the ridge gold.*

GETTING THERE

From the junction of US Highway 395 with State Route 20 west of Kettle Falls, follow US 395 north for 16 miles and turn left onto Boulder Creek Road (County Road 602). Drive west 8.8 miles, turning left onto FR 6113 (signed Bulldog Cabin). (From Republic, drive 2.8 miles east on SR 20, turning left onto SR 21. Continue 18.4 miles to Curlew and turn right onto Boulder Creek Road/CR 602. Proceed 13.9 miles, 2.8 miles beyond Deer Creek Summit, turning right

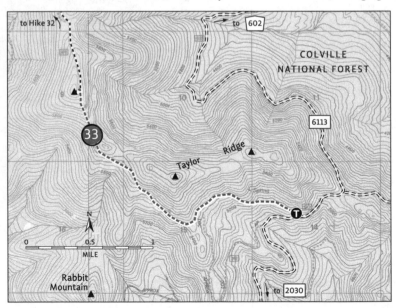

Good views south to King Mountain, US Mountain, and the Kettle Crest from Taylor Ridge

onto FR 6113.) Follow this good gravel road for 8.9 miles to a cattle guard near a road spur and trailhead for Taylor Ridge east. Continue south 0.4 mile to the trailhead for Taylor Ridge west (elev. 5050 ft) and limited parking on the left-side road shoulder.

ON THE TRAIL

The trail over Taylor Ridge is in decent shape. Word is slowly getting out among mountain bikers about this trail's riding appeal. And a fair number of hunters visit each fall, enough so that the path usually gets brushed out each season. But for the most part, this is one of the lonelier trails in the Kettles.

Starting nearly a mile high, gradually climb along the edge of an old clear-cut, passing by some big western larches. The forest is fairly open and, like much of Kettle country, is open to cattle grazing. Watch your step! At 1.1 miles, come to an old road (elev. 5400 ft). Walk left for a few steps and then resume your way back on the trail.

At about 1.4 miles, reach an opening with nice viewing south along the Kettle Crest. Continue steadily climbing through open forest, rounding one of the many knobs and summits along Taylor Ridge. After a slight descent and a few minor ups and down, continue upward toward the ridge's high point. Skirt meadows graced with juniper and wildflowers, and then briefly climb steeply to just below the ridge's high point, 2.8 miles from the trailhead and just before the trail transforms into an old jeep track. Look for a faint path heading left. Follow it a mere 0.1 mile over ledges to reach Taylor Ridge's 6190-foot high point.

Most of the summit is treed, but there are good views south to King, Mack, Twin Sisters, and US Mountains as well as along the Kettle Crest from Snow Peak to Profanity Peak. Snoop around and you'll find an old cabin foundation and other remnants of a long-gone fire lookout. This country is pretty wild now, but for much of the past century it saw its share of miners, trappers, and loggers.

EXTENDING YOUR TRIP

Continue west 3 miles or so along Taylor Ridge on old road to reach the Kettle Crest Trail. If you can arrange transportation for a pickup at Deer Creek Summit, it makes for a good one-way adventure. Or follow the eastern section of the ridge trail for a couple of miles, but be aware that it has become abandoned and obstructed by logging near Bulldog Mountain.

34 US Mountain

RATING/ DIFFICULTY	ROUND-TRIP	ELEV GAIN/ HIGH POINT	SEASON
**/3	5.8 miles	1450 feet/ 6232 feet	mid-June– Nov

Map: USGS Copper Butte; **Contact:** Colville National Forest, Three Rivers Ranger District, Kettle Falls, (509) 775-3305, www.fs.fed.us /r6/colville; **Notes:** Open to mountain bikes, horses, motorized use. Range area; **GPS:** N 48 42.846 W 118 26.634

An obscure but prominent peak just east of the Kettle Crest, US Mountain sees more bovine than boot prints. Follow an old jeep track through forests of pine and larch to high-country meadows with good views of the lofty Kettles and the thickly wooded Twin Sisters. Once worked by miners and now grazed by cattle, US is a great peak for wandering back into the past. It's also an excellent hike for solitude.

GETTING THERE

From Republic, head east on State Route 20 for 21 miles, turning left onto Albian Hill Road (FR 2030) (4.2 miles beyond Sherman Pass). (From Kettle Falls, head west on SR 20 for 22 miles, turning right onto FR 2030.) Follow FR 2030 for 7.5 miles to an obscure road on right signed "600" (0.4 mile north of the Old Stage trailhead). This is the trailhead (elev. 5350 ft). Park in a small clearing just up the road or in a small pullout along Albian Hill Road. Do not block FR Spur 600.

Meadows below the summit of US Mountain offer good views south into the Twin Sisters Roadless Area.

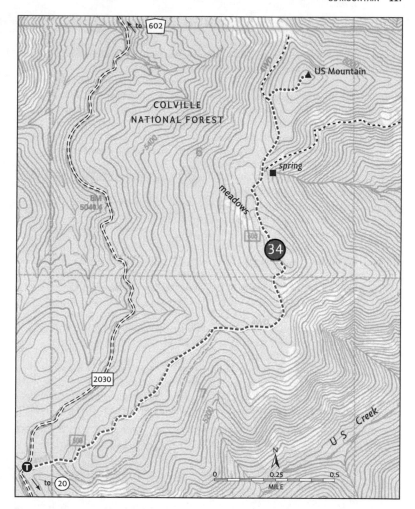

ON THE TRAIL

While this trail is open to four-wheel-drive recreationists (and snowmobiles when snow-covered), outside of deer season and winter, the chances of encountering motorists, or anyone for that matter, is slim. Most of the way is on an old road, and if it wasn't for the occasional 4x4-er, alders would have overtaken it long ago.

Head up the double-track, bearing right at a junction in 0.1 mile. From here the way climbs steeply. Don't let the grade and the tunnel of alders discourage you—this is the only lousy section, and it's short. The way soon levels out, with some minor ups and downs through stands of lodgepole pine and western larch.

At 1.3 miles the grade steepens, leaving thick woods for pocket meadows. Soon afterward, skirt a big meadow that invites ambling across it for good views of the Twin Sisters, and King and Mack Mountains. At 1.9 miles, crest a 6125-foot knoll. Then start descending, skirting ledges along the ridgeline. Look for openings in the forest to your left. Views are excellent here of Copper Butte, Midnight Mountain, and the impacts of a 1994 forest fire.

At 2.2 miles, come to a faint trail junction. The trail right drops to a fence-enclosed spring and then continues down the east side of US Mountain, ending at FR Spur 500 off Boulder Creek Road (FR 6110). It is lightly traveled and maintained. Continue left on the road track instead, reaching a saddle (elev. 5940 ft), and then resume climbing.

At 2.5 miles (elev. 6025 ft) the track once again descends (rapidly and dead-ending shortly afterward). Don't continue after descending about 50 feet—instead look for a small track right leading to an old mining

area. Now off-trail, angle to the right of the old mine and through open forest and meadow to reach US Mountain's 6232-foot summit after 0.4 mile.

Views are extremely limited from the summit, but meadows just below the high point on the south side grant wonderful viewing of the 13,000-acre Twin Sisters Roadless Area and high Kettle Crest summits from Copper Butte to Snow Peak.

35 King Mountain

RATING/ DIFFICULTY	ROUND-TRIP	ELEV GAIN/ HIGH POINT	SEASON
***/3	7.4 miles	1520 feet/ 6660 feet	mid-June– Nov

Map: USGS Copper Butte; **Contact:** Colville National Forest, Three Rivers Ranger District, Kettle Falls, (509) 775-3305, www.fs.fed.us /r6/colville; **Notes:** Open to mountain bikes, horses, motorized use; **GPS:** N 48 40.885 W 118 26.577

The highest peak in the Kettle River Range not situated along the Kettle Crest, King Mountain provides royal views of the lofty crest and of scores of equally

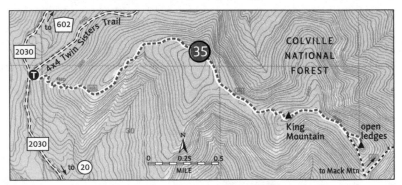

Lifting clouds reveal a rugged and wild landscape surrounding King Mountain.

impressive and intriguing surrounding summits. Follow a rarely traveled old jeep track along a thickly timbered ridgeline to a rocky pinnacle rarely set foot upon by human feet, and gaze upon some of the loneliest and wildest country in the region.

GETTING THERE

From Republic, head east on State Route 20 for 21 miles, turning left onto Albian Hill Road (FR 2030) (4.2 miles beyond Sherman Pass). (From Kettle Falls, head west on SR 20 for 22 miles, turning right onto FR 2030.) Follow FR 2030 for 4.8 miles to the trailhead (elev. 5500 ft), located at junction with the Twin Sisters Motorized Trail. Do not block this trail when parking.

ON THE TRAIL

Your route begins immediately to the right (south) of the 4x4 Twin Sisters Trail (Spur 200). The way to King Mountain is also open to motorized use, but don't let that discourage you. Outside of deer season, this route sees very little use, motorized or non. You're far more likely to encounter a four-legged trail user.

The way starts out in a thick forest of lodgepole pine. Dependent on frequent fires for seed germination and to suppress competing species, lodgepole pine is ubiquitous in the Kettles, often growing in thick dog-haired stands. First Peoples of the Rocky Mountains and Great Plains favored this tree's straight and slender trunks for teepee construction, hence its name.

Climb steadily and steeply at times. A few short switchbacks break up the grunt. Keep your mind off the climb by looking for spruce grouse and listening for nuthatches. At about 0.8 mile, come to the first of several small openings in the forest. Take in views of the southern Kettle Crest, and in early summer admire a carpet of wildflowers.

At about 1.1 miles, the trail crests a ridge (elev. 6250 ft), bringing respite from the climbing. Wander a short distance off-trail to the south for some nice views. Then continue along the trail through thick stands of pine

and fir. At 2.1 miles, round a lesser summit (elev. 6500 ft) and begin a slow descent. After passing a waterless campsite in a broad saddle (elev. 6335 ft), resume climbing, reaching King's western summit (elev. 6640 ft) at 3 miles. Mostly treed, the summit may perhaps disappoint you. However, look southeast across the small summit meadow and notice a rocky and intriguing nearby peak. That's King's slightly higher eastern summit, and that's where the extensive views are—keep hiking!

After passing over a small knob, rapidly drop to a saddle (elev. 6525 ft), coming to a junction soon afterward at 3.5 miles. The main trail continues right, skirting the rocky pinnacle on its eastward march toward Mack Mountain. Veer left on a rougher track, soon coming to an excellent viewpoint north. Directly across the North Fork Deadman Creek valley locate the Twin Sisters—centerpiece of the 13,300-acre roadless area you have been trudging across. Identify Profanity Peak to the north, with its sun-kissed meadows, and emerald Taylor Ridge to its east. Scattered about are other little-known peaks sporting colorful names—Alligator Ridge, Jackknife Mountain, US Mountain, and Bulldog Mountain.

Notice a trail taking off from the viewpoint. Take it and carefully pick your way up an outcropping of crumbling rock to King's 6660-foot eastern summit. Here is your true visual reward for all your effort: the Kettle Crest from White Mountain to Copper Butte, and obscure summits with intriguing names like Graves Mountain, Scalawag Ridge, and Bangs Mountain, to name a few.

With the old rotten rock below your feet and the rounded well-worn summits surrounding you, it's easy to see that these mountains are the oldest in the state, at over

60 million years old and rich in biological diversity.

36 Sherman Creek and Log Flume Heritage Site

RATING/ DIFFICULTY	ROUND-TRIP	ELEV GAIN/ HIGH POINT	SEASON
**/1	1.6 miles	60 feet/ 2230 feet	Mar–Dec

Map: USGS South Huckleberry Mountain; **Contact:** Colville National Forest, Three Rivers Ranger District, Kettle Falls, (509) 775-3305, www.fs.fed.us/r6/colville; **Notes:** Wheelchair-accessible. Dogs permitted on-leash; **GPS:** N 48 34.922 W 118 13.618

A delightful path along a tumbling waterway, the paved Sherman Creek Trail is perfect for children and

hikers of all ages who may want to stretch their legs while out on a trip along the Sherman Pass National Scenic Byway. One of the few nonmountainous hikes in the region, this trail is exceptionally attractive in spring when woodland flowers add cheer to the terrain, and snowmelt from the Kettles adds a roar to the river.

GETTING THERE
From Republic, head east on State Route 20 for 32.3 miles, turning right into the Log Flume Heritage Site. (From Kettle Falls, head west on SR 20 for 10.7 miles, turning left into the Log Flume Heritage Site.) The trailhead is at the southwest end of the parking area (elev. 2170 ft). Privy available.

ON THE TRAIL
Sherman Creek starts in the high meadows of Jungle Hill and Columbia Peak, its South Fork in the high basins beneath Snow Peak,

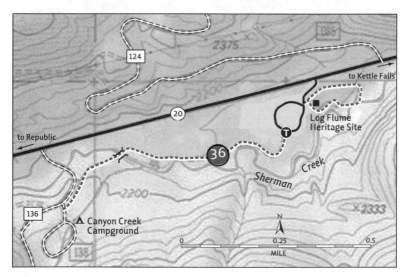

A silhouette from the past works the old sluiceway.

Nootka roses perfume the air, while aspen and cottonwood leaves rustling in the warm breezes add a nice background score. The creek itself plays a fine melody, its mood varying with the season and snowmelt.

At about 0.6 mile, cross the river on a nice bridge and continue walking upstream through a meadow of lupine shaded by big cottonwoods. The trail ends in the Canyon Creek Campground along the banks of Canyon Creek, which drains the northern slopes of South Huckleberry Mountain. Contemplate spending the night here as you saunter back to the trailhead.

EXTENDING YOUR TRIP
Take the time to walk the 0.4-mile loop through the Log Flume Heritage Site. Learn about early logging operations that included sluicing logs down a large flume, remnants of which still exist and can be seen along the trail.

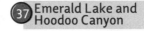

37 Emerald Lake and Hoodoo Canyon

RATING/ DIFFICULTY	ROUND-TRIP	ELEV GAIN/ HIGH POINT	SEASON
****/2	6.2 miles	825 feet/ 3500 feet	Apr–Nov

Map: USGS Jackknife; **Contact:** Colville National Forest, Three Rivers Ranger District, Kettle Falls, (509) 775-3305, www.fs .fed.us/r6/colville; **Notes:** Open to mountain bikes. Access road gated in winter to protect wildlife. Watch for ticks; **GPS:** N 48 37.429 W 118 14.384

A surprisingly lush canyon at the eastern edge of the Kettle River Range, Hoodoo houses wildlife-rich lakes

Bald Mountain, and the Barnaby Buttes, and together they drain a large area of the southern Kettles. Paralleling SR 20 for a good portion of its way to the Columbia River, Sherman Creek cuts through larch groves and cottonwood flats, cascades over ledges and careens through chasms. It's a sight to see, but not when you're buzzing by at 50 miles per hour. This trail enables you to enjoy it safely, at your own pace.

From the parking lot, the trail heads through open forest to immediately reach the river bank. Head west and upstream through meadow and open forest, savoring the sweet serenity of Sherman Creek.

tucked below shiny granite ledges. The trail through this slot in the mountains is a pure delight: gorgeous groves of towering pines and cedars year-round. In springtime, a riot of wildflowers brighten the canyon floor. And in autumn, aspen, Douglas maple, birch, and serviceberry streak Hoodoo red and gold.

GETTING THERE

From Republic, head east on State Route 20 for 34 miles, turning left onto Trout Lake Road (FR 020), 1.7 miles beyond the Log Flume Heritage Site. (From Kettle Falls, head west on SR 20 for 9 miles, turning right onto FR 020.) Follow FR 020 for 5.1 miles to its end at the Trout Lake Campground and Hoodoo Canyon trailhead (elev. 3050 ft). Privy available.

ON THE TRAIL

Emerald Lake sits about halfway in Hoodoo Canyon and can be accessed from either north or south. The northern approach from Deadman Creek is lightly used but involves more elevation gain and is steeper. The approach here from Trout Lake sees more use but is easier to get to and easier to hike. You can't go wrong either way, and strong hikers can easily hike the entire trail round-trip.

From the south end of the little car campground on the south shore of Trout Lake, find the start of the Hoodoo Canyon Trail and immediately come to the lake's outlet.

A hiker surveys Hoodoo Canyon from high on the trail. (Photo by Aaron Theisen)

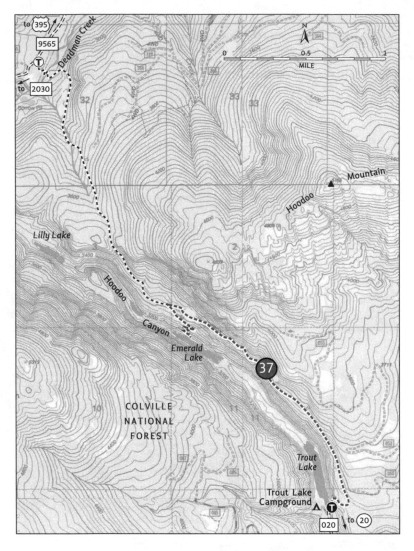

Cross it on a log bridge and then begin climbing. The way switchbacks from the cool canyon floor, cutting through Oregon grape, snowberry, current, thimbleberry, and dogwood. After about 0.4 mile, the climb eases and you are now high above Trout Lake.

Heading north now, along the canyon's sun-catching slopes, hike through very different vegetation than below. Beneath giant ponderosa pines lined with tall grasses (watch for ticks in the spring—they're profuse), traverse the canyon's eastern wall. If it's early in the season, admire the floral show—arnica, paintbrush, lupine, larkspur, balsamroot, buttercup, and more.

After reaching 3500 feet elevation, the way descends slightly. At 2.6 miles, shortly after crossing a small creek (dry later in the season), come to the junction with the Emerald Lake Trail (elev. 3450 ft). Turn left and head 0.6 mile, dropping a little more than 300 feet to reach the shores of the appropriately named lake at the bottom of the canyon (elev. 3125).

The water levels fluctuate throughout the year, either exposing big rocks or flooding shoreline birches and cottonwoods. Moose frequent the lake, as do various species of waterfowl. So sit quietly for awhile and observe some nature in action.

EXTENDING YOUR TRIP

From the Emerald Lake Trail junction, continue north on the Hoodoo Canyon Trail for 0.4 mile, climbing to a cliff overlooking the canyon (elev. 3700 ft). From there the trail leaves the canyon and rapidly descends through a lush forest of cedar and spruce to Deadman Creek (elev. 2825 ft). Cross the creek on a good bridge, and reach the northern trailhead (elev. 2900 ft) off of Deadman Creek Road (FR 9565) at 4.7 miles from the southern trailhead. If it's early in the season, mosquitoes are an annoyance.

38 Old Kettle Falls Trail

RATING/ DIFFICULTY	ROUND-TRIP	ELEV GAIN/ HIGH POINT	SEASON
*/1	2.6 miles	none/ 1300 feet	Mar–Dec

The trail crosses a channel before heading into a tunnel of aspen.

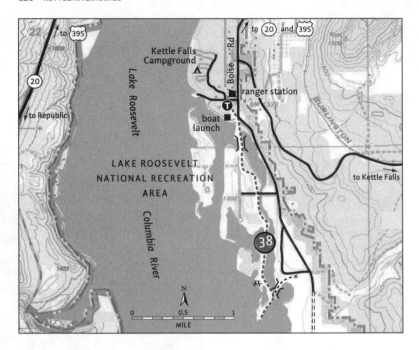

Map: USGS Kettle Falls; **Contact:** Lake Roosevelt National Recreation Area, (509) 633-9441, www.nps.gov/laro; **Notes:** Wheelchair-accessible. Dogs permitted on-leash; **GPS:** N48 35.953 W118 07.194

The falls are no more. Gone too is the original townsite of Kettle Falls. The impounded waters of the Grand Coulee Dam claimed them both in 1939. The town relocated to higher ground to the east. The falls receded into memory. One of the greatest fisheries on the Columbia River was claimed by the need for hydroelectric power. Walk the Old Kettle Falls Trail through abandoned homesteads and hallowed fishing grounds and let voices from the past cast insight, inquiry, and perhaps a little lament too.

GETTING THERE
From Colville, follow State Route 20/US Highway 395 west for 10 miles to the junction with SR 25 in Kettle Falls. Continue west on SR 20/US 395 for another 2.2 miles and turn left (south) onto Boise Road (just before the bridge over the Columbia River). Continue 1.6 miles, bearing right where Boise Road bears left to become the Old Kettle Falls Road. In 0.2 mile, come to the ranger station and the Kettle Falls Campground entrance. Park here. The trailhead (elev. 1300 ft) is just a few yards away on the south side of the campground entrance road. Privy available.

MAPMAKER, MAPMAKER, MAKE ME A MAP

While most Americans are familiar with Lewis and Clark and their 1804–1806 journey, few are familiar with David Thompson, who explored the vast Oregon Country around the same time, rivaling the Corps of Discovery in his mappings, findings, and influence on the American and European settlement of North America.

In 1784, the British-born Thompson came to British Canada (Churchill, in what is now Manitoba) at the age of fourteen. He apprenticed with the Hudson's Bay Company as a fur trader but quickly learned that his talents lay in surveying and mapmaking. In 1797, at age twenty-seven, he defected to Hudson's Bay Company's bitter rivals, the Northwest Company of Montreal, for whom he extensively mapped what is now northern Minnesota, eastern Ontario, and southern Manitoba.

In 1806, because of concerns of the Lewis and Clark Expedition and American claims to markets and settlements in the Northwest, Thompson set off for the Rocky Mountains to find a route to the Pacific Ocean. In 1807, he began exploring and mapping the head-waters of the Columbia River and the river's vast basin and tributaries. In 1811, the same year the Pacific Fur Company established Fort Astoria, the first American settlement in the Northwest at the mouth of the Columbia, the intrepid Thompson became the first recorded person to travel the entire length of the river. His 1814 map of the Columbia Basin was considered so accurate that the Canadian government continued to use it for nearly one hundred years.

In all, Thompson mapped a land mass of more than 1.5 million square miles. An accomplished and dedicated mapmaker, he was also a dedicated husband to his wife, Charlotte, for fifty-eight years. Thompson died in 1857 at the age of eighty-six. His legacy and accomplishments continue to intrigue historians and explorers—and many hikers and paddlers too.

Award-winning Spokane-based writer Jack Nisbit's *In The Mapmaker's Eye: David Thompson on the Columbia Plateau* (WSU Press, 2005) and *Sources of the River: Tracking David Thompson across North America* (Sasquatch Books, 2007) are excellent reads if you're interested in learning more about this fascinating individual.

—C. R.

ON THE TRAIL

This nearly perfectly flat trail is well used by locals walking their dogs and by campers on evening strolls. It may lack stunning scenery, but it's full of historical relics. The forest is pleasant too, and the surrounding wetlands great for bird-watching.

Head south on the wide trail, and after 0.1 mile cross the boat-launch access road.

Continue straight and soon come to a bridge spanning a draw lined with aspen. The water level fluctuates with the dam's drawdowns. The trail utilizes an old road briefly and then turns left, passing an old foundation and reaching the group-camp access road at 0.5 mile.

Cross the road and come to a much nicer stretch of trail. Pass by old homesteads and through pastures, orchards, and thickets of young pines and old locust trees. At 0.8 mile, cross another draw that may or may not be flowing with water. Continue along a piney "ridge" and then alongside a grassy marshy area that usually teems with wildlife.

At 1.1 miles, come to a junction. The trail left crosses a bridge over a cottonwood-lined draw, reaching a picnic area in 0.1 mile. Continue right instead, over sandy tread to a piney bluff. The trail ends at 1.3 miles, but when the water level is low you can walk out on the flats of the Columbia River. Just downstream is the Colville River. The town of Kettle Falls was relocated just upriver on this waterway, where the town of Meyers Falls once sat. The new transplants insisted on renaming Meyers Falls, Kettle Falls. They got their way.

EXTENDING YOUR TRIP

To see the site of the actual falls, visit the Saint Paul Mission located just north of the junction of Boise Road and SR 20/US 395. Check out the restored 1847 mission chapel built by Jesuit missionaries and Native Peoples. Then walk the 0.4-mile loop at the confluence of the Kettle and Columbia Rivers, where the famed explorer David Thompson, of the Northwest Company of Montreal, first passed by in 1811. His French Canadian fur traders named the falls Les Chaudieres—the Kettles—for the huge, kettle-shaped holes in the ledge below the falls. Occupied by Native Peoples for more than 9000 years, this spot was once the second-largest fishery on the Columbia River.

Opposite: The trail to the top of Hall Mountain near Sullivan Lake offers vast views of the Selkirk Mountains.

selkirk mountains

Eastern Washington and northern Idaho share the sprawling group of peaks known as the Selkirk Mountains. The southern end of the range is near Spokane (either at the granite climbing rocks on the north bank of the Spokane River or farther south at Mica Peak and the Rocks of Sharon, depending on which geologist you ask). From Spokane, the range stretches north into British Columbia, with notable landmarks such as Mount Spokane, Sullivan Lake, the Salmo-Priest Wilderness, and Gypsy Peak (elev. 7309 ft), the highest point in Eastern Washington.

The Salmo-Priest Wilderness is one of only three wilderness areas in Eastern Washington, so rugged that even the forest industry had little trouble bequeathing its 41,335 acres to preservation in 1984. The Pend Oreille County portion of the Selkirks is unique in Washington because of the critters that roam there. Forest roads are gated in certain high areas to curb motor-vehicle traffic and protect habitat for marquee species, including grizzly bears, gray wolves, bighorn sheep, and woodland caribou; the latter is one of the most critically endangered mammals in the United States.

39 Frater Lake

RATING/ DIFFICULTY	LOOP	ELEV GAIN/ HIGH POINT	SEASON
**/1	1.8 miles	125 feet/ 3318 feet	May–Nov

Maps: USGS Ione, Colville National Forest Frater Lake Sno-Park trail map; **Contact:** Colville National Forest, Three Rivers Ranger District, Colville, (509) 684-3711, www.fs .fed.us/r6/colville; **Notes:** Partly open to mountain bikes, motorized use; **GPS:** N 48 39.275 W 117 29.096

Trails circumnavigate Frater Lake.

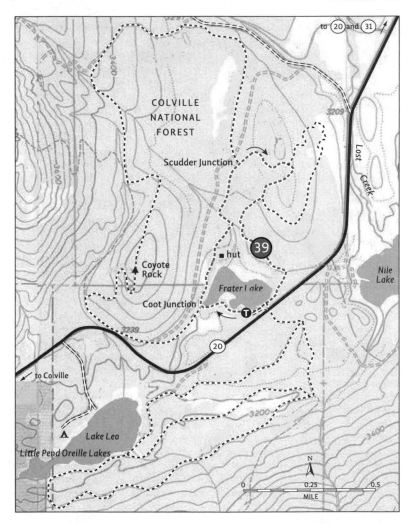

COLVILLE
NATIONAL
FOREST

Scudder Junction

Lost Creek

39

■ hut

Coyote
Rock

Frater Lake

Nile
Lake

Coot Junction

T

20

to Colville

Lake Leo

Little Pend Oreille Lakes

N

0   0.25   0.5
MILE

The kilometers on posted trail markers are a tip that this 10-mile system of forested loop trails was designed for cross-country skiing, a sport that clings to its metric European origin. While a part of this trail is open to motorcycles, the route featured here quickly whisks you into a peaceful forest to circumnavigate Frater Lake, one of seven lakes in a 6-mile stretch of the

Little Pend Oreille River valley. The lake is stocked with trout, dappled with lily pads, and home to a lodge of beavers, visiting waterfowl—and occasional hikers.

GETTING THERE
From State Route 20/31 about 47 miles north of Newport, turn west on SR 20 at Tiger. Drive 6.3 miles to the trailhead parking area (elev. 3270 ft) on the north side of the road at milepost 384. (From Colville, drive east on 3rd Avenue/SR 20 for 29 miles to the trailhead). Privy available.

ON THE TRAIL
The Tiger Loop Trail No. 150 begins between the kiosk and the restroom. It's a multiuse trail for nearly 0.2 mile to Coot Junction. Bear right on the nonmotorized trail along the lake. Pass between the log warming hut and outhouse, through the gate, and continue on the Tiger Loop.

Several bridges lead over a small creek. The strange boards on the railings are barriers to keep Nordic skiers from toppling over the bridges while making turns. Notice the carpet of kinnikinnick, a native ground cover that develops red berries (not poisonous, but not palatable either). The hoary elfin butterfly lays its eggs on its foliage.

At Scudder Junction, bear right. The trail leads to a fence with a view into the Teepee Seed Orchard, established in 1989. The Forest Service says that by 2020 this 24-acre tree farm will be producing enough Engelmann spruce and western white pine seeds to meet the reforestation needs of the eastern half of the 1.1-million-acre Colville National Forest.

From the fence, the trail doubles back into the forest as a pleasant single-track trail. Soon you'll come to a junction with the

option of turning left for a loop that adds 0.6 mile. Or bear right and follow the main trail back to the lake and trailhead.

EXTENDING YOUR TRIP
At Coot Junction, turn left and follow the 4.8-mile Coyote Rock Trail, which gains more elevation, offers some views, and adds more than 2 miles to your hike. Frater Lake parking area also is the base for Trail No. 155, a 2.5-mile network of loops starting just across SR 20 and extending southwest to Lake Leo.

40 Big Meadow Lake

RATING/ DIFFICULTY	LOOP	ELEV GAIN/ HIGH POINT	SEASON
****/2	2.8 miles	320 feet/ 3460 feet	May–Nov

Maps: USGS Aladdin Mtn, Colville National Forest map; **Contact:** Colville National Forest, Three Rivers Ranger District, Colville, (509) 684-3711, www.fs.fed.us/r6/colville; **Notes:** Partly wheelchair-accessible. Dogs permitted on-leash; **GPS:** N 48 43.768 W 117 33.866

 *Kids love this area, with its easy trails, fishing lake, and homestead cabin. The centerpiece is a wildlife-viewing platform overlooking Meadow Creek and the lake. The roofless tower is built from a fire lookout that once perched on North Baldy Mountain.*

GETTING THERE
From Colville, head east on 3rd Avenue/State Route 20 toward Ione. Drive 1.1 miles to the top of the hill across from the airport and turn left on Aladdin Road, which eventually

The Meadow Creek Trail features a replica homestead.

becomes Northport Road (CR 9435). Drive 19 miles and turn right on Big Meadow Creek Road (CR 2695). Drive 7.5 miles and turn right into the Big Meadow Lake Recreation Area (elev. 3300 ft). (From the Pend Oreille River valley at Ione, you can reach the lake by driving 7 miles west on gravel roads.) Privy available.

ON THE TRAIL

Start at the trailhead across from the parking area and vault toilet. Follow the paved path to the wildlife-viewing tower. Continue north on the wheelchair-accessible loop path for 0.2 mile and turn left through the gate onto Meadow Creek Trail No. 125.

Hike 0.3 mile and turn right on the 0.3-mile spur to the replica of a homestead cabin. Retrace your steps to the Meadow Creek Trail and turn right to continue the loop. After hiking a total of 1.6 miles, you'll reach the west end of the loop and cross Meadow Creek. Enjoy the changes in forest type as you hike back toward the lake. The trail drops past campsites to the campground access road. Turn left on the road and hike north along the lake, over the outlet, and past the shore-fishing area to the parking area.

EXTENDING YOUR TRIP

Add 1.5 miles by hiking around Big Meadow Lake if high water has not inundated the route. Connect to Lakeshore Trail No. 126 from the trailhead at the south-side campground. The trail merges with a road for a short way at the east end of the lake and then splits off left and follows the north shore back to the recreation area entrance road.

HIGH TIMES OVER FOR FIRE LOOKOUTS

Fire lookouts had their heyday in the first half of the twentieth century, especially during a Depression-era building boom. The Civilian Conservation Corps was dispatched to help erect cabins and towers for fire detection on accessible peaks with the best views of the landscape below. But after more than sixty years of service, most of the wooden sentinels and those who staffed them have met a foe more permanent than any wildfire: technology. Aircraft, computers, and imaging have taken over the lofty task.

Lookouts were torn down almost as quickly as they were built in a demolition campaign that surged across the country in the 1960s and 1970s. Of the 678 fire lookout sites in Washington, fewer than 90 still have standing structures. About 20 are staffed five days or more a season by various agencies or tribes. About 50 are maintained for emergency use.

To save some of the historic structures, the Forest Service and other agencies were convinced to rent some of the cabins and towers to campers. The Quartz Mountain Lookout in Mount Spokane State Park (Hike 67) is an excellent room with a view, available by reservation. The lookout was formerly on top of Mount Spokane. Instead of being destroyed, it was disassembled so State Parks staff and volunteers could relocate and rebuild it.

About two dozen of the hikes in this book lead to the eye-pleasing, lofty locations of fire lookout sites, former and active. Incidentally, the Idaho Panhandle was once the mecca of fire lookouts, with nearly 300 towers in roughly 150 miles from Priest Lake to the Saint Joe River country. Only about two dozen are still in use, nearly half of them as recreational rentals.
                                                                —R. L

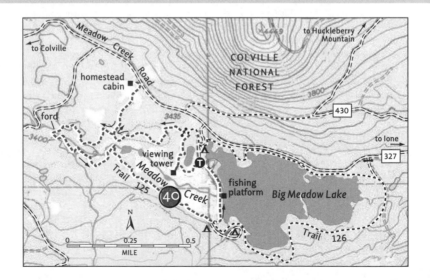

41 Rogers Mountain and Gillette Ridge

RATING/ DIFFICULTY	ROUND-TRIP	ELEV GAIN/ HIGH POINT	SEASON
****/3	5 miles	1200 feet/ 5770 feet	June–Oct

Maps: USGS Aladdin, USGS Gillette Mountain, Colville National Forest map; **Contact:** Colville National Forest, Three Rivers Ranger District, Colville, (509) 684-3711, www.fs .fed.us/r6/colville; **Notes:** Open to mountain bikes, motorized use; **GPS:** N 48 44.601 W 117 43.245

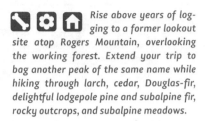

Rise above years of logging to a former lookout site atop Rogers Mountain, overlooking the working forest. Extend your trip to bag another peak of the same name while hiking through larch, cedar, Douglas-fir, delightful lodgepole pine and subalpine fir, rocky outcrops, and subalpine meadows.

GETTING THERE

From US Highway 395 in Colville, drive east on 3rd Avenue toward Ione and State Route 20 for 1 mile and turn left (north) across from the airport onto Aladdin Road. Go north 15 miles and turn left on unmarked

Cruising the trail between Rogers Mountain (background) to Mount Rogers

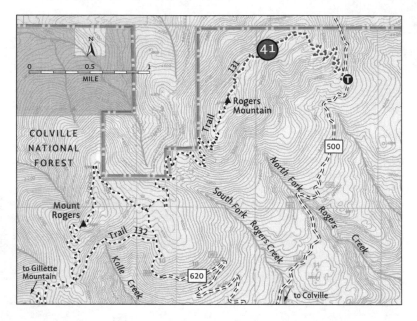

Forest Road 500. Cross the cattle guard and head up 3.3 miles. Bear right at the junction with FR 620 (which leads to an optional trailhead). Continue on FR 500 for 1.6 miles and turn left and uphill at a junction with an unmapped spur road. Go another 1.2 miles to the trailhead (elev. 4670 ft) off a short spur road to the left.

ON THE TRAIL

Gillette Ridge Trail No. 131 extends 9.7 miles from this trailhead to the Onion Creek trailhead (where the access road is no longer maintained) offering several options.

The trail heads up and switches back through a stand of larches (golden around the third week of October) and climbs out of a 2011 timber sale. Soon a switchback points you north, to look at Canadian peaks in the distance. Then the route bends decidedly

southwest, transitioning as it climbs into a forest of scattered lodgepole pine and low-growing huckleberry.

At 2 miles, cross the old lookout access road, which leads to the top, but the trail is a nicer route, leading 0.5 mile up to the broad summit of Rogers Mountain. Four cement anchors are all that remain of a lookout tower built in 1933. The tower blew down in 1959 and was never replaced. (Even the name of this 5770-foot mountain has been removed from the latest Colville National Forest map.) Enjoy the views and return to your car.

EXTENDING YOUR TRIP

For a highly recommended 12-mile round-trip, continue south and down off Rogers Mountain and follow the trail to Mount Rogers. The trail descends 2 miles to a saddle and a lush cedar forest before beginning a gradual 1.8-mile climb to the 5557-foot summit. (At 5.2 miles you'll pass the junction with the 0.6-mile trail to FR 620. Signs may still indicate Mount Rogers Loop Trail No. 130, but the lower segment of that loop appears to have been obliterated by logging.)

42 Sherlock Peak

RATING/ DIFFICULTY	ROUND-TRIP	ELEV GAIN/ HIGH POINT	SEASON
***/3	8.2 miles	2000 feet/ 6365 feet	late June– Oct

Maps: USGS Leadpoint, USGS Deep Lake, Colville National Forest map; **Contact:** Colville National Forest, Three Rivers Ranger District, Colville, (509) 684-3711, www.fs .fed.us/r6/colville; **Notes:** Open to mountain bikes, horses. High-clearance recommended; **GPS:** N 48 53.048 W 117 31.926

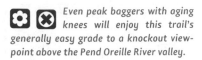 *Even peak baggers with aging knees will enjoy this trail's generally easy grade to a knockout viewpoint above the Pend Oreille River valley.*

GETTING THERE

From US Highway 395 in Colville, drive east on 3rd Avenue toward Ione and State Route 20 for 1 mile and turn left (north) across from the airport onto Aladdin Road. Go nearly 25 miles (the route becomes Aladdin-Northport Road/County Road 9435) to a Y and bear right onto Deep Lake–Boundary Road (CR 9445). (This area also is accessible via forest roads over Smackout Pass from Ione.) Continue 7.2 miles, passing Deep Lake, and turn right (east) at Leadpoint onto Silver Creek Road (CR 4720) Drive 0.5 mile and bear left at a Y, continuing on CR 4720. Go 1.3 miles and bear right at the next Y onto Forest Road 070 toward Silver Creek trailheads. Drive 0.4 mile and bear right onto

Sherlock Peak looms behind the snags.

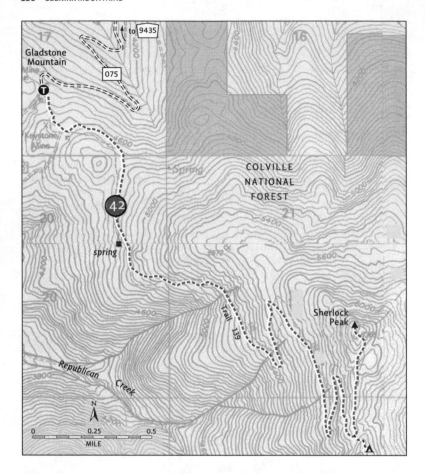

FR 075. Drive 4.5 slow miles to the trailhead at road's end (elev. 4540 ft).

ON THE TRAIL

Sherlock Peak Trail No. 139 heads up for the first 1.3 miles on a road that's fairly nondescript through the timber. A switchback leads to a single-track trail and the views start to open up.

At 2.3 miles the trail breaks into a glorious west-facing hillside of wildflowers above the headwaters of Republican Creek. As the route tops a ridge, check out the trail to the right that climbs briefly to a fine open vantage and campsite with views north to your destination at Sherlock Peak.

Then drop back down and follow the ridge and intermittent trail through the scattered subalpine fir, beargrass, and lupine. Go on the west side of the first knob and where the going gets steep, angle around the east side of the peak, skirt a bog, and begin angling up to a swale of green pine grass that leads to Sherlock's summit at 4.1 miles.

The view from the top is stunning: snowy peaks in Canada, Abercrombie Mountain, the Pend Oreille River valley, Crowell Ridge in the Salmo-Priest Wilderness, Idaho's Selkirk Crest in the distance to the east, the clear-cut swath of the international boundary, and when clear, the North Cascades to the west.

EXTENDING YOUR TRIP
From the campsite vista, explore the open untrailed ridge that extends south and southwest from Sherlock.

43 Abercrombie Mountain

RATING/ DIFFICULTY	ROUND-TRIP	ELEV GAIN/ HIGH POINT	SEASON
*****/3	7.3 miles	2350 feet/ 7308 feet	late June– Oct

Maps: USGS Abercrombie, Colville National Forest map; **Contact:** Colville National Forest, Three Rivers Ranger District, Colville, (509) 684-3711, www.fs.fed.us/r6/colville; **Notes:** Open to horses. Proposed wilderness; **GPS:** N 48 55.799 W 117 29.085

Abercrombie Mountain is the centerpiece of a lofty roadless area proposed for wilderness protection. It's the second-

Rocky rubble covers Abercrombie Mountain's summit; Hooknose Mountain is in the distance.

highest mountain in Eastern Washington (next to Gypsy Peak), joining its neighbors Sherlock Peak and Hooknose Mountain in a trio of prominent high points between the Columbia River to the west and the Pend Oreille River to the east. The open rocky summit offers great views in every direction.

GETTING THERE

From US Highway 395 in Colville, drive east on 3rd Avenue toward Ione and State Route 20. Near the edge of town, turn left (north) across from the airport onto Aladdin Road. Go nearly 25 miles (the route becomes Aladdin–Northport Road/County Road 9435) to a Y and bear right onto Deep Lake–Boundary Road (CR 9445). (This area also is accessible via forest roads over Smackout Pass from Ione.) Continue 7.3 miles, passing Deep Lake, and turn right (east) at Leadpoint onto Silver Creek Road (CR 4720). Drive 0.5 mile and bear left at a Y, continuing on CR 4720 about 1 mile. Cross a cattle guard onto national forest land. Drive 0.4 mile and turn left onto CR 7078. (Continuing straight onto FR 070 leads 1.3 miles to a campground and longer alternate route at Silver Creek Trailhead.) Drive 4.5 miles on CR 7078, turning right onto FR 300, a less-developed route, and drive about 3.3 miles to the trailhead at road's end (elev. 4990 ft).

ON THE TRAIL

Abercrombie Mountain Trail No. 117 angles uphill through cool forest and soon begins switchbacking to gain more than 900 feet of elevation in the 1.5 miles to the junction with Silver Creek Trail No. 119. Turn left, contouring before starting another series of nine well-graded switchbacks that lead to the open south ridge guarded by old silvery snags.

Head up the wide ridge. Soon start watching carefully for the junction with

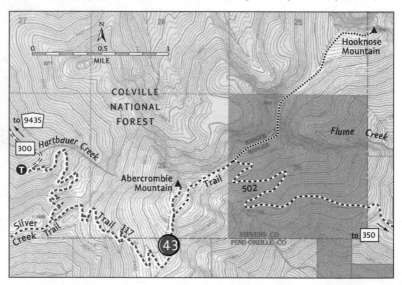

Flume Creek Trail No. 502, which contours off to the right at 3.5 miles. At this junction, turn left as Trail No. 117 leads uphill through snags and tenacious wildflowers on a route that's marked occasionally by cairns maintained by hikers. Finally, the route becomes a promenade over a rockway, past flat-stone hideouts to Abercrombie's broad 7308-foot summit, site of a dismantled fire lookout.

EXTENDING YOUR TRIP

For a rugged but excellent off-trail route to nearby Hooknose Mountain, go just south of the Abercrombie summit and follow Trail No. 502 down the mountain's northeast ridge for about 0.6 mile. Where the trail angles off the ridge to begin its descent into Flume Creek, bear left and stay on the ridge (a user trail is apparent in some places). From here it's 1.5 rough miles cross-country, skirting some of the rocky knobs and through trees, to the summit of Hooknose (elev. 7210 ft) and a precipitous 1100-foot drop-off overlooking tiny Hooknose Lake. You can supersize the Abercrombie Mountain mileage by starting from the Silver Creek Campground trailhead, for a round-trip of 16.4 miles.

44 Mill Butte

RATING/ DIFFICULTY	LOOP	ELEV GAIN/ HIGH POINT	SEASON
***/2	4.2 miles	680 feet/ 2615 feet	Mar–Nov

Maps: USGS Cliff Ridge, refuge map; **Contact:** Little Pend Oreille National Wildlife Refuge, (509) 684-8384, www.fws.gov /littlependoreille; **Notes:** Dogs permitted on-leash. Hunting allowed in most of refuge; **GPS:** N 48 27.687 W 117 43.846

Glaciers transported huge boulders and left them on Mill Butte.

Little Pend Oreille National Wildlife Refuge is a 41,568-acre jewel in northeastern Stevens County, with its namesake stream, lakes, and a wide range of wildlife. Hiking to Mill Butte offers lessons in modern habitat management by fire as well as prominent features left by glacial ice. The trail is the 2010 product of an active refuge friends group and the Washington Trails Association.

GETTING THERE

From Colville's Main Street (US Highway 395), turn east on 3rd Avenue (State Route 20) and drive nearly 6 miles. Just past White Mud Lake, turn right onto Artman–Gibson Road. Drive 1.5 miles to a four-way intersection and turn left onto Kitt–Narcisse Road. Drive 2.1 miles to a fork and bear right onto Bear Creek Road. Drive 2.5 miles and continue straight at an intersection another 0.6 mile to the parking area and kiosks at the refuge

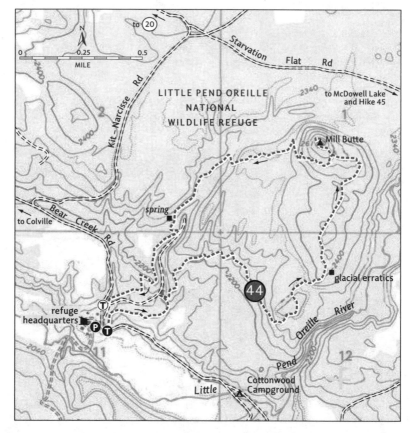

headquarters (elev. 2040 ft). Privy available at nearby Cottonwood Campground.

ON THE TRAIL
Check out the educational information at the parking area, then proceed to the trailheads across Bear Creek Road from the headquarters. Head out the parking area's lower entrance to the lower trailhead and hike the loop counterclockwise.

The trail leads up a ridge and into a thinned forest of ponderosa pine and western larch that's been treated with controlled burns to leave it open with good views. Wildflowers can be prolific at times, although Saint John's wort—a tall, yellow-blooming noxious weed—dominates some areas. Even when the hillsides dry out in midsummer, pockets of pine grass remain brilliant green. At 1.7 miles, the trail climbs to cross a small ridge and passes two large, out-of-place rocks. These glacial erratics were carried by glaciers some 10,000 years ago and deposited a considerable distance from their place of origin.

At 2.3 miles, continue up the short spur trail to Mill Butte for an open panorama of the vast forest landscape. Then head down and continue the loop. Notice the shrub clumps that start appearing. This is bitterbrush, introduced decades ago as winter food for the white-tailed deer the refuge was geared toward harboring. However, while mule deer eat bitterbrush (mule deer are rare on the refuge), the whitetails ignore this species of bitterbrush, refuge managers say.

The trail drops through carpets of kinnikinnick to an old roadbed that begins paralleling a spring-fed ravine on the left. The trail roughly follows the lush creek back to the upper trailhead across from the Little Pend Oreille refuge headquarters.

EXTENDING YOUR TRIP
See McDowell Lake (Hike 45).

45 McDowell Lake

RATING/ DIFFICULTY	LOOP	ELEV GAIN HIGH POINT	SEASON
****/1	1.3 miles	95 feet/ 2365 feet	Mar–Nov

Maps: USGS Cliff Ridge, refuge map; **Contact:** Little Pend Oreille National Wildlife Refuge, (509) 684-8384, www.fws.gov /littlependoreille; **Notes:** Partly wheelchair-accessible. Dogs permitted on-leash. Trout fishing allowed in main lake under special rules; **GPS:** N 48 28.513 W 117 41.142

This trail is prized as an environmental education destination. In the course of a mile, you'll see five distinct ecological habitats, from riparian to semi-arid. Thanks to the Friends of the LPO Refuge, a boardwalk leads over a cattail marsh and a group observation blind puts you in touch with the wide range of birds and other wildlife.

GETTING THERE
From Colville's Main Street (US Highway 395), turn east on 3rd Avenue (State Route 20) and drive 6 miles. Just past White Mud Lake, turn right onto Artman–Gibson Road. Drive 1.7 miles to a four-way intersection and turn left onto Kitt–Narcisse Road. Drive 2.2 miles to a fork and turn left on Narcisse Creek Road (straight takes you to refuge headquarters). Drive 1 mile to a Y and bear right. Bear right again toward McDowell Lake on the auto tour route. Go 1.7 miles to the trailhead on the right (elev. 2310 ft), just

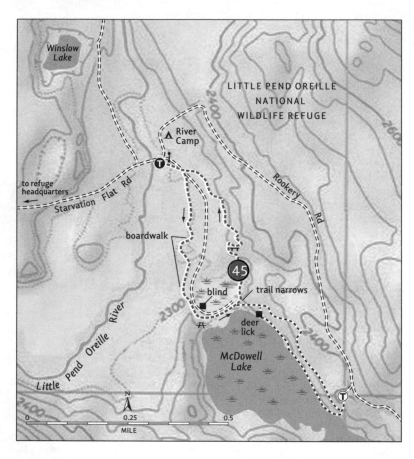

after the bridge over the Little Pend Oreille River. Privy available.

ON THE TRAIL

In early spring, be prepared to wade a few inches of water on the first part of the trail. Otherwise the first 0.6 mile is a breeze and universally accessible. Borrow a brochure from the trailhead and enjoy the interpretive stops along the way, including a chance to see rare marsh lupine, which blooms in late June or July.

Follow the boardwalk and then the dike road to a picnic area on the north end of McDowell Lake. An observation blind faces north over the marsh. Look for sign of moose, beavers, deer, great blue herons, ducks, dragonflies, and rising trout along the dike.

At the end of the dike road, the trail narrows into a single track and heads north.

The off-trail route along McDowell Lake goes by wildflowers and mineral licks.

SULLIVAN LAKE BASE CAMP

Base camps are remarkably enjoyable and efficient launch pads for day hiking. Get to where the action is, make a car camp with the comforts afforded by a cooler, camp stove, and lawn chairs, and then head out and gobble up some trail miles.

Of the many, many good base-camp options in Eastern Washington, Sullivan Lake stands out in the wild northeast corner of Pend Oreille County. For starters, the Nature Trail, Shoreline Trail, and Hall Mountain Trail are easily accessible from Colville National Forest developed campgrounds at both ends of the lake. The Forest Service ranger station is nearby for information during the week. A sandy swimming beach is prized by families.

A dozen of the Selkirk Mountain hikes in this book are either a short bike ride or easy drive from the lake, including trails into the Salmo-Priest Wilderness. Numerous other attractions are within easy striking distance, such as huckleberry picking, paddling the Z Canyon stretch of the Pend Oreille River starting from Metaline or taking a field trip to Gardner Cave at Crawford State Park off the Boundary Dam Road.

Sullivan Lake, which is remarkably clean and warm during summer, will be waiting to rinse off the trail dust in a posthike dip. Only a tiny section of the northeast corner is developed with a few cabins, helping this base-camp gem stay off the grid of power-boating maniacs. *Shhh.* Share this only with your most worthy friends.

—R. L.

Invasive species such as Saint John's wort and knapweed are taking over in a few areas, but in August, after many of the native wildflowers have gone to seed, these weeds are blooming and bustling with the activity of bees and butterflies.

The trail climbs higher to a bench for an overview of the marsh before winding back down to the trailhead.

EXTENDING YOUR TRIP

Where the dike road narrows to a single track, veer off the main loop and follow the user trail southeast on the bluffs above McDowell Lake. Follow a spine-like ridge (trail is faint) past the Rookery Road Auto Tour overlook almost to the water. Turn right and loop back on the faint shoreline game trail. As you approach the dike at the end of McDowell Lake, notice where deer regularly come to lick minerals from the soil. Near the last lick, climb the slope and turn left to rejoin the main loop.

Sullivan Creek enters the Mill Pond site.

46 Sullivan Mill Pond

RATING/ DIFFICULTY	ROUND-TRIP	ELEV GAIN/ HIGH POINT	SEASON
***/2	2 miles	280 feet/ 2575 feet	May–Nov

Maps: USGS Metaline Falls, Colville National Forest map; **Contact:** Colville National Forest, Sullivan Lake Ranger District, (509) 446-7500, www.fs.fed.us/r6/colville; **Notes:** Partly wheelchair-accessible. Dogs permitted on-leash. Trails subject to change after planned stream restoration; **GPS:** N 48 51 .528 W 117 17.992

 Big changes were underway for the Mill Pond Historic Site as this guidebook went to press. The pond—created in 1910 to store water for a mind-boggling 3-mile-long wood flume to supply hydropower to a Metaline Falls cement plant—was

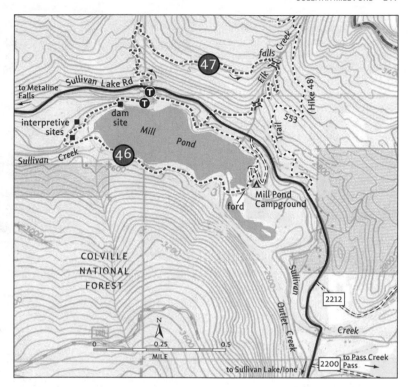

scheduled to be drained. Planning was underway to restore Sullivan Creek's winding path through the resulting meadow. But the trail, blacksmith cabin, and displays detailing the history of a unique hydroelectric system will remain. The best of the site is available only to hikers.

GETTING THERE

From Metaline Falls, drive north for 2 miles on State Route 31 and turn right onto Sullivan Lake Road (County Road 9345). Go 3.2 miles and turn right into the trailhead parking at Mill Pond Historic Site (elev. 2600 ft). Privy available.

ON THE TRAIL

From the parking area, head down to the right to begin the Mill Pond Flume Trail No. 520 interpretive walk. Signs detail the history of the area's first major development, starting in 1910 with a major wilderness work camp that used steam-powered machinery to build and service a covered wood aqueduct so large its roof became a boardwalk to Metaline Falls.

The trail leads across the dam site. At a junction, go right to reach the blacksmith shop and cabin displays. Read about the maintenance nightmares that ultimately doomed the flume project in 1956.

The trail then bends back and joins with Mill Pond Loop Trail No. 550, heading east through the trees above the Mill Pond site to Sullivan Creek, where most hikers will turn back for a 2-mile round-trip.

EXTENDING YOUR TRIP

In low water, Sullivan Creek can be forded. Cross the creek to the campground area and turn left on the trail that crosses Elk Creek and contours around the north side of the Mill Pond site back to the trailhead (see Hike 47).

47 Elk Creek Falls

RATING/ DIFFICULTY	LOOP	ELEV GAIN/ HIGH POINT	SEASON
****/2	2.1 miles	550 feet/ 3035 feet	May–Nov

Maps: USGS Metaline Falls, Colville National Forest map; **Contact:** Colville National Forest, Sullivan Lake Ranger District, (509) 446-7500, www.fs.fed.us/r6/colville; **Notes:** Dogs permitted on-leash. Use caution crossing highway; **GPS:** N 48 51.555 W 117 18.036

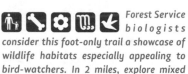 *Forest Service biologists consider this foot-only trail a showcase of wildlife habitats especially appealing to bird-watchers. In 2 miles, explore mixed deciduous and conifer forest, open shrublands, a riparian area, and a cool, cascading waterfall. The shrub field is the product of a 1980s controlled burn to revitalize habitat for elk.*

GETTING THERE

From Metaline Falls, drive north for 2 miles on State Route 31 and turn right onto Sullivan

Elk Creek Falls tumbles through cedars.

Lake Road (County Road 9345). Go 3.2 miles and turn right into the trailhead parking at Mill Pond Historic Site (elev. 2600 ft). Privy available.

ON THE TRAIL

From the parking area, Elk Creek Trail No. 560 heads uphill and crosses Sullivan Lake Road. The nicely routed single track is easy to follow as it winds through forest and open areas. It gains altitude for the first 0.6 mile before contouring into open areas and an overlook of the Mill Pond Historic Site below.

You'll encounter Douglas-fir and aspen as well as serviceberry, chokecherry, ninebark, ocean spray, snowberry, and flowers such as Indian paintbrush, lupine, larkspur, and queen's cup bead lily. A trail highlight—also the high point—is at Elk Creek Falls, which cascades refreshingly through cedars and below a footbridge at the halfway point of this hike.

Begin a winding descent, staying close to the creek and crossing another footbridge at 1.5 miles. Drop and cross Sullivan Lake Road. At a trail junction, you could turn left for a short walk to the Mill Pond Campground. But to finish the loop, turn right and hike west 0.3 mile to the trailhead.

EXTENDING YOUR TRIP
See Sullivan Mill Pond (Hike 46).

48 Red Bluff

RATING/ DIFFICULTY	ROUND-TRIP	ELEV GAIN/ HIGH POINT	SEASON
***/3	9 miles	2200 feet/ 3920 feet	May–Nov

Maps: USGS Boundary Dam, USGS Metaline Falls, Colville National Forest map; **Contact:** Colville National Forest, Sullivan Lake Ranger District, (509) 446-7500, www.fs.fed.us /r6/colville; **Notes:** Open to mountain bikes. Grizzly and wolf habitat; **GPS:** N 48 51.252 W 117 17.247

Take a pleasant walk through the woods—well-maintained and thoughtfully graded despite the total elevation gain—just outside the border of

Giant cedars line the banks of North Fork Sullivan Creek.

the Salmo-Priest Wilderness. The Red Bluff name derives from the reddish iron oxide in the Gypsy quartzite formations above. The trail is suitable for turning around at any point for a shorter hike, but ultimately it leads to the North Fork Sullivan Creek, a wild spot where we spotted a gray wolf while scouting this trek.

GETTING THERE

From Metaline Falls, drive north for 2 miles on State Route 31 and turn right onto Sullivan Lake Road (County Road 9345). Drive 4 miles and turn left into the small trailhead parking area (elev. 2720 ft). (From Sullivan Lake Ranger Station, drive 1.8 miles northwest to the trailhead.)

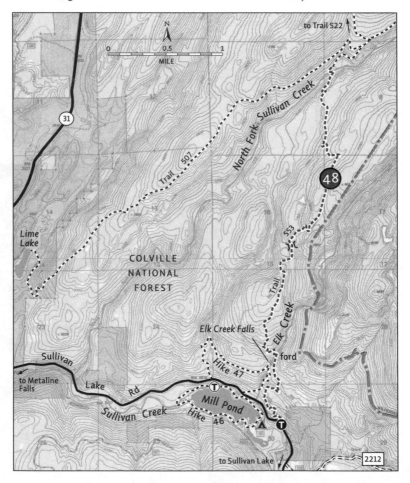

ON THE TRAIL

Red Bluff Trail No. 553 leads uphill on a knee-friendly grade past thimbleberry, queen's cup bead lily, wild strawberry and raspberry, lupine, and kinnikinnick as you weave through mountain maple, birch, and aspen mixed into the forest. Pearly everlasting graces trailside areas in summer through fall. And there's an assortment of mosses and fungi, along with long patches of twinflower, near the high point of the hike.

At 0.9 mile, ford Elk Creek, which is a dry hop on stepping stones for most of the season, but during spring look for a downed log bridge or plan on wading.

At 3 miles, the route tops out (elev. 3920 ft) and switchbacks down into darker forest of cedars and trees that choke out sunlight and limit forest-floor vegetation growth. Soon, after the last of several pleasant cruising stretches, the trail begins a long gradual descent to the North Fork Sullivan Creek, where a few giant cedars shade a pleasant break spot before you begin the hike back.

EXTENDING YOUR TRIP

Ford the creek and explore Halliday Trail No. 522 or North Fork Sullivan Creek Trail No. 507, which climbs all the way to Crowell Ridge. Or, cool off in a bathtub-size hole in the creek downstream from the trail crossing, but watch out for the devil's club along the shore.

49 Sullivan Lake Shoreline

RATING/ DIFFICULTY	ROUND-TRIP	ELEV GAIN/ HIGH POINT	SEASON
****/3	4.6 miles	650 feet/ 2835 feet	Apr–Nov

Viewpoint off Sullivan Lake Shoreline Trail

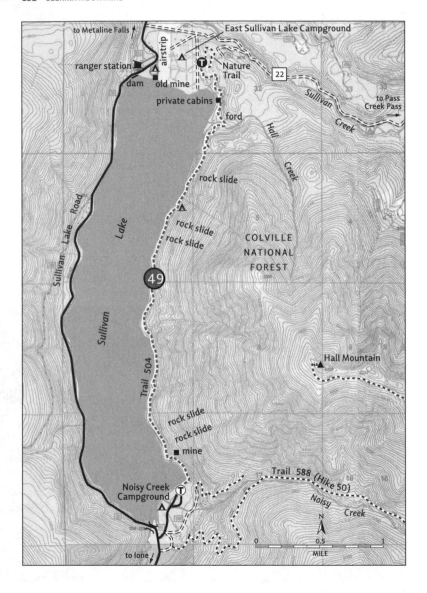

to Metaline Falls

East Sullivan Lake Campground

airstrip

ranger station

(T)

22

Nature Trail

dam   old mine

Sullivan   Creek

to Pass Creek Pass

private cabins

ford

Hall

Creek

rock slide

Sullivan   Lake   Road

Lake

rock slide

rock slide

COLVILLE

NATIONAL

FOREST

49

Sullivan

Trail 504

Hall Mountain

rock slide

rock slide

mine

Trail   588 (Hike 50)

Noisy Creek Campground

(T)

Noisy   Creek

N

to Ione

0   0.5   1

MILE

Maps: USGS Metaline Falls, Colville National Forest map; **Contact:** Colville National Forest, Sullivan Lake Ranger District, (509) 446-7500, www.fs.fed.us/r6/colville; **Notes:** Dogs permitted on-leash. Trail hikes equally well from north or south end of lake; **GPS:** N 48 50.420 W 117 16.712

   Countless calories from s'mores have been burned off on this route linking the campgrounds at the north and south ends of Sullivan Lake. An interpretive nature trail adds a shorter option and educational value, while the east shoreline trail can be a half-day experience. The trek offers a surprising smorgasbord of terrain, great views of Pend Oreille County's largest lake, plus swimming and even a peek into a bat cave. And don't worry about the occasional low-flying aircraft: Sullivan Lake is unique in the region for its north shoreline airstrip and campsites for pilots.

GETTING THERE
From Metaline Falls, drive north for 2 miles on State Route 31 and turn right onto Sullivan Lake Road (County Road 9345). Drive 4.7 miles and turn left onto Forest Road 22. Drive 0.4 mile and turn right into the East Sullivan Lake Campground. Drive 0.2 mile to the trailhead and free parking area for hikers on the left (elev. 2690 ft). Privy available. (See Hike 50 for directions to the south trailhead.)

ON THE TRAIL
From the north end of Lakeshore Trail No. 504, hike up a short distance and turn left on Nature Trail No. 509. Interpretive brochures are available at a kiosk (or from the ranger station on Sullivan Lake Road). Learn about springs, see remnant signs of a 1926 forest

fire, marvel at a 250-year-old western larch, and check out the "witches' broom" that's putting a spell on trees.

Finish the 0.6-mile loop (leave your brochure at the kiosk if you no longer need it) and continue hiking on the Lakeshore Trail. *Lakeshore* will seem a misnomer at first, as the trail gains elevation. Pass a trail that drops down to the right to a parking area for a remarkably small group of private cabins considering this is a 1550-acre lake.

The uphill effort soon proves worthwhile with a great down-lake view. Descend to cross a small creek and head up a mossy slope. At about 2 miles, the trail cuts across the first of five rock slides along the shoreline. Pass a small picnic area with access to the water and room for a small tent.

The trail has fewer ups and downs in the last mile as it heads into a birch forest and thimbleberries. Around the last bay, look for a path that heads up a short way to an old mining adit. Forest Service biologists have put a bat-friendly gate on the entrance to keep people out while allowing Townsend's big-eared bats to continue using the cave.

Just before reaching the south trailhead at the Noisy Creek Campground boat launch, the Lakeshore Trail passes a popular swimming area, usually equipped with a rope swing for launching out over the lake. Be wary of the condition of the rope—and the tree. Several former rope-swing trees have naturally toppled into the lake.

EXTENDING YOUR TRIP
Lock a bike near the trailhead at one end of the lake before hiking the Lakeshore Trail from the other end. Then pedal the paved, lightly traveled Sullivan Lake Road back to your starting point for a round-trip of 10 miles.

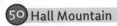

50 Hall Mountain

RATING/ DIFFICULTY	ROUND-TRIP	ELEV GAIN/ HIGH POINT	SEASON
*****/4	14 miles	4130 feet/ 6323 feet	July–Oct

Maps: USGS Metaline Falls, Colville National Forest map; **Contact:** Colville National Forest, Sullivan Lake Ranger District, (509) 446-7500, www.fs.fed.us/r6/colville; **Notes:** Open to mountain bikes, horses. Fording Noisy Creek can be difficult in high runoff; **GPS:** N 48 47.272 W 117 16.886

Hall Mountain casts its shadow on Sullivan Lake each morning, beckoning a few of the hearty visitors from the lakeside campgrounds. Being the former site of a fire lookout guarantees a view from the summit in all directions. The scene includes wilderness and proposed wilderness critical to megafauna, including bighorn sheep, grizzly bears, and rare woodland caribou.

GETTING THERE

From its junction with State Route 20 north of Cusick, drive SR 31 north toward Ione for 3.1 miles and turn right on Sullivan Lake Road (County Road 9345). Cross the Pend Oreille River and angle left, staying on Sullivan Lake Road (don't take a sharp left onto the river road). Drive 7.5 miles and turn into the Noisy Creek Campground Recreation Area at the south end of Sullivan Lake. Go a short way and turn right toward the Hall Mountain Trail. Follow the sign and another right turn into the trailhead and free parking area for hikers (elev. 2610 ft). Privy available.

Lupine along the last mile to Hall Mountain summit

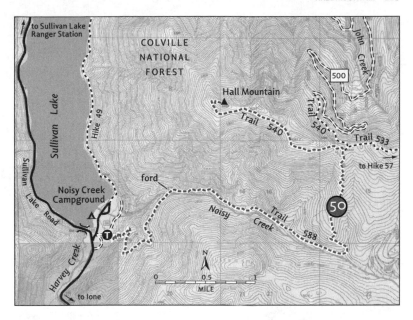

ON THE TRAIL

This hike heads immediately uphill through thimbleberries on Noisy Creek Trail No. 588 with eight nicely graded switchbacks in the first 0.8 mile. At 1.7 miles, ford Noisy Creek—easy rock-hopping most of the time but high and tricky in early season. Check out the remains of an old miner's cabin along the creek just below the ford.

The thimbleberries start giving way to devil's club as the trail follows Noisy Creek, climbing along with the sound of rushing water—yes, the creek's name is appropriate. You'll be treated to the din of countless little waterfalls roaring through the woods until the route finally bends northward at 3.8 miles to gain a ridge and higher, dryer ground. If you need more water, get it at Noisy Creek.

At 5.2 miles you'll hit the junction with Trails 533 and 540. Turn left (west) and continue on Hall Mountain Trail No. 540 for the last 1.8 miles to the summit. The route soon begins a broad sweep around the mountain through open slopes of grasses, lupine, other wildflowers, and even sage. Great views will start grabbing your attention even before the trail skirts past aspen stands to a lofty overlook of Sullivan Lake.

Pass silvery snags in the last few switchbacks through rock outcroppings to the broad summit, where concrete foundations are all that remain of the fire lookout built in 1930 and destroyed in the 1950s. Look north to see the still-used Sullivan Mountain Lookout and Crowell Ridge. Look northeast to Pass Creek Pass and the Shedroof Divide. Look east to Grassy Top and the Idaho

Selkirk Mountains. Look south to Molybdenite Mountain and the roaming area for one of the first wolf packs to repopulate Washington. Look west to the Pend Oreille Divide, Abercrombie Mountain, and the prominent silhouette of Hooknose.

EXTENDING YOUR TRIP

From the junction of Trails 588 and 540, head east on a third trail, Grassy Top Trail No. 533, which rolls delightfully over timbered high-ridge terrain for 5 miles to Trail No. 503 near Pass Creek Pass (Hike 57). **Tip:** For a 5-mile round-trip to Hall Mountain, with 75 percent less elevation gain, access the north side of the mountain via Johns Creek Road (FR 500), open only July 1–August 14.

51 Crowell Ridge

RATING/ DIFFICULTY	ROUND-TRIP	ELEV GAIN/ HIGH POINT	SEASON
****/3	8.4 miles	2700 feet/ 6880 feet	July–Oct

Maps: USGS Gypsy Peak, Colville National Forest map; **Contact:** Colville National Forest, Sullivan Lake Ranger District, (509) 446-7500, www.fs.fed.us/r6/colville; **Notes:** High-clearance recommended. Wilderness trail, mechanized equipment prohibited, grizzly habitat; **GPS:** N 48 52.696 W 117 14.691

🏠 ⭐ *Crowell Ridge is often admired from valley roads but rarely traversed by humans. Some vehicles can't even negotiate the rough access roads. Even fewer people head northeast on this spine of scattered trees and open rocky stretches that lead toward the highest peak in Eastern Washington. That's part of*

this trip's wonder and why this is one of the most lonesome and rewarding natural high routes in the Salmo-Priest Wilderness. Crowell Ridge is the parallel counterpart to Shedroof Divide to the east.

GETTING THERE

From Metaline Falls, drive north for 2 miles on State Route 31 and turn right on Sullivan Lake Road (County Road 9345). Drive 4.3 miles and turn left on Highline Road (FR 2212). Drive about 3 miles and turn left on Forest Road 245 toward the Sullivan Mountain Lookout (high-clearance vehicle recommended). The trailhead is on the north side of the road near the switchback below the lookout (elev. 6220 ft).

ON THE TRAIL

Crowell Ridge Trail No. 515 weaves through open timber before breaking into the openness of shrubs, rocks, and snags. On a good day, it's breathtaking, but bring appropriate clothing for a turn in the weather.

After 1 mile, the trail climbs for the next mile to 6740 feet and then heads down, but it skirts the rocky pinnacles of the ridgeline peaks. Continue on the ridge past an unmaintained trail on the right that heads down toward Smart Creek.

In a saddle at 3.9 miles, North Fork Sullivan Creek Trail No. 507 splits left and quickly plunges into the creek and roadless area below. Trail No. 515 bears right and contours around the east side of a knob. But for this hike, leave both trails and hike northward instead, straight up the ridge in front of you, for 0.3 mile to the site of a fire lookout abandoned around 1950 (elev. 6880 ft). This is a premium spot to size up the Salmo-Priest surroundings, including the Shedroof Divide to the east.

Crowell Ridge hikers see Idaho's Selkirk Mountains in distance.

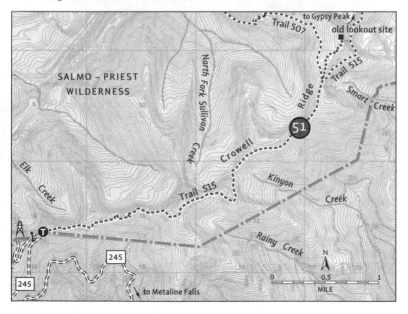

EXTENDING YOUR TRIP

Two other high spots beckon. Trail No. 515 leads toward 7309-foot Gypsy Peak, the highest point in Eastern Washington (map and compass or GPS essential; recommended for very fit hikers only). After 2 miles—at a saddle where the trail begins a notable descent toward Bear Pasture and FR 200—leave the trail and head north. See Hike 52 for the directions from here. Another option is back at the trailhead: hike 0.5 mile up the gated road to the Sullivan Mountain Lookout (elev. 6483 ft) and take in great views to Abercrombie and Hooknose Mountains to the southwest.

52 Gypsy Peak

RATING/ DIFFICULTY	ROUND-TRIP	ELEV GAIN/ HIGH POINT	SEASON
*****/5	6.5 miles	2000 feet/ 7000 feet	July– mid-Aug

Maps: USGS Gypsy Peak, Colville National Forest map; **Contact:** Colville National Forest, Sullivan Lake Ranger District, (509) 446-7500, www.fs.fed.us/r6/colville; **Notes:** FR 200 is rough in places, closed Aug 15–Nov 30. Wilderness trail, mechanized equipment prohibited. Cross-country scrambling involved. Grizzly habitat; **GPS:** N 48 55.040 W 117 08.370

⚙️ *Hikers have short window of opportunity to enjoy this relatively convenient access to the highest peak in Eastern Washington before the seasonal road closure to protect the occasional grizzly bear heading to the high berry fields. The first half of the hike climbs on an excellent subalpine route to the expanses of Crowell Ridge, one of two prominent spines in the*

Salmo-Priest Wilderness. From there, the trip requires open-ridge map navigation and cross-country travel over talus, leading to the best viewpoint of Gypsy Peak as it looms over Watch Lake. Most hikers can't resist a scramble to the summit.

GETTING THERE

From its junction with State Route 20 north of Cusick, drive SR 31 north toward Ione for 3.1 miles and turn right on Sullivan Lake Road (County Road 9345). Cross the bridge over the Pend Oreille River and angle left, staying on Sullivan Lake Road (don't take

Gypsy Peak looms over Watch Lake.

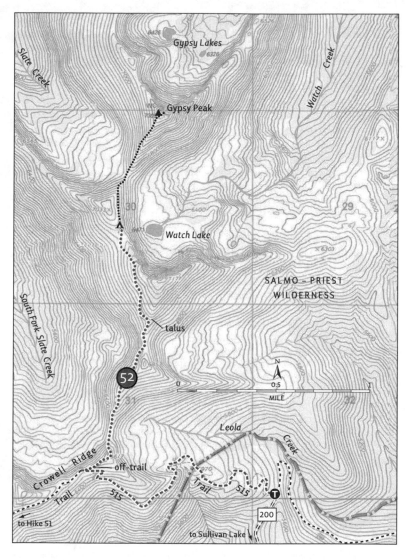

a sharp left on the river road). Drive 7.5 miles to Noisy Creek Campground and then another 4.5 miles along Sullivan Lake. Turn right on Forest Road 22. Drive 6 miles and bear left at the junction onto FR 2220 toward Salmo Mountain. Drive 1.5 miles and bear left on FR 2212. Drive 4.6 miles and continue straight on FR 200. Drive 6.5 miles (rough in places) to the trailhead at the road's end (elev. 5560 ft).

ON THE TRAIL

Crowell Ridge Trail No. 515 heads uphill on an old road that soon narrows to a single track through an already subalpine environment of scattered firs, beargrass, and huckleberries. Reach the wilderness boundary after about 15 minutes of walking with pleasant views of the open ridges that wait for you above.

Cross a tiny creek that drains one of several alpine wetlands you'll look down upon later. Head up a few switchbacks and then traverse an open slope with great views east to the Idaho Selkirk Mountains. Climb three switchbacks to the crest of Crowell Ridge at 1.6 miles, where the trail bends left and heads southwest on the ridge. Gypsy Peak seekers must turn right and begin cross-country hiking. Gypsy is hidden behind a distant ridge to the north.

Start by scrambling almost directly up (north), over, and down the ridge (a faint user trail shows occasionally). Immediately the route begins climbing the next ridge. Enjoy the rolling benches that stair-step up the ridge to a steep rock outcropping. Contour to the left (west) side of the ridge, angling toward the saddle ahead.

From the next saddle, hike up to where the ridge gets steep again and angle left (west), just below the talus. Then begin angling up the slope to the ridge that overlooks Watch Lake. Very little elevation gain is needed on this last traverse to reach a campsite at the low notch overlooking Watch Lake and the

spectacle of Gypsy Peak. However, it's more scenic to gain the ridge at around 7000 feet for the best views, before dropping down to the campsite. This campsite is a good rest stop for deciding whether to turn around—or to press on.

EXTENDING YOUR TRIP

To fulfill your Gypsy fortunes, from the campsite contour over onto the untrailed but easy-to-see south ridge that leads up open rocky slopes to the summit of Gypsy Peak. This highly recommended side trip adds 1.5 miles and 700 feet of elevation gain round-trip. For even more, scramble down the ridge northwest from the summit for views down to the Gypsy Lakes.

53 Salmo River

RATING/ DIFFICULTY	ROUND-TRIP	ELEV GAIN/ HIGH POINT	SEASON
****/3	6 miles	2110 feet/ 5920 feet	late July–Nov

Maps: USGS Salmo Mountain, Colville National Forest map; **Contact:** Colville National Forest, Sullivan Lake Ranger District, (509) 446-7500, www.fs.fed.us/r6 /colville; **Notes:** Open to horses. Wilderness trail, mechanized equipment prohibited. Grizzly habitat; **GPS:** N 48 57.328 W 117 04.888

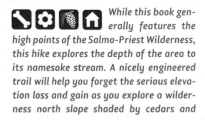 *While this book generally features the high points of the Salmo-Priest Wilderness, this hike explores the depth of the area to its namesake stream. A nicely engineered trail will help you forget the serious elevation loss and gain as you explore a wilderness north slope shaded by cedars and*

An abandoned cabin along Salmo River

hemlocks and graced with lacy ferns, fungi, and wildflowers. The soothing river is a magnet for overnight campers seeking a quick wilderness experience.

GETTING THERE

From its junction with State Route 20 north of Cusick, drive SR 31 north toward Ione for 3.1 miles and turn right on Sullivan Lake Road (County Road 9345). Cross the bridge over the Pend Oreille River and angle left, staying on Sullivan Lake Road (don't take a sharp left on the river road). Drive 7.5 miles to Noisy Creek Campground and then another 4.5 miles along Sullivan Lake. Turn right on Forest Road 22. Drive 6 miles and bear left at the junction onto FR 2220. Drive 12.8 miles to the trailhead near the road's end (elev. 5920 ft). Privy available. (**Tip:** In this last 12.8 miles, you'll pass several campsites, a good group site at Gypsy Meadows, trailheads for several other Salmo-Priest hikes, and the road to Salmo Mountain Lookout.)

ON THE TRAIL

The first half of this hike is all downhill, but on gently graded Salmo Basin Trail No. 506 leading into old-growth forest. You'll cross a small creek a few times and pass various wildflowers in the summer season.

After 3 miles, reach the Salmo River (elev. 4100 ft). Turn back if the river is high in early season. By midsummer the river is usually easy to ford; by late summer, you can usually hop across on configured stones. Campsites stretch along the river on a bench above the north shore.

EXTENDING YOUR TRIP

Once across the river, head downstream (left) through the campsites. Near the last heavily used campsite, hike off-trail up a short slope and continue downstream on another bench. Soon you'll cross a small stream channel. Then go across the flat about 400 yards and look for an old cabin (GPS: N 48 58.979 W 117 04.492). The

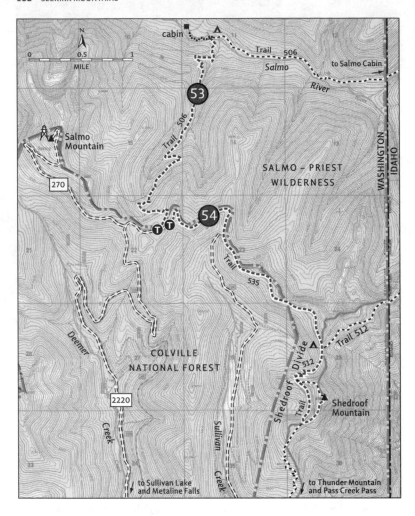

Forest Service has no solid information on the cabin's origins. For an on-trail extension from the Salmo River crossing, continue upstream on Trail No. 506 for 2.3 miles to a junction and spur leading to the meager remains of the Salmo Cabin, built in the 1930s as a Forest Service backcountry station and used until 1951. To take in a nearby fire lookout, on the return drive down from the trailhead on FR 2220, turn right on FR 270 and drive 2.1 miles to the Salmo Mountain Lookout.

54 Shedroof Mountain (Shedroof Divide)

RATING/ DIFFICULTY	ROUND-TRIP	ELEV GAIN/ HIGH POINT	SEASON
****/4	8.8 miles	1920 feet/ 6764 feet	July–Oct

Maps: USGS Salmo Mountain, Colville National Forest map; **Contact:** Colville National Forest, Sullivan Lake Ranger District, (509) 446-7500, www.fs.fed.us/r6 /colville; **Notes:** Open to horses. Wilderness trail, mechanized equipment prohibited. Grizzly habitat; **GPS:** N 48 57.333 W 117 04.857

Get the best Shedroof Divide views for the least output of energy. Starting from a high-elevation trailhead, the route winds through timber and open slopes to the summit of Shedroof Mountain for views into the Rockies of Canada and down on Upper Priest Lake in Idaho.

GETTING THERE

From its junction with State Route 20 north of Cusick, drive SR 31 north toward Ione for 3.1 miles and turn right on Sullivan Lake Road (County Road 9345). Cross the bridge over the Pend Oreille River and angle left, staying on Sullivan Lake Road (don't take a sharp left on the river road). Drive 7.5 miles to Noisy Creek Campground and then another 4.5 miles along Sullivan Lake. Turn right on Forest Road 22. Drive 6 miles and bear left at the junction onto FR 2220. Drive 12.8 miles to the trailhead at the end of the road (elev. 5940 ft). Privy available. (Note: In this last

Priest Lake and the Idaho Selkirks can be seen from Shedroof Mountain.

12.8 miles, you'll pass several campsites, a good group site at Gypsy Meadows, trailheads for several other Salmo-Priest hikes, and the road to Salmo Mountain Lookout.)

ON THE TRAIL

Salmo Divide Trail No. 535 begins as an old road for 1 mile to the wilderness boundary. The single-track trail then snakes through the woods along a ridge to an opening at 2 miles, with full views of Crowell Ridge, southern Shedroof Divide, and back over your shoulder to the gleaming Salmo Mountain Lookout.

At 3 miles, reach a small campsite and the junction with the Shedroof Divide Trail No. 512. Head right (south) toward Shedroof Mountain. In the next 0.5 mile, climb nine switchbacks and up a short, steep last gasp to a ridge. An unmaintained trail takes off to the left through false azalea and blowdowns and leads directly to the top of Shedroof Mountain in 0.4 mile. To take the longer, maintained route, continue on the main trail.

Hike nearly 0.5 mile and look for a trail branching off to the left just before the main trail crests a small ridge. The unsigned spur trail gains 320 feet and leads 0.4 mile to the summit (elev. 6764 ft).

Footings for the old fire lookout are still intact—the lookout started as a tent in 1915, became a cabin in 1918, sported a cupola in 1926, and graduated to a 30-foot pole-tower cabin in 1938, before its ultimate destruction in the 1950s. Marvelous views remain: Snowy Top Mountain and far into Canada to the north; the Idaho Selkirks to the east; Upper Priest and Priest Lakes to the southeast. You can see the Shedroof Divide Trail skirting a slope to the north, and even farther north the clear-cut swath that indicates the US-Canada boundary.

EXTENDING YOUR TRIP

Hike north or south on the Shedroof Divide Trail as far as your endurance, water, and daylight allow. It's more than 6 miles north (elev. +1280/-800 ft) to the spur trail up to the Little Snowy Top Mountain Lookout. See also Hikes 53 and 55. And on the return drive from the trailhead down FR 2220, turn right on FR 270 and drive 2.1 miles to the Salmo Mountain Lookout.

55 Thunder Creek and Mountain (Shedroof Divide)

RATING/ DIFFICULTY	ROUND-TRIP	ELEV GAIN/ HIGH POINT	SEASON
****/5	14.4 miles	2485 feet/ 6560 feet	mid-July– mid-Oct

Maps: USGS Salmo Mtn, USGS Helmer Mtn; **Contact:** Colville National Forest, Sullivan Lake Ranger District, (509) 446-7500, www .fs.fed.us/r6/colville; **Notes:** Open to horses. Wilderness trail, mechanized equipment prohibited. Grizzly habitat; **GPS:** N 48 54.033 W 117 04.896

    Hike to a lonely lookout site along the Shedroof Divide within the grizzly bear and woodland caribou–harboring Salmo-Priest Wilderness. Wander through groves of giant cedars and catch good views of the surrounding wild country. Savor succulent huckleberries in fall and cherish solitude no matter the season.

GETTING THERE

From Metaline Falls, drive 2 miles north on State Route 31, turning right onto Sullivan Lake Road (County Road 9345). Proceed 4.7 miles, turning left onto FR 22 just before

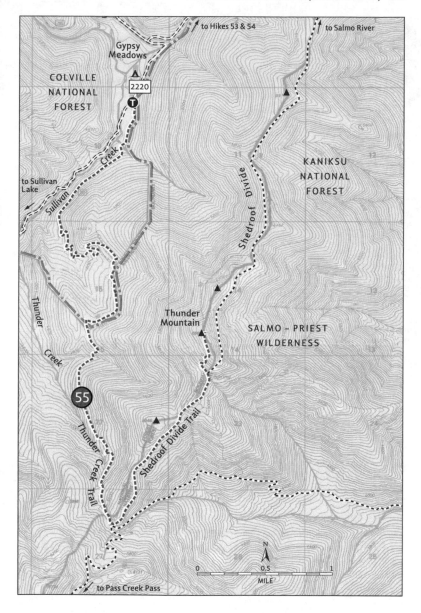

Old cedars line the way.

Sullivan Lake. Continue 6 miles to a junction just after the Sullivan Creek bridge crossing. Bear left onto FR 2220 and proceed 6 miles to the Thunder Creek trailhead (elev. 4300 ft) located across from the Gypsy Meadows camping area.

ON THE TRAIL

Starting on a decommissioned logging road, head west through old growth and cross a small creek. Soon begin traversing an old clear-cut on a well-graded route through rapidly regenerating forest. When not hiking through an alder tunnel, you can catch some sunlight along the way and views of Prouty and Gypsy Peaks across the valley. Cottonwoods and larches make this Salmo-Priest portal a golden entryway come October.

At 2.3 miles, the road walking ends (elev. 4740 ft) and a well-built single-track leads into old growth. Bridges over the numerous creeks and cribbage and puncheon through the boggy areas help keep you dry and mud free.

At 3.1 miles (elev. 4900 ft), in a small saddle, enter the Salmo-Priest Wilderness. Then begin to descend through thick forest that bears scars from past fires. The large square holes on some of the cedars and big snags are old traps for pine martens, a member of the weasel family that's an agile tree climber.

At 3.6 miles, cross a side creek (elev. 4675 ft) in a dark cedar grove and resume climbing. Come upon Thunder Creek in a spectacular grove of ancient forest at 4.1 miles. Now following alongside the creek, traverse some of the grandest old growth in Eastern Washington. Precipitation and moisture retention in this valley give it a west-of-the-Cascade-Crest appearance, but the larches make it solidly east side.

At 5.5 miles, reach Shedroof Divide Trail No. 512 in a narrow saddle (elev. 5525 ft). Gently climb through open forest with views out to Idaho peaks. After a saddle at about 6.2 miles, the way climbs more steadily and the forest grows thicker. Skirt beneath some cliffs and pass through patches of mature timber, eventually reaching an unmarked junction (look for nails in a tree) at 6.5 miles (elev. 6075 ft).

Head left for 0.7 mile on the unmaintained and slightly brushy path to the 6560-foot summit of Thunder Mountain. The fire lookout is long gone and trees obscure the views, but decent gazing can be had northeast and southwest along the Shedroof Divide. Blueberries grow on the summit in profusion and you can share them with the abundant grouse.

EXTENDING YOUR TRIP

From the Thunder Creek Trail junction on the Shedroof Divide, head west along the divide for about 1.7 miles to the saddle between Helmer Mountain's two summits. The 6734-foot high point is an easy off-trail romp to the right. Or for a nice loop from Thunder Mountain, head east on the Shedroof Divide Trail. After soon passing a good spring, follow, dip and climb along the high divide, passing good viewpoints out to the Priest and Sullivan River valleys. At 5.2 miles, head left on the Shedroof Cut-Off Trail (Sullivan Creek is unbridged). At 7.2 miles, reach FR 2220. Turn left and walk the road 0.6 mile to close the loop. It's only slightly longer than returning the way you came but involves more elevation gain.

56 Mankato Mountain (Shedroof Divide)

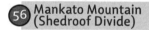

RATING/ DIFFICULTY	ROUND-TRIP	ELEV GAIN/ HIGH POINT	SEASON
*****/3	7 miles	2220 feet/ 6590 feet	July–Oct

Maps: USGS Pass Creek Pass, USGS Salmo Mountain, Colville National Forest map; **Contact:** Colville National Forest, Sullivan Lake Ranger District, (509) 446-7500, www .fs.fed.us/r6/colville; **Notes:** Open to horses. Wilderness trail, mechanized equipment prohibited. Grizzly habitat; **GPS:** N 48 47.860 W 117 07.667

This easy-access trip samples the best of the Salmo-Priest's Shedroof Divide Trail: ridge walking around peaks, expansive views, moose and black-bear sightings, and thermal-riding hawks and ravens. This route tops out on the summit of Mankato Mountain, where a lifetime of future hikes can be seen and planned in every direction.

GETTING THERE

From Metaline Falls, drive north 2 miles on State Route 31 and turn right on Sullivan Lake Road (County Road 9345). Drive 4.7 miles and turn left on Forest Road 22. Drive 6 miles and bear right at the junction on FR 22. Drive 7.9 miles to Pass Creek Pass, where several cars can be thoughtfully parked. The trailhead (elev 5410 ft) is on the east side of the pass, up the road a short way from parking for another two vehicles. (This area is also accessible from the east side of the pass via Priest Lake, Idaho.)

ON THE TRAIL

Start hiking up Shedroof Divide Trail No. 512, which is notched into steep hillside through a landscape familiar with lightning-caused forest fires. Fireweed is prolific. Just when you want a change from looking east to the crest of Idaho's Selkirk Mountains, the trail winds past Round Top Mountain for views toward the west.

The Shedroof Divide is a regular hangout for a few moose. Bears are not uncommon, especially when huckleberries are ripe in August and September.

Soon the trail weaves along the center of a ridge, with views both east and west, before it skirts left on the west side of the divide, again through an old burn. Mankato Mountain's grassy slopes are dead ahead,

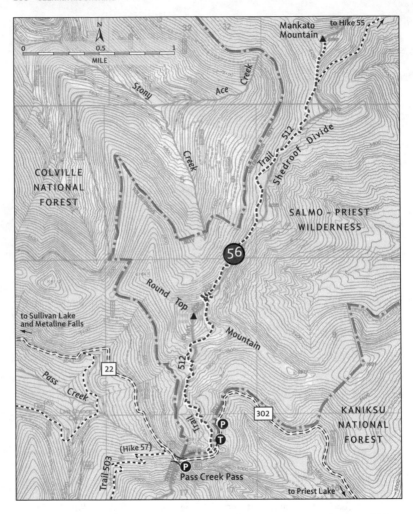

upstaging the more timbered slopes of Helmer Mountain farther along to the left.

At 3.2 miles, you'll be at the base of Mankato where the trail bends around to the east side of the divide. Leave the trail and hike up the semi-open south slope. Gain 345 feet in 0.3 mile through scattered blow-downs, huckleberry, beargrass, fescue, and lupine. The open 6590-foot summit offers a delicious panorama. On a nice day, gaze at Gypsy Peak and Bear Pasture to the north-west; Salmo Mountain Lookout and Snowy

Bull moose along Shedroof Divide Trail

Top and the Canadian Selkirks to the north; miles of Idaho Selkirks like the edge of a battered saw blade to the east; and Grassy Top and Molybdenite to the south.

EXTENDING YOUR TRIP
Follow the mostly open ridge cross-country from Mankato's summit northwest to the top of an unnamed but attractive peak (elev. 6680 ft).

57 Grassy Top Mountain

RATING/ DIFFICULTY	ROUND-TRIP	ELEV GAIN/ HIGH POINT	SEASON
***/3	7.8 miles	1470 feet/ 6253 feet	July–Nov

Maps: USGS Pass Creek, Colville National Forest map; **Contact:** Colville National Forest, Sullivan Lake Ranger District, (509) 446-7500, www.fs.fed.us/r6/colville; **Notes:**

Open to mountain bikes, horses. Grizzly habitat. Proposed wilderness; **GPS:** N 48 47.897 W 117 08.048

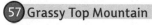 *Grassy Top is a timbered mountain that doesn't have the airy feeling of open peaks, but this beautifully maintained trail has a wild flavor because of views to the east and west of roadless forest proposed for wilderness protection. The route is especially colorful in late autumn, when huckleberry bushes are crimson and western larches are golden yellow.*

GETTING THERE
From Metaline Falls, drive 2 miles north on State Route 31 and turn right on Sullivan Lake Road (County Road 9345). Drive 4.7 miles and turn left on Forest Road 22. Drive 6 miles and bear right at the junction on FR 22. Drive 7.8 miles to the trailhead (elev. 5355 ft) on

Grassy Top larch turn gold in October.

the right. But park a short way farther at Pass Creek Pass, where thoughtful drivers can park several cars. (This area is also accessible from the east side of the pass via Priest Lake, Idaho.)

ON THE TRAIL

Grassy Top Trail No. 503 drops from the road and soon begins gaining a ridge in four long, gentle switchbacks above the Pass Creek drainage. Once on the ridge, cruise a fine trail that weaves to the east and west sides of knobby peaks.

At 2.7 miles, continue straight past the junction with Trail No. 533 (which heads toward Hall Mountain). Soon Trail No. 503

sidehills across a grassy slope above the Middle Fork Harvey Creek drainage. This stretch is particularly impressive from mid-October to November, when fall colors are glowing.

Soon the trail leads into the woods on a timbered ridge, with sheltered views to the east. The trail splits at a grassy opening: Left goes unceremoniously to the summit of Grassy Top, with views to the east. The right fork is worth exploring to see the views it offers to the south.

EXTENDING YOUR TRIP

Trail No. 503 leads 3 miles to Harvey Creek Road, the quickest route to Grassy Top for

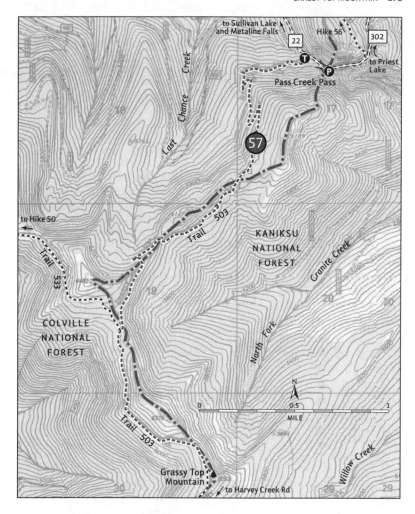

people camping at Sullivan Lake, but not as rewarding. For an excellent 8-mile ridge walk, drop a car at the end of FR 500 (open July 1–August 14) on your way to Pass Creek Pass and hike out on Trail No. 533: 5.1 miles toward Hall Mountain, turn right on Trail No. 540, and hike 0.5 mile to your shuttle car; or add 3 miles round-trip by continuing straight on Trail No. 533 and taking the spur to Hall Mountain (elev. 6323 ft).

58 Roosevelt Grove of Ancient Cedars

RATING/ DIFFICULTY	LOOP	ELEV GAIN/ HIGH POINT	SEASON
***/2	2.5 miles	300 feet/ 3600 feet	May–Nov

Maps: USGS Helmer Mtn, Kaniksu National Forest map; **Contact:** Kaniksu National Forest, Priest Lake Ranger District, (208) 443-2512, www.fs.usda.gov/ipnf; **Notes:** Dogs permitted on-leash. Supervise children closely on overlook trail; **GPS:** N 48 45.990 W 117 03.743

Around 1919, foresters in the business of cutting down trees recognized the aesthetic value of this stand of old-growth cedars and appealed for its protection. A 1926 forest fire destroyed about 75 percent of the grove, but 22 acres attest to its original majesty. The trees are 800 years old on average, and a few may be more than 2000 years old. The whitewater rush of Granite Falls adds to the ambiance. Incidentally, Stagger Inn was the name given to the camp at this site for workers fighting that 1926 fire, describing the condition of the exhausted crews.

GETTING THERE

From Metaline Falls, drive north 2 miles on State Route 31. Turn right on Sullivan Lake Road (County Road 9345). At Sullivan Lake, turn east on Forest Road 22 toward Priest Lake, Idaho. Drive 21 miles (over Pass Creek Pass), and turn south at Granite Pass toward Nordman, Idaho. Go 1.7 miles on FR 302 and turn into Stagger Inn Campground and trailhead (elev. 3300 ft). (From Priest River,

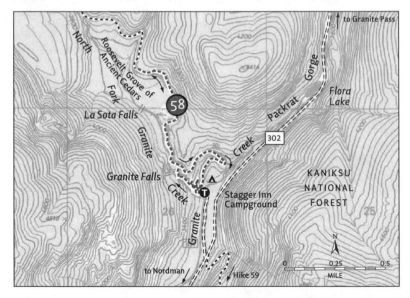

Cascades below Granite Falls near Roosevelt Grove of Ancient Cedars

Idaho—the best access in early season, when Pass Creek Pass can be snowbound—drive north 36 miles on SR 57 to Nordman. Continue on SR 57 another 2 miles and bear left on FR 302 for 11 miles to the campground and trailhead.) Privy available.

ON THE TRAIL

From the trailhead kiosk, start with a short side trip to the left. Follow your ears to the rush of water tumbling through the rocks below the 70-foot slide of Granite Falls. Then return to the trailhead and head up the Overlook Trail, which quickly leads to a view of the lower falls from a platform that hangs over the rock cliff. The trail then gets more rocky and rugged up to a natural overlook of Granite Creek plunging into pools.

Soon the Overlook Trail joins with the main trail, a smooth, wide path born from an old logging road. Turn left and hike 0.5 mile to the upper cedar grove, which covers about 20 acres between the trail and the creek. A few paths wander through the peacefulness of the giant trees, and so should you before hiking the main trail back 1 mile to the trailhead. Follow your ears to the 20-foot drop of La Sota Falls.

EXTENDING YOUR TRIP

The Granite Falls Trail continues past the upper cedar grove for miles.

59 Little Grass Mountain

RATING/ DIFFICULTY	ROUND-TRIP	ELEV GAIN/ HIGH POINT	SEASON
****/5	10.5 miles	2520 feet/ 5695 feet	July–Oct

Maps: USGS Helmer Mtn, Kaniksu National Forest map; **Contact:** Kaniksu National Forest, Priest Lake Ranger District, (208) 443-2512, www.fs.usda.gov/ipnf; **Notes:** Open to horses. Grizzly habitat. Last 0.8 mile of trail may not be maintained; **GPS:** N 48 45.784 W 117 03.661

🔧⚙️🌲🏠❌ A former fire lookout site, Little Grass Mountain offers vast views of the northeastern Washington and Idaho Panhandle forests, a sweeping stretch of the Idaho Selkirk Crest, and Priest Lake. On the way, get a healthy dose of mileage and elevation gain, cross a few creeks, and feast on the sight of an enchanting cedar grove and the flavor of late-season huckleberries. There's little competition for any of it.

GETTING THERE

From Metaline Falls, drive 2 miles north on State Route 31. Turn right on Sullivan Lake Road (County Road 9345). At Sullivan Lake, turn east on Forest Road 22 toward Priest Lake, Idaho. Drive 21 miles (over Pass Creek Pass), and turn south at Granite Pass toward Nordman, Idaho. Go 1.7 miles on FR 302. The trailhead (elev. 3310 ft) is 100 yards north of Stagger Inn Campground. (From Priest River, Idaho—the best access in early season, when Pass Creek Pass can be snowbound—drive north 36 miles on SR 57 to Nordman. Continue on SR 57 for 2 miles and bear left on FR 302 for 11 miles to the campground.) Privy available.

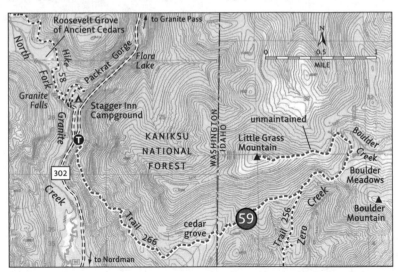

Lush ferns feather Little Grass Mountain trail.

ON THE TRAIL

Trail No. 266 heads steeply up into the trees and some switchbacks before continuing up in a long traverse. After 2 miles, it eases onto a bench with a creek, where water spreads to nourish fern meadows and a long grove of ancient cedars that extends up and across the Washington–Idaho state line at 2.5 miles. Huckleberries that don't ripen until late in the season begin showing up among the beargrass. Usually there's no shortage of evidence that elk are in the area.

Drop down a slope and then start up again to the left as you pass the junction with Trail No. 256. Continue straight across a slope of springs and lush vegetation (including stinging nettles) that often obscures the trail. Soon you'll be in a narrow ravine that leads up to Boulder Meadows.

The trail bends northwest and soon ends at decommissioned FR 1014. If you reach the road, you've gone about 100 yards past the unmaintained 0.8-mile spur that heads southwest and then west up a ridge to the summit of Little Grass Mountain. If you lose the trail, use your map and compass to help you navigate up the ridge. The south side of the ridge is more open. Soon you'll break out into open grassy slopes for an easy walk up through wildflowers to the concrete footings of a lookout tower built in 1934 and destroyed in 1960.

EXTENDING YOUR TRIP

Check out the Huff Lake Interpretive Site 0.2 mile south on FR 302. It's a peatland study of at least five rare plant species: bristle-stalked sedge, creeping snowberry, northern starflower, bog willow, and bog cranberry.

60 Kalispell Rock

RATING/ DIFFICULTY	ROUND-TRIP	ELEV GAIN/ HIGH POINT	SEASON
****/3	5.6 miles	1490 feet/ 5200 feet	June–Oct

Maps: USGS Monumental Mtn, Colville and Kaniksu National Forest maps; **Contact:** Kaniksu National Forest, Priest Lake Ranger District, (208) 443-2512, www.fs.usda.gov /ipnf; **Notes:** Open to mountain bikes, horses. Trails east of Pend Oreille Divide are maintained by the Idaho Panhandle national forests; **GPS:** N 48 38.021 W 117 06.101

  This once-popular hiking area lost its charm in the early 1980s when clear-cutting was rampant. But the wildlife-rich forest is reviving and the attraction is back. Kalispell Rock sports the remains of a Forest Service cabin in the shadow of massive mushrooms of granite overlooking the Priest River drainage. Deer and moose frequent this route, as do, possibly, elk and bear.

GETTING THERE
From State Route 20 north of Newport, turn east into Usk. Follow Kings Lake Road over the Pend Oreille River and turn left on Leclerc Road (also known as Newport–Ione Road). Drive 16 miles and bear right on Leclerc Creek Road. Drive 0.9 mile and bear right on East Branch Road (becomes Forest Road 1934). Drive 14.1 miles (the road becomes FR 308 at a pass) and bear right at a Y. Go 0.1 mile, still on FR 308, to the guardrail blocking a spur road on the right. This is the trailhead (elev. 3910 ft).

ON THE TRAIL
Go past the gate, over the earthen berm that blocks motor vehicles, and head up Kalispell Rock Trail No. 370, a former logging road. At 0.5 mile, bear left at the junction with another old road and continue up. (Take care to note the road junctions heading up the ridge; they can be easy to miss on the way down.)

At 1.5 miles, just after the road slips over to the north side of the ridge, turn left on a lesser road that climbs sharply to the spine of the ridge. This is the sweet section of the

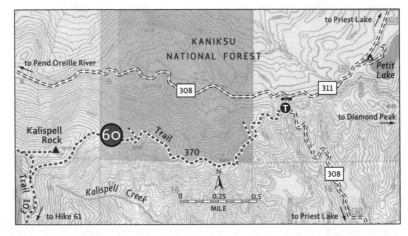

The old lookout tender's cabin is decomposing below Kalispell Rock.

old-road portion of the route. At 2.3 miles, the route drops to a grassy opening and a trail junction. Trail No. 103 continues ahead (south), but Trail No. 370 makes a turn to the right and up on single-track. Ah, now the hike is getting good.

But pay attention. After hiking and climbing 0.2 mile, the trail levels and descends slightly. Just before reaching a more open area (where the trail eventually fades away), look for the main trail doubling back sharply to the right. This easy final 0.3 mile to the old lookout cabin site is the sweetest part of the hike.

The tallest granite slabs at the lookout site are dangerous to climb. But just below the cabin site to the east is a rock slab that makes a great lunch spot. The cabin was built in 1927 as a refuge for the lookout staffer, who would climb a ladder to the alidade (firefinder) shelter on top of Kalispell Rock.

The shelter was removed and the cabin left to decay after 1935. On the fourth log up the north inside-wall of the old cabin, for as long as it lasts, is the inscription "Pete van Gelder" followed by a string of dates, '48–'81. Van Gelder was a legendary member of the Spokane Mountaineers. The dates indicate his visits, leading volunteer groups, often with lookout historian Ray Kresek, to maintain this trail and others.

EXTENDING YOUR TRIP

Trail No. 103 to the south eventually becomes a single-track that follows the divide toward Hungry Mountain and North Baldy Mountain (Hike 61). Or spend some time at tiny Petit Lake, east from the trailhead on FR 311, with its low-key campsite and good trout fishing, especially in late summer and early fall. Bring a small boat to enjoy it fully.

61 Hungry Mountain

RATING/ DIFFICULTY	ROUND-TRIP	ELEV GAIN / HIGH POINT	SEASON
***/3	8.4 miles	2180 feet/ 5955 feet	June–Oct

Maps: USGS North Baldy, Colville and Kaniksu National Forest maps; **Contact:** Kaniksu National Forest, Priest Lake Ranger District, (208) 443-2512, www.fs.usda.gov /ipnf; **Notes:** Park before trailhead to avoid rough road. High-clearance recommended regardless. Trail open to mountain bikes, horses. Trails east of Pend Oreille Divide are maintained by Idaho Panhandle national forests; **GPS:** N 48 32.784 W 117 09.482

❌ *If you love ridge rambling, don't overlook this lightly used north– south trail. It caters to serious leg stretching on top of a timbered divide between the Pend Oreille River drainage to the west and the Priest Lake and River drainage to the east. We saw elk, moose, and deer on a* single trip. We also saw scats or tracks from predators taking an interest in those animals, including black bears and a mountain lion.

GETTING THERE
From State Route 20 north of Newport, bear right and head east through Usk on Kings Lake Road. Cross the bridge over the Pend Oreille River and turn left on Leclerc Road (also known as Newport–Ione Road). Drive 13 miles and just after crossing Mill Creek, turn right on Mill Creek Road (Forest Road 1200). Drive 10 sometimes dusty miles to Pyramid Pass junction. Turn left onto FR 306 toward North Baldy Mountain. Drive 4 miles and park at turnouts on the right (elev. 5725 ft); the road heads left and traverses the west-facing slope of North Baldy, becoming extremely rough.

ON THE TRAIL
Hike 0.5 mile up the rough road and look for Trail No. 103 taking off down to the left. This is the trip high point (elev. 5955 ft). The trail

Looking south to North Baldy from Hungry Mountain

heads downhill for more than a mile through timber and beargrass before coming to a gated logging road. Turn right on the road and walk about 20 yards. Then turn left off the road and hike north on Trail No. 103.

The route from here has gentle ups and downs through beargrass and huckleberries. It passes a startling outcropping of granite boulders in a small meadow and then heads up and cruises along a ridge. To the east, the timber is mostly intact to protect the Priest Lake watershed. To the west, second growth is healing the landscape nuked by ill-conceived clear-cutting. Let's hope we learned our lesson.

At 4 miles, reach a junction. Turn right, leaving Trail No. 103, and head up Stateline Trail No. 162, cross a small meadow where the trail briefly fades, and bear left up the fall line, reaching the top of Hungry Mountain (elev. 5541 ft) 0.2 mile from the trail junction. From the granite slabs on the timbered summit, look south to the trailhead at North Baldy Mountain.

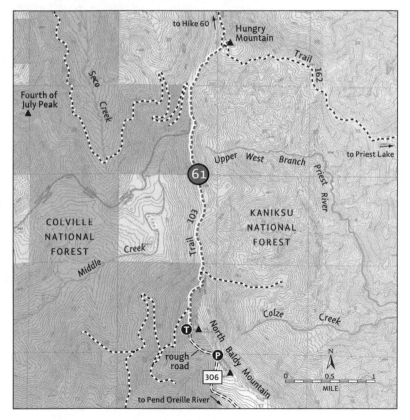

EXTENDING YOUR TRIP

Stateline Trail No. 162, which descends significantly from Hungry Mountain, is worth exploring. You can also continue north on Trail No. 103 to Kalispell Rock (Hike 60) and back for a rewarding 16-mile round-trip. For a shorter side trip, from the Hungry Mountain trailhead hike 0.3 mile up the rough access road to the top of North Baldy Mountain (elev. 6173 ft).

62 Bead Lake

RATING/ DIFFICULTY	ROUND-TRIP	ELEV GAIN / HIGH POINT	SEASON
****/3	11.2 miles	2100 feet/ 3100 feet	Mar–Nov

Maps: USGS Bead Lake, Colville National Forest map; **Contact:** Colville National Forest, Newport Ranger District, (509) 447-7300, www.fs.fed.us/r6/colville; **Notes:** NW Forest Pass required Apr 15–Oct 1, only at boat-launch trailhead. Open to mountain bikes, horses; **GPS:** N 48 17.195 W 117 06.556

At 720 acres, Bead Lake is the second largest lake in Pend Oreille County (behind Sullivan), yet it has a deep, clear high-mountain feel. Explore its east shore's rocky points, wildflowers, cedar groves, campsites, and notable giant white pine. This trip is a gem, whether the water beckons for a summer dip or awes you with its glimmering ice cap in early spring.

Early spring hiking at Bead Lake

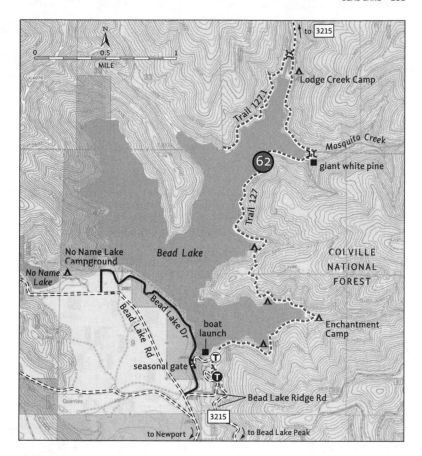

GETTING THERE

From Newport, follow US Highway 2 across the Pend Oreille River into Idaho and take the first left onto Leclerc Road. Continue north 2.7 miles and turn right on Bead Lake Road. Drive 6.1 miles and choose from two options: To reach the boat-launch trailhead, turn right on paved Bead Lake Drive (Loop Road) and drive 0.2 mile. To reach the no-fee upper trailhead, turn right just before Bead

Lake Drive on gravel Bead Lake Ridge Road (FR 3215), and drive 0.5 mile to a small parking area for several cars (elev. 3015 ft). Privy available in season (near the boat launch).

ON THE TRAIL

Bead Lake Trail No. 127 switchbacks down toward the lake from the upper trailhead. At 0.2 mile and the junction with the trail from the boat-launch trailhead, continue ahead, with the lake on your left. At 0.7 mile, pass the spur down to the Mineral Bay boat-in campsite. At 1.2 miles, the trail passes through a cedar grove and the hike-in Enchantment Camp at the end of the anchor-shaped lake's southeast arm.

Hike overland through a saddle in a peninsula, and drop to a gully with a path that leads to the water and another boat-in campsite. At 3.5 miles, after the trail passes through a cedar grove flat—just before reaching a series of footbridges—look upslope to the right for a giant white pine more than 15 feet in circumference.

At about 4.6 miles, the trail passes Lodge Creek Camp. Head left, leaving the main trail and cross the footbridge over Lodge Creek. This Spur Trail No. 127.1 travels above the shoreline, affording good views of the lake, before it dead-ends in 1.1 miles.

EXTENDING YOUR TRIP
From the Lodge Creek footbridge, Trail No. 127 heads up the east side of the creek, first gently through cedars, then crossing the creek and gaining 600 feet to end at FR 3215 in 1.5 miles.

63 Pend Oreille County Park

RATING/ DIFFICULTY	LOOP	ELEV GAIN/ HIGH POINT	SEASON
***/3	4.1 miles	750 feet/ 2780 feet	Mar–Nov

Maps: USGS Elk, Pend Oreille County Park trails map; **Contact:** Pend Oreille County Works Department, (509) 447-4513, www .pendoreilleco.org/county/parks.asp; **Notes:** Facilities open Memorial Day–Labor Day. Trail open to mountain bikes, horses. Dogs

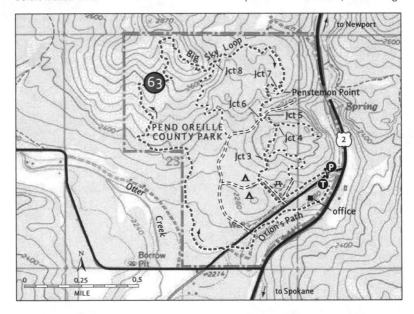

Arrowleaf balsamroot in Pend Oreille County Park

permitted on-leash. Watch for ticks; **GPS:** N 48 04.825 W 117 19.558

The Back Country Horsemen *of Washington, schools, and service groups rescued this fine 440-acre park from neglect. Although the picnic area and rustic campground are open only during summer, the 7-mile trail system is open year-round. Explore wildflower areas, old-growth pines, cedars, and high overlooks above the valley.*

GETTING THERE
North of Spokane, from the intersection of Deer Park–Milan Road (at Riverside Schools), drive 8.2 miles north on US Highway 2 and turn west at milepost 318 into the entrance of Pend Oreille County Park. Leave your car in the lot next to the highway before going through the gate, which is locked to keep out motor vehicles except in summer. Walk past the gate on the paved road 100 yards to the unmarked trailhead on the left (elev. 2340 ft). Privy available.

ON THE TRAIL
Leave the paved entrance road (a portion of the old Newport Highway) on Orion's Path, which soon becomes single-track. At a meadow, the route continues ahead on a double-track that leads to the paved entrance road 0.7 mile later. Turn left on the old highway for a short way and then turn right on the double-track trail, which soon funnels into the sweet, single-track Big Sky Loop.

MOUNT SPOKANE TRAILHEADS

Mount Spokane State Park offers a wealth of day-hiking options, most accessible from the main Mount Spokane Park Drive, open year-round, and Summit Road, open during summer.

From the park entrance at milepost 15.4 of Mount Spokane Park Drive (State Route 206), set your vehicle trip odometer and find the following trailheads (Discover Pass required):

At 0.2 mile: The park's first public parking spot accesses Trail No. 110, the main trail linking to upper-mountain destinations.

At 1.7 miles: The hairpin-turn parking lot offers trailhead access to the Mount Kit Carson Lower Loop Road, Burping Brook picnic area, and Trail Nos. 100, 110, and 140 and others that link to three of the park's most popular summits.

At 3 miles: A four-way junction offers several options.

- Go straight to reach the downhill ski area.
- Turn right to reach the Selkirk Lodge and cross-country ski trails, including the trailhead for Quartz Mountain.
- Park at this junction to access Trail Nos. 100 and 130 for longer hikes to Day Mountain, Mount Kit Carson, the Mount Spokane summit, or other destinations in the core trails area.
- Turn left to drive up Summit Road to more trailheads.

At 1 mile up Summit Road: Turn right for Bald Knob picnic area parking to access Trail No. 130 to the CCC Cabin and Day Mountain.

At 1.6 miles up Summit Road: A small parking area offers access to shorter routes to the CCC Cabin and Trail No. 140 to the top of Mount Spokane.

At 3 miles up Summit Road: The road ends at the top of the mountain near the lovely stone Vista House. Here you will find restrooms near the top of the chairlift and the summit trailhead for Trail No. 140. It's all downhill from here.

—R. L

The trail climbs in short bursts for 1.5 miles almost to the park's high point on a brushy ridge overlooking the valley. Then it drops quickly. At 2.5 miles from the start, continue past a post marking Junction 8 (a shortcut back, called Arrowleaf Ridge Trail) as the Big Sky Loop contours over to a bench before dropping again. Check out the short Penstemon Point Loop at the Junction 7 marker.

At Junction 6, bear left on the double-track for a short way, and then turn right onto the single-track at Junction 5. At Junction 4, continue straight as the Big Sky Loop bends into a lusher area with cedars.

Soon the trail bears left and heads down to the campground. Turn left on the campground road, and then turn left on the old highway and follow the pavement back to your car.

EXTENDING YOUR TRIP

Explore up to 3 more miles of fire roads, connectors, and spur trails in the park.

64 Mount Spokane Summit

RATING/ DIFFICULTY	ROUND-TRIP	ELEV GAIN/ HIGH POINT	SEASON
***/3	2.4 miles	700 feet/ 5880 feet	June–Oct

Maps: USGS Mt Spokane, state park map from Friends of Mount Spokane State Park, www.mountspokane.org; **Contact:** Mount Spokane State Park, (509) 238-4258, www .parks.wa.gov/parks; **Notes:** Discover Pass required. Park open 6:30AM–dusk. Trail open to mountain bikes, horses. Dogs permitted on-leash. Privy at summit; **GPS:** N 47 55.070 W 117 07.367

Mount Spokane is the high point in the Spokane region, and the summit is a highlight destination, where hikers, bikers, and drivers converge to be on top of it all. This hike in Washington's standout year-round state park provides plenty of options for savoring the forest, wildflowers, and critters before emerging at the top, where chairlifts deposit skiers during winter. The Vista House near the summit is a tribute to the craftsmanship of 1930s Civilian Conservation Corps stone masons.

GETTING THERE

From US Highway 2 north of Spokane (or take the Argonne Road exit from I-90 and go north on Argonne and Bruce Roads), head east on Mount Spokane Park Drive (State Route 206) to the park entrance at milepost 15.4. Continue 3 miles on Mount Spokane Park Drive and turn left onto Summit Road. Drive 1.6 miles (passing the campground) to the parking area (elev. 5190 ft) before a hairpin turn.

The stone Vista House on Mount Spokane

ON THE TRAIL

Walk up the paved road a short way to the hairpin turn. The gated Mount Kit Carson Loop Road on the left is an option for your return route.

Head up the double-track just to the right of the Mount Kit Carson Loop Road. Go a short way to a communications tower structure and walk straight through it, continuing up through the ferns to connect with Trail

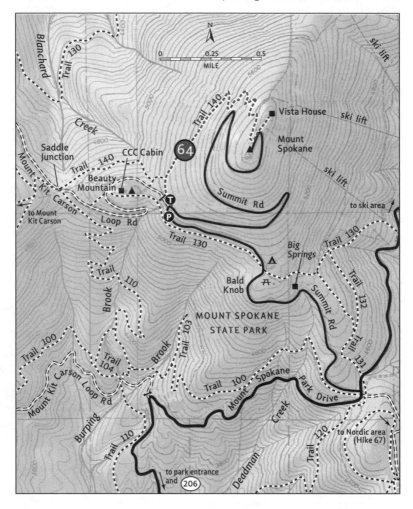

No. 140. Turn right and head uphill about 1 mile on switchbacks to the summit of Mount Spokane.

Turn left at the road, walk through a parking area, past a vault toilet and Chairlift 1, to the Vista House. This stone structure, built on a granite outcropping by the Civilian Conservation Corps in 1934, is open for shelter and picnicking. The views are excellent toward Spirit Lake to the east, as well as a portion of Twin Lakes and south to Newman Lake.

Return the way you came, or add a slight variation by bypassing the spur you came up from the trailhead and continuing on Trail No. 140 and a spur out to the Mount Kit Carson Loop Road. Turn left on the road to walk back out to the trailhead.

EXTENDING YOUR TRIP

If you make the alternate return, turn right on the loop road and then left to visit the CCC Cabin at Beauty Mountain (elev. 5180 ft). For a bottom-to-top summit hike, leave your vehicle at the first trailhead 0.2 mile from the park entrance, and hike Trail No. 110, crossing Lower Kit Carson Loop Road and continuing up to Upper Kit Carson Loop Road and a junction with several trails. Cross the road and head up Trail No. 140 to the summit. This route to the top is about 11 miles round-trip and gains 3100 feet. For a 5.4-mile round-trip to the summit, start on Trail No. 130 at the junction with Summit Road, 3 miles from the park entrance.

65 Day Mountain

RATING/ DIFFICULTY	ROUND-TRIP	ELEV GAIN/ HIGH POINT	SEASON
****/2	6 miles	880 feet/ 5170 feet	June–Oct

Maps: USGS Mt Kit Carson, USGS Mt Spokane, state park map from Friends of Mount Spokane State Park, www.mountspokane.org;

Spokane Valley looms below Day Mountain.

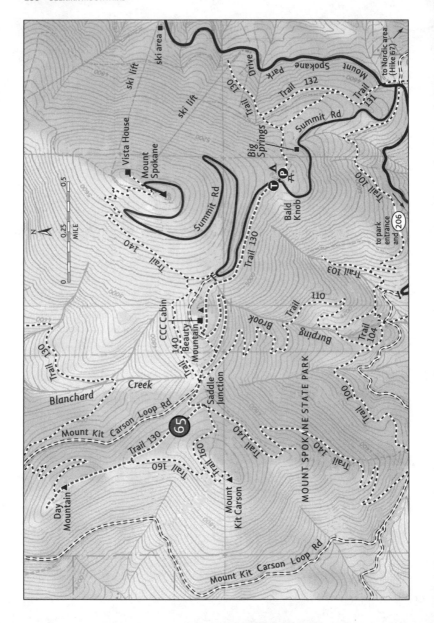

Contact: Mount Spokane State Park, (509) 238-4258, www.parks.wa.gov/parks; **Notes:** Discover Pass required. Park open 6:30AM–dusk. Trail open to mountain bikes, horses. Dogs permitted on-leash; **GPS:** N47 54.774 W117 06.774

 *While most of the trails in Mount Spokane State Park seem to go up and down, this choice route follows a ridge, minimizing elevation gain but still getting to the top of a mountain! Can't beat that. Open slopes, pleasant timbered stretches, hillside springs, and wildflowers greet you, as well as some nifty stonework steps, handiwork of the 1930s Civilian Conservation Corps. Day Mountain, 800 feet lower than Mount Spokane, offers a pleasant view of the Spokane Valley below.*

GETTING THERE

From US Highway 2 north of Spokane (or take the Argonne Road exit from I-90 and go north on Argonne and Bruce Roads), head east on Mount Spokane Park Drive (State Route 206) to the park entrance at milepost 15.4. Continue 3 miles on Mount Spokane Park Drive and turn left on Summit Road. Drive 1 mile, turn right at the trailhead (elev. 5120 ft), and park at the Bald Knob picnic site. Privy available.

ON THE TRAIL

Walk back out the parking lot entrance and cross Summit Road to Trail No. 130, a nice single-track that starts in an old burn area with open views of the Spokane Valley. Soon the openings trend to grassy meadows and then turn to a forest of older, more scattered trees.

At 1 mile, reach a junction. The right fork heads up a couple of hundred yards to the rock steps and pathway leading to the CCC Cabin on Beauty Mountain (elev. 5180 ft). Some two hundred members of the Civilian Conservation Corps built these area roads and other facilities during the Great Depression. They used stone to build the Vista House on the Mount Spokane summit in 1933 (Hike 64). The CCC Cabin was rebuilt on its original site in 1998.

For Day Mountain, bear left at the fork and drop immediately to Mount Kit Carson Loop Road, where you have two options: Turn left and hike down the road, which switches down to Saddle Junction at 1.7 miles from the trailhead. Or, turn right, hike about 20 yards, and look for a trail that drops steeply to "cut the switchback" to the road below. Trail Nos. 110, 130, 140, and 160 meet at Saddle Junction, where there's a privy and signs.

Continue left and up past the outhouse toward Mount Kit Carson. Go about 20 yards and bear right on the newer trail built in 2010. After making a switchback and angling upslope, come to a junction with the old trail. Turn right, staying on Trail No. 160. Go about 20 yards and turn right on single-track Trail No. 130 toward Day Mountain.

At 2.4 miles, reach another junction with Trail No. 160. Continue straight. Hike through a fairly thick stand of lodgepole pine before breaking into a more parklike grassy forest of older Douglas-firs. Head uphill.

As the trail rounds the top of Day Mountain, you're still in the trees. Continue downhill on the other side until the trail leads to an open ridge. At 3 miles, the trail fades into a rocky outcropping—a good place for a break with good views below of Peone Prairie and the Spokane Valley.

EXTENDING YOUR TRIP

Look carefully and you'll find Trail No. 130 continuing northward; follow it for a while if you wish. On your return to the trailhead turn right off of Trail No. 130 onto Trail No. 160 and make a short climb to the summit of Mount Kit Carson. Enjoy another view, and another summit, before continuing on Trail No. 160 northeast back to Saddle Junction and then back to the trailhead.

66 Burping Brook Basin

RATING/ DIFFICULTY	LOOP	ELEV GAIN/ HIGH POINT	SEASON
****/3	6.2 miles	1660 feet/ 5020 feet	June–Oct

Maps: USGS Mt Kit Carson, state park map from Friends of Mount Spokane State Park, www.mountspokane.org; **Contact:** Mount Spokane State Park, (509) 238-4258, www .parks.wa.gov/parks; **Notes:** Discover Pass required. Park open 6:30AM–dusk. Trail open to mountain bikes, horses. Dogs permitted on-leash; **GPS:** N 47 54.271 W 117 07.489

This route is the core of the Mount Spokane State Park single-track trail system. It appeals to people who relish variety in a good forest walk, with liberal doses of ups, downs, terrain changes, running water, and extension options. Explore the three forks in the Burping Brook headwaters on trails beautifully thought out and routed by volunteers through firs, cedars, and hemlocks, with sites for picnicking.

GETTING THERE

From US Highway 2 north of Spokane (or take the Argonne Road exit from I-90 and go north on Argonne and Bruce Roads), head east on Mount Spokane Park Drive (State Route 206) to the park entrance at milepost 15.4. Continue 1.7 miles on Mount Spokane Park Drive to a parking area before a hairpin turn (elev. 3860 ft).

ON THE TRAIL

From the parking area, use caution as you walk uphill and cross the road. The route begins at the hairpin turn, through the gate on Mount Kit Carson Loop Road. Hike the road 50 paces and bear right on Trail No. 103. Go another 50 yards, bear left onto Trail No. 100, and cross the creek. Hike 0.35 mile and bear right to leave Trail No. 100 and continue uphill on Trail No. 110. Contour and switchback nearly 2 miles to reunite with Mount Kit Carson Road at Saddle Junction.

Turn left (west) onto Trail No. 140, being careful not to branch out on Trail Nos. 130 to Day Mountain or 160 to Mount Kit Carson (unless you want to take side trips). Trail No. 140 contours along the flank of Kit Carson and then drops down: Look for a left turn onto the newer single-track. (Continue on the decommissioned double-track for a short way if you want a meadow view.)

Trail No. 140 switches back southward to Mount Kit Carson Loop Road at Smith Gap. Hike the road a short way, and then turn left onto Trail No. 100. Contour above the road for 1.1 miles, take the Trail No. 104 connector trail down a few switchbacks to the Burping Brook picnic site, and then hike 0.3 mile up Mount Kit Carson Loop Road to the trailhead.

EXTENDING YOUR TRIP

From Saddle Junction, out-and-back trails lead to good views at Mount Kit Carson,

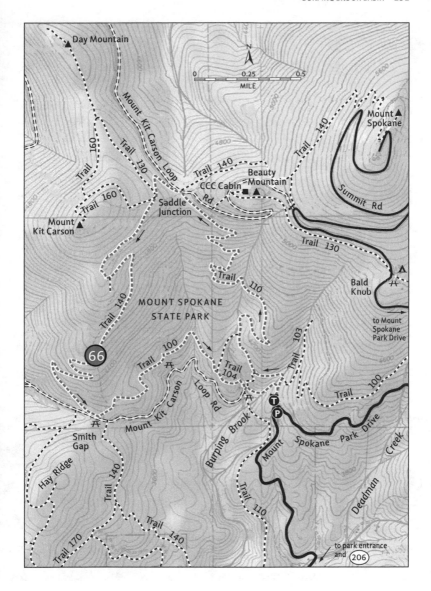

Day Mountain

N

0   0.25   0.5
MILE

Mount Spokane

Trail 140

Trail 160

Mount Kit Carson Loop

Trail 130

Trail 160

Trail 140

CCC Cabin

Beauty Mountain

Summit Rd

Saddle Junction

Mount Kit Carson

Trail 130

Trail 140

Bald Knob

Trail 110

MOUNT SPOKANE STATE PARK

66

Trail 103

to Mount Spokane Park Drive

Trail 100

Trail 104

Trail 100

Mount Kit Carson Loop Rd

T
P

Burping Brook

Mount Spokane Park Drive

Creek

Smith Gap

Deadman

Hay Ridge

Trail 140

Trail 110

Trail 170

Trail 140

to park entrance and 206

Enjoying sunset on Mount Kit Carson

Day Mountain, or Mount Spokane's summit. At the least, make a side trip to Kit Carson's rock outcropping overlooking Spokane Valley.

67 Quartz Mountain

RATING/ DIFFICULTY	LOOP	ELEV GAIN/ HIGH POINT	SEASON
***/2	5.5 miles	860 feet/ 5160 feet	June–Oct

Maps: USGS Mt Kit Spokane, state park map from Friends of Mount Spokane State Park, www.mountspokane.org; **Contact:** Mount Spokane State Park, (509) 238-4258, www .parks.wa.gov/parks; **Notes:** Discover Pass required. Park open 6:30AM–dusk. Trail open to mountain bikes, horses. Dogs permitted on-leash. Reserve Quartz Mountain Lookout at (888) 226-7688, www.parks.wa.gov; **GPS:** N47 54.188 W117 05.992

A fire lookout that once stood on Mount Spokane was retired and reassembled in 2005 for recreation on Quartz Mountain. You can rent the lookout or simply visit for one of the best views of Mount Spokane and northern Idaho below. The hike takes advantage of the state park's 25-mile core Nordic ski trail system, which is rich with wildlife, wildflowers, and huckleberries.

GETTING THERE

From US Highway 2 north of Spokane (or take the Argonne Road exit from I-90 and go north on Argonne and Bruce Roads), head east on Mount Spokane Park Drive (State Route 206) to the park entrance at milepost 15.4. Continue 3 miles on Mount Spokane

Park Drive. Drive to a four-way junction. Turn right and drive 0.1 mile through the large parking lot. At a junction, make a right-hand hairpin turn and park by Selkirk Lodge, the base area for the cross-country trail system, and the trailhead (elev. 4630 ft). Privy available.

ON THE TRAIL

Find the large trail system signboard and map above the lodge. From this trailhead, five double-track trails lead to Junction 1. For simplicity, go left on the Mountain View Trail and follow it 0.3 mile to Junction 1, a large grassy meadow. From here, stay left and walk up a road for a short way, bearing left on the first trail, called Sam's Swoop (Sam is a perennial volunteer, worthy of a trail name). Note the diversity of plants: huckleberry, beargrass, wild strawberry, ferns, and much more.

At 1 mile, reach Junction 2, another meadow, where seven trails meet with a road (Lodgepole Trail) running through the middle. Bearing left on the road is the fastest way to Quartz Mountain, but it's more interesting to hike the Eagle Crest Trail, just to the right of the road.

At 1.6 miles, the Eagle Crest Trail peaks at a meadow and viewpoint worth a stop. Then the trail heads down. At about 2 miles, the trail ends at the Nova Hut warming shelter and privy. Turn left at the junction. Go about 30 yards and turn right on the road that services the Quartz Mountain Lookout. Continue straight past a junction with a double-track trail that heads left. In another 60 yards, at a junction of two trails, bear left on the single-track. The gravel below your feet indicates why it's called Quartz Mountain.

At 2.5 miles, the single-track trail meets

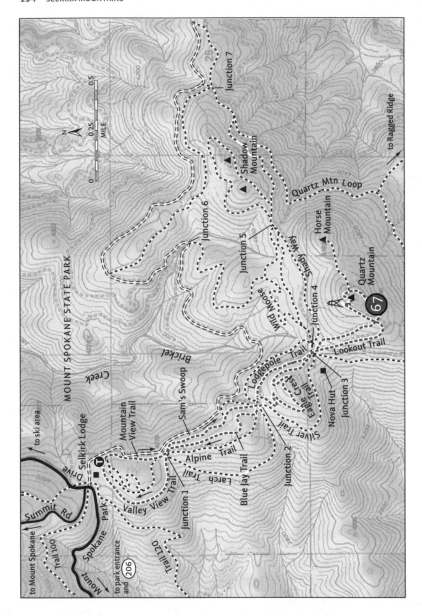

The Quartz Mountain Lookout is a rental room with a view.

the lookout access road. Turn immediately left and continue uphill. The trail eventually ends at 2.9 miles at the Quartz Mountain Lookout, where there's a picnic table and privy.

If the lookout is not occupied by renters, climb up for a view: Mount Spokane, with its ski lifts and transmission towers, looms large to the north. Mount Kit Carson is the knob to the left of the big mountain. The Idaho Selkirks look jagged in the distance to the northeast. From the south-facing catwalk,

you can see three lakes below (left to right): Twin Lakes and Hauser Lake in Idaho, then Newman Lake in Washington.

Follow the road to loop off the summit back to Junction 3. Explore some of the other cross-country trails to loop your way back to your car. Signs and maps at the major junctions help keep you oriented. Lodgepole Trail is the shortest way back to Junction 2. Or try Blue Jay back to Junction 1 and the Valley View Trail from Junction 1 to the trailhead to enjoy open views to the south.

EXTENDING YOUR TRIP

If you're good with map and compass, explore the Ragged Ridge Natural Area Preserve. A trail can be followed off and on to the scenic rocky ridge. You can also explore other ski trails on the way back to the trailhead.

Oppostie: McLellan Conservation Area overlooks Lake Spokane, an impoundment on the Spokane River.

around spokane

The local visitors center describes Spokane as *Near nature, near perfect.* At least half of that slogan is indisputable. Wildness is just out the door in every quadrant of the city and all around the county, protected in havens such as Riverside and Mount Spokane State Parks, the Little Spokane River Natural Area, and more than two dozen Spokane County Conservation Futures areas. Turnbull National Wildlife Refuge and its abundance of wildlife on display is just another feather in the areas near-nature cap. Best of all, public routes ranging from pine-needle-padded footpaths to the paved Fish Lake Trail and Spokane River Centennial Trail beckon visitors to all the best spots.

Maps: USGS Greenacres, Antoine Peak Conservation Area map; **Contact:** Spokane County Parks and Recreation, (509) 477-4730, www.spokanecounty.org/parks; **Notes:** Open to mountain bikes, horses. Dogs permitted on-leash; **GPS:** N 47 43.257 W 117 11.817

Minutes from I-90, Antoine Peak is a 1066-acre sanctuary for wildlife watching secured by the Spokane County Conservation Futures program. We have seen turkey vultures, hawks, and ravens soaring over the peak, all at one time; a days-old whitetail fawn 50 yards from the summit towers; and tracks of wild turkey, quail, deer, moose, elk, and bear. Did we mention this is just minutes from the Spokane Valley Mall?

GETTING THERE
From I-90 in Spokane Valley, take exit 291B and drive 2.2 miles north on Sullivan Road.

68 Antoine Peak

RATING/ DIFFICULTY	LOOP	ELEV GAIN/ HIGH POINT	SEASON
***/3	6.8 miles	1230 feet/ 3375 feet	May–Nov

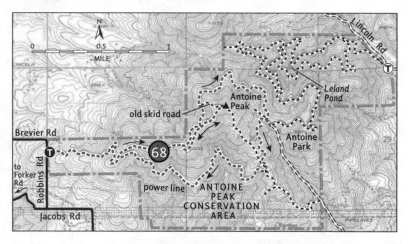

Antoine Peak trails are ideal for groups.

SPOKANE COUNTY INVESTS IN CONSERVATION FUTURES

The Spokane County Conservation Futures program has opened the doors to hiking several of the choice routes featured in this book. Private land destined for subdivision and development was preserved as open space for wildlife to roam and muscle-powered visitors to enjoy.

The program, administered by Spokane County Parks and Recreation, preserves open spaces with a voter-approved property tax of up to 6.25 cents per $1000 of assessed value. The funds are earmarked for acquiring property and development rights to benefit wildlife, conserve natural resources, increase passive recreation, provide educational opportunities, and improve the quality of life for area residents. From its inception in 1994 through 2012, the program purchased about 6300 acres in about thirty acquisitions. Hikers, equestrians, and outdoor groups often chip in to build or maintain trails in the areas.

The conservation areas are public, but they are nestled amid private property that must be respected by visitors. Park carefully to the side of the road when parking lots are not available, and don't block gates or stray onto private property.

Natural areas purchased or expanded by Conservation Futures funding include Antoine Peak (Hike 68), Liberty Lake County Park (Hike 69), Saltese Uplands (Hike 70), Iller Creek (Hike 71), Dishman Hills Natural Area (Hike 72), South Hill Bluff (Hike 75), Slavin Conservation Area (Hike 77), and Palisades Park (Hike 78). Keep these prime areas in mind for your next hike—and the next time the program comes up for a vote.

More conservation areas worthy of visits are listed on the Spokane County Parks and Recreation website (www.spokanecounty.org/parks). —R. L.

Turn left on Wellesley Avenue, go to a four-way stop, and turn right on Progress Street. At the next stop sign, turn right on Forker Road. Go uphill 0.4 mile and turn right on Jacobs Road. Drive 0.7 mile and turn left on Robbins Road. Drive 0.4 mile to the west-side trailhead (elev. 2500 ft) at the top of the hill.

ON THE TRAIL
Go through the gate and head 0.8 mile up the summit access road (closed to unauthorized vehicles) to a fork. Bear left (you'll return to this junction near the end of the loop). At 1.3 miles, bear right at a fork (you'll be returning to this road soon too), continuing up another 0.5 mile to the summit.

Walk past the first radio tower (if you listen, you might hear FM radio tunes), catch the great views looking north to Mount Spokane and south to Liberty Lake. Then head to the second tower. A road heading down to the right is a shortcut to the loop road.

To continue the circumnavigation of the peak, retrace your steps down the way you came and take a sharp right (passing another shortcut on the right, down an old skid road that starts near the first tower's southwest guyline anchor). The trail soon begins climbing around the west side of the peak, and then it angles down and bends around the cooler, lusher, more heavily timbered north side.

At 3.9 miles, the loop road meets a junction on the east side of the peak. An eroded skid trail comes down steeply from above, and a road heads down to the left toward a broad ridge called Antoine Park, then to a pond and the east trailhead. Bear right at this junction to continue the loop, reaching another junction in about a half mile with the road shortcut from the summit. About

100 yards farther along the loop, reach yet another junction and take a sharp right.

From here, at 4.6 miles, the loop road has its ups and downs, but it primarily contours around the mountain for another 1.4 miles to a familiar junction. Turn left and hike the last 0.8 mile to the trailhead.

EXTENDING YOUR TRIP
From the east side of Antoine Peak, take the old road that leads to the east trailhead and reach Leland Pond in 2.2 miles (look for turtles). It's another mile to the east trailhead off Lincoln Road (accessed by leaving I-90 at exit 293, driving north on Barker Road, turning right on Trent Avenue, driving 1 mile east to turn left on Campbell Road, driving north 1.6 miles to turn left at Lincoln Road, and finally driving 0.6 mile to the parking area on the left; privy available).

69 Liberty Lake

RATING/ DIFFICULTY	LOOP	ELEV GAIN/ HIGH POINT	SEASON
****/3	9 miles	1550 feet/ 3280 feet	May–Oct

Maps: USGS Liberty Lake, USGS Mica Peak; **Contact:** Spokane County Parks and Recreation, (509) 477-4730, www.spokane county.org/parks; **Notes:** $2 entrance fee Memorial Day–Labor Day. Open to horses. Dogs permitted on-leash; **GPS:** N 47 37.866 W 117 03.517

 A Spokane County park and a 455-acre county conservation area join at a clear-water lake to create one of the region's most diverse and refreshing hiking areas. The developed

area ranges from a sandy swimming beach to a campground and picnic area. Then the wilderness begins on trail that leads past beaver dams, into an ancient cedar grove, past a cascading waterfall, and up to scenic views down onto Liberty Lake.

GETTING THERE

From I-90 east of Spokane, take Liberty Lake exit 296. Turn south on Liberty Lake Road. Drive 1 mile and turn left on Sprague Avenue, which becomes Neyland Road in another mile. Continue another 0.8 mile,

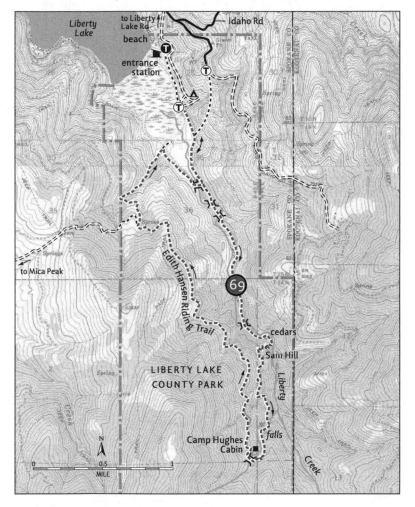

bear right at the Y, and then turn right on Lakeside Road. Drive 0.7 mile and turn right on Zephyr Road to reach the Liberty Lake County Park entrance parking area (elev. 2090 ft). Privy available. An alternate connector trail is planned from the equestrian trailhead parking area on the road above the main entrance.

ON THE TRAIL

From the pay station, follow the route past the day-use restrooms and picnic shelter for 0.5 mile to the restrooms area at the far end of the campground. Look for the main trailhead kiosk and gate (near campsite 21), and head up along Liberty Creek. At 0.8 mile pass a junction with the old trail coming in from the right. A new route was built in

2011 so hikers could avoid the lower portion of the creek, home to busy beavers.

At 1.1 miles, reach a junction that starts the loop (you'll be returning from the right). Continue straight and cross the little footbridge over Split Creek (the trail fork leads to the horse ford).

Climb steadily, now along Liberty Creek, and at 2.5 miles reach an open grove of large cedars, one of the first acquisitions of Spokane County Conservation Futures (see the sidebar in this section). This is a popular destination for picnicking under towering giants.

To continue the loop, bear right on the footbridge across the creek and begin the twelve switchbacks up Sam Hill. A viewpoint looking northwest to Liberty Lake is on the

Hikers continue above the Liberty Creek Falls.

twelfth one. Antoine Peak is straight down the valley in the distance, and Mount Spokane is the highest point to the right.

At 3.5 miles, come to the cool respite at the base of cascades known as Liberty Falls. The vast majority of hikers turn around here for a 7-mile round trip. But for the full loop, switchback up from the falls. Hike through a more open forest and cross the creek on a bridge at about 4 miles.

A short way farther, continue straight at a trail crossing and go uphill to the high point of this hike near an old outhouse. Turn right here and head down to the Camp Hughes Cabin (elev. 3250 ft), a shelter built in the mid-1970s.

Back on the main loop, head downhill on the Edith Hansen Riding Trail, occasionally used by horse riders. At 6.3 miles, stay right at a fork (the trail left is worth exploring all the way to Mica Peak). At 7.1 miles, come to a junction just past the horse trail sign and a big wooden wall structure. Turn right on the single-track to avoid the boggy area of Liberty Creek flooded by beaver activity. Soon you'll cross a footbridge over Liberty Creek and then come to the main trail you hiked up earlier. Turn left and return to the trailhead.

EXTENDING YOUR TRIP
Hikers with good endurance and map-reading skills can hike all the way to Mica Peak. Take a trail south off the Edith Hansen Riding Trail. Follow the route uphill to a saddle south of Boundary Mountain and along the west side of Stump Ridge to a main ridge at about 4700 feet. Soon the route up the ridge follows jeep roads. Stay on the ridge, heading up the steepest routes to a better road that leads to the FAA radar dome at 5205 feet.

70 Saltese Uplands

RATING/ DIFFICULTY	LOOP	ELEV GAIN/ HIGH POINT	SEASON
***/3	7.3 miles	1185 feet/ 2640 feet	Mar–Dec

Maps: USGS Greenacres, USGS Liberty Lake, Spokane County Conservation Futures map; **Contact:** Spokane County Parks and Recreation, (509) 477-4730, www.spokanecounty.org/parks; **Notes:** Open to mountain bikes, horses. Dogs permitted on-leash; **GPS:** N 47 38.625 W 117 07.872

 Spokane County delivered a one-two punch for conservation and recreation in 2010–11, first by securing 510 acres of wetlands on Saltese Flats, then by acquiring the adjacent 552-acre Saltese Uplands Conservation Area overlooking the flats. From top to bottom, the uplands are a gem for walkers and wildlife watchers, with more than 9 miles of trails and roads for nonmotorized recreation. Mountain biking and horse riding are allowed, but the sight lines are good in this mostly open terrain, making it easy for everyone to share the trail.

GETTING THERE
From I-90 east of Spokane, take Barker Road exit 293 and drive 0.5 mile south on Barker Road. Turn left on Sprague Avenue and Drive 0.9 mile. Turn right on Henry Road and go 0.8 mile to the trailhead parking area on the left (elev. 2070 ft). Privy available.

ON THE TRAIL
Follow the trail south paralleling Henry Road and turn left at a junction, onto an old

road. Go up a short way to a junction with two single-track trails. If you like, make an out-and-back side trip by going left on the Mulligan Trail for 0.5 mile to where the trail dead-ends in a basin at a big pear tree—attractive to deer in the early fall.

Back at the junction, cross the old fire road and take the other single-track, the Palisades Trail, which quickly starts gaining elevation in big switchbacks. Enjoy the curvy trail, which keeps serving up a different view ahead.

Pass a spring. When the single-track joins a road, look for the single-track splitting off to the left and heading uphill to a fence near the water tank for the private Legacy

Ridge Estates development on the other side of the ridge. Take a break here to drink in views over Saltese Flats. Follow the fence westward a couple hundred yards to look down the Spokane Valley: Antoine Peak (Hike 68) lies to the north, Palisades Park (Hike 78) is in the distance to the west, Iller Creek Conservation Area and Dishman Hills near Tower Mountain (Hikes 71 and 72) are closer to the west.

The open slopes of the Saltese Uplands generate updrafts that attract numerous raptors, which feast on the bounty of rodents and ground squirrels that find easy burrowing in the fine Palouse topsoil. The trails were lumpy with critter burrows—and

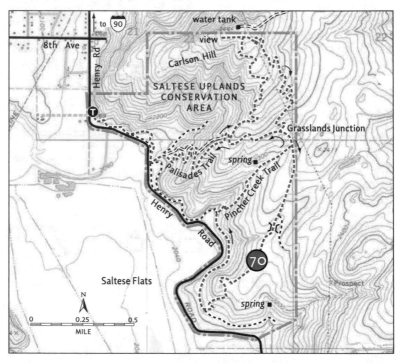

Mark Pinch designed and labored on Saltese Uplands trails.

coyote scat—just weeks after they were originally carved out of the hillside with pulaskis in 2011.

Now follow the fence line to the east and pick up the trail again. Shortly you'll go over the crest for a great view of Liberty Lake, and then the single-track winds down off the ridge. Cross the rough power-line road and wind down to a junction at another double-track. (The right-hand road is a shortcut back to the trailhead, but you'll get to hike it later in this trip.) Go left to continue the longer loop, and follow the old farm road down to another fence.

Pass the junction with a single-track trail (you'll return to this spot in 2.3 miles) and continue straight on the double-track over the open hillside. Bear right on the next single-track and go down. Turn right at a junction with the trail that parallels the road and hike 0.5 mile north to another junction.

Straight ahead is a the easiest walk back to the trailhead. But to get the most out of this hike, turn right and head 0.6 mile up the single-track Pincher Creek Trail to a familiar junction. Bear left and follow the double-track back to Henry Road, turning right on the single-track that leads to the trailhead.

EXTENDING YOUR TRIP

Trails and old ranch roads crisscross and connect, for even more exploring of the Saltese Uplands.

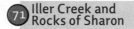

Iller Creek and Rocks of Sharon

RATING/ DIFFICULTY	LOOP	ELEV GAIN/ HIGH POINT	SEASON
★★★★★/3	5.5 miles	1250 feet/ 3580 feet	Apr–Dec

Maps: USGS Spokane SE, Spokane County Conservation Futures map; **Contact:** Spokane County Parks and Recreation, (509) 477-4730, www.spokanecounty.org/parks; **Notes:** Open to mountain bikes. Dogs permitted on-leash; **GPS:** N 47 36.089 W 117 16.903

 *You'll find yourself between a Big Rock and a hard place to leave as you explore some of the wild and lofty 950+ acres in Spokane Valley preserved for nature lovers and critters, including moose. Spokane County secured the Iller Creek Unit of the Dishman Hills Conservation Area, and Dishman Hills Conservancy preserved the adjacent Rocks of Sharon. This hike has it all, from a dank creek bottom to scenic granite-quartzite rock outcroppings and a glorious view of the Palouse region.*

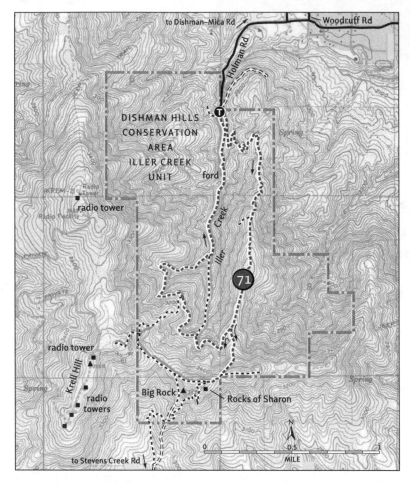

GETTING THERE

From I-90 in Spokane Valley, take Argonne Road exit 287 and head south. At the intersection with Sprague Avenue, continue straight onto Dishman–Mica Road. Go 2.4 miles and turn right at the traffic light onto Schafer Road. Drive 0.8 mile and turn right on 44th Avenue. Go one block and take the first left on Woodruff Road. Go 0.3 mile, turn right on Holman Road, and follow it about 0.7 mile to the trailhead (elev. 2400 ft). Don't block the private road. Privy available.

ON THE TRAIL

Head through the gate and immediately turn left. The trail soon begins switchbacking up

Big Rock stands out among the Rocks of Sharon.

a brushy open slope. At 0.8 mile, the trail gains the ridge, with views to the east (left) of Mica Peak (elev. 5205 ft) and its summit FAA radar dome. Follow the ridge, soon heading into scattered ponderosa pines and eventually Douglas-firs. At 1.5 miles the trail forks. Continue left.

Soon the ridge trail flattens into a park-like setting with views to both sides. Walk through balsamroot, lupine, ocean spray, serviceberry, and other classic native plants of this region. Ease down into a saddle and then begin climbing again. At 1.9 miles, come to another junction. Stay left for now, but take note for the return trip.

At nearly 2.4 miles, turn right at a T junction on an east–west ridge and head up. The trail forks into parallel trails that rejoin at the first big outcropping of the Rocks of Sharon (elev. 3530 ft). Protruding from an east ridge off Tower Mountain, the Rocks of Sharon

perhaps got their name in the early 1900s, when weekend visitors would detrain from the old Spokane-to-Pullman electric line at the long-gone Sharon store and hike up to picnic in the rocks.

Scramble around for views of the Palouse farmlands to the south, with Steptoe Butte (elev. 3612 ft) jutting up like a distant spike in the middle of nowhere. Just below you is Big Rock, a granite-quartzite monolith and playground for rock climbers. Down from the rocks is Stevens Creek Road, another access to this area off the Palouse Highway.

Begin your return by heading back the way you came for nearly 0.5 mile and take the sharp left on the single-track trail you noted on the way up. The trail leads down into a lusher forest, including hemlock, grand fir, and Pacific yew. Cross the creek and continue down.

At the junction with an old eroded trail

that drops to the right along the main creek, bear left on a niftier hiking route into an area damp with little creeks. Numerous dips in the trail attract mountain bikers.

Soon you'll merge with the creekside trail and continue down. A short way before reaching the trailhead, you'll come to a creek ford that's easy most of the year, but during runoff it can be over your boots.

EXTENDING YOUR TRIP
From the Rocks of Sharon, the trail continues west. A left fork drops down, angles to the base of Big Rock, and loops back up from a junction with the access trail coming from Stevens Creek Road. A right fork eventually drops steeply to Iller Creek. The main trail heads up to communication towers on East Tower Mountain (Krell Hill). Tower Mountain ridges are good for cruising north and south, but they are private land and access is not assured.

72 Eagle Peak

RATING/ DIFFICULTY	LOOP	ELEV GAIN/ HIGH POINT	SEASON
****/3	4 miles	690 feet/ 2425 feet	Mar–Dec

Maps: USGS Spokane NE, Dishman Hills Conservancy map, www.dhnaa.org; **Contact:** Spokane County Parks and Recreation, (509) 477-4730, www.spokanecounty.org /parks; **Notes:** Dogs permitted on-leash; **GPS:** N 47 39.249 W 117 17.366

 *Citizens rallied in the 1960s to preserve 530 acres of choice Spokane Valley real estate for wildlife and walkers instead of trophy homes and pavement.*

Bitterroots bloom early spring in Dishman Hills; watch your step!

The Dishman Hills Natural Area is a staple for school field trips and nature observations, starting from the green lawn at Camp Caro and ranging into an urban wilderness. You can devote days to exploring here, from damp nooks to basalt crannies. This hike hits many highlights, including ponds, a high-peak overlook, springs, and all the wildlife opportunities in between.

GETTING THERE
From Spokane on eastbound I-90, take Sprague Avenue exit 285 and continue straight on Appleway Boulevard. Go past Vista Road 0.3 mile and turn right on Sargent Road, and then immediately right again into the Camp Caro–Dishman Hills parking area (625 South Sargent Road). The trailhead (elev. 1960 ft) is at the south end. Privy available at Camp Caro in summer.

ON THE TRAIL

You can become disoriented in this area's maze of trails. Trail signs were planned as this book went to press. Meanwhile, keep this in mind: Any trail heading north will eventually lead back to Camp Caro or at least to Appleway Boulevard. Let this route description guide your first trek to Eagle Peak, then unleash yourself in this rich wild area.

Follow the path from the south end of the gravel parking area to a paved parking area

and go through (yes, through) the Camp Caro lodge. Continue straight, leaving the paved path and going onto the dirt trail past the kiosk.

Hike up some steps and continue toward Goldback Spring, staying on the main trail with the rimrock on your left. At a fork near a park bench, bear left and continue toward Goldback Spring. (The right fork leads into Enchanted Ravine.) At the next junction, bear left again toward Goldback Spring.

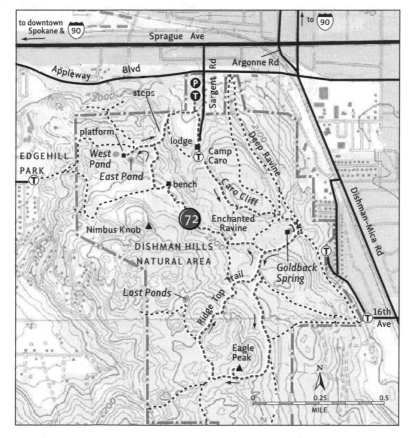

The trail crosses a footbridge over the spring and lush vegetation. Turn right and climb the steps on the trail heading to East/West Ponds and Eagle Peak. At the next intersection with a trail that heads back to Camp Caro, bear left and continue hiking uphill.

Bear left at another junction just a short way up the trail. (Take note: you'll return to this junction later.) Just a short way farther, turn right at another junction with the less obvious Eagle Peak Loop Trail and begin climbing. Bear right at the next two intersections, continuing the uphill trend.

The trail finally tops a ridge of basalt outcroppings at yet another junction. Before continuing the loop to the left, follow the spur trail straight ahead that leads to the top of Eagle Peak (elev. 2425 ft), the highest point in the Dishman Hills Natural Area, with a great view of the Spokane Valley, Mount Spokane to the north, Antoine Peak closer to the northeast, and Mica Peak to the east. The higher areas south of Eagle Peak are private property, where you can see signs of the 2008 wildfire that burned several acres and homes.

Retrace your steps back to the last junction, turn right and head through the basalt formations. Turn right at the next trail junction as you drop from the rocky ridge and begin heading north. Soon you'll come to a fork. Go left to explore Lost Ponds if you wish, but to continue the loop trail, bear right and stay on the Ridge Top Trail.

Soon begin a long descent to a junction you passed earlier. Bear left toward Camp Caro. Go a short way to another familiar junction and bear left again toward East/West Ponds. Also go left at the next two junctions. (Trails heading right, including to Enchanted Ravine, are quick exits to Camp Caro.)

Pass a viewpoint with a bench on the right, and then wind up onto a flat of basalt. Continue on the trail straight and down a slab of rock at this junction toward East/West Ponds. Pass a spur trail heading left and soon drop down another tier to a junction at stair steps. Turn left here to visit East/West Ponds, which are just up the trail to the left at the next junction.

After checking out the ponds (chorus frogs sing here in April or May, ducklings swim in July, and moose pay occasional visits), retrace your route to the junction above the steps and head down the wood-beam staircase—one of many Eagle Scout projects in the natural area.

Bear right at the next two junctions down through the series of steps and water bars, go through the chain link fence, and turn left on the paved path along the green lawn at Camp Caro.

EXTENDING YOUR TRIP

At some point, you must hike the Enchanted Ravine and explore the rocky spine of Deep Ravine on the east side of the natural area.

73 Beacon Hill

RATING/ DIFFICULTY	ROUND-TRIP	ELEV GAIN/ HIGH POINT	SEASON
**/3	4.2 miles	780 feet/ 2600 feet	Mar–Dec

Maps: USGS Spokane NE, Beacon Hill Recreation Area map; **Contact:** Spokane City Parks and Recreation Department, (509) 625-6200, www.spokaneparks.org, and Fat Tire Trail Riders Club, www.fttrc.org; **Notes:** Open to mountain bikes. Dogs permitted on-leash; **GPS:** N 47 41.203 W 117 20.808

🧑‍🧒 🔪 🌸 *Beacon Hill's summit is swarmed by communications towers and transmission lines, and the slopes around it tend to be dominated by mountain bikers. But hikers find plenty of room and a surprising amount of beauty in more than 900 acres of city, county, and private land just north of the Spokane River near Upriver Dam. Ponderosa pines dominate slopes distinguished by granite outcroppings near this southern extent of the Selkirk Mountains. The area is a riot of wildflowers from late April into June.*

GETTING THERE

From I-90 in Spokane, take exit 283B. Go straight along the highway and turn north on Freya Street, which eventually becomes Greene Street. At 2.3 miles, the road bends left and then right (up a hill) and becomes Market Street. Turn right at the stoplight and head east on Euclid Avenue. Go 0.8 mile (Euclid becomes Frederick Avenue) and turn left on Havana Street. Drive two blocks to the dirt parking area (elev. 1990 ft) for Minnehaha Park.

ON THE TRAIL

The west side of Beacon Hill has fewer trails than other areas here, but the trails and old jeep roads still can be confusing. Signage has been proposed. If you get off track on your way to Beacon Hill summit, just head up.

Start at the gate on the paved trail along the grassy developed park. At the ball field, just past rock pillars, bear right off the paved trail onto a wide dirt path that heads up. Soon skirt the Esmeralda Golf Course parking lot and stay left, paralleling it (in this case, *don't* take the double-track routes that head up).

Beacon Hill is a quick hiking getaway in Spokane.

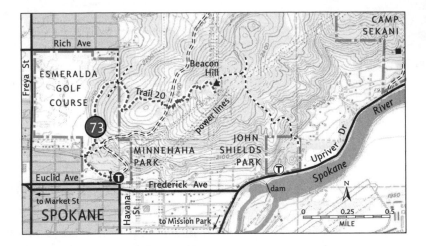

Go through some concrete barriers, then up. When you come to a jeep road that continues up, turn left on the single-track Trail No. 20, which continues north, paralleling the golf course.

This single-track generally bears left at most intersections, climbing gently as it contours northward. As you make a sweeping bend to the east, continue straight up on the single-track at a five-prong junction of trails and jeep roads. After a dogleg south and then north, come to a bench before the power lines. The single-track continues straight across two jeep roads in fairly quick succession.

From here, the single-track is easy to follow as it snakes up the steeper hillside eastward to a rim of rocks south of Beacon Hill summit, which is dominated by com-munication towers. Enjoy expansive views (albeit through power lines and other man-made obstacles). Few places in Spokane's urban area have such a sweeping view of the Spokane Valley east and west.

EXTENDING YOUR TRIP

Explore to your heart's content. Private landowners ask the public to stay out of some parcels in the low areas directly south of Beacon Hill. But some of the most captivating nooks in the area are in the rock outcroppings found on myriad paths gener-ally heading southeast toward John Shields Park (locally known as Minnehaha Rocks), a training area for rock climbers. The Shields Park parking area on Upriver Drive also offers good hiker access to Beacon Hill trails.

74 Downtown Spokane Bridges

RATING/ DIFFICULTY	LOOP	ELEV GAIN/ HIGH POINT	SEASON
***/2	7.7 miles	430 feet/ 1880 feet	Year-round

Maps: USGS Spokane NW, Spokane city map; **Contact:** Spokane Regional Convention and Visitors Bureau, (509) 624-1341, www .visitspokane.com; **Notes:** Partly wheelchair-

Don Kardong Bridge over Spokane River

accessible. Dogs permitted on-leash. Watch for city traffic; **GPS:** N 47 39.348 W 117 27.236

 *Marmots, deer, waterfowl, and fish are more common on this urban route than on many remote wilderness trails. The route takes you over 18 of downtown Spokane's 22 river bridges, joining with the Spokane River Centennial Trail and making a grand tour of Riverfront Park en route. Spokane Falls is a highlight, the Spokane River your constant companion. And as near to nature as you are on this hike, you're also never far from a place to eat, drink, or shop.*

GETTING THERE

From Monroe Street in downtown Spokane, drive 1.3 miles west on Riverside Avenue. Just

before crossing the Hangman Creek Bridge, turn right on Clark Avenue to reach the trailhead parking area (elev. 1750 ft).

ON THE TRAIL

Follow the paved path and cross the Sandifur Bridge over the Spokane River. The path winds up to Ohio Avenue. Follow the sidewalk upstream, overlooking the river gorge. Pass a scenic rest spot at the Hamblen Conservation Area overlook.

Cross the Maple Street Bridge overpass and continue straight on Ohio through the Kendall Yards development. An extension of the Spokane River Centennial Trail is planned here, leading all the way under the Monroe Street Bridge. Until that's complete, work your way upstream and carefully cross Monroe Street to the small bridge-side memorial park. Turn south to cross the Monroe Street Bridge, enjoying a view of Spokane Falls.

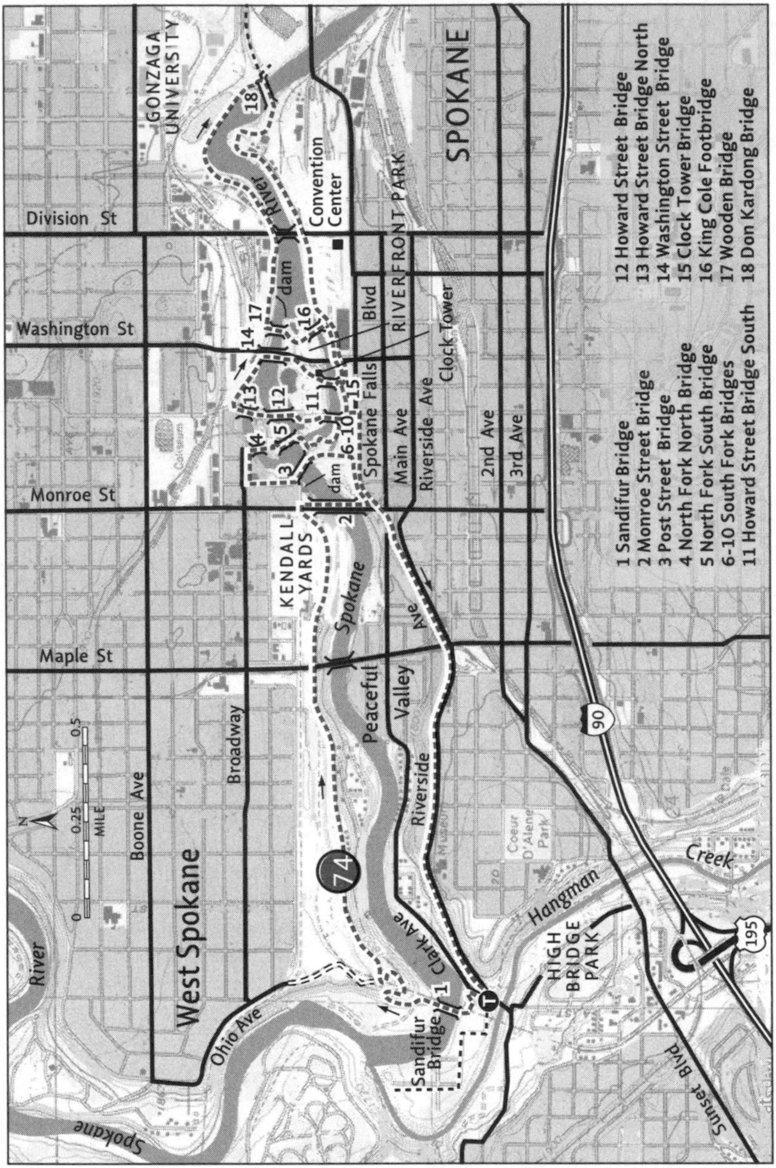

GONZAGA UNIVERSITY

SPOKANE

Division St

Convention Center

RIVERFRONT PARK

Washington St

Blvd

Clock Tower

Spokane Falls

Monroe St

Main Ave

Riverside Ave

2nd Ave

3rd Ave

KENDALL YARDS

Maple St

Peaceful Valley

Broadway

Riverside

90

Coeur d'Alene Park

Clark Ave

Hangman

HIGH BRIDGE PARK

Creek

195

Ohio Ave

Sandifur Bridge

Sunset Blvd

West Spokane

River

Spokane

N

0.25   0.5
MILE

Boone Ave

74

1 Sandifur Bridge
2 Monroe Street Bridge
3 Post Street Bridge
4 North Fork North Bridge
5 North Fork South Bridge
6-10 South Fork Footbridges
11 Howard Street Bridge South
12 Howard Street Bridge
13 Howard Street Bridge North
14 Washington Street Bridge
15 Clock Tower Bridge
16 King Cole Footbridge
17 Wooden Bridge
18 Don Kardong Bridge

At the south end of the bridge, follow the sidewalk left and continue upstream along Spokane Falls Boulevard. Cross Post Street and turn left on the sidewalk, heading north along the Bloomsday runner sculptures.

The sidewalk leads north across the Post Street Bridge up to Broadway. Turn right for a block and head straight ahead and down the paved path that leads back to the river. Cross North Fork North Bridge (bridge no. 4) and then immediately turn right to cross the North Fork South Bridge, where spring-runoff walkers can get wet with spray from water roaring over the "fang" of basalt in the falls just upstream.

Hike past the "Washington Water Power Upper Falls Power Plant" and immediately turn right along the access road. Cross a South Fork bridge (no. 6) and turn left, switchbacking up the path built during Expo '74 that loops up and crosses the little river fork four more times, bringing the bridge count to 10. At the top, bend left along the big pool toward the Rotary Fountain.

Just before the Carrousel, turn left (north) to cross the Howard Street Bridge South. At the end, bear left on the path that soon continues northward (toward the Spokane Arena), crossing the Howard Street Bridge and the Howard Street Bridge North in quick succession. Then turn right (upstream) on the path along the river. Go through the underpass and take the upstream stairs to cross the Washington Street Bridge (no. 14). On the other side, exit on the stairs to the left and then immediately turn right to follow the path up (restrooms to the left). Then bend right, along the Pavilion, for a short way. Turn left on the path down through the grass. Cross the Clock Tower Footbridge and turn left.

Hike upstream past the Red Wagon and the INB Performing Arts Center and turn left to cross the King Cole Footbridge (no. 16). Bear right and wind down, heading northward to cross the wooden bridge leading to a group of hotels. Immediately turn right and follow the walkway upstream on the north riverbank. Bear right onto the pedestrian trail that leads under the Division Street Bridge. Continue on a boardwalk. Then follow the paved path upstream through open expanses of the Gonzaga University campus.

Where the paved path comes to the Don Kardong Bridge, scramble up the short gravel path and turn right on the Centennial Trail to cross the bridge. Congratulations, this is bridge no. 18. Now you're headed back downstream.

Follow the trail, staying right at junctions to stay along the river's south shore. Soon you'll be back at the INB Performing Arts Center. Continue straight downstream and eventually cross Post Street at the Bloomsday runner sculptures. Continue west and carefully follow the two pedestrian crossings to the west side of Monroe Street.

Turn left (south) across Main Avenue and follow the sidewalk around to the right in front of the Spokane Club. Follow Riverside Avenue all the way back through Brown's Addition to the trailhead, with only one more traffic crossing at the Maple Street Bridge onramp.

EXTENDING YOUR TRIP
When you first reach the Don Kardong Bridge (no. 18), head east (upstream) and hike the Centennial Trail to Mission Street, where you could bag another bridge. Serious bridge baggers can hit 21 spans by making sidewalk detours to cross the Maple and Division Street Bridges.

75 South Hill Bluff

RATING/ DIFFICULTY	ROUND-TRIP	ELEV GAIN/ HIGH POINT	SEASON
****/1	3 miles	350 feet/ 2340	Feb–Dec

Maps: USGS Spokane NW, USGS Spokane SW, and Spokane city map; **Contact:** Spokane Regional Convention and Visitors Bureau, (509) 624-1341, www.visitspokane .com; **Notes:** Open to mountain bikes. Dogs permitted on-leash; **GPS:** N 47 37.714 W 117 25.780

More than 23 miles of trails grace the steep swath of undeveloped Spokane City Parks land between High Drive and the Hangman Creek/US Highway 195 corridor below. The trails initially were built on the sly by volunteer biker-hikers who had a vision long before the city thought sustainable trails could be carved into the steep, sandy slopes. This is the place to be for a stunning sunset, and the bluff is especially brilliant with blooming arrowleaf balsamroot and serviceberry in April and May.

GETTING THERE
From Monroe Street, drive west on 29th Avenue three blocks to the end of the road. Turn right at High Drive and then immediately left into a South Hill Bluff trailhead parking area (elev. 2290 ft). More parking is available near Bernard Street, close to the turnaround for this hike.

ON THE TRAIL
This is the easiest of the *many* hiking options on the South Hill Bluff. Walk this route with a map in hand, and soon you'll start to put together the many trail combinations that make for invigorating hikes between the rim and the valley. You can't get lost. Paved roads are above, Hangman Creek below.

From the 29th and High Drive trailhead, follow the concrete sidewalk down and then left, and start walking on a trail. It angles

South Hill Bluff Trail above Hangman Creek

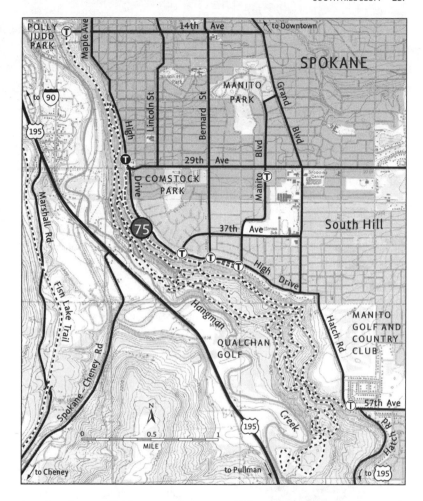

down for a short way but then generally traverses the slope, roughly paralleling below High Drive with gentle ups and downs. You'll pass a few trails heading back up to High Drive and several trails forking down to the lower slopes and Hangman Creek. Stay on this upper-tier trail.

After 1.4 miles, the trail angles up to High Drive near the intersection with Manito Boulevard. This is the turnaround point. Drop back down and hike the same trail back. Or drop down to a lower-level trail that contours back. Several trails eventually will lead you up to High Drive again and the trailhead.

EXTENDING YOUR TRIP

Explore any of the trails branching down off the top-tier trail. Or, from the 29th and High Drive trailhead, drop down the concrete path and continue straight on the trail that heads north along High Drive. This trail offers a pleasant walk to Polly Judd Park trailhead at the west end of 14th Avenue.

76 Fish Lake Trail

RATING / DIFFICULTY	ROUND-TRIP	ELEV GAIN/ HIGH POINT	SEASON
**/1	15 miles	375 feet/ 2155 feet	Mar–Nov

Maps: USGS Spokane NW, Spokane SW, Fish Lake Trail brochure; **Contact:** Spokane City Parks and Recreation Department, (509) 625-6200, www.spokaneparks.org; **Notes:** Wheelchair-accessible. Dogs permitted on-leash. Hikers stay right, share route with cyclists and skaters; **GPS:** N 47 38.829 W 117 27.172

Fish Lake Trail users make use of abandoned railroad bridges.

The Fish Lake Trail has been a public route since 1991, when Spokane assumed ownership of the abandoned Union Pacific Railway that runs 10.2 miles from Spokane to Cheney. Sections near Cheney and Marshall were paved around 1995, but the trail's popularity soared when this section leading out of Spokane was developed and paved in 2009–10. Walkers and bicyclists of all types enjoy out-and-back treks of any length on this gentle ribbon of flatness through the ponderosa pines.

GETTING THERE

From Maple or Ash Street near downtown Spokane, drive west on 2nd Avenue, which bends left after a few blocks and becomes Sunset Boulevard. Stay right on Sunset Boulevard (do not drop down below the underpass). Drive to the stoplight and turn left at Government Way. Then take the first left, on Milton Street. (Alternate access comes from US Highway 195 via 16th Avenue to Lindeke Street and Government Way.) Drive into the trailhead parking area (elev. 1900 ft). Privy available.

ON THE TRAIL

Fish Lake Trail immediately leads to restructured railroad bridges that cross I-90. The paved trail eases through a neighborhood of scattered homes and across another bridge over 16th Avenue at 0.5 mile. By the time you cross the Thorpe Road overpass at 1 mile, you're pretty much into the woods.

The trail parallels US 195 for about 2 miles, buffered by ponderosa pines and basalt walls. Buttercups bloom here in March or April. Cross Marshall Road at 2.1 miles as

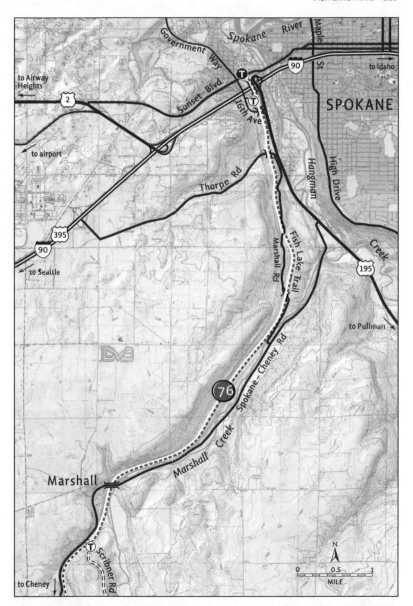

the trail bends away from US 195 and takes you farther away from it all.

Between Marshall Road and the small town of Marshall, hikers aching for more ups and downs can sneak off the flat, paved Fish Lake Trail and walk the rocky fire-break road separating the west side of the trail from the active railway above.

At 6.8 miles, go under the Cheney–Spokane Road overpass. Exit the tunnel-like structure and hike a short way farther to the Scribner Road trailhead. The slight grade on this trail is imperceptible, but relish the fact that you've hiked uphill all the way from Spokane, and the return trip is all downhill.

EXTENDING YOUR TRIP

Someday the trail may go all the way to Cheney without a gap. Until funding is available, the 2.5 miles from Scribner Road to Fish Lake are undeveloped and blocked. The 3-mile section from Fish Lake to Cheney is developed and paved. At Cheney, the Fish Lake Trail transforms into the unpaved Columbia Plateau Trail, managed by Washington State Parks. For a hike with less bicycle traffic, drive to the southeast end of Cheney's main drag (State Route 904) and park at the Cheney–Plaza Road trailhead. The developed portion of the Columbia Plateau Trail heads westward for 23 miles, including part of Turnbull National Wildlife Refuge.

77 James T. Slavin Conservation Area

RATING/ DIFFICULTY	ROUND-TRIP	ELEV GAIN/ HIGH POINT	SEASON
***/2	5.5 miles	370 feet/ 2415 feet	Feb–Dec

Maps: USGS Spokane SW, Spokane County Conservation Futures map; **Contact:** Spokane County Parks and Recreation, (509) 477-4730, www.spokanecounty.org/parks; **Notes:** Open to horses. Dogs permitted on-leash. Watch for ticks; **GPS:** N 47 32.223 W 117 24.733

Restored wetlands at James T. Slavin Conservation Area

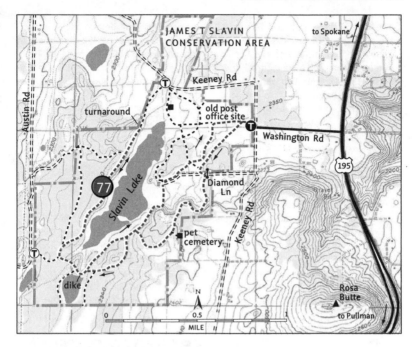

Wetlands and water-fowl abound in this 628-acre preserve secured by Spokane County Conservation Futures in the Rosa Butte area south of Spokane. Restoration projects put water back where it belongs: in a 5-acre lake and nearly 200 acres of seasonal ponds and wetlands. The result is a natural scabland of pines, aspens, rocky bluffs, wildflowers, and wetness that attracts everything from songbirds to elk—plus hikers and equestrians who enjoy the trails.

GETTING THERE

From I-90 in Spokane, take exit 279. Drive south on US Highway 195 about 8.4 miles and turn west at milepost 87.5 onto Washington Road. Drive 0.5 mile and turn right on Keeney Road, and then immediately turn left into the James T. Slavin Conservation Area parking lot and trailhead (elev. 2170 ft). Privy available.

ON THE TRAIL

From the trailhead, walk into the open meadow about 20 yards and go left at the first junction on a single-track trail that heads southwest toward aspens. At 0.5 mile, by a contorted pine, the trail meets an old farm access road (Diamond Lane). Turn left, hike the road about 60 yards and turn right on a single-track trail just before reaching a fence.

The trail winds up and at 0.7 mile makes a short climb to an open, rocky bluff. The trail traces the rim briefly before angling over a flat and into the forest. Signs memorialize the pets the Slavin family buried in the area in the 1900s.

At a fork, bear left and continue south along the wetlands on a double-track trail. Go a short way to a junction with a single-track trail that heads right. This is a good option in early spring or fall, but portions can be marshy in spring or shrouded with tall grass in summer. Stay left for the more dependable 0.5-mile route to the dike at the upper end of the main lake. Turn around here for a round-trip of nearly 4 miles.

But if conditions allow, continue across the earthen dike and bear right into the woods. The trail here dips and can be knee-deep in water during spring.

Turn right at a junction to head north on high ground on the west side of the main lake. (Shorebirds join waterfowl here, as water recedes and exposes mud along the lake's edge.) Bear right at the next two junctions, keeping the water almost always in sight to your right as you wind through the pine woodlands to the end of the main lake and your turnaround point at 2.9 miles. Although the trail continues down into deep grass and loops into a meadow and back to the trailhead, it's a better hike to retrace your steps.

Return to the dike, cross it, and take the familiar high (dry) or low (may be wet or grassy) route. To make a loop, stay straight at the junction with the trail that leads to the unofficial pet cemetery. The way wraps below a bluff and into the woods. Then it turns sharply left and crosses a meadow (can be wet in spring). Bear right onto Diamond Lane. Shortly after, bear left onto a single-track through a timbered flat and continue straight past spur trails. The trail winds through hawthorns, aspens, and prolific spring wildflowers.

Soon the trail breaks into the open meadow. Halfway across the open area, turn right and walk 0.2 mile east to the trailhead. A small post office once sat near the high point of the meadow, about 100 yards from the trailhead.

78 Palisades Park

RATING/ DIFFICULTY	LOOP	ELEV GAIN/ HIGH POINT	SEASON
***/3	4.2 miles	520 feet/ 2200 feet	Mar–Dec

Maps: USGS Spokane SW, and Palisades Park map, www.palisadesnw.com; **Contact:** Spokane City Parks and Recreation Department, (509) 625-6200, www.spokaneparks .org; **Notes:** Partly wheelchair-accessible. Open to mountain bikes, horses. Dogs permitted on-leash; **GPS:** N 47 39.281 W 117 29.175

Palisades Park offers one of the best cityscape views of Spokane while also letting you slip away into native wildlands. And don't miss the outstanding example of 1930s Civilian Conservation Corps rock masonry that many visitors overlook. This city park is a walker's gift, rescued from trash dumpers and partiers by citizen volunteers working with the city to block out motorized vehicles.

GETTING THERE
From southwest Spokane at the intersection of Government Way and Sunset Boulevard, drive 0.8 mile north on Government Way. Turn left (west) on Greenwood Road. Drive 1 mile on Greenwood, bearing right at the fork with Indian Canyon Road, and turn

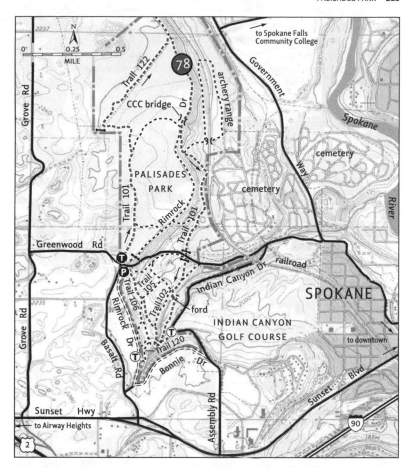

left on the gravel road to the parking spots (elev. 2175 ft).

ON THE TRAIL

Walk across Greenwood Road to the trailhead sign on Rimrock Drive. This area is brilliant with blooming balsamroot in April. Portions of trails can be wet or muddy in spring. Begin hiking to the left of the signs on Trail No. 101. Go nearly 0.3 mile and turn left at a junction with a spur trail coming from Rimrock Drive. The route forks at about 0.8 mile. Go left on Trail No. 122. (Trail No. 101 to the right is a shortcut).

Trail No. 122 follows a fence line and crosses a seasonal wet spot. At a T with the Fairchild Air Force Base water pipeline road, turn right. At the junction with Rimrock Drive (overlooking Fort Wright and Spokane Falls Community College), turn right again and soak in views from Spokane all the way to Mount Spokane in the distance.

Rimrock Drive traverses a splendid bit of CCC stone work, forming a bridge over a small seasonal creek. Cross the bridge and walk out on the point to look back and appreciate it.

Continue on Rimrock Drive about 60 yards to the end of the roadside boulders and drop left sharply into a slot onto Trail No. 101. As the trail begins bending left, take the single-track to the right. At the next junction with double-track Trail No. 123/101, turn right and follow No. 101 as it goes up, then down into an open ponderosa pine forest, generally paralleling the railroad south to Greenwood Road.

Cross the paved road and walk through the gates to continue straight on a fire road (Trail No. 102). Where the fire road begins going up to the right, bear left and down onto the single-track connector trail, which soon switchbacks left and down to ford a creek on slippery stones. Climb up. Turn right at a trail junction and head upstream, staying above

the creek on Trail No. 121 through a pleasant open-timber area.

The trail merges into the Trail No. 102 fire road near a waterfall viewpoint. The falls is a trickle in summer, but flows can be good in spring. Ice climbers practice here in winter. A steep, dangerous trail goes to the base of the falls.

To continue the loop, follow the fire road as it bends right over the top of the falls and head back downstream (north). When you reach an open flat on your left—once used as a winter camp by the Spokane Indian Tribe—look for a sometimes faint trail heading left through the meadow. Hike through the open area, under the power lines and into the trees, where the trail becomes more obvious.

Bear left at the junction with Trail No. 105 and continue toward the bluff on Trail No. 106, which climbs briefly through thick shrubs to the Greenwood parking area.

EXTENDING YOUR TRIP
Trail No. 120 offers interesting single-track alternatives for getting off the fire road near the waterfall.

Civilian Conservation Corps built this rock bridge in Palisades Park.

T. J. Meenach Bridge–Fort George Wright (Spokane River)

RATING/ DIFFICULTY	LOOP	ELEV GAIN/ HIGH POINT	SEASON
***/2	4.3 miles	500 feet/ 1860 feet	Feb–Dec

Maps: USGS Spokane NW, state park map; **Contact:** Riverside State Park, (509) 465-5064, www.parks.wa.gov/parks; **Notes:** Discover Pass required. Partly wheelchair-accessible. Open to mountain bikes. Dogs permitted on-leash; **GPS:** N 47 40.730 W 117 27.196

This unsung city walk starts on a sidewalk, enters quiet woods, and offers a chance to splash in the Spokane River before climbing to overlooks of the river valley. The loop route joins the paved Cen-

tennial Tail and passes a military cemetery that dates back to the 1800s. A neat side trip leads to a rare glimpse of where the Spokane Aquifer—source of the city's drinking water—springs out of a hillside.

GETTING THERE
From I-90 in Spokane, take exit 280 and drive about 1.3 miles north on Maple Street, crossing the Spokane River on the Maple Street Bridge. Turn left (west) on Maxwell Avenue and drive 1.1 miles (the road becomes Pettet Drive). Near the bottom of the grade, turn left into the parking area (elev. 1710 ft) before reaching the T. J. Meenach Bridge.

ON THE TRAIL
From the parking area, use the crosswalk and follow the sidewalk up and along the upstream side of the T. J. Meenach Bridge for 0.2 mile to the south side of the river. The trail starts here (elev. 1740 ft) as part

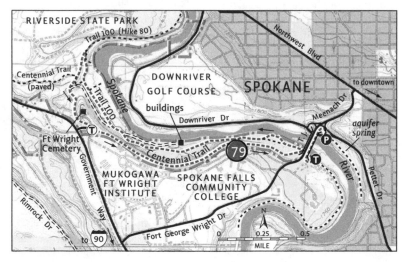

Spring runoff floods a Spokane River beach below Fort George Wright Cemetery.

of the paved Spokane River Centennial Trail, bending left and heading downstream. After passing under the bridge, bear right off the Centennial Trail and onto single-track Trail No. 100.

Suddenly you're in the woods, away from traffic. At 0.4 mile, a trail angles off the main trail to descend closer to the shoreline. Follow it if you wish. It loops back to the main trail after a few hundred yards.

At 0.9 mile, the main trail continues past the rock foundation of a long-gone house. At 1.2 miles, angle left above the first of several utility buildings for a power substation. At 1.4 miles the trail sweeps down past the last of the buildings, out of the woods, and joins the gravel road that serves the utility site. Bear left and follow the road about a 100 yards, bearing right on a double-track trail.

Several spur trails head to the right, to the shoreline. While the river can be fast and dangerous in high spring runoff and early summer flows, a large eddy quiets down by midsummer, making a good place to picnic or let dogs frolic.

Soon you'll come to a trail heading steeply left to the Centennial Trail and the service road to the Fort George Wright Cemetery trailhead. Continue straight, climbing a single-track to a trail junction on the bluff above the river at 2 miles (elev. 1745 ft). This scenic viewpoint is a good turnaround point for a shorter hike.

To make a loop, turn left and follow the single-track to the paved Centennial Trail. Follow the Centennial Trail past the Fort George Wright Cemetery and trailhead for 2.3 miles to your car.

EXTENDING YOUR TRIP

From the turnaround, the trail continues on Trail No. 100 in Riverside State Park

(Hike 80). From the south end of T. J. Meenach Bridge, a route starts below the fenced river-gauge facility and continues upstream to Riverside Memorial Park (it involves some private land). And from the parking lot on Pettet Drive, a trail runs upstream for miles, paved at first and leading in 0.1 mile to a rare opening to the Spokane Aquifer, which spills clear, cold spring water into the Spokane River.

80 Fort George Wright–Bowl and Pitcher (Spokane River)

RATING/ DIFFICULTY	ROUND-TRIP	ELEV GAIN/ HIGH POINT	SEASON
***/3	6.8 miles	680 feet/ 1850 feet	Mar–Dec

Maps: USGS Spokane NW, state park map; **Contact:** Riverside State Park, (509) 465-5064, www.parks.wa.gov/parks; **Notes:** Discover Pass required. Open 6:30AM–dusk. Partly wheelchair-accessible. Open to mountain bikes, horses. Dogs permitted on-leash; **GPS:** N 47 40.864 W 117 28.756

   Starting at the old Fort George Wright Cemetery, opened in 1899 and overlooking the Spokane River, hikers get a brief taste of the paved Spokane River Centennial Trail before breaking off on a dirt trail that's a constant companion to the Spokane River as it winds its way to the roar of the Bowl and Pitcher rapids.

GETTING THERE
From just west of Spokane Falls Community College, at the intersection of Government Way with Fort George Wright Drive, head 0.6 mile north on Government Way. Turn

Groomed grounds at Fort George Wright Cemetery; Mount Spokane in background

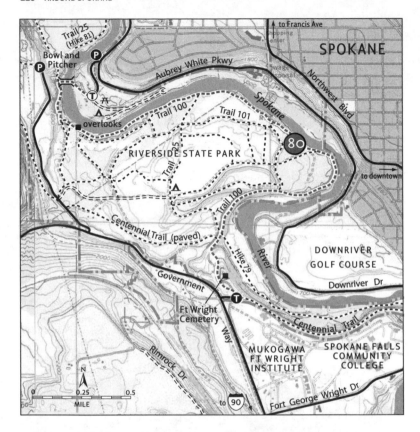

right on Houston Road into the Centennial Trail parking area at Fort George Wright Cemetery (elev. 1850 ft). Privy available.

ON THE TRAIL

From the parking lot, bow briefly to about 650 graves of soldiers and some family members with birth dates as early as 1832.

Head left (west) on the paved Centennial Trail, down a gully and up. Where the paved trail bends left, bear right past a bench and along a fence overlooking the Spokane River onto a single-track trail (Trail No. 100, likely unsigned). Pass a trail that drops to the river and a nice swimming beach in low-water conditions (part of Hike 79).

Stay on the main trail as it heads downstream and slices across a steep slope. Watch out for poison ivy. At 0.9 mile, the trail forks. Left goes up to more trails and a loftier view; take the right fork and drop to old ponderosa pines along the rocky shoreline just above the river. Head up an incline. You'll pass several road or trail junctions in quick succession. The rule: Stay right, keeping to the trail on the rim above the river.

At 1.5 miles, pass the Spokane sewage treatment plant across the river. It's surprisingly uneventful. At 1.9 miles, pass the junction with Trail No. 101. At 2.5 miles, pass another junction, following the rule of staying to the right, along the river. At this point, Trail No. 100 is also part of the 25-Mile Loop Trail around the core of Riverside State Park. (Another day, maybe?) Historically, the Spokane Indian Tribe stored roots in cool talus areas at the base of basalt rock formations in this area.

At 2.8 miles, a short spur goes to the right to a good overlook of the river—a sweet spot to be snacking if river rafters are heading into the rapids downstream at the Bowl and Pitcher, named for the shapes of the huge basalt formations.

At about 3 miles, the trail forks, but both trails reunite shortly. (The left fork along the scree slope is easiest.) A short way farther, the trail drops to a junction. Turn right and down the steps, so you can cross the footbridge over the Spokane River and enjoy the rapids below. The Bowl and Pitcher Recreation Area here has water, toilets, and a picnic area, should you have such needs before you turn around and retrace your route.

EXTENDING YOUR TRIP

Enjoy trails downstream from the Bowl and Pitcher (Hike 81) or farther upstream from the Fort Wright Cemetery trailhead (Hike 79). Some walkers enjoy the paved Centennial Trail in either direction from the trailhead.

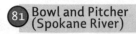

81 Bowl and Pitcher (Spokane River)

RATING / DIFFICULTY	LOOP	ELEV GAIN/ HIGH POINT	SEASON
****/3	5.1 miles	180 feet/ 1760 feet	Mar–Dec

Maps: USGS Airway Heights, USGS Spokane NW, state park map; **Contact:** Riverside State Park, (509) 465-5064, www.parks.wa.gov /parks; **Notes:** Discover Pass required. Open 6:30 AM–dusk. Partly wheelchair-accessible. Open to mountain bikes, horses. Dogs permitted on-leash. Shots might be heard from nearby shooting range; **GPS:** N 47 41.775 W 117 29.746

   This hike has something for everyone—and it's along the Spokane city limits in a choice niche of Riverside State Park. From a developed picnic area and campground, the trail crosses a footbridge over Spokane River rapids at the iconic Bowl and Pitcher basalt formations. The route hugs the river to one of the area's most notable white-water landmarks and secluded shoreline break spots. Then it climbs to overlooks and an old cliff-hanging railroad grade unknown to most park visitors.

GETTING THERE

From west Spokane, follow Fort George Wright Drive or Pettet Drive to the T. J. Meenach Bridge over the Spokane River and head downstream on Downriver Drive. Bear left onto Aubrey White Parkway into Riverside State Park. Drive 2 miles and turn left into the Bowl and Pitcher Recreation Area. (From northwest Spokane, drive west

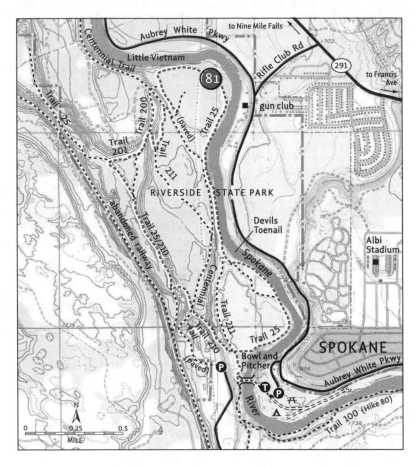

on Francis Avenue to Assembly Street, where Francis becomes Nine Mile Road (State Route 291). Continue 0.8 mile on Nine Mile Road and turn left on Rifle Club Road. Drive 0.5 mile and turn left on Aubrey White Parkway. Drive 1.3 miles and turn right into the Bowl and Pitcher Recreation Area.) Drive to the day-use parking area just past the entry station. The trailhead (elev. 1760 ft) is

near a kiosk across the parking lot below the restrooms (which are closed in winter).

ON THE TRAIL
Follow a wheelchair-accessible path across the suspension bridge over the Spokane River. Enjoy the rapids and the Bowl and Pitcher's namesake basalt formations.

On the west side of the river, head up the

Rafters head toward Spokane River footbridge at Bowl and Pitcher basalt formations.

steps and bear right on Trail No. 25 above the picnic shelter. At 0.3 mile, turn right at the junction with Trail Nos. 210 and 211 to continue on Trail No. 25. Bear right at any spur-trail junctions to stay along the river.

At 1.2 miles, pass mile marker 20 (and a spur to a low-water riverside beach). There's a good view downstream to the Devils Toenail Rapid. Its namesake basalt rock spikes out of the middle of the river, creating a white-knuckle rafting attraction. Bear right at the next two forks to a nifty overlook at Devils Toenail. From the overlook, the trail drops on a rocky stretch along the river. At high spring flows, this section can be inundated, forcing hikers up (left) to the paved Spokane River Centennial Trail.

At 1.75 miles, the trail angles up from the river and skirts the edge of the Centennial Trail before splitting right as a single-track down to a flat. At 2.5 miles, the trail forks just

after coming close to the river again. A side trip right and down leads to Little Vietnam, with lush vegetation and several places to enjoy the river shoreline in low flows.

To complete the loop and get the "high view" of the river, bear left at this junction and again at the next one (don't go right on a trail that angles up to Gate 36). Shortly after, turn right on another trail that leads gently up to the pavement, and turn right for 50 yards on the Centennial Trail. Then turn sharply left on Trail No. 211, heading southwest along a flat for a few hundred yards to a sharp right turn on Trail No. 200. Turn left on Trail No. 201 and head up the spine of the ridge to another stair-step plateau—a sweet spot between the river flats and the vertical basalt rimrock.

Stay right at the first unmarked fork. Hike a short way to another fork and go left on Trail No. 25/210 (right leads to a neat spur, at

Trail No. 25 mile-marker 3, built by mountain bikers). As the way bends left and begins heading downhill, Trail Nos. 210 and 25 split. Continue straight on Trail No. 210, cross the Centennial Trail, and come to a familiar junction with Trail Nos. 211 and 25. Turn right to return to your car.

EXTENDING YOUR TRIP

From the junction of Trail Nos. 210 and 25 near the end of the loop, turn right and head uphill on Trail No. 25 to an abandoned railway that hangs almost imperceptibly on a ledge around the rimrock. Explore it in either direction.

82 Deep Creek Canyon

RATING/ DIFFICULTY	LOOP	ELEV GAIN/ HIGH POINT	SEASON
****/4	4.6 miles	900 feet/ 2200 feet	Apr–Dec

Maps: USGS Nine Mile Falls, state park map; **Contact:** Riverside State Park, (509) 465-5064, www.parks.wa.gov/parks; **Notes:** Discover Pass required. Open 6:30AM–dusk. Partly wheelchair-accessible. Open to mountain bikes, horses. Dogs permitted on-leash; **GPS:** N 47 46.319 W 117 33.128

Deep Creek Canyon is its own little world within sprawling Riverside State Park. An intermittent stream dropping decisively to join the Spokane River is confined by basalt cliffs towering as high as 300 feet above and narrowing as close as 60 feet across. Lush greenery is unceremoniously interrupted by bulging basalt outcroppings and swaths of scree resembling explosion rubble. Blue-green swal-

lows swoop through the canyon and ospreys nest nearby. The highlight might be climbing from the bowels of Deep Creek Canyon to Pine Bluff and savoring where you've been from a bird's-eye view.

GETTING THERE

From the intersection of Francis Avenue and Assembly Street in northwest Spokane, head west toward Nine Mile Falls on Francis Avenue, which becomes Nine Mile Road (State Route 291). Drive 6.1 miles and turn left at Nine Mile Dam onto Charles Road. Drive 0.1 mile, crossing the Spokane River, and turn left on Carlson Road. Drive 0.4 mile and turn right into the Spokane River

Basalt towers stand guard over Deep Creek.

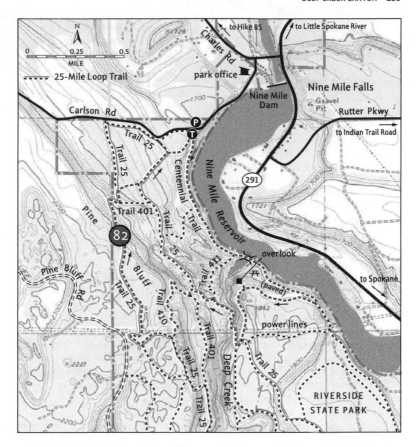

Centennial Trail trailhead parking area (elev. 1590 ft). Privy available.

ON THE TRAIL

Hike back down the road a short way and descend through the gate on the Centennial Trail. Follow the paved route above the Nine Mile Reservoir portion of the Spokane River. Taking note of trail options on the right to explore later, cross the bridge, pass the picnic site at Deep Creek, and continue on the Centennial Trail up the hill. At 1.1 miles, turn right and hike the road that leads 0.4 mile to the Deep Creek Overlook. Enjoy the views of unique basalt formations and down into Deep Creek Canyon.

Continue up the road another 0.3 mile and drop sharply to the right on Trail No. 25, which plunges to the canyon bottom. This trail is part of a 25-mile loop through Riverside State Park, and you'll encounter it several times on this hike.

Turn right and follow the creekbed a short distance before the trail heads up the other side. Gain a bluff to the junction with Trail No. 411 (a side trip right leads into a moonscape of basalt outcroppings and scree). Continue on Trail No. 25 uphill to a junction and turn left on the connector trail that leads up toward Pine Bluff.

At the top of the switchbacks, turn right on Trail No. 410. Go a few hundred yards up to an opening and take the trail to the right to an overlook of the Spokane River and Nine Mile Dam. The trail works up a secondary bluff to the higher Pine Bluff and another good overlook. Ospreys nest on the power-line poles below. Bring binoculars in summer for the rare opportunity to look *down* into a nest and possibly see osprey chicks.

Past the power lines, reach a junction that reunites you with Trail No. 25. Turn right on the double-track trail. It heads up and then loops down through the ponderosa pines along the power lines, winding to a T junction with a service road.

Turn right, go 30 yards, and turn right again to continue on Trail No. 25. Go another 30 yards and turn right yet again, to continue on Trail No. 25. Eventually the trail drops to a junction with Trail No. 401. Bear left and continue down to another junction, where you turn right on Trail No. 402.

As you descend and pass another junction with Trail No. 25, Trail 402 narrows to a single-track for its last leg—with a view over Nine Mile Reservoir—to the trailhead.

EXTENDING YOUR TRIP

Restart the loop along the Centennial Trail to Deep Creek Bridge and enjoy a well-deserved picnic. Then explore trails up from the picnic area into interesting rock formations.

83 Indian Painted Rocks–Saint George's School (Little Spokane River)

RATING/ DIFFICULTY	ROUND-TRIP	ELEV GAIN/ HIGH POINT	SEASON
***/3	4.7 miles	600 feet/ 1790 feet	Mar–Nov

Maps: USGS Dartford, state park map; **Contact:** Riverside State Park, (509) 465-5064, www.parks.wa.gov/parks; **Notes:** Discover Pass required. Open 6:30AM–dusk. No dogs or bikes allowed in natural area. Buggy in summer; **GPS:** N 47 46.826 W 117 29.745

The 1993-acre Little Spokane River Natural Area, protecting more than 7 miles of the serpentine river's corridor on the north edge of Spokane, is one of the region's richest wildlife habitats. It's distinguished for attracting a spring-summer diversity of bird species unmatched in the region. This route explores the best hiking along the river stretch between Indian Painted Rocks and the Saint George's School area.

GETTING THERE

From Maple Street in north Spokane, head 1 mile west on Francis Avenue (State Route 291). Turn right (north) on Indian Trail Road and drive 4.7 miles to a junction with Rutter Parkway. Continue straight onto the parkway, dropping down to the Little Spokane River. Shortly after crossing a bridge, turn left into the Indian Painted Rocks parking area (also popular with river paddlers) and trailhead (elev. 1420 ft). Privy available.

ON THE TRAIL

From the Indian Painted Rocks trailhead,

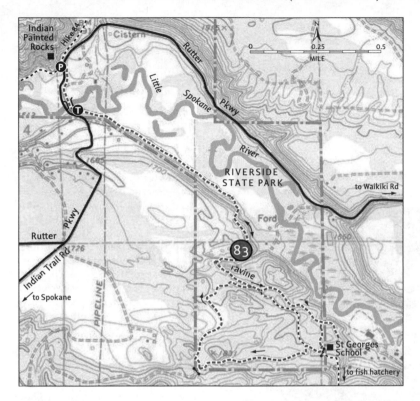

walk south on Rutter Parkway (stay to the edge of the road and be careful of traffic), cross to the south side of the Little Spokane River, and look for the trailhead to the left. The trail leads upstream and across a huge meadow that gets tall with grass during summer.

At 0.7 mile, the trail begins ascending a single-track into a forest of granite outcroppings and gullies, passing a cattail-lined wetland. After hiking up and out of an enchanting ravine at 1.3 miles, bear left at a fork. Hike 0.3 mile to an overlook of Saint George's School. Then backtrack a short way and look for the easy-to-miss trail heading left (south) up to a gated double-track trail.

At the gate, turn right on the double-track and hike a short way to a junction with another double-track. Right heads back to the trailhead. To make a loop, turn left on the double-track and hike through a section of thinned forest to another gate. Turn right at the gate onto a single-track that leads back to the granite-lined "enchanted ravine."

Turn left at the ravine and follow the main trail 1.3 miles back to the trailhead.

EXTENDING YOUR TRIP

From the gate above Saint George's School, go left through the gate instead of right. The mostly double-track trail leads 2.5 miles upstream to a trailhead near the Spokane Fish Hatchery, with a spur option to a view of Mount Spokane. This route includes an abrupt 500-foot ascent followed by easy walking below Five Mile Prairie to a prettier but similarly abrupt 540-foot descent to the hatchery trailhead off Waikiki Road. The hatchery, fed by a pure spring right out of the Spokane Aquifer, is worth a visit.

Wild turkey gobbler on Little Spokane River Trail

84 Little Spokane River Overlook

RATING/ DIFFICULTY	LOOP	ELEV GAIN/ HIGH POINT	SEASON
****/3	6.4 miles	1150 feet/ 2470 feet	Apr–Nov

Maps: USGS Dartford, USGS Nine Mile Falls, state park map; **Contact:** Riverside State Park, (509) 465-5064, www.parks.wa.gov /parks; **Notes:** Discover Pass required. Open 6:30AM–dusk. No dogs or bikes allowed in natural area. Watch for rattlesnakes; **GPS:** N 47 46.973 W 117 29.788

The Little Spokane River Natural Area, managed by Riverside State Park, got an upland boost with the addition of the Van Horn, Edburg, Bass woodlands secured through Spokane County Conservation Futures. While most visitors hike or paddle in the river valley, this 701-acre property takes you from the depths of the river canyon to a high overlook, offering a top-to-bottom perspective of the habitats that attract waterfowl and eagles, muskrats and beavers, raccoons and coyotes, rattlesnakes and mountain lions, deer and moose.

GETTING THERE

From Maple Street in north Spokane, head 1 mile west on Francis Avenue (State Route 291). Turn right (north) on Indian Trail Road. Drive 4.7 miles to a junction with Rutter Parkway. Continue straight onto the parkway, dropping down to the Little Spokane River. Shortly after crossing a bridge, turn left into the parking area (popular with river paddlers) and trailhead (elev. 1420 ft). Privy available.

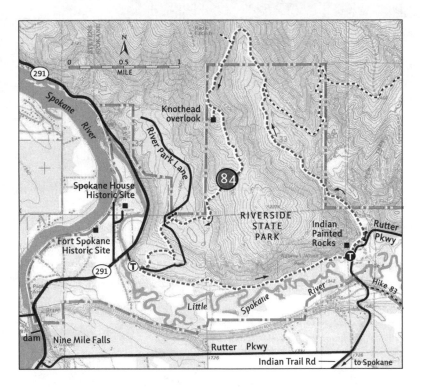

ON THE TRAIL

From the Indian Painted Rocks trailhead, the kid-friendly version of this hike simply follows the trail along the Little Spokane River as far out and back as the kids want to go. For the longer loop, head the other way, north past the toilets, away from the river. After a short way, the trail bends back to a gate off Rutter Parkway. Turn left here onto the double-track trail. (This is an alternate access point, with limited parking.)

The route goes up a draw, previously logged but regaining its natural, wild stature. The trail sweeps left across the head of the timbered draw and angles up toward the ridge. At 2 miles, stay left at a junction with a logging road coming in from the right, and continue up. This can be a midday hot stretch, but by evening it's shady. At 2.5 miles, the trail gains the ridge, a mostly untouched area of timber, native plants, and basalt outcroppings. Views to the right include the Spokane River and down into Lake Spokane (Long Lake).

Continue up to a bench, where the trail bends left and off the ridge. At this point, a single-track spur trail heads to the right a couple hundred yards to big granite boulders for an excellent vista at 2.7 miles. This knob is locally known as Knothead. Look south to

Near Knothead, overlooking Spokane River

the Deep Creek basalt outcroppings (Hike 82) and the Nine Mile area of Riverside State Park, location of the Spokane River Centennial Trail terminus. Look southwest to the Spokane airport area and down to SR 291 and the boat launch at the confluence of the Spokane and Little Spokane Rivers (a short off-trail walk southeast to another knob offers a view down toward the Little Spokane River to where you began).

Backtrack to the junction at the bench and turn right. Hike through parklike openings on the south-facing slope. Just before reaching a gate at River Park Lane, which accesses private property, the trail turns left toward SR 291. Drop a couple hundred yards, cross the paved road, and descend toward the Little Spokane River.

Down in a little meadow, keep an eye out for a marker where the trail makes a 90-degree right turn. The trail winds around a bluff with a good view up the Little Spokane River valley before making another drop down to River Park Lane and a trailhead off of SR 291 at 4.8 miles. Make a hard left turn off the pavement onto the trail that

parallels the river back to Indian Painted Rocks, returning to your start in 1.6 miles.

EXTENDING YOUR TRIP
See Indian Painted Rocks (Hike 83).

85 McLellan Conservation Area

RATING/ DIFFICULTY	LOOP	ELEV GAIN/ HIGH POINT	SEASON
***/3	3.8 miles	380 feet/ 1760 feet	Mar–Dec

Maps: USGS Tumtum, USGS Four Mound Prairie, McLellan Conservation Area map; **Contact:** Spokane County Parks and Recreation, (509) 477-4730, www.spokanecounty .org/parks; **Notes:** Open to mountain bikes, horses. Dogs permitted on-leash. Shots might be heard from distant shooting range; **GPS:** N 47 52.489 W 117 41.463

  Just west of Riverside State Park, the McLellan Conservation Area—secured by Spokane County Conservation Futures—preserves

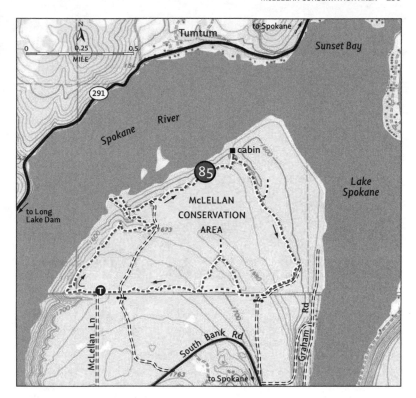

410 acres on a scenic bend of Lake Spokane (the confusing name for the Spokane River reservoir behind Long Lake Dam). The area includes 1.5 miles of shoreline and adjoins a 640-acre parcel managed by the Department of Natural Resources. The thinned ponderosa and Douglas-fir forest and shoreline habitats are important year-round for wildlife large and small. April through May is prime time to enjoy the riot of wildflowers. At the time of this writing, no formal trail was maintained. But the route is easy to find.

GETTING THERE

From the intersection of Francis Avenue and Assembly Street in northwest Spokane, drive 6.1 miles west toward Nine Mile Falls on Francis Avenue, which becomes Nine Mile Road (State Route 291). At Nine Mile Dam, turn left on Charles Road. Cross the Spokane River, continue 5 miles (passing Sontag County Park), and turn right onto South Bank Road. Go 5.8 miles, turn right onto McLellan Lane, and drive 0.8 mile to the trailhead at road's end (elev. 1760 ft).

McLellan hikers rise above Lake Spokane anglers.

ON THE TRAIL

At the gate, follow the fence to the left (west), after which there's a more discernible trail. Leave this trail where it bends right and continue straight along the bluff to a natural overlook by an old-growth tree above Lake Spokane (previously called Long Lake). Turn right from the overlook and hike cross-country, keeping the bluff and the reservoir on your left and letting them be your guide.

Contour to the right along a deep ravine until it's shallow enough to let you drop down to an old road. Follow the road left and down to a parklike spot at the water's edge. Then either backtrack up the road or walk a short way upstream and climb a steep ridge back up. Either way, continue following the bluff. After a long flat area, the route stairsteps down to a lower bluff. (Look for a pet memorial.) Drop down to the lower bluff when convenient and look for an old cabin site at 2 miles.

Then follow the faint road southeastward from the cabin. The old track is often littered with downfall and droppings from wild turkeys. Bear right at a junction with another faint road (it heads left toward the reservoir and fades away). Soon you'll enter a more open area of timber thinned for fire control. Some private buildings stand along the shore to the left.

Continue up on the road and bear right. The road eventually leads to a gate. From here, the road swings to the right and then back up to the fence and the trailhead. Or, leave the road and head cross-country, keeping the fence on your left.

Opposite: Big Sky Country—the Beezley Hills

columbia plateau

The Columbia Plateau (also referred to as the Columbia Basin) is a sprawling area south and east of the Columbia River consisting of ancient basalt flows scoured and shaped by Ice Age floods into channeled scablands. Within the rain shadow of the Cascade Mountains, the Columbia Plateau sees the lowest amount of rainfall in the state. But massive irrigation projects have transformed large parts of it into croplands and vineyards. Sparsely populated in its northern reaches, its southern reaches consist of one of the fastest growing metropolitan areas in the country. A land of sagebrush-steppe, canyons, coulees, sand dunes, and mesas, the plateau possesses incredible geological and biological diversity. Public lands scattered across it provide excellent hiking opportunities for discovering a land that lacks big mountains—but is big on wide-open spaces and scenic delights.

86 Turnbull National Wildlife Refuge Auto Tour Trails

RATING/ DIFFICULTY	ROUND-TRIP	ELEV GAIN/ HIGH POINT	SEASON
***/1	3 miles	110 feet/ 2290 feet	Mar–Dec

Maps: USGS Cheney, refuge brochure; **Contact:** Turnbull National Wildlife Refuge, (509) 235-4723, www.fws.gov/turnbull; **Notes:** Federal pass or $3 vehicle fee Mar 1–Oct 31. Open daylight hours. Partly wheelchair-accessible. Dogs permitted on-leash. Stay on designated roads and trails; **GPS:** N 47 26.321 W 117 32.052

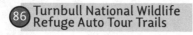 *This easy-going hike combines two trails that are part of an auto tour in the Turn-*

bull National Wildlife Refuge. The Kepple Peninsula Trail leads to a wildlife observation blind as it loops from open area, into pine forest, and along the shore of Kepple Lake. Then hike (or drive) 0.4 mile to the 30-Acre Lake Trail for an out-and-back walk featuring aspens and cattails.

GETTING THERE

From the intersection of 1st and K Streets at the south end of Cheney's business district, turn east onto Cheney-Plaza Road toward Williams Lake. Drive 4.2 miles south and turn left on Smith Road toward Turnbull Refuge headquarters. Stop at the self-pay station on the right and check the maps. Continue 1.8 miles (past a parking area, kiosks, and restrooms), and turn left on the Pine Creek Auto Tour route. Drive past the Blackhorse Lake trailhead at 0.7 mile on the tour route, then pass the south trailhead for 30-Acre Lake at 1.1 miles, then pass the Kepple Lake Overlook trailhead at 2.3 miles. Finally, after 2.6 miles, pull into the Kepple Peninsula Interpretive Trail parking area (elev. 2280 ft). Privy available.

ON THE TRAIL

Start on the paved wheelchair-accessible trail with interpretive signs for an easy walk to a wildlife-viewing blind at the far end of the peninsula that juts into Kepple Lake. Continue the loop clockwise by following the single-track dirt trail along the wetlands from the waterfowl exhibit back to the trailhead.

Then walk (or drive) another 0.4 mile on the tour route to the 30-Acre Lake north trailhead. Hike through the gate onto the double-track trail that heads through open forest and past aspens and scablands.

Soon you'll see a fenced enclosure on the

Kepple Lake is one of Turnbull's easy strolls.

MIMA MOUNDS: A MYSTERY

On hikes such as the Pine Lakes Loop (Hike 87) in Turnbull National Wildlife Refuge and Fishtrap Lake (Hike 109), hikers will notice mima (MY-ma) mounds and wonder: What created these clumps of rock and grass that can be 4–6 feet tall and 30 feet wide, together looking like a junkyard of giant baseball pitcher's mounds? Scientists wonder too.

Researchers who looked into the matter by digging through mima mounds debunked the myth that they're Native American burial sites. But they turned up no conclusive answers, just dozens of hypotheses: freeze-and-thaw cycles, erosion, wind working with vegetation, earthquakes, flood cycles, volcanic eruptions—giant prehistoric prairie dogs? Your guess is as good as theirs.

Although Eastern Washington offers many examples of these geological attractions, a 445-acre Mima Mounds Natural Area Preserve in Western Washington south of Olympia is dedicated to revealing them to the public. The state-protected area has a good walking path.

For information, visit Washington Trails Association, www.wta.org/go-hiking/hikes/mima-mounds.

—R. L.

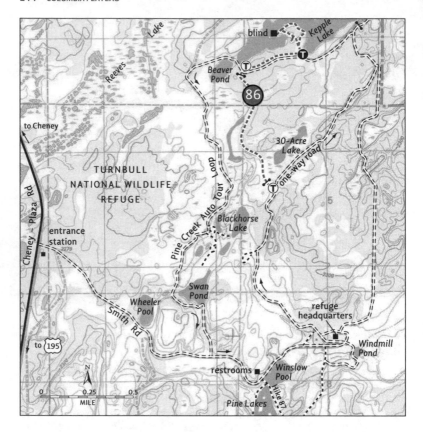

right that's part of a study to see how well aspens regenerate when they're protected from elk foraging. The plots indicate that elk have had a devastating impact on the aspens, which are important to a variety of wildlife. The research was part of the scientific justification for allowing controlled hunting seasons on portions of the refuge (not around the auto tour route or public-use trails).

Tules gobble up most of 30-Acre Lake, with little water showing much of the year.

Reach the south trailhead after 0.75 mile and retrace your steps. Consider leaving a bike at the south trailhead during your drive in and pedaling the tour route back to the Kepple Peninsula trailhead.

EXTENDING YOUR TRIP

Hike the other three short trails along the auto tour route mentioned in the Getting There directions. On the drive out, stop at 4.4 miles around the tour loop to bag the Blackhorse Lake Boardwalk.

87 Pine Lakes

RATING/ DIFFICULTY	LOOP	ELEV GAIN/ HIGH POINT	SEASON
***/3	6 miles	400 feet/ 2375 feet	Mar–Dec

Maps: USGS Cheney, refuge brochure; **Contact:** Turnbull National Wildlife Refuge, (509) 235-4723, www.fws.gov/turnbull; **Notes:** Federal pass or $3 vehicle fee Mar 1–Oct 31. Open daylight hours. Partly wheelchair-accessible. Dogs permitted on-leash. Stay on designated roads and trails; **GPS:** N47 24.891 W117 32.283

The diked lakes and marshes on Pine Creek are a magnet for waterfowl and other wildlife, including some standouts, such as trumpeter swans. You'll get a flavor for the refuge's habitat diversity by following the featured loop as it ranges from the creek basin to the open grasslands and potholes that border farmed fields.

GETTING THERE

From the intersection of 1st and K Streets at the south end of Cheney's business district, turn east onto Cheney-Plaza Road toward Williams Lake. Drive 4.2 miles south and turn left on Smith Road toward Turnbull Refuge headquarters. Stop at the self-pay station on the right and check the maps. Continue 1.5 miles to the trailhead parking area and kiosk (elev. 2260 ft). Privy available.

ON THE TRAIL

From the parking area, cross the road to the Pine Lakes Loop trailhead and check out Winslow Pool observation area before proceeding down on the paved path. Hike past Winslow Pool, a favorite area for red-wing blackbirds and a variety of waterfowl,

Trumpeter swans return to Turnbull as soon as winter ice recedes.

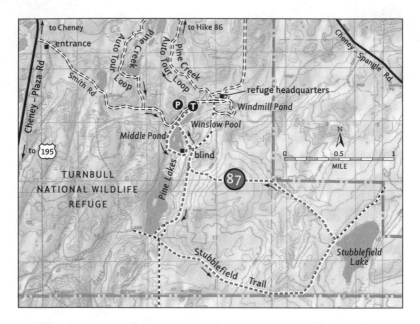

including migrating tundra and nesting trumpeter swans. At the first junction, bear right and continue down along the next pool. During spring and early summer, the paved trail is often littered with the droppings of geese and coyotes. The trail soon bends left and crosses the earthen dike at the end of Middle Pond.

At a Y junction, bear right onto the gravel path (left leads to an observation blind and the way you'll return to the trailhead at the end of this hike). Go a short way to a junction and turn right at 0.75 mile. Go a short way farther to another junction, and turn right onto a gravel roadway that is your path heading south into a more open area along the Pine Lakes. Scoured by Ice Age floods, the landscape features "scabs" of basalt rock exposed above rich soil and wetlands.

At the next junction, make a mental note that you'll return here, from the left. Continue straight, and at 1.6 miles come to the dike at the end of Pine Lakes. Turn left and head up onto the Stubblefield Trail. Hike briefly to the next junction and turn left through the former fence gate and into a pine forest thinned for fire control in the years just after 2000.

Soon the trail breaks into open range land. The route can have numerous wet spots during spring, as the scablands basalt foundation prevents water from soaking into the ground. At the next junction, bear left away from the fence. Stubblefield Lake, on your right, dries up significantly by late summer.

The trail stays in the open, but tracks of critters such as elk and deer suggest that you may have observers just inside the forests on each side. Soon the route arches gradually over the trek's high point (elev. 2375 ft) before bending down to a familiar junction. Turn right on the Pine Lakes Trail and return to the trailhead, looping by the observation blind to return via the east side of Middle Pond.

EXTENDING YOUR TRIP

Five short trails can be accessed along the refuge's 5.4-mile Pine Creek Auto Tour (see Hike 86, Turnball National Wildlife Refuge).

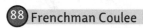

88 Frenchman Coulee

RATING/ DIFFICULTY	ROUND-TRIP	ELEV GAIN/ HIGH POINT	SEASON
***/2	4 miles	100 feet/ 875 feet	Mar–Dec

Map: USGS Babcock Ridge; **Contact:** Washington Department of Fish and Wildlife, Columbia Basin Wildlife Area, Moses Lake, 509-765-6641, http://wdfw.wa.gov/lands /wildlife_areas; **Notes:** Discover Pass required; **GPS:** N 4701.381 W 119 59.516

 *Follow an old jeep track on an easy journey through a harsh landscape of sage, sand, and basalt. Frenchman Coulee is small but impressive, with its imposing canyon walls, sculptured rock formations, and plummeting waterfall. Marvel at the old highway blasted into steep canyon walls and spanning deep clefts. Summer can be blistering hot and winter blustery and bone-chilling. But fall is delightful, with agreeable temperatures, and spring simply divine, when the canyon floor comes alive in a dazzling display of blossoms.*

GETTING THERE

From Moses Lake, follow I-90 west to exit 143, turning right (north) onto Silica Road. (From Ellensburg, follow I-90 east to exit 143, turning left onto Silica Road.) Proceed 0.8 mile and turn left onto Vantage Road (old Highway 10). Follow this road west for 3.6 miles down into Frenchman Coulee, passing popular pull-outs for climbers and coming to the trailhead on your right (elev. 875 ft).

ON THE TRAIL

Starting on a shelf at the edge of the Columbia River, head east on an old jeep track. Closed to motorized travel, it's obvious from the tire tracks that scofflaws can't read or

Seasonal waterfall at the head of Frenchman Coulee

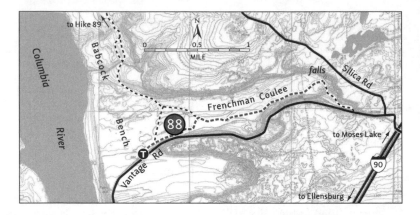

don't care about this regulation meant to protect this fragile environment. Managed by the Washington Department of Fish and Wildlife, Frenchman Coulee is part of the multiunit 192,000-acre Columbia Basin Wildlife Area, consisting of outstanding sagebrush-steppe ecosystems, including the nearby Ancient and Dusty Lakes. A popular hunting area, be sure to don orange when hiking here in the fall.

At just shy of 0.2 mile, come to a Y junction (elev. 845 ft). The way left travels north along Babcock Bench, offering some good views of the Columbia River (here dammed as Wanapum Lake) and Whiskey Dick Mountain (long-winded here, with its turbines) rising behind it. Bear right instead to journey up the coulee.

The track parallels the old highway, coming pretty close to it at about 0.4 mile before the road pulls away to start climbing out of the coulee. The old jeep track stays pretty level while canyon walls flanking the north and south rise precipitously. At 0.8 mile, come to another jeep-track junction (elev. 825 ft). The track left leads back to meet the one you started on 0.4 mile north of where

you left it. Consider returning that way for some variation. Meanwhile, head right to continue your journey into the heart of the coulee.

At 0.9 mile, skirt the base of some steep, stark basalt cliffs littered with rusting car parts and other debris. Look up at the old highway blasted into ledges and spanning deep chasms. Try to envision cars puttering up this highway back in the 1930s and 1940s under a scorching hot sun, pulling over in distress with steam spouting from radiator caps.

The tread now gets a little sandier and softer, hence the slower walking. Skirt big talus slopes that harbor reptiles and small mammals. Now well below the highway and away from popular climbing spots, engine and human sounds are replaced by wind and birdsong and the falling water from the nearing cascade.

Pass beneath high-tension power lines and begin angling north toward a creek cascading from the coulee rim. At 2 miles, reach the base (elev. 875 ft) of the cascade near a big talus slope. The flow is regulated by runoff and by irrigation needs from above, which means it sometimes dries up. Willows

KLAHOWYA TILLICUM: CHINOOK JARGON

Many place names in Eastern Washington, like much of the Pacific Northwest, come from the Chinook Jargon. Not an actual language, Chinook is a collection of several hundred words drawn from various Native American languages (primarily Coast Salish) as well as English and French. It was used as a trade language among Native peoples, Europeans, and American settlers and explorers in the Pacific Northwest throughout the nineteenth century. A unique part of our Pacific Northwest cultural heritage, Chinook names are sprinkled throughout our landscape. Below are some Chinook words you may encounter when hiking in Eastern Washington:

chuck	water, river, stream
cultus	bad, worthless
elip	first, in front of
hyas	big, powerful, mighty
ipsoot	hidden
kimtah	behind, after
klahowya	hello, greetings, how are you?
klip	deep, sunken
lemolo	wild, crazy
lolo	carry, lift
memaloose	dead
mesachie	bad, evil, dangerous
moolock	elk
muckamuck	food
ollalie	berries
pil	red
saghalie	above, high, on top, sacred
sitkum	half of something, part of something
skookum	big, strong, mighty
tenas	small, weak, children
tillicum	friend, people
tupso	pasture, grass
tyee	chief, leader

—C. R.

and sage along the outflow indicate that water does flow this way on occasion.

Admire the falls and the ravens and raptors that ride the thermals above it. Marvel, too, at the depth and scope of the coulee from here, deep inside it. Scout around, noting the scattered debris warranting a much needed cleanup of the canyon. During springtime delight in the dazzling floral carpet.

EXTENDING YOUR TRIP

It is possible to continue beyond the waterfall, picking up a good jeep track once more and following it for about 0.4 mile up and out of the coulee. It emerges 2 miles east from the trailhead. Return the same way or walk the road back for a loop. Consider hiking the track along Babcock Bench to a nice knoll about 1.3 miles from the trailhead, with good views of the Columbia River.

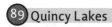 Quincy Lakes

Ancient Lakes

RATING/ DIFFICULTY	ROUND-TRIP	ELEV GAIN/ HIGH POINT	SEASON
****/2	4.4 miles	280 feet/ 1000 feet	Feb–Nov

Dusty Lake

RATING/ DIFFICULTY	ROUND-TRIP	ELEV GAIN/ HIGH POINT	SEASON
****/3	6 miles	350 feet/ 1000 feet	Feb–Nov

Map: USGS Babcock Ridge; **Contact:** Washington Department of Fish and Wildlife, Columbia Basin Wildlife Area, Moses Lake, 509-765-6641, http://wdfw.wa.gov/lands /wildlife_areas; **Notes:** Discover Pass required. Watch for rattlesnakes; **GPS:** N 47 09.610 W 119 58.845

     *Hike to a series of pothole lakes lying within deep basalt canyons carved by ancient glacial floodwaters. Follow old jeep tracks beneath stark cliffs and across sage-scented flats and along grassy slopes. One of the most popular hiking destinations in the Channeled Scab-* *lands and Columbia Basin, the Quincy Lakes are especially delightful in spring, with its ample sunshine and profuse wildflowers.*

GETTING THERE

From Moses Lake, follow I-90 west to exit 151. (From Ellensburg, follow I-90 east to exit 149). Then head north on State Route 281 for 5 miles, turning left onto White Trail Road (Rd 5 NW). Continue 7.8 miles, turning left onto Rd 9 NW. (From Wenatchee, follow SR 28 east for 26 miles to White Trail Road, 0.7 mile beyond the rest area. Then proceed south 1 mile, turning right onto Rd 9 NW.) After 2.2 miles, the pavement ends and the road becomes Ancient Lakes Road. Continue 3.7 miles to the road's end and trailhead (elev. 1000 ft). Privy available.

ON THE TRAIL

Start on an old jeep track long closed to vehicles and head south through open country along the Babcock Bench, which rises several hundred feet above the Columbia River. The wide track is perfect for those skittish about hiking in snake country. Winter is best for totally avoiding these necessary components of this ecosystem as well as for escaping the stifling heat of summer.

Meander beneath a mesa, across sage flats, and along wetlands of cattails and willows. The wetlands as well as the lakes were an unintended consequence of irrigation projects begun in the 1940s in the Columbia Basin. Seepage from canals created these oases, which have since become wildlife havens.

At 0.4 mile, pass a not-so-obvious trail leading left for the Ancient Lakes. The main (preferred) way (elev. 940 ft) to the lakes is reached at 0.6 mile. Turn left here,

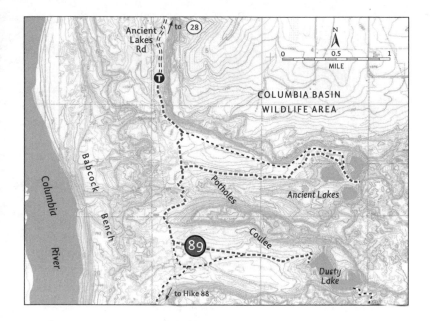

following a secondary jeep track into the well-vegetated Potholes Coulee. The way descends about 40 feet and then regains it, climbing a small knoll that overlooks the first of the three Ancient Lakes.

Then follow a boot-beaten path down off the knoll to a small grassy rise (elev. 830 ft) between the lakes. The path ends at 2.2 miles at the base (elev. 860 ft) of the coulee wall, where there are some good views overlooking two of the lakes and a waterfall crashing from above the coulee rim. Roam at will, letting western meadowlarks serenade you.

For Dusty Lake, which attracts fewer visitors because of its longer approach and harsher setting, bypass the Ancient Lakes turnoff and continue straight. Ignoring side tracks, round a ridge (elev. 990 ft) that separates the coulees housing Dusty and

the Ancient Lakes, and take in good views west of Whiskey Dick's wind farm and the Colockum country. Then descend and cross beneath some high-tension power lines (ubiquitous in the Columbia Basin). And at 1.5 miles, near a power-line tower, come to a junction (elev. 900 ft).

Bear left, following a good track into Potholes Coulee, slowly climbing its broad sage-filled bottom (elev. 950 ft) before descending to Dusty Lake (elev. 850 ft) at 3 miles. The lake is set beneath talus slopes and stark canyon walls. Listen to water crashing from the rim, to wind whistling across the coulee bottom, to the birds and insects of the sagebrush-steppe. Good campsites (often occupied on weekend nights) invite you to hang around and listen to coyotes' and owls' calls all night.

Dusty Lake lies beneath stark basalt walls.

EXTENDING YOUR TRIP

A short but highly scenic trail starts from the coulee rim and drops into the canyon, passing several small ponds on its way to the east shore of Dusty Lake. Trail access is from the U road that traverses the Quincy Lakes Unit of the Columbia Basin Wildlife Area. Due to repeated vandalism, the road may be closed, but it's open to foot traffic.

90 Beezley Hills

RATING/ DIFFICULTY	ROUND-TRIP	ELEV GAIN/ HIGH POINT	SEASON
**/2	2.2 miles	250 feet/ 2800 feet	Mar–Nov

Maps: USGS Monument Hills, USGS Ephrata SW; **Contact:** Washington Nature Conservancy, (206) 343-4345, www.nature.org /washington; **GPS:** N 47 19.109 W 119 47.982

The Beezley Hills stretch from the Columbia River to Ephrata and consist of some of the finest and wildest sagebrush-steppe habitat remaining in the state. Named after an early rancher, the hills are dotted with springs that provide exceptional breeding and foraging grounds for a wide array of species, including pygmy rabbits, badgers, sage grouse, and prairie falcons. The Nature Conservancy began establishing a preserve here in the late 1990s, and it now totals more than 30,000 acres. The preserve also harbors rare plants, including sulphur lupine, which sports white blossoms. The pink-blossomed hedgehog cactus grows in profusion. Listen for bluebird song in the windswept, sage-scented slopes. Watch the sun rise above the channeled Columbia Plateau, or watch it set behind a frosty wall of Cascade peaks.

GETTING THERE

From Moses Lake, follow I-90 west to exit 151. (From Ellensburg, follow I-90 east to exit 149.) Then head north on State Route 281 for 10 miles to its junction with SR 28 in Quincy. Turn right (east) on SR 28 (F Street SE), continuing 0.8 mile. Just before reaching West Canal, turn left onto Columbia Way (which becomes P Street) and continue north. At 3.1 miles, the pavement ends and the road becomes Monument Hill Road. Follow this good gravel road for 4.1 miles to the

trailhead (elev. 2800 ft), located near a spur road to communication towers. Park on the road shoulder.

ON THE TRAIL

Pass through a stile and follow an old jeep track through wide-open country. A fainter set of tracks diverge left—it meets back up with the main track after 0.25 mile. Soak up the sun and breezes and admire the farmed plains to the south, Moses Lake to the east, and lofty Mission Ridge to the west. In spring

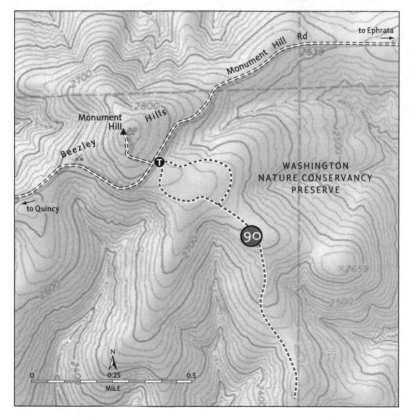

This Nature Conservancy Preserve is renowned for its hedgehog cacti.

the way is muddy, with fresh imprints from passing critters. By later in the summer the ground is hard and cracked.

The way bends southeast and slowly descends. Early in the season the hills can appear drab. But come here in April and May and be treated to a dazzling floral display. Balsamroot, buckwheat, bitterroot, bluebells, lupine, phlox, desert parsley, larkspur, prairie starflower, and others brighten the landscape. Start looking for hedgehog cacti as you approach a flat after a short little drop. They appear as spiny little barrels perched among lichen-covered rocks.

At about 1.1 miles, the old jeep track reaches a small knoll (elev. 2550 ft) and then peters out. Return the way you came.

EXTENDING YOUR TRIP

It's possible to continue exploring by following game trails, but be sure to walk softly on the land, and don't leave the preserve and stray onto abutting private property. In nearby Ephrata you can hike through the eastern extent of the Beezley Hills on a series of service roads and trails. Access is from Cyrus Road (reached from 1st Avenue near the canal). Trails are numerous and unmarked, but city officials hope to eventually develop the area into a major park. Also consider exploring the Moses Coulee section of the Nature Conservancy Preserve. Dutch Henry Falls near Jameson Lake (accessed from Jameson Lake Road off of US Highway 2) offers some nice roaming on quiet trails through spectacular canyon country.

91 Steamboat Rock

RATING/ DIFFICULTY	ROUND-TRIP	ELEV GAIN/ HIGH POINT	SEASON
****/2	3.2 miles	760 feet/ 2300 feet	Year-round

Maps: USGS Steamboat Rock SW, USGS Steamboat Rock SE, state park map online (not accurate); **Contact:** Steamboat Rock State Park, (509) 663-1304, www.parks .wa.gov/parks; **Notes:** Discover Pass required. Dogs permitted on-leash. Watch for rattlesnakes; **GPS:** N 47 51.837 W 119 07.305

 *Stand upon this massive basaltic butte within the Grand Coulee and try to visualize the floods of biblical proportions that carved out the Channeled Scablands of the Columbia Plateau. Marvel at the man-made lake now flooding the surrounding canyon, and cherish the extraor-*

dinary beauty of this harsh but ecologi-
cally vibrant landscape. Roam Steamboat
Rock's rim, watching for deer, jackrabbits,
wrens, and swallows. And come in spring
when the rock is awash in a riot of
blossoms.

GETTING THERE

From Spokane, follow US Highway 2 west
to Wilbur and turn right (north) onto State
Route 21. After 0.25 mile, bear left onto SR
174 and follow it for 19 miles to its junction
with SR 155 in Grand Coulee. Turn left and

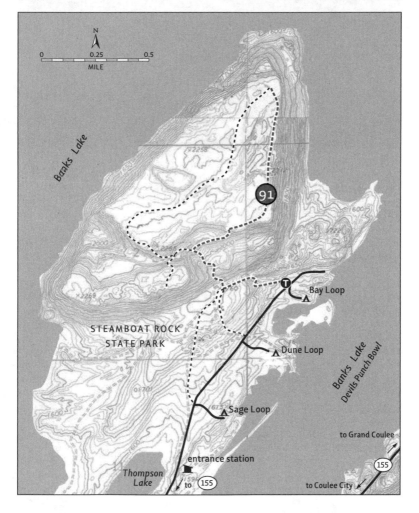

Dramatic views of Banks Lake from Steamboat Rock

follow SR 155 south for 10.1 miles, turning right onto the Steamboat Rock State Park entrance road. (From Wenatchee, follow SR 2 east to 2 miles beyond Coulee City, bearing left onto SR 155. Continue 15.6 miles north on SR 155, turning left onto the park entrance road.) Proceed 2 miles to park entrance gate. Continue another mile, passing campgrounds, to the day-use area and trailhead (elev. 1580 ft). Privy available.

ON THE TRAIL

Starting in open sagebrush-steppe that comes alive in April, particularly with lupine and balsamroot blossoms, hike toward the basaltic behemoth. The trail heads for a gap between the two "summits" of the mesa-like rock. Pass a draw harboring a few pines and trudge across some sandy tread before marching beneath the base of the hulking rock.

At 0.3 mile, come to a junction (elev. 1750 ft) at a couple of picnic tables set among five lonely ponderosa pines. The trail left leads to the Dune Loop Campground. The trail and service road straight lead to the Sage Loop Campground. You want to head right—straight up a steep scree slope to a small cleft in the wall of the rock. Watch your footing; you'll need the use of your hands in a few places. Admire Steamboat Rock's stark face as you clamber up this passage to its heights. Notice all the lichens growing on the basalt and adding blotches of green and orange to the gray.

The grade eases after 0.1 mile. Grasses and flowers and big glacial erratics line the way. At 0.6 mile on a shelf, high on the rock, reach a junction (elev. 2100 ft). Maps show either two loops or one giant loop circling the top of the rock. Don't believe them—it's more like one obscure loop and one out-and-back. But you really can't get lost on this 600-plus-acre rock, since steep drop-offs keep you from wandering too far!

The best explorations lie to the right

IN THE WAKE OF ICE AGE FLOODS

While not obvious at first glance, Eastern Washington is a geological wonder as awesome as the Grand Canyon, considering how the landscape was formed. The rimrock lakes, potholes, coulees, canyons, and dry waterfalls aren't the product of wind and raindrops over millennia. Rather, they were created by Ice Age floods that scoured the region 15,000–18,000 years ago. The floods rank as one of the earth's most significant geological events in the past two million years.

The Channeled Scablands, which begin just south of Spokane and spread over more than 3000 square miles, were created by torrents of biblical proportions. Waters burst from ice dams near Clark Fork, Idaho, and emptied Glacial Lake Missoula several times over a couple thousand years with unimaginable force. Scientists say the floodwaters raced over Steamboat Rock at 65 miles per hour—nearly ten times faster than any flood modern humans might see. The volume of water in one of these floods was roughly equivalent to ten times the combined flow of all the rivers of the world.

Evidence of the sudden, violent flooding is apparent throughout Eastern Washington, including lake-size potholes created by the mortar-and-pestle grinding of rocks in whirlpools; steep basalt cliffs bordering wide, flat channels; megaripples and thousands of foreign granite boulders that floods carried from hundreds of miles away and deposited in unlikely places, such as a current wheat field.

Congress has created an Ice Age Floods National Geologic Trail that someday may be enhanced by visitors centers, highway signage, printed materials, and maps to guide tourists from one point of interest to another. Check out the enlightening guidebook, *Washington's Channeled Scablands Guide*, by John Soennichsen (Mountaineers Books, 2012), and the Cheney-Spokane Chapter of the Ice Age Floods Institute, with its active programs and field trips (www.iceagefloodsewa.org).

Meanwhile, about two dozen of the hikes in this book put walkers on the path of the Ice Age floods, no life jacket required.

—R. L.

along a well-defined path, so follow it. After a short, steep climb, crest the grassy plateau (elev. 2270 ft). Now walk along the rim (use caution), watching swallows skim the sky. Admire Northrup Canyon directly east and Banks Lake, which nearly surrounds you. Nature made the coulee thanks to great Ice Age floods (see "In the Wake of Ice Age Floods" sidebar). But man made the nearly 30-mile-long lake, part of the massive Columbia Basin Project. Water from the Columbia River is pumped into the Grand Coulee and stored for irrigation for nearly 700,000 acres across the Columbia Plateau. It is the largest water-reclamation project in the country and it has brought great changes, both positive and negative, to the basin. Steamboat Rock, once an island in the Columbia River (when it flowed through the Grand Coulee), is once again surrounded (almost) by water.

At 1.4 miles, reach one of the rock's high

points (elev. 2300 ft) and admire sweeping views north to the Columbia River cut (but the river isn't visible), Moses Mountain, and the Kettle River Range. West lie the North Cascades' serrated silhouette.

At 1.6 miles, good tread ends at the north tip of the plateau (elev. 2260 ft). Retrace your steps or consider the loop option described below.

EXTENDING YOUR TRIP

A faint path leads south from where the good tread ends on the rock's northern tip. Follow it along a shelf across ledge and by erratics, coming to a junction in 0.5 mile. The way left leads back to the main trail in 0.25 mile. The way right travels for about 0.8 mile to return to the junction with the trail coming up from below. About 0.1 mile before that junction is a well-defined trail that climbs right 0.2 mile to a huge erratic and great viewpoint south down the Grand Coulee. You can continue 0.6 mile beyond to the southern tip of the rock on very faint (if any) tread, where a colony of marmots may greet you.

92 Northrup Canyon

RATING/ DIFFICULTY	ROUND-TRIP	ELEV GAIN/ HIGH POINT	SEASON
***/2	6.2 miles	685 feet/ 2260 feet	Year-round

Maps: USGS Steamboat Rock SE, USGS Electric City, state park map online (not accurate); **Contact:** Steamboat Rock State Park, (509) 663-1304, www.parks.wa.gov /parks; **Notes:** Discover Pass required. Partly wheelchair-accessible. Dogs permitted on-leash. Watch for rattlesnakes. Old Wagon Road Trail closed Nov 15–Mar 15 to protect

wintering eagles; **GPS:** N 47 51.960 W 119 04.950

 *An old home-stead, fish-hopping lake, pine and aspen groves, and a few other surprises make this dramatic subcanyon of the Grand Coulee a delight to hike. But not in summer, when temperatures soar and rattlesnakes abound. Come in spring for the blossoms, fall for golden aspens, or winter for a profusion of bald eagles.*

GETTING THERE

From Spokane, follow US Highway 2 west to Wilbur, turning right (north) onto State Route 21. After 0.25 mile, bear left onto SR 174 and drive 19 miles to its junction with SR 155 in Grand Coulee. Turn left and follow SR 155 south for 6.8 miles, turning left onto Northrup Canyon Road. (From Wenatchee, follow SR 2 east to 2 miles beyond Coulee City, bearing left onto SR 155. Continue 18.9 miles north on SR 155, turning right onto Northrup Canyon Road.) Proceed 0.6 mile to the trailhead (elev. 1800 ft). Privy available.

ON THE TRAIL

Added to Steamboat Rock State Park in the 1970s, Northrup Canyon contains a small lake, a reliably flowing stream, and one of the few forested areas within the Columbia Plateau. Perhaps the canyon's most notable feature is that it's one of the most important roosts in Eastern Washington for wintering bald eagles. From late fall to early spring, up to two hundred of them spend the night in the canyon's tall pines and firs after fishing in the nearby Columbia River and Banks Lake.

Before heading up the gated road, check out the kiosk with information on

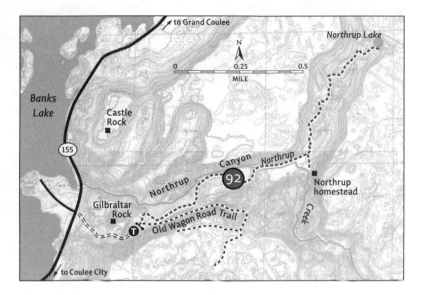

the Northrup family who homesteaded in the canyon. Then start hiking. Just after the gate, a short path diverges left to a spot used for winter eagle observation. Shortly after that, the Old Wagon Road Trail leaves right and makes an excellent side trip. Consider coming back again if you don't have time or energy for it on this trip.

Continue on the old road left, through open sage with good views up the canyon. The way then bends right and descends 50 feet, passing an old dump site from the Coulee Dam construction days. Soon pass beneath a cool canopy of ponderosa pine and Douglas-fir. Stands of aspen light up with the canyon with brilliant yellows come October.

Follow the road along the base of the north canyon walls, undulating between forest groves and sagebrush-steppe. After a short climb, skirt a grassy wetland, and

then climb again to cross Northrup Creek on a plank bridge. Continue upcanyon, across fertile flats, reaching the old Northrup homestead (elev. 1870 ft) at 1.8 miles. Snoop around the former park residence and older homestead buildings before heading to Northrup Lake.

Locate the lake trail taking off left from the old chicken coop. Now traversing much rougher terrain, wind up a thinly forested tight draw, going up and over and around ledges and boulders. Sections are like a labyrinth that should intrigue young explorers.

At 2.1 miles, crest a small rise (elev. 2100 ft) before descending to a wetland (elev. 2025 ft) ringed with cattails. Pass more wetland pools, and after traversing a grassy flat begin a rather steep climb up ledges that showcase pretty blossoms in spring. At 2.8 miles, crest a pine-shrouded ridge (elev. 2260 ft) within the canyon walls. Then descend,

Ruins of the original Northrup homestead

passing through grassy flats before coming to Northrup Lake (elev. 2160 ft) at 3.1 miles.

Set in a basaltic bowl lined with scree, reeds, dogwoods, and pines, the lake is scenic and serene. Grab some lunch and watch fish jump while listening to blackbird song.

EXTENDING YOUR TRIP

From the lake, a rough path continues above it if you're inclined to go farther. From the homestead, a primitive path continues along Northrup Creek, but it can be tricky to find and follow. Instead, hike the Old Wagon Road Trail (note seasonal closures), which served as a freight line for wagons between Almira and Bridgeport in the 1880s. The way traverses the south canyon wall, across scree slopes and ledges, and must have been quite a task to complete. At 0.9 mile, it leaves the canyon for a sage-covered draw, reaching the canyon rim and a junction (elev. 2275 ft)

at 1.1 miles, where the old wagon route continues left, leaving state park property. Follow the lightly used path straight for 0.4 mile to a 2325-foot overlook and breathtaking view on the canyon rim (use caution). In spring, the canyon rim bursts with bitterroot and other blossoms.

93 Fort Spokane

RATING/ DIFFICULTY	LOOP	ELEV GAIN/ HIGH POINT	SEASON
***/1	2.5 miles	260 feet/ 1660 feet	Mar–Dec

Map: USGS Fort Spokane; **Contact:** Lake Roosevelt National Recreation Area, (509) 633-9441, www.nps.gov/laro; **Notes:** Visitors center usually open mid-June–Labor Day. Partly wheelchair-accessible. Dogs permitted on-leash; **GPS:** N 47 54.184 W 118 18.529

Wander through the grounds of one of the last frontier forts built in the West. Pause at interpretive plaques, peek into restored buildings, and peer out over a bunchgrass bench above the Columbia River. Then climb to a bluff above the fort to survey the surroundings. Aside from excellent views of the 1880 fort grounds, admire the landscape here at the confluence of the Columbia and Spokane Rivers, where sagebrush-steppe transitions into ponderosa pine forest.

GETTING THERE

From Spokane, follow US Highway 2 west for 35 miles to Davenport. (From Wenatchee, follow US 2 east for 125 miles to Davenport.) Then head north on State Route 25 for 22.4 miles, turning left into Fort Spokane. Continue 0.3 mile to the parking lot and trailhead (elev. 1400 ft). Privy available.

ON THE TRAIL

Part history walk and part nature walk, this hike incorporates two of the three trails traversing the grounds of Fort Spokane. Located within the Lake Roosevelt National Recreation Area, a 129-mile long corridor along the Columbia River from the Grand Coulee Dam to Onion Creek just south of Northport on the Canadian border, the fort is one of several historic sites within this national park unit. Established in 1946 after the flooding of the river by the Grand Coulee Dam, Lake Roosevelt is a very different environment than the free-flowing river that was here in 1880 when the US Army began construction of Fort Spokane.

Strategically built at the confluence of the Spokane and Columbia Rivers, the infantry and cavalry stationed here were in charge of keeping the peace between the seminomadic Spokane and Colville Tribes, who had been relegated to reservations,

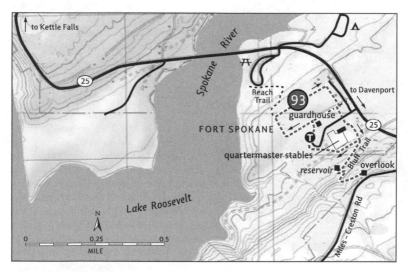

and land-seeking settlers encroaching upon Native lands. But the Fort saw no skirmishes. In 1898 most of the fort's troops deployed for combat in the Spanish-American War, and the fort was soon decommissioned and transferred to the Bureau of Indian Affairs. After serving as a boarding school, tuberculosis sanatorium, and hospital, the fort was closed in 1929. Grab the excellent free booklet at the trailhead to get the most out of your trip around the fort.

The recommended route begins on the wide, well-groomed, and perfectly flat Sen-

A lone pine stands watch over Fort Spokane.

tinel Trail and follows the interpretive posts (there are plenty of options for shortening or lengthening this hike). At 0.1 mile, reach the guardhouse (a visitors center in the summer). Turn left and walk the periphery of the fort grounds. The Park Service has replanted the grounds with native plants and grasses. Admire flowers in late spring and early summer and enjoy the sweet melodies of various breeding birds.

At 0.3 mile, near the Bachelor Officers Quarters, the Beach Trail descends 100 feet off the bluff, coming to a beach on the river at 0.4 mile. The Sentinel Trail continues straight, passing the officers' row and parade grounds. At 0.75 mile, cross the park road and continue walking through the fort grounds to the quartermaster stables and the powder magazine.

At 1.1 miles, in a ponderosa pine grove that once fed the fort sawmill, come to the junction with the Bluff Trail. Turn left on it and enjoy hiking through one of the few forests in Lincoln County. Savor the cooler air trapped within the pine groves. After skirting a scree slope. come to the old reservoir and pump house at 1.3 miles.

The trail resumes beyond the pump house, climbing steeply (but paved and utilizing some staircases) up a scree slope before resuming natural tread upon cresting the bluff. The way then turns eastward through pines and flower gardens, reaching a wonderful viewpoint at 1.6 miles at its terminus (elev. 1660 ft). Try to imagine what the fort looked like in its heyday in the 1890s, when forty-five buildings once stood on the grounds.

Retrace your steps back to the beginning of the Bluff Trail and finish the Sentinel Trail loop by walking past the stables and orchard, returning to your vehicle at 2.5 miles.

EXTENDING YOUR TRIP
Add another 0.8 mile by heading down the Beach Trail and back. Enjoy big pines and look for roosting eagles and osprey.

94 Crab Creek(Columbia National Wildlife Refuge)

RATING/ DIFFICULTY	ROUND-TRIP	ELEV GAIN/ HIGH POINT	SEASON
**/1	2.6 miles	40 feet/ 870 feet	Year-round

Maps: USGS Corfu, USGS Soda Lake; **Contact:** Columbia National Wildlife Refuge, (509) 546-8300, www.fws.gov/colum bla; **Notes:** Dogs permitted on-leash; **GPS:** N 17 46 57.009 W 119 15.286

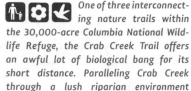 *One of three interconnecting nature trails within the 30,000-acre Columbia National Wildlife Refuge, the Crab Creek Trail offers an awful lot of biological bang for its short distance. Paralleling Crab Creek through a lush riparian environment within a sagebrush-steppe coulee, enjoy the contrasts—and birds. This is one of the best bird-watching hikes on the Columbia Plateau—and one of the easiest to hike, with its near-level course.*

GETTING THERE
From Spokane, take I-90 west to exit 179 in Moses Lake. Head south on State Route 17 for 2 miles, turning right onto Road M SE. Follow it for 6.4 miles, turning right onto

Crab Creek provides excellent habitat for birds and amphibians.

SR 262. Continue west for 2.4 miles, turning left (directly across from a large boat launch and just before reaching the O'Sullivan Dam), into the Columbia National Wildlife Refuge. (From Ellensburg, take I-90 east to exit 137. Then follow SR 26 for 25 miles east, turning left onto SR 262. Proceed 17.7 miles to the refuge road.) Follow this gravel road

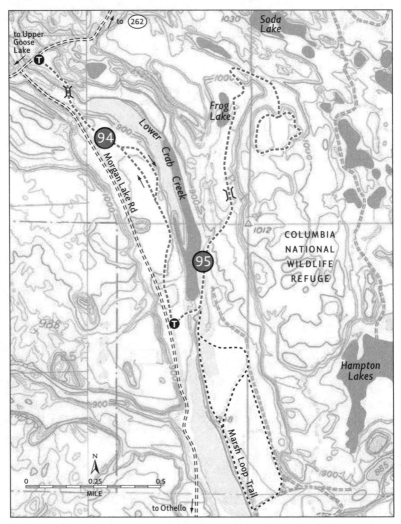

south, passing a spur to Soda Lake Campground, and come to a junction at 2.2 miles. Turn right and bear left in 0.2 mile, reaching the trailhead (elev. 860 ft) on your left in another 0.4 mile (2.8 miles from SR 262), just before a junction with Morgan Lake Road.

ON THE TRAIL

The Columbia National Wildlife Refuge is a land of imposing basaltic coulees within the heart of the Columbia Plateau. Despite receiving less than 8 inches of rain a year, the refuge is littered with lakes and marshes thanks to seepage from surrounding reclamation and irrigation projects. Its canyons, lakes, wetlands, and sagebrush-steppe environment provide important habitat for a wide array of species. Located along the Pacific Flyway, the refuge is a stop over and wintering ground for many migratory birds, including thousands of lesser sandhill cranes. Visit in fall and spring for the best bird-watching. Most of the refuge is within the Drumheller Channels, a national natural landmark within the Channeled Scablands, which were formed by ancient cataclysmic floods. Both nature and humans have left a large imprint here, benefiting scores of avian residents.

Head south on the wide and well-groomed trail, soon coming to a kiosk. Then cross Crab Creek (elev. 850 ft) on a bridge and scan the shorelines cloaked in reeds and cattails for songbirds and waterfowl. Crab Creek used to be an ephemeral stream, but thanks to constant seepage, it runs yearlong. Take time to read the interpretive signs along the way.

At 0.4 mile, the trail splits. Go left—you'll be returning right. Follow the rose-lined path along the creek. Depending on time of year, a small waterfall may be flowing

into the creek from the canyon wall to the east. At 0.6 mile, come to another junction. Right leads back to the trailhead—head left first, through thick riparian vegetation lining the bottom of the coulee. Mosquitoes can be fierce here in spring and early summer. While you're swatting at them, remember that they feed all of those birds and amphibians in the refuge.

At 0.9 mile, the trail climbs some steps to travel along a sage-shrouded bench (elev. 870 ft) above the creek bottom. Enjoy good views of the coulee and Marsh Lake to the south. At 1.3 miles, reach the trailhead (elev. 860 ft) for the Frog and Marsh Lake Trails (Hike 95). Continue farther or return to your trailhead and save these great trails for another visit.

95 Frog Lake

RATING/ DIFFICULTY	ROUND-TRIP	ELEV GAIN/ HIGH POINT	SEASON
***/2	3 miles	235 feet/ 1055 feet	Year-round

Maps: USGS Corfu, USGS Soda Lake; **Contact:** Columbia National Wildlife Refuge, (509) 546-8300, www.fws.gov/columbia; **Notes:** Dogs permitted on-leash; **GPS:** N 46 56.207 W 119 14.667

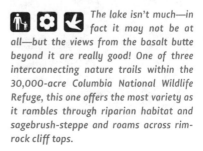 *The lake isn't much—in fact it may not be at all—but the views from the basalt butte beyond it are really good! One of three interconnecting nature trails within the 30,000-acre Columbia National Wildlife Refuge, this one offers the most variety as it rambles through riparian habitat and sagebrush-steppe and roams across rimrock cliff tops.*

GETTING THERE

From Spokane, take I-90 west to exit 179 in Moses Lake. Head south on State Route 17 for 2 miles, turning right onto Road M SE. Follow it for 6.4 miles, turning right onto SR 262. Continue west for 2.4 miles, turning left (directly across from large boat launch and just before reaching the O'Sullivan Dam), into the Columbia National Wildlife Refuge. (From Ellensburg, take I-90 east to exit 137. Then follow SR 26 for 25 miles east, turning left onto SR 262. Proceed 17.7 miles to the refuge road.) Follow this gravel road south, passing a spur to Soda Lake Campground, and come to a junction at 2.2 miles. Turn right and bear left in 0.2 mile. Pass the Crab Creek trailhead in another 0.4 mile, and come to a junction with Morgan Lake Road shortly

Co-author Craig Romano checks out the basalt butte above Frog Lake.

afterward. Turn left and reach the trailhead (elev. 860 ft) in another mile (3.9 miles from SR 262).

ON THE TRAIL

From the trailhead kiosk two trails diverge. The trail left heads north along Crab Creek (Hike 94). The trail straight drops off the small bench you're on, leading to the Frog Lake and Marsh Loop Trails. Go straight and walk across an earthen dam (elev. 840 ft), one of several responsible for the nearby large wetland ponds teeming with birdlife. The refuge is a bird lover's delight. Between its diverse habitats and being located along the Pacific Flyway, more than 225 species of birds have been recorded on the refuge, including burrowing owls, prairie falcons, and ferruginous hawks. But the refuge's most famous avian resident is its migratory lesser sandhill cranes. Arriving in March and flying in large flocks resembling phalanxes of pterodactyls (and sounding like them), they are spectacular to watch.

After a little more than 0.1 mile, come to a junction. The Marsh Loop Trail (an excellent add-on to this hike) heads right. Hop along left on the Frog Lake Trail. After a short walk along a pond dike, the trail heads into the sagebrush-steppe and begins to climb. Be sure to read the interpretive displays along the way. Notice all the canine scat in the tread. Coyotes are abundant here. Other mammals too—look for yellow-bellied marmots and, if you're lucky, Washington ground squirrels, a threatened species.

Cross a bridge over a draw and continue climbing, enjoying nice views of the Crab Creek drainage. At 0.7 mile, reach Frog Lake (elev. 920 ft) in a small basin, which will more than likely be dry. Not exactly an amphibian's delight. Follow the trail up a small cleft in the basalt wall behind the lake. The way then bends right, following along basalt cliffs before climbing once again to reach a junction at 1.2 miles.

Here a trail loops 0.6 mile around the 1055-foot mesa. Go either way. The views are wonderful in every direction. Look out over the Drumheller Channels surrounding you. A significant part of the Channeled Scablands, these basalt buttes and canyons were scoured by ancient giant floods. In the 1940s significant change occurred again as the US Bureau of Reclamation's Columbia Basin Project inadvertently created hundreds of lakes and wetlands within the channels, through seepage.

As you walk along the mesa rim counting lakes below, watch for raptors, swallows, and other birds that make their homes in the cliffs. Close the loop and return to your vehicle once you're content with your nature observations.

EXTENDING YOUR TRIP

By all means hike the Marsh Loop Trail while you're here. The trail—actually a wide service road—loops 1.8 miles (with a shortcut option) around large wetland ponds that harbor hundreds of waterfowl and other birds. There are nice interpretive displays along the way too.

96 Hanford Reach North

RATING/ DIFFICULTY	ROUND-TRIP	ELEV GAIN/ HIGH POINT	SEASON
*****/3	7 miles	500 feet/ 725 feet	Year-round

Map: USGS Locke Island; **Contact:** Hanford Reach National Monument, Mid-Columbia River National Wildlife Recreation Com-plex, (509) 546-8300, www.fws.gov/hanford reach; **Note:** Watch for rattlesnakes; **GPS:** N 46 40.630 W 119 26.673

Towering white bluffs, massive sand dunes, pelican colonies, brilliant wildflowers, and the last free-flowing nontidal section of the Columbia River all help make the Hanford Reach one of the most dramatic natural areas in the state. Follow a rudimentary trail across bluff tops and to shifting dunes. Survey a wild riverbank and a restricted area across the Columbia, where the atomic age was born.

GETTING THERE

From Spokane, follow I-90 west to Ritzville. Continue 30 miles south on US Highway 395 to its junction with State Route 26. Follow SR 26 west for 21 miles to its junction with SR 24 in Othello. Continue west on SR 24 for 16 miles, turning left onto an unmarked gravel road just before milepost 63. (From Ellensburg, follow I-90 east to exit 137, heading south on SR 26 for one mile. Bear right onto SR 243 and after 14 miles turn left onto the 24SW Road. Follow it for 13.7 miles to SR 24, first passing through Mattawa. Turn left and continue 10 miles east to the turnoff right, just past milepost 63.) Pass through a solar-powered gate (closed at night), following a good gravel road 3.9 miles south to a four-way junction. Turn right and continue 1.3 miles to the trailhead (elev. 400 ft) located on the right (before the boat launch at the old ferry crossing), near a locust grove.

ON THE TRAIL

Since the Hanford Reach became a national monument in 2000 (see "From Manhattan

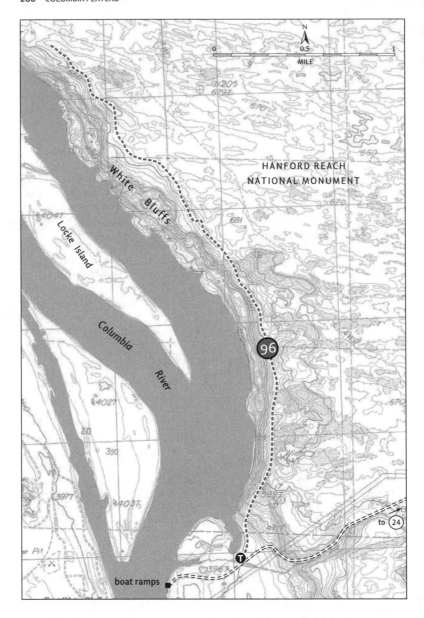

N
0   0.5   1
MILE

HANFORD REACH
NATIONAL MONUMENT

White Bluffs

Locke Island

Columbia River

96

to 24

boat ramps

FROM MANHATTAN PROJECT TO NATIONAL MONUMENT

In 1943, in the midst of World War II, the US government launched the Manhattan Project, which would forever change the course of history with the birth of the atomic bomb—and forever change the landscape of the lower Columbia River basin. To facilitate the processing of plutonium, a large remote area was needed, with an ample nearby power source. The federal government chose the Hanford Site, an area of more than 428,000 acres mostly in Benton County. Two communities—Hanford and White Bluffs—were condemned, and the little town of Richland was transformed into a government city of 25,000.

Operations at Hanford were expanded during the Cold War to ultimately include nine nuclear reactors and five plutonium-processing complexes responsible for supplying the US nuclear weapons arsenal. As the Cold War dissipated, Hanford's weapons-production reactors were decommissioned, leaving behind significant amounts of radioactive waste and contaminated groundwater. Today the site is one of the nation's largest Superfund cleanup areas. The site still hosts one nuclear power plant as well as numerous scientific research and development labs.

Ironically, this massive government project with its large buffer zones ended up preserving large tracts of natural habitat—some of the last significant undeveloped sections of the Columbia Plateau's sagebrush-steppe ecosystem. In 2000, President Clinton invoked the Antiquities Act of 1906 (which President Teddy Roosevelt used to protect the Grand Canyon and other major natural sites) and proclaimed 195,000 acres of the buffer zone around the Hanford Site as a national monument.

As well as containing rare plants, endemic species, elk herds, and more than 250 species of birds, the monument also contains a 51-mile free-flowing stretch of the Columbia River. The monument is managed by the US Fish and Wildlife Service, and 57,000 acres of it are open to the public. In 2011, Congressman Doc Hastings began procedures to open to the public the section of the monument housing Rattlesnake Mountain. While this could potentially create new hiking opportunities, it may also open the mountain to ORV use, threatening the integrity of this important and shrinking ecosystem.

—C. R.

Project to National Monument" sidebar), more and more hikers are discovering that what they thought would be a desolate part of the state is actually thriving with fauna and flora. Thanks to being withdrawn from the public for decades and remaining in a relatively natural state, the Hanford Reach represents one of the last large undeveloped and uncultivated parts of the Columbia Plateau. One of the driest

parts of the state (annual rainfall averages 7 inches), the Hanford Reach is a harsh but fragile environment. Tread softly. And be sure you're well prepared with ample water and sun protection.

The unsigned and unofficial trail starts by a post near a grove of locust trees. At first grassy, then more defined, the path heads up an open slope that dazzles with flowers in spring. The impressive White

A hiker enjoys a Sahara-like hike across the sand dunes of the Hanford Reach.

Bluffs immediately come into view. So does the Columbia River. Watch for white pelicans below and swallows along the bluffs. At about 0.5 mile, stay on a path right, staying clear of the steep and prone-to-erosion bluff face. The path can be sketchy, vanishing at times in dunes. Just work your way up and down along the bluff tops, staying away from cliff edges.

Enjoy excellent views of Locke Island below, Rattlesnake Mountain west, and Saddle Mountain north. At about 2 miles, reach impressive dunes that may make you feel like you're in the Sahara. Walk across the dunes, continuing north. While always shifting, some of the higher dunes form pyramidal "summits," topping out at elevations of more than 725 feet.

From these vantages more than 300 feet above the river, you have commanding views of the shoreline below the bluffs. Scan it and the wetland pockets between the dunes for deer, coyotes, jackrabbits, and mice—there are three species of the latter: deer, western harvest, and the northern grasshopper mouse.

At 3.5 miles, the dunes end. While you can continue hiking another mile farther north, paths are practically nonexistent and brush can be thick. Best to return to the trailhead instead, slowly sauntering back across this dramatic landscape.

97 Hanford Reach South

RATING/ DIFFICULTY	ROUND-TRIP	ELEV GAIN/ HIGH POINT	SEASON
****/3	5.4 miles	700 feet/ 880 feet	Year-round

Maps: USGS Locke Island, USGS Hanford; **Contact:** Hanford Reach National Monument, Mid-Columbia River National Wildlife Recreation Complex, (509) 546-8300, www .fws.gov/hanfordreach; **Notes:** Watch for rattlesnakes; **GPS:** N 46 37.9710 W 119 23.729

 *Follow an abandoned highway down to the last free-flowing section of the Columbia River. Listen to birdsong and to cottonwood leaves bristling in warm afternoon breezes—and to the heavy machinery across the river that's cleaning up the contaminated remains of the world's first plutonium production reactor. Then explore the canyons and fluted ridges of the White Bluffs, a dramatic badlands of sandstone that gives off a muted glow in the hot sun and in spring comes to life in a dazzling carpet of wildflowers.*

GETTING THERE

From Spokane, follow I-90 west to Ritzville. Continue 30 miles south on US Highway 395 to its junction with State Route 26. Follow SR 26 west for 21 miles to its junction with SR 24 in Othello. Continue west on SR 24 for 16 miles, turning left onto an unmarked gravel road just before milepost 63. (From Ellensburg, follow I-90 east to exit 137, heading south on SR 26 for one mile. Bear right onto SR 243 and after 14 miles turn left onto the 24SW Road. Follow it for 13.7 miles to SR 24, first passing through Mattawa. Turn left and continue 10 miles east to the turnoff right, just past milepost 63.) Pass through a solar-powered gate (closed at night), following a good gravel road 3.9 miles south to a four-way junction. Continue straight for another 4 miles to road's end and trailhead (elev. 880 ft) at an overlook.

ON THE TRAIL

Pass a gate and follow an old paved road south. The road was closed when the US government, during World War II, chose the surrounding area to host a massive plutonium-processing complex and several nuclear reactors. The towns of Hanford and White Bluffs were condemned and evacuated. All that remains of them are a schoolhouse and several roads and sidewalks. As you saunter down this road, try to imagine what life was like for those two rural communities on the Reach in 1942—and how quickly life changed when the Manhattan Project went into effect in 1943 (see "From Manhattan Project to National Monument" sidebar).

In 2000, land use on the Reach changed again when President Clinton declared 195,000 acres of the buffer zone around the Hanford site a national monument, permanently protecting the last free-flowing nontidal stretch of the Columbia and some of the last large undisturbed tracts of sagebrush-steppe in the state. The Reach is a harsh but delicate environment; walk softly and be sufficiently prepared for extreme weather. Fall and spring can be delightful times to explore the area.

Follow the old road downward, taking in excellent views of the White Bluffs and subsidiary bluffs and dunes. Look for white pelicans on the river's islands. Look out across the flats housing the Hanford complex and west to Rattlesnake Mountain (also within the monument and currently closed to public entry) and north to Saddle Mountain (within the monument and open to the public). On clear days you can see Mount Rainier hovering in the distance. Heat can be intense here—so too the winds. Notice the old guard railings being swallowed by sand.

At 1 mile, just beyond a gully to the left and guardrail to the right, and just before the road drops through a cut to the river, locate a faint trail (elev. 590 ft) heading left

across a grassy flat. Take it, traversing a level bench. Round a gully and at 1.5 miles pass a spur trail leading to the right, to the road. Continue straight on a now-obvious trail along a ridgeline of sorts. To the right, enjoy sweeping views across the Columbia River; to the left, an isolated valley comes into view, backed by bigger and higher bluffs.

Crest a 625-foot high point and then drop a little before steeply climbing, reaching a 750-foot high point on the ridge with commanding views at 2.1 miles. Continue south another 0.3 mile, dropping into a small gap (elev. 650 ft) and reaching a junction. You can continue hiking along the ridge straight if you'd like. The suggested route is to head right 0.4 mile, descending off the bluff and returning to the road (elev. 400 ft).

When you reach the road, the way left shortly comes to a gate and is an alternative starting point near some transmission lines. Turn right instead to head back to your starting point. Here, at near river level, watch for cormorants fishing and terns diving for fish. Watch for raptors too.

The White Bluffs make for a striking backdrop against the Columbia River.

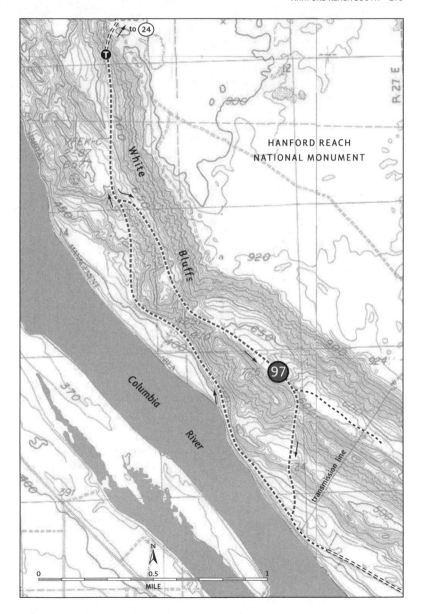

Enjoy a nice walk along the base of the bluffs. Notice the locust groves, remnants of the area's agricultural past before being transformed into an atomic energy center. Eventually you'll leave the riverbank and begin climbing again. At 4.4 miles, pass a familiar trail junction. From here it's 1 more mile and 300 feet of climbing back to your vehicle.

EXTENDING YOUR TRIP
You may want to wander (no formal trails) other parts of the national monument. Saddle Mountain and Wahluke Lake offer some decent exploring options.

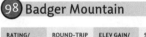 **Badger Mountain**

RATING/ DIFFICULTY	ROUND-TRIP	ELEV GAIN/ HIGH POINT	SEASON
*****/2	4.4 miles	675 feet/ 1550 feet	Year-round

Maps: USGS Badger Mountain, Friends of Badger Mountain map online; **Contact:** Friends of Badger Mountain, www.friendsof badger.org; **Notes:** Open to mountain bikes, horses. Dogs permitted on-leash; **GPS:** N 46 14.534 W 119 20.565

   *Marvel at horizon-spanning views, from the sun-baked Hanford Reach to snowy Cascades volcanoes, all from a windswept and wildflower-carpeted mountain at the edge of the Tri-Cities. One of the region's newest parks and trail systems, Badger Mountain is already a classic Washington hiking destination. Three trails ascend this landmark above the Columbia River, allowing for a satisfying loop or a stunning ridgeline traverse.*

GETTING THERE
From Pasco, follow I-182 west to I-82, proceeding east on I-82 to exit 104. (From Yakima, follow I-82 east to exit 104.) Turn left onto Dallas Road and drive 1.8 miles, turning right onto a dirt road. Be sure to follow the middle road of the three that diverge from this spot. Reach the Westgate trailhead (elev. 875 ft) in 0.1 mile. Privy available.

ON THE TRAIL
There are three ways to the summit. The Canyon Trail, which starts from a Richland city park on the mountain's northeastern slopes, is the most popular. The Skyline Trail from the east is another way up—and combined with the Sagebrush Trail makes a nice loop with the Canyon Trail. These ways are wonderful and well-hiked and are accessed right from the city of Richland. The approach described here is the preferred route for first-time Badger Mountain hikers and its access is much easier to find for out-of-towners.

Follow the wide and well-built Skyline Trail through sagebrush-steppe bordered by orchards. Badger Mountain stands as an oasis of natural habitat in an area rapidly being paved over and converted to agricultural uses. Alarmed citizens feared the loss of this locally prominent peak to development and in 2003 formed the Friends of Badger Mountain, which helped spearhead the creation of the 650-acre Badger Mountain Centennial Preserve. Conservationists and public officials continue to work on expanding the preserve as well as protecting adjacent peaks and ridges through the Ridges to River Open Space Network. There is great potential for an expanded trail system through their efforts.

On a good grade, wind up the mountain's

The Tri-Cities sprawl out below Badger Mountain.

western shoulder, crossing a service road after about 0.5 mile. Volunteers from the Friends of Badger Mountain, Washington Trails Association, and REI are responsible for constructing this multiuse, nonmotorized trail as well as the hiker-only Canyon Trail. At 0.8 mile, reach a marker denoting the maximum elevation of Lake Lewis (elev. 1250 ft) formed during the Missoula Floods 16,000 years ago (see "In the Wake of Ice Age Floods" sidebar).

While Badger appears barren from a distance, a walk on this mountain in spring reveals a different story. Wildflowers are profuse: lupine, vetch, balsamroot, phlox, larkspur, fleabane, bluebell, prairie star, hawksbeard, lomatium, and many more. And if you can lift your eyes from the ground, cast a glance or two outward to breathtaking

views of the Columbia River just below, all the way to Mounts Rainier, Adams, and Hood in the distance. The Horse Heaven Hills lie to the west, the Blue Mountains east, and Candy, Red, and Rattlesnake Mountains north.

Continue across an open slope of swaying grasses and sweet-scented sage. At 1.4 miles, once again cross a service road (elev. 1500 ft). Now traverse along the south face of the mountain, staying below a handful of communications towers and the peak's 1579-foot summit. At 2.1 miles, reach a junction (elev. 1530 ft) with the Canyon Trail. Turn left, continuing for 0.1 mile to a service road just below the summit tower (elev. 1550 ft). This is a good place to turn around (as the trail descends beyond), after absorbing a wonderful view of the Tri-Cities spread out below.

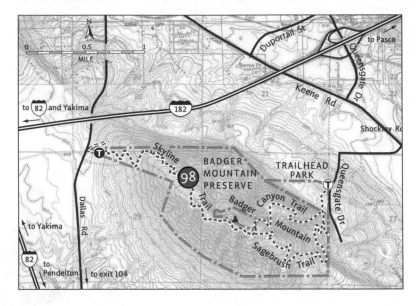

EXTENDING YOUR TRIP

From Richland's Trailhead Park (elev. 700 ft) at the mountain's eastern base, make a nice 3.3-mile loop by following the recently refurbished Canyon Trail west to the Skyline Trail, then to the Sagebrush Trail, and then back to Trailhead Park. Strong hikers can do all of the Badger Mountain trails in a day for a up-and-over-the-mountain-twice 7.7-mile lollipop loop.

99 Chamna Natural Preserve

RATING / DIFFICULTY	LOOP	ELEV GAIN/ HIGH POINT	SEASON
**/1	3.6 miles	none/ 360 feet	Year-round

Maps: USGS Richland, USGS Badger Mountain, Tapteal Greenway Association map online; **Contact:** Tapteal Greenway Association, (509) 637-3621, www.tapteal.org /pages/chamna.html; **Notes:** Dogs permitted on-leash. Watch for rattlesnakes; **GPS:** N 46 15.447 W 119 17.211

Wander on miles of trail through a rich riparian zone and wildlife haven right in the middle of the Tri-Cities. The Chamna Natural Preserve protects 276 acres at the confluence of the Yakima and Columbia Rivers. The preserve used to be overwhelmed by illegal dumping and dirt biking, but a coalition of concerned citizens started cleaning up the place in the late 1990s, transforming it into an inviting greenbelt where birds are prolific.

GETTING THERE

From Pasco, follow I-182 west to exit 5B. (From Yakima, follow I-82 east to I-182 east and exit 5B.) Exit onto George Washington Way, merging into the left lane and proceeding to the first set of traffic lights. Turn left onto Adams Street, and then immediately turn left onto Aaron Drive. Continue 0.6 mile on Aaron Drive, turning left onto Jadwin Avenue. Proceed 0.2 mile, crossing the interstate and coming to a junction with Carrier Road. Turn right and continue 0.5 mile (follow signs for Chamna Natural Preserve) to the trailhead (elev. 360 ft). Privy available.

ON THE TRAIL

One of several preserves and parks spearheaded by the Tapteal Greenway Association, Chamna is an important link in an emerging 30-mile greenbelt along the Yakima River from Bateman Island, at the confluence of the river with the Columbia, to the Kiona Bend in Benton City. Tapteal is the original name of the Yakima River.

The Tapteal Greenway Association is busy working with government officials and private citizens to create this greenbelt, not only for environmental protection, but also to provide recreational opportunities. The master plan includes a long-distance interconnected trail system. But no need to wait, for there are currently miles of trails in place. The Chamna Natural Preserve alone boasts more than 11 miles of nonmotorized trails.

The trail system is well marked. Hike as long and as much as you'd like, from a quick lunch-break stroll to an all-day, leave-no-tread-untouched expedition! The hike recommended here travels the periphery of the preserve and can be shortened (or lengthened) at will along the way.

Starting on the River Trail, head east. The Yakima River soon comes into view. The plain you're hiking across was known to the Cham-na-pam peoples as Chem-na.

A young hiker looks for wildlife along the River Trail in Chamna Natural Preserve.

It was the site of a Catholic mission before it was farmed by early settler families. More recently, volunteers have removed more than sixteen tons of trash and Chamna is once again becoming a vibrant ecosystem.

Soon come to the first of many junctions, this one with the Jack Rabbit Trail. Stay right here and at the next several trail and service-road junctions, remaining on the River Trail. Pass benches for resting and watching kingfishers and waterfowl. Come upon old foundations and irrigation ditches. Silver maples introduced from the eastern United States and Russian olives from Asia line the way. While both are nonnative,

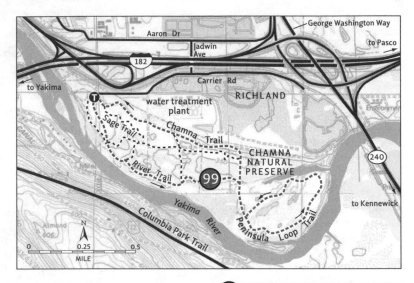

certain native wildlife species have adapted to and benefited from these trees.

At about 1.3 miles, the River Trail ends at an old service road. Turn right and access the 0.8-mile Peninsula Loop Trail, continuing east along the river and then looping back west to the service road. Look for beavers, otters, deer, and coyotes. Did you see any ospreys? Now walk the old service road north to either the Sage Trail or the more direct Chamna Trail (passing the Midpoint Trailhead, an alternative starting point near the water-treatment plant) back to the trailhead, for a grand loop of about 3.6 miles.

EXTENDING YOUR TRIP

Sample the other trails on the preserve as well as the other nearby Tapteal Greenway parks and preserves. The Duportail Trail leads 2.3 miles north from Chamna to Richland's 236-acre W. E. Johnson Park, with its several miles of trails.

100 Amon Basin

RATING/ DIFFICULTY	ROUND-TRIP	ELEV GAIN/ HIGH POINT	SEASON
*/1	2.3 miles	50 feet/ 525 feet	Year-round

Map: USGS Badger Mountain; **Contact:** Tapteal Greenway Association, (509) 627-3621, www.tapteal.org; **Notes:** Dogs permitted on-leash; **GPS:** N 46 12.981 W 119 15.155

One of the last large undeveloped parcels remaining within the Tri-Cities, Amon Basin consists of old-growth sage and riparian sagebrush-steppe—crucial habitat for badgers, river otters, and black-tailed jackrabbits. The Tapteal Greenway Association has been developing trails within the basin and advocating for its protection. Hike this threatened area

*and decide if you'd like to see it paved over
or forever protected as a natural area.*

GETTING THERE

From Pasco, follow I-182 west to exit 5A
onto State Route 240. Continue east on SR
240 for 1.5 miles to the Columbia Park Trail
exit. Turn right (west) onto Columbia Park
Trail and continue 0.6 mile, turning left
onto Leslie Road. Follow it 1.9 miles south,
turning left onto Broadmoor Street (0.7 mile
beyond the Gage Boulevard intersection).
(From Yakima, follow I-82 east to exit 109.
Turn right onto Badger Road and proceed 0.2
mile, turning left onto Leslie Road. Continue
1.5 miles, passing the southern trailhead
at 0.6 mile, and turn right onto Broadmoor
Street.) Follow Broadmoor Street for 0.6
mile to Claybell Park and the trailhead (elev.
475 ft). Privy available.

ON THE TRAIL

From the east end of the parking lot, follow
the blocked roadway south, quickly coming
to a junction. You'll be heading right on the
wide trail into the 100-acre Amon Basin
Nature Preserve. Much of the land to the
southeast of here may soon end up sprouting more than four hundred houses, seriously
compromising the ecological integrity of the
existing preserve and forever diminishing
the prospects of what the Tapteal Greenway
Association (TGA) envisions as a Central
Natural Park for the Tri-Cities. The TGA has
been working with the Washington Department of Fish and Wildlife, the Trust for Public
Lands, and other agencies and citizens trying
to secure $2 million to purchase the 119-acre
parcel slated for development.

Walk the wide trail west along the
demarcation of natural sagebrush-steppe
and the manicured lawns of Claybell Park.

Several parallel and diverging trails lead
from this path into the sage and you may
want to explore them, although they may
be confusing to follow. At 0.2 mile, turn left
on a wide path along the sewer line, paralleling the West Fork Amon Creek. The Amon
Creek corridor is the last natural connection
within the Tri-Cities between the Columbia
River and the basalt ridges to the west. Like
nearby Little Badger Mountain hovering over
this basin, development pressure is great
here, threatening to turn this entire locale
into housing and pavement. Not good for
the resident jackrabbits, badgers, and more
than 150 species of birds.

*Amon Basin consists of rich riparian
habitat threatened by development.*

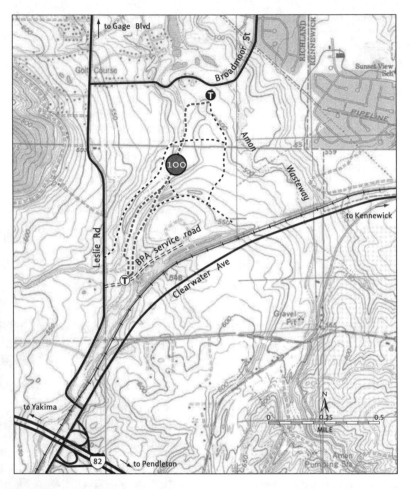

At 0.4 mile, intersect a wide east–west trail. Continue south along the sewer line through rows of recently planted native species, compliments of the TGA. At 0.5 mile, come to a pump house and more trail options. The wide sewer-line path veers right, crossing the creek to terminate on Leslie Road near the south trailhead. It can be followed for an alternative loop. The path left heads across sage into the heart of what will either be a grand park or a grand development. Continue south along the irrigation retention pool, coming to an easy-to-miss junction at 0.6 mile.

You'll be returning on the trail right, so keep hiking straight uphill to a junction (elev. 525 ft) with an old road at 0.7 mile. Turn right and on a near level track enjoy excellent views of the Amon Creek drainage below and Little Badger Mountain to the west. At 1 mile, just before a bench, come to a junction with a trail leading down to the creekside trail you'll be returning on. Continue straight on the old road, coming to the BPA service road at 1.1 miles.

Turn right and within a few hundred feet come to a trail junction. The road continues straight a few hundred more feet, crossing Amon Creek and reaching the south trailhead located off of Leslie Road (an alternative starting point). Head right on the trail along a lovely wetland bursting with blackbird song. The way weaves around and over bluffs along the wetland's east shore, providing excellent bird-watching.

At 1.3 miles, come to the first of two viewing platforms. The second one is 0.1 mile farther, just before a junction with the

way leading right back to the old road. Stay left and continue on a grassy bluff, eventually dropping down to creek level. Notice all of the beaver sign. At 1.6 miles, return to a familiar junction just south of the retention pool. Turn left and retrace your steps 0.7 mile to Claybell Park.

EXTENDING YOUR TRIP

Explore some of the radiating trails if the preserve has been successfully expanded.

101 Bateman Island

RATING/ DIFFICULTY	LOOP	ELEV GAIN/ HIGH POINT	SEASON
**/1	2.4 miles	20 feet / 370 feet	Year-round

Map: USGS Kennewick, **Contact:** Richland Parks and Recreation, (509) 942-7529, http://richlandparksandrec.com; **Notes:** Dogs permitted on-leash; **GPS:** N 46 14.288 W 119 13.536

Bateman Island is connected to the mainland by a tree-lined causeway.

Hike across a small causeway to a 160-acre island in the Columbia River. The Yakima River flows into the Columbia here, creating a delta rich with wildlife—and surrounded by one of the fastest-growing metropolitan areas in the country. Enjoy good views to the west of the sage-covered hills and mountains flanking the Tri-Cities and to the east the stately homes lining the Columbia. Embrace the wind, the sun, and the West's grandest river from this easy and interesting hike in the heart of the Tri-Cities.

GETTING THERE

From Pasco, follow US Highway 395 south across the Columbia River into Kennewick, bearing right onto State Route 240. Continue 4 miles west to the Columbia Center Boulevard exit and turn right. (From Yakima, follow I-82 east to I-182 east and take exit 5A. Continue 2.7 miles east on SR 240 to the Columbia Center Boulevard exit and turn left.) Proceed 0.3 mile (0.4 mile if coming from Yakima) to the Columbia Park Trail and turn left, driving 0.1 mile to Wye Park and the trailhead (elev. 370 ft). Privy available.

SCOUTING TRAILS IN THE TRI-CITIES

Nearly the entire length of the Columbia River within Kennewick, Pasco, and Richland is graced with paved trails, making the Tri-Cities a wonderful place to bring your bike or walking and running shoes. The bulk of this trail system consists of the Sacagawea Heritage Trail, a 23-mile lollipop loop that travels through all three cities and across two of its vehicle bridges. It's named for the young Lemhi Shoshone woman who, with her infant son, accompanied Lewis and Clark as a scout and interpreter. Sacagawea visited the area on October 16 and 17, 1805, on the expedition's way to the Pacific. They made camp at the confluence of the Snake and Columbia Rivers at what is now Sacajawea State Park.

The heritage trail begins at the state park and travels north along the Columbia through Pasco, before crossing the river on the I-182 bridge. Here you can veer north along the Columbia on the 7-mile Richland Riverfront Trail. The Sacagawea Heritage Trail continues south through nature preserves on the Yakima River delta and then on through Kennewick's sprawling Columbia Park, before crossing the Columbia on the cable bridge and returning to Pasco. There are lots of wonderful interpretive sites, displays, and sculptures along the way.

At the 284-acre Sacajawea State Park, you can visit the Sacajawea Interpretive Center as well as one of the seven interpretive displays that make up the Confluence Project, which was commissioned for the bicentennial of the Lewis and Clark Expedition. Designed by famed Chinese American artist Maya Lin, these outdoor displays located at seven major confluences draw on history, Native American lore and culture, and from the diary entries of both Lewis and Clark.

Note that the state park and the trail have two different spellings of the scout's name. This reflects a pronunciation controversy. While the state park contains the traditional spelling, pronounced sack-uh-juh-WEE-uh, the heritage trail represents the traditional pronunciation, tsa-caw-gaw-WEE-aw, derived from the Hidatsa words for bird (*cagàga*) and woman (*mìà*) for which Sacagawea was named.

For more information about the trail, visit the Tri-Cities Visitor and Convention Bureau "Friends of Our Trail" page (www.visittri-cities.com/visitors/heritage-&-eco-tourism /friends-of-our-trail).

—C. R.

ON THE TRAIL

Before dropping 20 feet down the riverbank to Bateman Island, read the informative sign at the Wye Park parking lot. There's a lot of history and birdlife waiting for you on that small island. Cross the paved 23-mile Sacagawea Heritage Trail (see "Scouting Trails in the Tri-Cities" sidebar) and pass a gate at the entrance to the causeway. Bateman Island was farmed from the 1870s to the 1950s, and you'll see plenty of evidence of this—old roads, foundations, nonnative trees. A fire swept the island in 2001, and you'll see evidence of that too.

Soon after reaching the island, a side trail bears right. Many of these trails are brushy and unmaintained. It's best to stay on the old farm roads that make up this loop. At 0.3 mile, bear left at a junction (you'll be returning on the old road to your right). Continue left on the south side of the island, through high reeds and grasses and groves of locust trees. Pass thickets of dogwoods and Russian olives too. Stop occasionally to hear birdsong against the background noises of the surrounding urban area.

Ignore side trails and stay on the wide old road. At 0.8 mile, pass an old foundation and a handful of catalpa trees, native to the American South and often referred to as cigar trees after their long, bean like seedpods. At 1 mile, come to a junction near a nice beach. Stay straight and venture 0.2 mile to the northern tip of the island, taking in good views of the I-182 bridge and Badger, Candy, and Rattlesnake Mountains. Lewis and Clark visited the island in October 1805, the farthest up the Columbia River they explored after paddling down the Snake River.

Return to the junction and follow the road-trail east across open fields. It soon bends south, passing through burned and recovering forest. Bear right at a junction at 1.6 miles, rounding a wetland flush with avian activity. At 1.9 miles, bear right again, returning to the main trail in another 0.2 mile. Turn left and cross the sumac-lined causeway once more, returning to your vehicle in 0.3 mile.

EXTENDING YOUR TRIP
Stretch your legs further by walking along the Sacagawea Heritage Trail. Nearby Columbia Park is a well-shaded, well-liked, and lovely park for hiking, running, cycling, and lethargically whiling away the day.

102 Burbank Slough Wildlife Trail

RATING/ DIFFICULTY	ROUND-TRIP	ELEV GAIN/ HIGH POINT	SEASON
**/1	2.8 miles	25 feet/ 355 feet	Year-round

Maps: USGS Humorist, refuge brochure
Contact: McNary National Wildlife Refuge, (509) 546-8300, www.fws.gov/mcnary;
Notes: Partly wheelchair-accessible. Dogs permitted on-leash. Watch for rattlesnakes;
GPS: N 46 12.070 W 118 59.588

  More than 250 bird species frequent the McNary National Wildlife Refuge. The Burbank Slough Wildlife Trail is a good place to start looking for them. From the refuge's new environmental education and administrative center, head out on this easy and inviting shoreline trail. Be sure to visit the native plant garden; children will enjoy the on-site teepee.

GETTING THERE
From the junction of US Highway 395 and I-182/US 12 (exit 14) in Pasco, follow US 12 4.4 miles east to a junction with SR 124 (shortly after the Snake River Bridge). Continue 1.2 miles east on US 12, turning left onto East Humorist Road. After 0.1 mile, turn left (north) onto Lake Road and proceed 0.3 mile to the trailhead at McNary National Wildlife Refuge headquarters and education center (elev. 350 ft). Privy available.

ON THE TRAIL
Be sure to grab a pamphlet at the parking lot kiosk before you start exploring. You may want to snoop around the environmental

The Burbank Slough is an old river oxbow that teems with birdlife.

education center too, before taking to the trail. Opened in 2009, this facility has been a real boon to area schoolchildren, helping them bond with the outdoors. The nicely displayed and labeled native plant garden is a great way to become familiar with the flora of the lower Columbia Basin. Kids will enjoy the animal tracks in the pathway.

Then head out 0.2 mile on a paved path to the bird blind on Burbank Slough (elev. 340 ft). How many red-winged and yellow-headed blackbirds do you see in the reeds and tules? Any teals, shovlers, canvasbacks, or scaups on the water? How many mallards? More than half of the mallards that use the Pacific Flyway winter in and near the refuge. The refuge was established in 1956 to replace habitat lost downstream to the McNary Dam. It consists of more than 15,000 acres within several units, including the one here that protects the long Burbank Slough.

Continue on a grassy jeep track, heading west along the slough and at the edge of a cornfield. Human activity has greatly altered this landscape, changing drainage patterns and introducing exotic species, such as the prolific Russian olive. But that riparian shrub has actually benefited some native species, such as magpies that build their nests in them.

At 0.6 mile, a spur heads out to the water's edge. Just beyond is a junction with a small loop trail near some big Chinese elm trees. You'll return left—so head right on sandy tread, soon coming to a small bridge. At 0.9 mile, near a nest platform, come to a junction with the loop. But first head right, along the northern shore of the slough. Look for burrowing owls—they nest here—and prickly pear cactus, which provides fruit favored by many refuge birds and animals.

At 1.3 miles, the trail ends at a gate near Lake Road (elev. 355 ft). Enjoy a good view of the eastern end of the slough and out to the towered Jump-off Joe, a peak across the Columbia River. Traffic and no shoulder

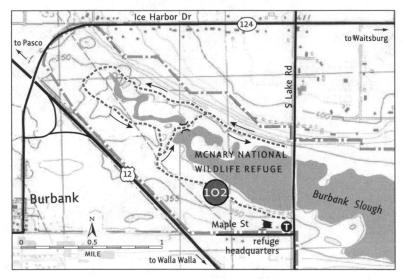

make it inadvisable to walk the road back to the refuge center. Besides, you have the loop still left to hike, so double back 0.3 mile to the previous junction and continue straight.

Hike past sand dunes and patches of sweet-scented sage bushes, their trunks blotched with red lichen. And angle around wetland pools shaded by cottonwoods. Look for harriers above and amphibians and reptiles below. At 2.1 miles, return to the main trail. From here it's 0.7 mile back to the trailhead. If it isn't too hazy out, you should be able to see the Blue Mountains in the distance to the east. If it's early morning or evening, you should be able to see plenty of birds on the way back to your vehicle.

EXTENDING YOUR TRIP

Hike the 4-mile horse trail along the Walla Walla River in the Wallula Unit of the refuge. Access it from Madam Dorian Park, located about 10 miles south on US 12.

103 Juniper Dunes Wilderness

RATING/ DIFFICULTY	ROUND-TRIP	ELEV GAIN/ HIGH POINT	SEASON
***/2	2 miles	200 feet/ 1000 feet	Mar–May

Map: USGS Levey NE; **Contact:** BLM Spokane District, (509) 536-1200, www .blm.gov/or/districts/spokane/index.php; **Notes:** Access is via private land. Southern approach not recommended due to poor roads, changing landownership stipulations. Northern approach recommended, only permissible Mar 1–May 31. No overnight parking. Respect private property. Wilderness trail, mechanized equipment prohibited. Pack sufficient water. Watch for rattlesnakes; **GPS:** N 46 25.721 W 118 49.518

  Enclosed by fences and containing no mountains, no

lakes, no rivers, and practically no trails, Juniper Dunes is an anomaly among our state's wilderness areas. Surrounded by agricultural lands and adjacent dune areas ravaged by off-road vehicles, the 7140-acre Juniper Dunes Wilderness protects the state's largest remaining natural groves of junipers and some of its biggest dunes. And while this landscape may appear harsh, it's actually a pretty sensitive environment—one harboring a plethora of fauna and flora.

GETTING THERE

From Spokane, follow I-90 west to exit 220 in Ritzville, continuing 14 miles south on US Highway 395. Take the Lind exit and follow SR 21 24 miles south to Kahlotus. Turn left onto SR 260, and after 0.2 mile turn right onto SR 263. Follow it for 0.7 mile, bearing right onto the Pasco–Kahlotus Road. Continue 16.5 miles south on this good road, turning right at the Star School District House onto Snake River Road. (From Pasco, follow US 12

east, exiting onto the Pasco–Kahlotus Road. Follow it 24 miles north, turning left at the Star School District House onto Snake River Road.) Follow Snake River Road 3.4 miles west, turning left onto graveled Blackman Ridge Road. Continue 2.4 miles, turning left onto graveled Joy Road and driving 2 miles to the road's end and trailhead (elev. 800 ft).

ON THE TRAIL

This hike begins on private land owned by the Juniper Dunes Ranch. Access is only from March 1 until May 31 and only during daylight hours. Please respect all posted rules and close all gates. The owners can deny access at any time, so it's important to be a good guest on their land. The access window is short, but it's during the spring months when temperatures aren't too extreme and the dunes are awash in wildflowers.

From the trailhead you can see the dunes rising in the immediate distance. Walk through a gate, crossing a small corner of the ranch, and within 0.2 mile come to another

The Juniper Dunes Wilderness contains one of the largest dune complexes in the state.

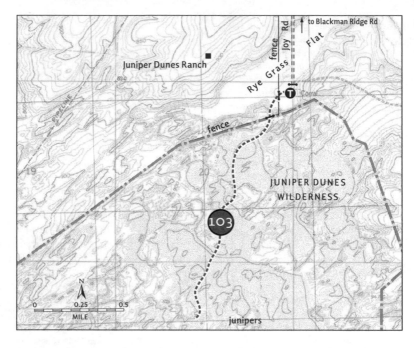

gate. Pass through it and enter the 7140-acre wilderness area, the only one within Washington administered by the Bureau of Land Management and the only one completely enclosed by fences. The fences ensure that off-road-vehicle riders on adjacent BLM-administered dune lands don't encroach upon this protected environment. The wilderness still sports scars from ORVs that traversed it before it became protected in 1984.

Trails of sorts traverse the dunes, but generally the exploring is cross-country across what can be a forbidding land when temperatures soar. Pack plenty of water and sunscreen and note markers so as not to get lost. If you do get disoriented, you'll eventually come to a fence line, which you can follow back to the trailhead. It's not a bad idea to have a GPS unit on hand.

The dunes are fascinating to explore. Winds sculpt beautiful patterns in them. Check out parabolic mounds and sandy bowls. Lizards and small mammals such as pocket gophers and kangaroo rats leave their signatures in the sand. Bigger mammals too—like badgers, coyotes, bobcats, and deer. Look for flowering plants in spring: sandwort, milk vetch, prickly pear cactus, penstemon, balsamroot buckwheat, larkspur, and many others. And the dunes support rabbitbrush, wheatgrass, ricegrass, and of course the area's namesake western junipers.

From the wilderness boundary, follow a path of sorts 0.3 mile up a sprawling dune (elev. 1000 ft) that rises well over 150 feet above the adjacent farmland. Views are good of the Sahara-like terrain as well as of the Saddle Mountains to the north and the Blue Mountains to the southeast.

Drop down, passing by grassy pockets and continuing west to some nice juniper groves at about 1 mile. These trees are adapted to dry habitat, so this area's 8 inches of annual rainfall suits them just fine. This is a good turnaround point, giving you a nice taste of this wilderness. However, the biggest junipers are located farther to your south, if you feel inclined to locate them.

104 Z Lake

RATING/ DIFFICULTY	ONE-WAY	ELEV GAIN/ HIGH POINT	SEASON
**/3	3.5 miles	275 feet/ 2310 feet	Mar–Dec

Maps: USGS Rocklyn SW, BLM Spokane District Telford Recreation Area map; **Contact:** Washington Department of Fish and Wildlife, Swanson Lake Wildlife Area, (509) 636-2344, www.wdfw.wa.gov/lands/wildlife _areas; **Notes:** Discover Pass required. Open to mountain bikes, horses. Range area. Watch for rattlesnakes, ticks. **GPS:** N 47 36.774 W 118 24.029

This long, skinny rimrock lake with a crook and narrows in the middle was out-of-sight and off-limits on private land for decades. It doesn't even have an official name. Locally known as Z Lake, the area has gradually gained attention since being acquired by the Washington Department of Fish and Wildlife and added to the 21,000-acre Swanson Lakes Wildlife Area. The area

merges with the Bureau of Land Management Telford Recreation Area. One study pegged Z Lake as the most productive habitat for aquatic invertebrates in the region, luring walk-in anglers to cast for the few but plump trout. The management priority is protecting wildlife habitat, but cattle are still allowed to graze here—and they make most of the trails. Explore this area wearing sturdy boots.

GETTING THERE
From Davenport, drive 13.5 miles west on US Highway 2. Just west of the highway rest area, turn south on Telford Road. Drive 7.5 miles to the trailhead parking area (elev. 2300 ft) at Whittaker Lake Road.

ON THE TRAIL
This hike can be done as an out-and-back from either the north or south trailhead. It's described here as a one-way hike from the north trailhead, easily accomplished by leaving a vehicle or bicycle on Telford Road, just 1.5 miles along the road from your starting trailhead.

Go through the gate and head west on Whittaker Lake Road (closed to unauthorized motor vehicles). At 0.5 mile, continue straight where the gravel portion of the road bends north. Soon, a bit of the long north–south ribbon of a lake will come into view below the basalt cliffs in the distance. This is a good point to pause with binoculars. Mule deer, coyotes, and other critters often can be seen taking cover when there's movement on the horizon—including you.

Continue down to a fence corner and go through the gate. There's no defined trail at this point. Continue straight west, weaving through the mounds on game trails. Rugged boots are recommended for hiking because

A dogleg gives narrow Z Lake its name.

of the basalt scree that must be negotiated through the flats.

Hike to the water and then turn south. It's easy to find your own path along the east shore above the lake. Pass the old windmill tower and the solar panels that power the lake aerator, which helps provide oxygen for trout during the winter freeze-up.

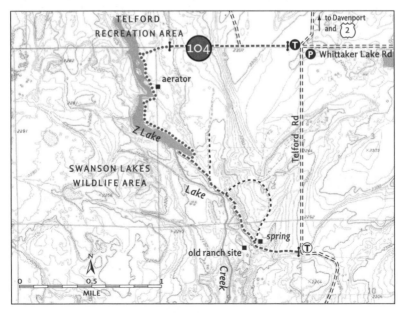

A little farther south, an aluminum rowboat has traditionally been left for anglers to use. Check it out if it's still there. Use it if you like, but bring it back off the water and turn it upside down with the oars inside—just as you should have found it.

Soon you'll come to the zigzag feature that gives the lake its name. Turn west and hike up into the rocky outcropping where the lake makes two right-angle turns. This is a great spot for a break and watching up and down the lake: look up for kestrels, marsh hawks, and opsreys; and look down to the water for waterfowl, turtles, and fish.

Continue south along the shoreline. The walking gets easier. At the south end of the lake (can be wet in spring), eventually bend right to hit a ranch road. The way goes right briefly and dead-ends at the lake.

To finish the hike, continue south on the road. At an old corral area near some tall trees, follow the road as it bends left past a spring and eastward to the south trailhead and limited parking at Telford Road.

EXTENDING YOUR TRIP

Cross-country hikers can circumnavigate the lake. The west side has higher bluffs for loftier views.

105 Twin Lakes

RATING/ DIFFICULTY	LOOP	ELEV GAIN/ HIGH POINT	SEASON
***/3	10 miles	830 feet/ 2250 feet	Mar–Dec

Maps: USGS Rocklyn SW, USGS Swanson Lakes, BLM Spokane District Twin Lakes Recreation Area map; **Contact:** BLM Spokane District, (509) 536-1200, www.blm .gov/or/districts/spokane; **Notes:** Open to

mountain bikes, horses. Range area. Watch for rattlesnakes, ticks; **GPS:** N 47 31.795 W 118 30.352

Get your fix of wide-open spaces in this hike that links Channeled Scablands water features in Lake Creek Canyon with the surrounding sage and grazing lands. Starting from a fishing lake and small campground, follow old jeep tracks through a portion of 14,000 acres of range and wetlands managed by the Bureau of Land Management for recreation and wildlife. Cattle are allowed to graze here among the deer and other wildlife. Spring is prime time for hiking, as the sagebrush-steppe blooms and migrant waterfowl pass through.

GETTING THERE

From its junction with US Highway 2 in Davenport, head south on State Route 28. Drive 12.7 miles to Harrington and turn right (west) onto Coffeepot Road. Drive 13.5 miles and turn right (north) onto Highline Road. Drive 1.3 miles and turn right (east) onto the BLM Twin Lakes access road. Drive 2 miles down to the lakeside campground and go past the boat ramp. The trailhead (elev. 1915 ft) is in the second big parking area near the outlet creek on the left. Privy available.

ON THE TRAIL

The trail starts at a footbridge across the creek between Upper and Lower Twin Lakes. Cross the bridge and bear right on the south side of Upper Twin. Go through a gate. Gain a little elevation and look down on the lake where anglers come to catch bass, crappie, perch, and trout. Soon the trail bends south away from the lake and heads right and

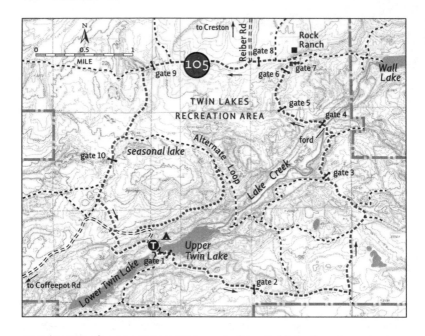

around a grove of aspens. Pass a spring—source of the wet spot producing the aspens.

The trail works up a small draw onto a broad sagebrush plateau. The area has numerous wildflowers in the spring, but it can be desertlike in the summer. Hot-weather hikers should take a cue from the wildlife and be hiking at sunrise.

At 1.2 miles, pass through another gate. (For a shorter loop hike, take the road [or trail] on the left that is a few hundred yards farther on.) In late May or early June, you might see bitterroots blooming directly in the trail. At 2.9 miles, the trail skirts the right side of a wetland and trees. Look for wild iris and wild onion blooming in spring. At 3.1 miles, continue straight on the main track at a faint junction. At 3.3 miles, the track turns right around some rock-filled fence-corner

anchors. Suddenly the scenery becomes more interesting as the topography breaks up with basalt cliffs along the drainage between Wall Lake and Upper Twin Lake. A few pine trees crop into the picture as the trail drops into the canyon.

At 3.8 miles, go through a gate and continue down through a wildlife-rich area and then up to a ford over Lake Creek at 4.6 miles. In all but the highest spring water, there are usually enough rocks here to hop across without getting boots too wet.

When you reach a fence, go up through the sagebrush to the left and parallel the fence a short way to the walk-through gate. (The road gate usually is locked.) Pass through several more gates on the way toward the deserted buildings of the old Rock Ranch. At the corrals of a formerly

A campground at Upper Twin Lake

bustling cattle operation at 5.5 miles, turn left through another gate toward the house.

To continue the loop, head left (west) from the house, up the access road (open to vehicles) and past the metal buildings. At 6.1 miles, go through gate no. 8. Continue to a kiosk at the junction with Reiber Road and go through another gate to get back on a nonmotorized track. Continue west through reclaimed farmland for 1 mile before going through a gate and coming to more interesting native rangeland. At 7.7 miles, bear right at a fork. Pass a seasonal lake in a pasture at 8.2 miles.

At 8.4 miles, pass through the tenth gate of the trek. At 9.2 miles, the trail intersects the Twin Lakes access road. You can turn left and head directly down to the lake and trailhead, or end the hike on a sweeter trail by turning right on the access road, going 100 yards, and turning left off the road onto

a trail. It drops into the Twin Lakes canyon before hooking back to join the access road again at nearly 10 miles. Turn right and follow the access road down to the trailhead.

EXTENDING YOUR TRIP
From the corral and buildings at Rock Ranch, a track heads 1 mile east to Wall Lake, a nice side trip.

106 Lakeview Ranch

RATING/ DIFFICULTY	ROUND-TRIP	ELEV GAIN/ HIGH POINT	SEASON
****/3	13 miles	600 feet/ 1800 feet	Year-round

Maps: USGS Pacific Lake, USGS Sullivan Lake, BLM map online, www.blm.gov/or /resources/recreation/site_info.php ?siteid=275; **Contact:** BLM Spokane District,

(509) 536-1200; www.blm.gov/or/districts
/spokane; **Notes:** Open to horses. Partly
open to mountain bikes, motorized use.
Watch for rattlesnakes. Pack sufficient water;
GPS: N 47 24.830 W 118 44.474

*You'll get more than
just a lake view
hiking this 12,000+-acre former ranch.
Canyons, craters, grasslands, and bluffs
await—and lots of wildlife too. Hike one of
the longest trails on the Columbia Plateau*

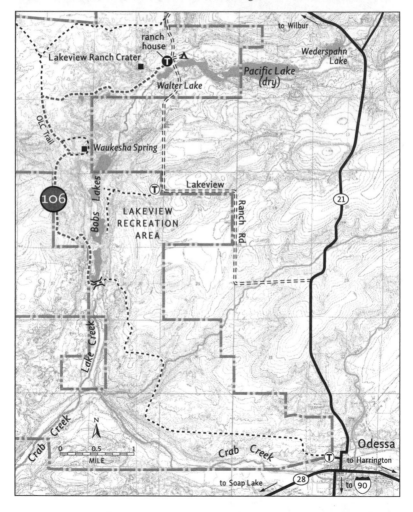

and with each step through this varied terrain, scenic surprises greet you. The several lakes in the area, including 1.5-mile-long Pacific Lake, have mostly gone dry because of controversial deep-well irrigation that has lowered the vast Odessa Aquifer. Still, the lakes and their basalt cliff surroundings are fascinating flashbacks to a prehistoric time.

GETTING THERE

From Spokane, follow I-90 west to exit 245 at Sprague. Head for about 13 miles north on State Route 23, turning left onto Mohler Road. After about 10 miles, reach SR 28. Turn left and drive 16 miles to Odessa. (From Ellensburg, follow I-90 east to exit 206. Then drive 18 miles north on SR 21 to Odessa.) Head 2.8 miles north on SR 21, turning left onto graveled Lakeview Ranch Road. Go 3.3 miles and just before a right-angle turn, note an alternate access for a quick walk down to Bobs Lakes. Then continue 1.9 miles on Lakeview Ranch Road to Lakeview Ranch and the trailhead (elev. 1600 ft) on the left behind the barns.

ON THE TRAIL

Acquired for the public by the Bureau of Land Management in the 1990s, this former working ranch offers miles of roads and trails to explore. The hike described here utilizes part of the 12.9-mile Odessa–Lake Creek (OLC) Trail to travel into the Lake Creek Coulee. That trail begins just north of the ranch buildings—but its first few miles are open to motorized use, posing little interest to hikers.

Start your hike instead by following the old jeep track west from the trailhead. You can make a short side trip north to Lakeview Ranch Crater. This crater, like the nearby and

A hiker climbs out of a large canyon on the Odessa-Lake Creek Trail.

more defined Odessa Craters, was created not by meteor activity but by scouring from Ice Age floods. The Odessa Crater in Texas, however, was formed by a meteor hit.

Traversing open grasslands teeming with birds and wildflowers (in spring), pass Walter Lake on your left—which may be a dry lake bed. After about 1 mile of level terrain, the path swings into some low rolling hills and comes to a good-sized lake on your right.

BLM RANGE LANDS INVITE HIKERS

A new era started in 1987 with 156 acres purchased at the Lakeview Ranch near Pacific Lake north of Odessa. The US Bureau of Land Management—once the runt of land-management agencies in Eastern Washington—began a campaign to build its stature one parcel at a time.

Two decades later, after a series of land trades, acquisitions, and consolidations, the agency has become a regional giant for wildlife habitat restoration and public access to sagebrush-steppe wild lands. The BLM has increased its Washington landholdings from about 308,000 acres in 1985 to about 446,000 acres. More importantly, instead of being small parcels, scattered and sometimes inaccessible, the acreage is largely consolidated into large tracts in Eastern Washington, especially in Lincoln County. All of it is open to hikers.

By seeking willing sellers and acquiring an 8000-acre ranch here and a 10,000-acre ranch there, the BLM built a handsome spread where fish and wildlife can be housed and managed on equal or higher terms with livestock. In many cases, the agency has offered lease-back arrangements so ranchers selling land can continue ranging livestock, although the amount of grazing is reduced by up to 60 percent. Hunters, hikers, equestrians, and mountain bikers can enter through gates and travel freely all day through the scablands without stepping off public land.

Standout examples include more than 20,000 acres in the Odessa area near Lakeview Ranch (Hike 106), about 17,000 acres in the Coffeepot–Twin Lakes areas west of Harrington (Hike 105), and about 8000 acres along Hog Canyon and Fishtrap Lakes off I-90 (Hikes 108 and 109). The 14,000-acre Escure Ranch straddling the Adams-Whitman county line south of Lamont, a former sheep and cattle operation, is a public plum that includes 8 miles of Rock Creek, along with Wall Lake (Hike 110).

For more information, contact the US Bureau of Land Management, Spokane District, (509) 536-1200, www.blm.gov/or/districts/spokane.

—R. L.

Pass several more smaller lakes that vary in size depending on the season and amount of recent rainfall. Good opportunities for bird-watching here. The surrounding sage-dotted hills also harbor numerous bird species and mammals—look for jackrabbits.

At 2.1 miles, reach a junction with the OLC Trail (elev. 1700 ft). It's a jeep track here and open to motorized travel. Don't let that discourage you though—use is fairly light. Turn left and hike the track, coming to a junction

at 2.6 miles. The way left is the OLC route. It drops 100 feet to Waukesha Spring along a fence line (private property beyond, so don't think of walking on the paths heading east); then it climbs back up. Skip it, saving 0.6 mile and a small climb. Instead, continue straight on a shortcut that meets back up with the OLC Trail in 0.4 mile.

Then continue right, coming to the end of motorized use at an old rusty combine part at 3.5 miles. The views here are pretty decent east across the small coulee housing Lake Creek and out to distant wheat fields. Now follow the trail along a fence line, climbing higher on a slope of golden grasses. At 4.5 miles, reach a hillcrest (elev. 1800 ft) and begin descending into the coulee. Aside from not losing the sketchy tread (pay attention for trail markers), take care not to twist an ankle in the numerous burrows in the trail. Enjoy good views of imposing basalt cliffs and the wide canyon floor housing Bobs Lakes, a series of shallow bodies of water (or salt flats).

After descending a steep draw, reach a gate at 5.8 miles at a bench above the coulee floor. The way turns right along the bench, eventually dropping to the grassy coulee bottom and reaching a bridge over Lake Creek (elev. 1425 ft) at 6.5 miles. For most day hikers, this is a good spot to turn around. But first feel free to explore the canyon.

EXTENDING YOUR TRIP

Make a loop by walking north along the Bobs Lakes to an old jeep track, reaching the Lakeview Ranch Road in about 2.5 miles. It's then a 2 mile walk north on that road back to your vehicle. Better yet, leave a car at the Odessa trailhead for the OLC Trail (0.3 mile west of Birch Street) and make a one-way journey. From the bridge, the way climbs out of the coulee, passing a spring and good views of the Odessa Towers rock formations. An up-and-down course across grassy hills and sagebrush-steppe leads toward Crab Creek Coulee before following a utility road a short way, then trail again, to reach the trailhead in 6.2 miles—12.7 miles from the ranch trailhead. Also, go to the campground area just a few hundred yards northeast of the Lakeview Ranch buildings and hike the north rim of dry but scenic Pacific Lake.

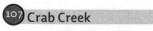

Crab Creek

RATING/ DIFFICULTY	ROUND-TRIP	ELEV GAIN/ HIGH POINT	SEASON
***/3	6 miles	320 feet/ 1830 feet	Feb–Dec

Maps: USGS Harrington SE, BLM Spokane District Rocky Ford map; **Contact:** BLM Spokane District, (509) 536-1200, www.blm.gov/or/districts/spokane; **Notes:** Open to horses. Watch for rattlesnakes, ticks. Safest for dogs in late fall or winter. Range area; **GPS:** N 47 18.092 W 118 15.298

 *Water in a desertlike environment creates a wildlife magnet as Crab Creek flows through this stretch of public land in Lincoln County. Transitions are dramatic, from winter brown to the lush spring greenery that virtually hides the creek in some areas. While the route can be hiked almost year-round, it's especially pleasing as the area blooms with life from March through early May and again in late fall, when ticks and rattlesnakes have retreated.*

GETTING THERE

From I-90 east of Ritzville, take Tokio exit 231 and head north. The road becomes Danekas Road. Follow it about 1.4 miles and turn right on Hills Road (also known as the Harrington–Tokio Road). Drive north over the railway, go 6 miles. Just after crossing a bridge over Crab Creek, pass a parking area and kiosk on the right (upstream side of the road) and turn left. (From Harrington, head south on State Route 23. At the edge of town, turn right toward Ritzville on the Harrington–Tokio Road. Drive 12 miles to the

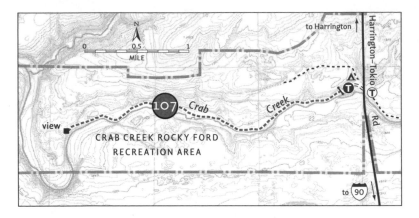

Crab Creek access on the right.) Drive to the end of the large undeveloped BLM camping area and the trailhead (elev. 1825 ft). Privy available.

ON THE TRAIL

The trailhead is near a corralled spring. Go through the gate and follow the stock trail downstream. This trail can fade or braid

A mallard hen distracts hikers from her nearby brood.

in places, but the route generally heads downstream on the first bench level above the creek. It's much easier to follow from fall through early spring than it is from late spring through summer, when the creekside grass and vegetation leafs out thick.

Basalt outcroppings rise on the right, forming condo sites for swallows and other nesting birds. The trail soon heads to the edge of the creek, and then it skirts to the right of the first large thicket of wild roses and hawthorns by angling away from the creek and hugging the basalt outcropping.

Soon the creek returns to greet the trail. If the grass isn't too high, you'll see waterfowl. Many ducks hatch here in May and early June. If you see an adult duck splashing downstream in a broken-wing act, just keep hiking. The parent is luring you from the clutch of ducklings hidden in the grass. It will return to its brood after you pass.

The trail fades in and out in a series of game and stock trails. At 1 mile, pass through a creekside opening in a fence. Although this is classic mule deer country, we have seen whitetails up a draw across the creek at 2.5 miles.

At 2.7 miles, as the trail fades, the terrain offers an easy angle to the top of a basalt ledge, where you can continue hiking downstream for a change of scenery just above the creek. At 2.9 miles, the creek begins a big sweeping left turn. Angle uphill, keeping the creek in view, for an easy, gradual cross-country climb to the top of the bluffs overlooking the creek.

The bluff top is a good place for further exploration, or simply pull up a rock and enjoy a snack and the vista of the creek below. Return from here for a round-trip trek of 6 miles.

EXTENDING YOUR TRIP
From the parking area, cross the highway to another trailhead and hike a similar trail along Crab Creek upstream for about 1 mile.

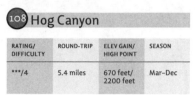
108 Hog Canyon

RATING/ DIFFICULTY	ROUND-TRIP	ELEV GAIN/ HIGH POINT	SEASON
***/4	5.4 miles	670 feet/ 2200 feet	Mar–Dec

Maps: USGS Fishtrap, BLM Spokane District Fishtrap map; **Contact:** BLM Spokane District, (509) 536-1200, www.blm.gov/or /districts/spokane; **Notes:** Open to mountain bikes, horses. Range area. Watch for ticks; **GPS:** N 47 21.672 W 117 49.721

 Every season has its moment on this showcase in the Channeled Scablands scoured by the great Ice Age floods. March to early May is prime time to catch the blooming arrowleaf balsamroot and other wildflowers in the open ponderosa pine forest and to see the waterfall at the north end of Hog Canyon. Hog Lake is one of just four in the region designated for winter fishing (December 1–March 31), which overlaps with the end and the beginning of hiking season. Aspens brighten the route in October. Deer, coyotes, and other wildlife are active early on summer mornings, which also is the best time to hike the open portions of this route when daytime temperatures soar.

GETTING THERE
From I-90 about 25 miles west of Spokane, take Fishtrap exit 254 and head south on Sprague Highway. Drive nearly 2.5 miles and

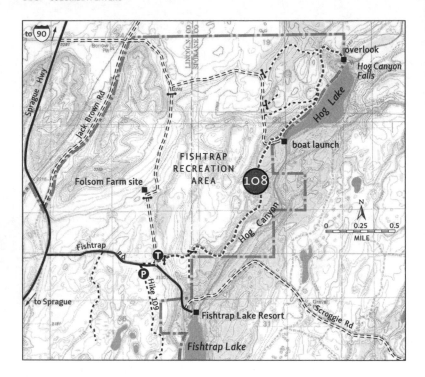

turn left on Fishtrap Road. Drive 0.6 mile to a multi-trailhead parking area on the right (elev. 2170 ft).

ON THE TRAIL

From the parking area, walk the paved road 0.1 mile toward Fishtrap Lake Resort. Turn left on the first dirt road. Take the first or second gate on the right through the barbed-wire fence (the gate paths merge in about 100 ft) to begin hiking the single-track trail toward Hog Lake.

The trail drops into a grassy draw and then climbs the slope on the opposite side and through a fence gate. Take note of the single-track's direction here to avoid

confusion on the way back. Soon the trail heads down to the right and quickly changes character as it drops into the ponderosa pines. This area is open to periodic livestock grazing and cattle trails could cause occasional confusion. When in doubt, look for the vertical trail posts the BLM uses to mark the route.

The trail bends left, levels onto a bench, and contours along Hog Canyon, which is not too deep at this point. Cattails vegetate the canyon bottom, and the wildlife tracks and beauty of the scabland terrain make it easy to overlook the cow pies. The trail then steps down to another broader, more meadowlike bench. At 1.5 miles, pass a little aspen grove

A scablands waterfall is a highlight of the Hog Lake hike.

that's luscious green in spring and summer, stunning yellow in October, and almost as eye-catching as naked white-barked skeletons for the next five months.

The trail continues a short way on a double-track. Then bear right on the single-track as it enters the Hog Lake access site. Walk to the boat launch and bear left onto the angler trail along the lake's northwest shore. After a few hundred yards, the user trail angles up toward the rim. It fades as it crosses a short patch of scree near the top but becomes evident again as it follows the edge of the bluff, with great views looking down on the lake and across Hog Canyon. Where the user trail finally peters out above the wide bend in the lake, head left 30 yards or so to the main double-track trail and continue up-lake, although the water will not be in view.

Hike a few hundred yards. Just as the double-track enters scattered timber, about 60 yards before it switchbacks up toward the rim on the left, take the cow trail that gently drops to the right. Contour past the first little draw and around a little knob where the trail becomes a more obvious single-track again and climbs a short slope to a ridge. From here, drop down the ridge toward the lake to an excellent viewpoint overlooking Hog Canyon Falls. Best viewing is in late winter or spring, when the runoff is surging. The falls, virtually dry in summer and autumn, is on private land.

EXTENDING YOUR TRIP

From the trailhead gate, walk north on the access road to the old buildings of Folsom Farm.

109 Fishtrap Lake

RATING/ DIFFICULTY	ROUND-TRIP	ELEV GAIN/ HIGH POINT	SEASON
***/2	6.4 miles	350 feet/ 2180 feet	Mar–Dec

Maps: USGS Fishtrap, BLM Spokane District Fishtrap map; **Contact:** BLM Spokane District, (509) 536-1200, www.blm.gov/or /districts/spokane; **Notes:** Open to mountain bikes, horses. Range area. Watch for ticks; **GPS:** N 47 21.635, W 117 49.844

A trail along old ranch roads runs the length of Fishtrap Lake, a remnant of the Ice Age floods and center- piece of the Bureau of Land Management's 7000-acre Fishtrap Recreation Area. The sageland scenery is spectacular during spring wildflower blooming and colorful during fall foliage. The lake is stocked with rainbow trout and is especially popular with anglers late April–May. Most anglers concentrate at the north end out of Fish- trap Lake Resort, where patrons from

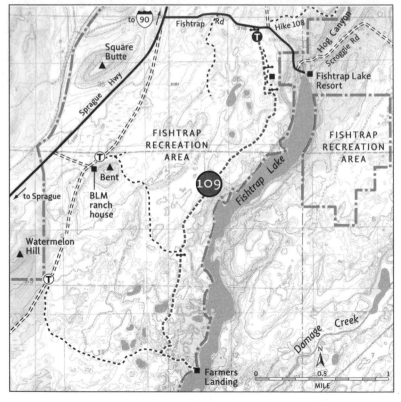

Fishtrap Lake from Farmers Landing

Spokane once came by train to dine and dance. But this hike strides away from the lakeshore, hooking back at the south end of the lake to Farmers Landing, an ideal tranquil lakeshore site for a picnic and waterfowl watching.

GETTING THERE

From I-90 about 25 miles west of Spokane, take Fishtrap exit 254 and head south on Sprague Highway. Drive nearly 2.5 miles and turn left on Fishtrap Road. Drive 0.6 mile to a multi-trailhead parking area on the right (elev. 2170 ft).

ON THE TRAIL

From the trailhead parking lot, go through the gate and follow the double-track trail

that heads south toward a lakeside residence surrounded by trees. When the road reaches a fence around the private property, just walk along the right side of the enclosure and pick up the trail again as it exits the enclosure on the south side.

The route parallels the shoreline of Fishtrap Lake, but you won't see the water until you gain a little elevation in an open area after hiking 1.5 miles. At 2 miles, the trail forks. (Right goes 1.2 miles to the BLM Ranch House trailhead and the area manager's residence.) Take the left fork, go through a gate, and continue toward Farmers Landing. (If you hiked cross-country to the east, you'd come to the narrows of Fishtrap Lake.)

Go through some timber and past a seasonal wetland on the right. At 2.9 miles, come to a junction in a grove of older pines. (The double-track to the right heads 1.4 miles to the Farmers Landing trailhead.) Head left and hike 0.3 mile to the lakeshore at Farmers Landing. This open spot overlooking the south end of the lake is ideal for picnics. You'll likely be alone, except on the fourth weekend in April when the fishing season opens.

EXTENDING YOUR TRIP

Horse riders have pioneered some single-track trails that run north from the BLM Ranch House trail. If you're up for some exploring, give one of them a try, or just head north cross-country from the Ranch House trail. Use a compass to make sure you keep heading north as you skirt scabland ponds and meadows, and you'll eventually hit Fishtrap Road near the trailhead. Other options: Shuttle a bicycle or vehicle to the Ranch House trailhead for a one-way hike of 2.2 miles, or to the Farmers Landing trailhead for a one-way hike of 4.4 miles.

110 Escure Ranch–Towell Falls

RATING/ DIFFICULTY	ROUND-TRIP	ELEV GAIN/ HIGH POINT	SEASON
***/2	6.4 miles	530 feet/ 1565 feet	Feb–Dec

Maps: USGS Honn Lakes, USGS Revere, BLM Spokane District Escure Ranch map; **Contact:** BLM Spokane District, (509) 536-1200, www.blm.gov/or/districts/spokane; **Notes:** Open to mountain bikes, horses, hunting. Partly open to motorized use. Range area. Watch for rattlesnakes, ticks; **GPS:** N 47 00.856 W 117 56.613

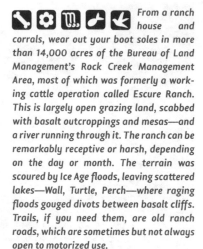 *From a ranch house and corrals, wear out your boot soles in more than 14,000 acres of the Bureau of Land Management's Rock Creek Management Area, most of which was formerly a working cattle operation called Escure Ranch. This is largely open grazing land, scabbed with basalt outcroppings and mesas—and a river running through it. The ranch can be remarkably receptive or harsh, depending on the day or month. The terrain was scoured by Ice Age floods, leaving scattered lakes—Wall, Turtle, Perch—where raging floods gouged divots between basalt cliffs. Trails, if you need them, are old ranch roads, which are sometimes but not always open to motorized use.*

GETTING THERE

From I-90 at Sprague, take exit 245 and head south (through town) on State Route 23 toward Saint John and Steptoe. Drive 12 miles from I-90 and, at a sharp left bend in the highway, turn right onto Davis Road. Drive 6.8 miles and turn left on Jordan–Knott Road. Head south 2.2 miles, crossing the bridge over Rock Creek, and turn right into the Rock Creek Management Area. Drive another 2.4 miles on a sometimes rough road to the trailhead (elev. 1460 ft). Privy available.

ON THE TRAIL

The trail to Towell Falls starts through the gate near the kiosk and heads south on an old ranch road. This road is open to motorized use roughly from April, when the ground dries, to early June, when it's closed to prevent fires. Wildflowers peak in April and early May. Common wildlife sightings include

Rock Creek's Towell Falls at Escure Ranch

coyotes, mule deer, and hawks. Rock Creek holds rainbow and brown trout, and some of the ranch lakes hold bass and panfish. Special Washington fishing regulations apply. Keep dogs on-leash to protect them during snake season.

The route parallels Rock Creek before the stream bends west and away from the road. After hiking 2.8 miles, ascend to a basalt bluff overlooking the creek and affording the first glimpse of Towell Falls in the distance. The route then drops to a small seasonal parking area.

A marker leads you on a faint trail straight toward the larger lower falls. Take the faint path down toward the creek and bend to the right along a small basalt cliff, heading upstream. Skirt right onto an old road cut around a small grove of aspens, and then drop off the bluff onto the scabrock bench that leads to the creek. You can walk to the edge of the upper falls.

EXTENDING YOUR TRIP

Explore another mile downstream to the south end of the BLM property. For a real workout, add the 8-mile round-trip to Wall Lake. From the Ranch House trailhead, cross the bridge over Rock Creek, follow the road through the old ranch house gates, and continue west up the hill. Follow the vertical trail signs across the upper flats. Pass

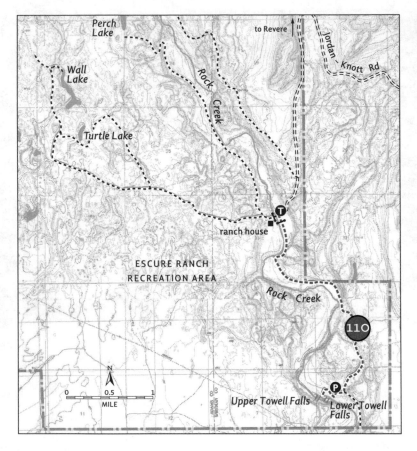

through four more gates en route to Wall Lake. If you can navigate well with map and compass or GPS, a nifty 11-mile loop can be made by hiking from Wall Lake cross-country (rugged) to Perch Lake and then following an old ranch road southeast, parallel to Rock Creek, a short way back to the trailhead.

Opposite: Palouse River upper falls

palouse hills

The Palouse is a fertile farming area that resembles an ocean of waves whipped up in a major storm. The Ice Age floods that scoured the Channeled Scablands deposited rich ripples of silt over about 3000 square miles of Eastern Washington land just north of the Snake River. Those rolling hills have been developed into rich fields of wheat, lentils, and canola, along with thousands of acres seeded to grass under the federal Conservation Reserve Program.

The Palouse is the darling of landscape photographers trying to capture subtle light, shadows, and textures. Fingers of forest and streams string through the rough seas of farm fields. Images change character hourly with the movement of the sun and seasonally with the different shades of crop ripeness and harvest. Steptoe Butte and Kamiak Butte are prime unfarmed natural-area destinations for overlooking the spectacle from remnant preserves of native grasses and wildflowers.

What's the wildest area in the Palouse? The Palouse River and 186-foot-high Palouse Falls are top candidates, but the distinction should likely go to the Washington State University campus in Pullman, home of the Cougars.

111 Kamiak Butte

RATING / DIFFICULTY	LOOP	ELEV GAIN/ HIGH POINT	SEASON
***/2	2.9 miles	800 feet/ 3641 feet	Mar–Oct

Maps: USGS Albion, Kamiak Butte County Park brochure online; **Contact:** Whitman County Parks and Recreation Department, Colfax, (509) 397-6238, www.whitmacounty .org; **Notes:** Park and picnic area open 7AM–dusk, spring–fall. Campers must stay inside closed gate at night. Park subject to closure if fire danger is extreme. Picnic shelters can be rented. Dogs permitted on-leash; **GPS:** N 46 52.214 W 117 09.187

Kamiak Butte is a natural-area island that rises abruptly from a sea of wavelike Palouse hills. Textures of fertile grain fields below create a stunning landscape. Shadows on the rolling hills change by the hour, sometimes as dramatically as the green-to-gold of the growing season. Because of the sweeping monocultures below, the native flora of the timbered mountain (a more precise term than "butte") is especially attractive to wildlife. About 130 bird species have been documented living or pit-stopping in the 298-acre county park, along with several endangered plant species and all sorts of other critters, including white-tailed deer and the occasional moose. This hike leads to the 3641-foot summit of Kamiak Butte, the second-highest point in Whitman County. Bring a wildflower field guide.

GETTING THERE

From downtown Colfax, turn east on Canyon Street and continue as it becomes State Route 272 (Palouse Highway) for 5.3 miles. Turn right on Clear Creek Road. Go 8.1 miles and make a sharp right onto Fugate Road (County Road 5100), continuing 0.5 mile. (From Pullman, take State Route 27 north 11.6 miles. Turn left on Clear Creek Road and drive 0.4 mile. Turn left on Fugate Road and drive 0.6 mile.) Turn south into Kamiak Butte County Park and drive to the trailhead (elev. 2900 ft) at the day-use area. Privy available.

Palouse farm fields look like ocean waves below Kamiak Butte.

ON THE TRAIL

A map sign marks the Pine Ridge trailhead from the day-use area. The trail heads up a wide path, making several long switchbacks to the top of the ridge. Here you can begin to understand why this island of habitat is designated a national natural landmark for its natural and geologic significance. The cooler, denser north side of the ridge (including some cedars) you just ascended gives way to a dryer remnant grassland prairie habitat facing south, including arrowleaf balsamroot and other plants associated with lower sagelands. Wildflowers bloom here as early as February, peaking in May and June.

Kamiak Butte, a name honoring Chief Kamiakin of the Yakama Tribe, can be seen in the distance from this ridge. Steptoe Butte is the prominent peak 15 miles to the northwest. The Blue Mountains can be seen far to the south on a clear day.

Explore the trail that heads left (east) on the ridge spine for a short walk to the park boundary, and then return to the junction, where a few braided trails head southwest. Take the most traveled trail upward and stay near the spine of the ridge. After a long, gradual climb, contour on the south side of a knob and begin dropping to a saddle and junction. Continue left on the short spur to the rocky and sparsely timbered Kamiak Butte summit at 3641 feet. The ridge trail splits around both sides of the summit but merges into one trail. Stretch your legs for another 0.25 mile west to the fence that blocks access to private land and communications towers at the end of the butte.

Double back to the summit and back to the saddle junction. Bear left and downhill to leave Pine Ridge and continue the loop. The downhill return on the north side of the ridge leads pleasantly through a lusher, wetter habitat. Halfway down, a denser stand of

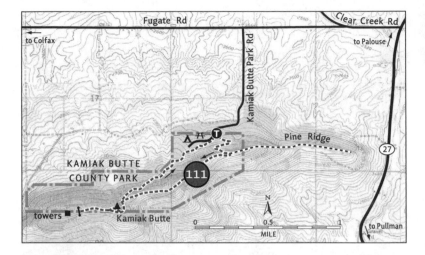

smaller trees indicates where a short-lived ski run was cut in the 1950s. From here to the trailhead, two spur trails drop downhill to the campground.

EXTENDING YOUR TRIP

Several trails wander around the campground, offering more views. Expect to see deer at the forest edges moving in and out of the grain fields early and late in the day.

112 Palouse Falls

RATING/ DIFFICULTY	ROUND-TRIP	ELEV GAIN/ HIGH POINT	SEASON
****/2	1.3 miles	150 feet/ 925 feet	Year-round

Maps: USGS Palouse Falls, state park map online; **Contact:** Palouse Falls State Park, (509) 646-9218, www.parks.wa.gov/parks; **Notes:** Discover Pass required. Dogs permitted on-leash. Watch for rattlesnakes; **GPS:** N 46 39.835 W 118 13.637

Plummeting nearly 186 feet within a stark canyon of basalt, Palouse Falls is one of the most striking waterfalls in the Pacific Northwest. Here the Palouse River thunders through a deep channel that was scoured across the Palouse Hills during the great Ice Age floods. While you can easily view this spectacle of nature from the parking lot, a couple of enticing trails lead along the canyon rim high above the plunging waters—and deep into the canyon to a series of rapids upriver from the awesome falls.

GETTING THERE

From Spokane, follow I-90 west to exit 221 in Ritzville. Then drive 41.5 miles south on SR 261, turning left onto Palouse Falls Road. Reach the trailhead (elev. 900 ft) in Palouse Falls State Park after 2.4 miles. (From Pasco, take US Highway 395 north to Connell. Then follow SR 260 east for 25 miles, turning right onto SR 261. Reach the state park turnoff after 8.6 miles.)

ON THE TRAIL

Upon exiting your vehicle, you'll immediately be greeted by the roar of the Palouse River dropping 186 feet into a plunge pool beneath steep-shelved cliff walls. The First Peoples of the Palouse called these falls *Aputaput*, meaning "falling water." They tell of how the falls was created by four giant brothers pursuing a mythological creature called the Big Beaver. The river once flowed smoothly into the Snake River, the story goes, until the Big Beaver was pursued and speared five times. Wounded, he gouged out canyon walls and forced the river to change course to plummet over a cliff. Big Beaver's claw marks can still be seen in the canyon walls—the basalt columns. And the river indeed changed course. It once flowed through the Washtucna Coulee until the Ice Age floods forced its relocation to where you are now standing.

Feel free to first walk the paved path to falls vistas and interpretive signs. Then start this hike, which begins on a service road at the north end of the parking area. Saunter past willows and through sage and flowers—lots of them. Depending on the season, look for camas, lupine, desert parsley, arrowleaf balsamroot, bluebells, yellow bells, and more.

At 0.1 mile, a well-defined path branches right along the canyon rim above the falls. You'll be returning left, so take the path right and proceed with caution, staying a safe distance away from the canyon's edge. Avoid the social paths that head into the canyon, as they can be extremely dangerous. Look for snakes and yellow-bellied marmots along the way—and of course stop to marvel at the river below.

At 0.25 mile, reach a spot above the thundering falls. Peer down at Castle Rock with its turrets and parapets. Then continue along the rim, enjoying vertigo-inducing views into the chasm below. A series of rapids in a bend in the river beneath an impressive face of columnar basalt soon comes into view. That's your destination.

At 0.5 mile, come to the end of a service road (elev. 925 ft). The trail continues right through a small gap, steeply dropping (use caution) to a set of railroad tracks. The line is still in use, so stay clear. Walk to the right, along the tracks, for 0.1 mile and then pick up trail again. Descend across a basalt talus slope, reaching the canyon floor in another 0.1 mile. Then on easy trail continue through

While not as breathtaking as Palouse Falls, the upper falls sit in a wild and gorgeous canyon.

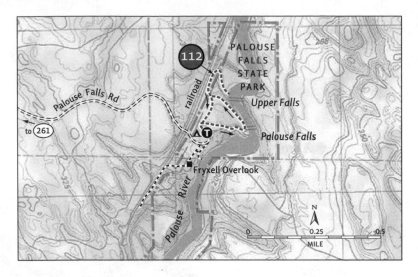

pockets of head-high sage, reaching the river's edge at the rapids (elev. 775 ft). This is a nice spot to sit and ponder. Or feel free to scout around the canyon floor, but stay snake awake! When ready to return, retrace your steps to the service road and follow it 0.3 mile back to the trailhead.

EXTENDING YOUR TRIP

From the trailhead, take a short trail south to the Fryxell Overlook. From there a trail heads a short distance south along the railroad tracks before descending to a bench in the canyon. Adventurous and sure-footed souls may want to check it out.

Opposite: Sulphur buckwheat brightens the rugged terrain near Deadman Peak in the Blue Mountains.

blue mountains

Plateaus flanked by narrow ridges and slopes that drop steeply into deep canyons characterize the Washington portion of the Blue Mountains. Stray from the river drainages or high plateaus and the terrain falls into the general category of vertical. The range stretches about 190 miles from central Oregon into southeastern Washington, where the Blues are the headwaters for Snake and Columbia River tributaries sought by steelhead returning from the ocean to spawn.

While just a fraction of the 1.4 million-acre Umatilla National Forest, the Pomeroy and Walla Walla Ranger Districts maintain hundreds of miles of trails in the Eastern Washington portion of the Blues. The marquee destination for hikers and horse packers is the 177,465-acre Wenaha-Tucannon Wilderness, named for the area's two major river drainages. The Washington Department of Fish and Wildlife also manages 70,000 acres of public land primarily for fish and wildlife habitat in the Blue Mountains Wildlife Area Complex. The busiest period in the Blues is October through early November, when most campsites and turnouts are filled with hunters pursuing Rocky Mountain elk.

113 Lewis and Clark Trail State Park

RATING/ DIFFICULTY	LOOP	ELEV GAIN/ HIGH POINT	SEASON
*/1	0.8 mile	none/ 1400 feet	Year-round

Maps: USGS Huntsville, state park map online; **Contact:** Lewis and Clark Trail State Park, (509) 337-6457, www.parks.wa.gov /parks; **Notes:** Discover Pass required. Dogs permitted on-leash; **GPS:** N 46 17.376 W 118 04.281

Saunter through a lush forest that embraces the trout-filled Touchet River. Surrounded by sun-baked hills of golden grasses, this small forested tract retains moisture, making it a cool green haven on a hot summer's day. Old-growth ponderosa pines and cottonwoods help shade the way. Some of them graced this grove when Lewis and Clark passed through on May 2, 1806, on their return from the Pacific.

GETTING THERE

From Pasco, head east on US Highway 12, turning left onto State Route 124 just after crossing the Snake River Bridge. Follow SR 124 for 45 miles to Waitsburg, picking up US 12 once again and continuing east 4.3 miles to the Lewis and Clark Trail State Park. (From Dayton, travel west on US 12 for 5.3 miles.) Turn left (north) into the park, proceeding to the campground restroom building and trailhead (elev. 1400 ft).

ON THE TRAIL

Behind the restrooms, with silhouettes of the intrepid duo Lewis and Clark pointing the way, find the trailhead for the Fur, Fins, and Feathers Nature Trail. Grab an interpretive brochure (or ask the ranger for one), and then set out west (right) on this delightful little loop. You'll immediately notice how thick the vegetation is. Nettles grow head high—stay on the trail or be zapped. The trail circles the campground, often resonating with the sounds of happy families. During quieter times, birdsong fills the air.

After crossing a service road and the campground loop road, begin circling back under an impressive canopy of cottonwoods. The trail brushes alongside the Touchet River, providing good views out to the open

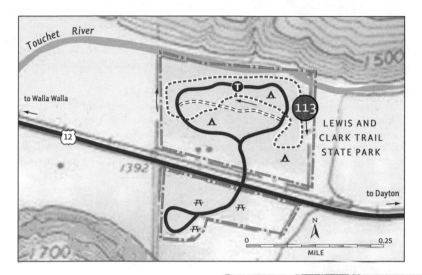

countryside beyond. It was this promising countryside that attracted early settlers to the region, particularly French Canadians who came with the early fur brigades. Touchet is derived from the French word *toucheur*, which means "cattle driver."

But long before the fur trappers and Lewis and Clark, this region bustled with the activity of First Peoples. They traversed the area via the Nimipooiskit Trail, which extended from the Rocky Mountains to the Pacific Ocean. Remnants of this trail still exist in the valley.

Notice the heavy sediment along the riverbank, evidence of past flooding and the reason why this area is so lush with vegetation and hosts a healthy assortment of birds. Look up at overhanging limbs for osprey. Look in the grasses for scurrying quails. And look out in the open fields for magpies. The delightful trail soon skirts the group camp

A giant cottonwood along the Touchet River

before turning away from the river to head back west. Cross the campground loop road once more and return to your start.

EXTENDING YOUR TRIP
The park continues on the south side of US 12, where there's a short but nice nature trail and interpretive displays on Lewis and Clark. Learn, too, about the Bateman family who homesteaded this tract in 1864 and sold it to the state during the Great Depression. During this austere time, park officials and townsfolk constructed the restroom building from 10,000 stones acquired from the Touchet River. During summer months, park personnel provide historical interpretation and guided walks.

114 Mill Creek

RATING/ DIFFICULTY	LOOP	ELEV GAIN/ HIGH POINT	SEASON
***/1	5.2 miles	155 feet/ 1270 feet	Year-round

Maps: USGS Walla Walla, Army Corps trail map available online; **Contact:** US Army Corps of Engineers, Walla Walla District, (509) 527-7160, www.nww.usace.army.mil; **Notes:** Bennington Lake open 5:00AM–10:00PM. Partly open to mountain bikes, horses. Partly wheelchair-accessible. Dogs permitted on-leash; **GPS:** N 46 04.575 118 16.371

Thanks to damaging floods during the late eighteenth and early nineteenth centuries, Walla Walla residents now have in their backyard a 612-acre public tract of rolling hills, forested creeks, and trails. More than 20 miles worth,

actually, embracing Mill Creek and circling Bennington Lake—all part of a flood-control project that overflows with great hiking opportunities.

GETTING THERE
From Walla Walla, head east on US Highway 12, exiting onto Airport Way. Head south on Airport Way, reaching intersection with Isaacs Avenue in 0.2 mile. Proceed straight onto Tausick Way, pass Walla Walla Community College, and cross Mill Creek and turn left on Reservoir Road after 0.4 mile. Continue 0.5 mile to parking and the trailhead (elev. 1160 ft) at the Mill Creek Office. Privy available.

Concrete blocks across the spillway make for a fun (or nerve-wracking) crossing.

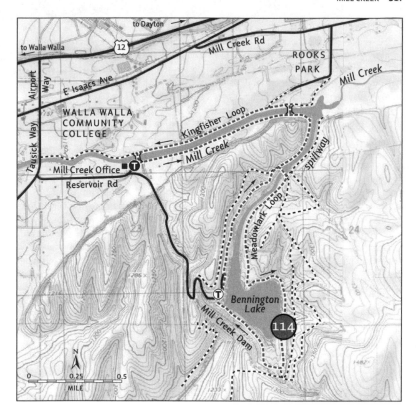

ON THE TRAIL

More than 20 miles of multiuse, nonmotorized trails, and service roads traverse Mill Creek, the largest tract of public land in the Walla Walla Valley. The suggested hike here incorporates two of the three loop trails within the complex, offering a nice half-day hike. Feel free to shorten, lengthen, or create your own loops and combinations.

From the trailhead, head east on the Kingfisher Loop, following a service road along the creek, tiered and between levees (you're on one) as part of the flood-control project.

Originating high in the Blue Mountains, the creek's waters are clean and sparkling. The way is practically level and lined with cottonwoods and other greenery. At 0.8 mile, come to a bridge and a junction. If you're just out for a short hike, cross the bridge and head left downstream (right leads to Rooks Park, another alternative trailhead). The paved Mill Creek Recreation Trail comes to another bridge that takes you back to the trailhead for a 1.7-mile loop.

The suggested hike continues straight 0.1 mile to a diversion dam and a service road (part of the Whitetail Trail loop). Head right on the service road over a grassy hillside that parallels a diversion spillway and reach a junction (elev. 1270 ft) with the Meadowlark Loop trail at 1.3 miles. Turn left and walk across the spillway, getting your feet wet or, if you're determined not to, hopping across a series of concrete blocks. Ignore side trails and stay on the Meadowlark Loop alongside and encircling Bennington Lake. While motor-free, the lake isn't quiet, echoing with the sounds of happy paddlers and swimmers—much to the chagrin of fishermen and women in pursuit of rainbows.

Pass through pockets of deciduous trees—pretty in fall and shade-granting in summer. The way is near level. Cross the Mill Creek Dam (elev. 1225 ft) and pass through the busy parking lots and picnic areas along the lake's southwest shore. Catch some nice views of the Blues across the lake. Then resume quieter ambling through fields, returning to the spillway junction at 3.9 miles. Return to Mill Creek and take the Kingfisher Loop back to your vehicle for a hike of 5.2 miles.

EXTENDING YOUR TRIP
For near-shoreline access to Bennington Lake, from the Mill Creek trailhead drive 1 mile east on Reservoir Road to parking and trailheads at Bennington Lake.

115 Deadman Peak

RATING/ DIFFICULTY	ROUND-TRIP	ELEV GAIN/ HIGH POINT	SEASON
***/3	6 miles	1780 feet/ 5960 feet	late June–Oct

Maps: USGS Deadman Peak, Umatilla National Forest map; **Contact:** Umatilla National Forest, Walla Walla Ranger District, (509) 522-6290, www.fs.fed.us/r6/uma/walla2; **Notes:** Open to mountain bikes, horses. Rough access road. Access restricted south of trail into Mill Creek watershed; **GPS:** N 46 03.765 W 117 54.891

Except for a few dozen hunters who get special permits to probe this area in late October, the Intake–Deadman Peak Trail is rarely tramped by hikers. It has no trailhead sign and is not clearly listed among hiking options on the Forest Service website. The route forms the boundary around a portion of the pristine Mill Creek Watershed, which is monitored occasionally by patrols to keep people away from the drinking-water source for Walla Walla. Vehicle access includes a few miles on the rough but scenic mile-high Kendall Skyline Road, completed in 1928. A short side trip leads to the Table Rock Lookout. Like forbidden fruit, you can look at Deadman Peak from the lookout and hike within a couple hundred feet of its summit on the trail, but the top is just inside the watershed boundary and off-limits.

GETTING THERE
From US Highway 12 in Dayton, turn south toward Bluewood Ski Area on 4th Street, which eventually becomes Kendall Skyline Road (Forest Road 64). Drive 23.2 miles to a junction with FR 46 and continue straight. Go 0.3 mile farther and turn left, continuing on FR 64 toward the Table Rock Lookout. Drive 2 miles on this rough, talcum-powder-dusty road segment and look for an unauthorized road heading up the open slope to the right just past Blakely Spring. This is a possible

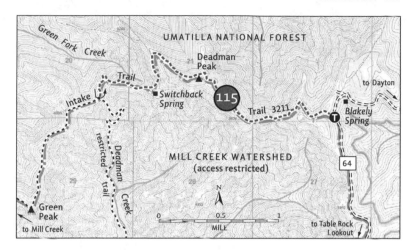

parking spot. Continue as FR 64 bends south for 0.2 mile and look to the uphill side for the first of many steel posts with 12-inch-wide signs designating the Mill Creek Watershed Boundary. This first sign is the trailhead, with room for one vehicle to park clear of the road if two wheels are up on the slope (elev. 5820 ft).

ON THE TRAIL

The Forest Service clearly makes no effort to make the beginning of the route apparent. But another watershed boundary sign up the slope helps get hikers on course. Intake Trail No. 3211 soon becomes a single-track route, with boundary signs on your left every few tenths of a mile or so.

Deadman Peak is seen in the distance beyond Table Rock Lookout.

The trail undulates on a north slope lush with shrubs, including huckleberry and false hellebore. Columbines might catch your eye in August. Soon the landscape opens to sweeping views of the Columbia and Walla Walla County farmlands below. As the trail drops into a notch, Deadman Peak is in full view, about 0.8 mile ahead, distinguished by a bald basalt outcropping lapping over from the summit.

The trail contours around the north side of Deadman Peak, tantalizingly close to the summit. But anywhere there's a short scramble route to the peak, there's likely to be a watershed boundary sign reminding you that it's off-limits. The trail continues around to an open point on the west side of the peak and a ridge that would lead gently to the summit, if only it weren't forbidden.

Then the trail begins a long steady descent. It's a total of 2 miles to the open point of the ridge where the trail drops left and contours southward. Turn back here for a 4-mile round trip. However, the next mile is interesting for wildlife enthusiasts. The trail passes Switchback Spring at the headwaters of Green Fork Creek, where elk thoroughfares often can be seen. A bit farther, the trail breaks out onto an open ridge, where you can see back to the Table Rock Lookout without violating watershed restrictions.

At 3 miles you can see where the restricted Deadman Creek Trail starts up and over the lip and drops down into the restricted watershed. Turn back here for a 6-mile round trip.

EXTENDING YOUR TRIP

Drive south on FR 64 about 3 miles and hike or drive up the 0.2-mile spur (high-clearance required for driving) to the Table Rock Lookout (elev. 6250 ft) for the best view of Deadman Peak and the entire surrounding area. Privy available.

116 Middle Point Ridge

RATING/ DIFFICULTY	ROUND-TRIP	ELEV GAIN/ HIGH POINT	SEASON
***/3	5.5 miles	1730 feet/ 5130 feet	June–Nov

Maps: USGS Eckler Mountain, USGS Godman Spring, Umatilla National Forest map; **Contact:** Umatilla National Forest, Walla Walla Ranger District, (509) 522-6290, www .fs.fed.us/r6/uma/walla2; **Notes:** NW Forest Pass or federal equivalent required. Occasional motorcycle use; **GPS:** N 46 08.154 W 117 48.520

A paved road from Dayton leads to a route through forest that was burned—some old monarchs were spared—by the 110,000-acre Columbia Complex forest fires of 2006. Up from the North Fork Touchet River, the trail offers good views and an even better workout as it climbs to pleasant strolling on Middle Point Ridge. The entire hike is just a smidge off-piste from the Bluewood Ski Area.

GETTING THERE

From US Highway 12 in Dayton, turn south toward Bluewood Ski Area on 4th Street, which eventually becomes Kendall Skyline Road (Forest Road 64). Drive a total of 16.5 miles to the trailhead on the left (elev. 3390 ft). Privy available.

ON THE TRAIL

Middle Point Trail No. 3116 drops from the paved parking area, crosses a footbridge

Some hearty trees survived forest fire on Middle Point Ridge.

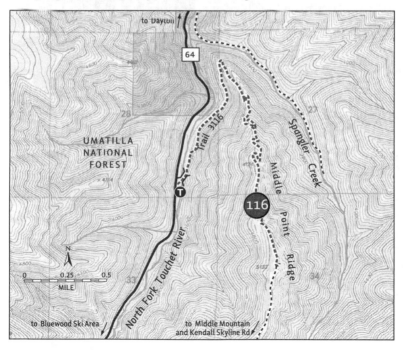

over the North Fork Touchet River, and heads down along the stream. Soon it begins a nicely graded climb to the first switchback. Then the grade steps up a notch, angling toward the ridge and switchbacking into rock bands.

At the ridge, you'll begin getting a close look at the aftermath of the 2006 fires. The trail becomes a pleasant walk on the ridge up to an open high point with distant views, a good turnaround point.

EXTENDING YOUR TRIP

Continue south on the trail 1.5 miles on a nice ridge route to the more timbered Middle Mountain (elev. 5724 ft). From there, you're more likely to encounter motorized vehicles as the trail heads toward Kendall Skyline Road.

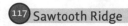 **117 Sawtooth Ridge**

RATING/ DIFFICULTY	ROUND-TRIP	ELEV GAIN / HIGH POINT	SEASON
***/3	5.8 miles	850 feet/ 5930 feet	June–Nov

Maps: USGS Godman Spring, Umatilla National Forest map; **Contact:** Umatilla National Forest, Pomeroy Ranger District, (509) 843-1891, www.fs.fed.us/r6/uma /pomeroy; **Notes:** NW Forest Pass or federal equivalent required. Open to horses. Wilderness trail, mechanized equipment prohibited; **GPS:** N 46 03.701 W 117 50.642

   This hike samples the scenic high portion of a trail that eventually drops 14

Early morning is prime time to hike Sawtooth Ridge.

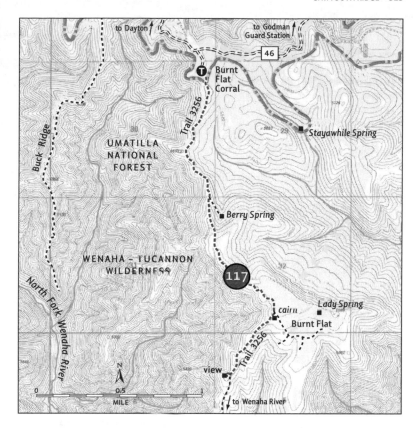

miles to the Wenaha River in the heart of the Wenaha-Tucannon Wilderness. Views constantly change. The Forest Service tends the trail well, yet use is light except for the occasional horse group.

GETTING THERE

From US Highway 12 in Dayton, turn south toward Bluewood Ski Area on 4th Street, which eventually becomes Kendall Skyline Road (Forest Road 64). Drive a total of 23.2 miles to a junction and turn left on FR 46 toward Godman Guard Station. Drive 3.7 miles and turn right into a large horse-staging area. Privy available. If your vehicle can climb the rocky little incline, continue 0.2 mile to the trailhead (elev. 5620 ft) and more parking at the end of Burnt Flat Road (FR 240).

ON THE TRAIL

From the Sawtooth Trail No. 3256 trailhead, go down into an open forest. At 1.5 miles, break into openings with big views out to adjacent canyon rims. The route assumes a ridge that alternates from desertlike landscape to lush woods. Sulfur buckwheat blooms from a rocky crust-like soil in a vibrant show, even in the heat of August.

At about 3 miles, take the right fork at a cairned junction. (Left goes to a horse-camping area on Burnt Flat.) Soon break out onto an open ridge. On a clear day the view to the south includes the Wallowa Mountains of northeastern Oregon.

Then the trail drops steeply into a notch. You may want to turn back here, but it's worthwhile to continue along the next finger ridge. Leave the trail when it begins dropping significantly again into the trees and wander for the views on both sides of the open ridge before hooking up with the trail again back to the trailhead.

EXTENDING YOUR TRIP

Take the left (southeast) fork at the cairned junction and explore the Burnt Flat area for interesting campsites and springs that attract wildlife. The trail isn't always maintained.

118 Twin Buttes

RATING/ DIFFICULTY	ROUND-TRIP	ELEV GAIN/ HIGH POINT	SEASON
***/3	3.8 miles	700 feet/ 5674 feet	June–Oct

Maps: USGS Godman Spring, USGS Oregon Butte, USFS Wenaha-Tucannon Wilderness map; **Contact:** Umatilla National Forest, Pomeroy Ranger District, (509) 843-1891, www.fs.fed.us/r6/uma/pomeroy; **Notes:** NW Forest Pass or federal equivalent required. Open to horses. Wilderness trail, mechanized equipment prohibited. Rough road; **GPS:** N 46 01.696, W 117 46.676

This trip is one of the most painless ways to experience the Wenaha-Tucannon Wilderness, considering the access road offers the deepest penetration into the otherwise roadless area. You'll be surrounded by wilderness as you leave the trailhead. The trail to Twin Buttes leads to views overlooking a wilderness known for its carved canyons rather than its peaks. Expect hunting camps at the trailhead when big-game seasons open in October.

GETTING THERE

From US Highway 12 about 4 miles west of Pomeroy (or 8 miles east of the junction with State Route 127), turn south near milepost 399 on Tatman Mountain Road. Follow the signs for Camp Wooten, joining the Tucannon River Road after 9 miles. (From points farther west, get on the Tucannon River Road at Dayton.) Turn south on Tucannon River Road. Pass Camp Wooten, drive about 2 miles, and turn right onto Forest Road 4620. Drive 4 miles and turn left on Kendall Skyline Road (FR 46). Go south on FR 46 for nearly 17 miles, passing the Godman Guard Station, and turn left onto rougher FR 300. Drive about 5 miles and bear left at a Y (may not be marked) to the trailhead and camping area at Twin Buttes Spring (elev. 5350 ft). Privy available.

ON THE TRAIL

Hike 0.3 mile on an old roadbed to a junction with the trail to Grizzly Bear Ridge (Hike 119) and turn left onto East Butte Creek Trail No. 3112. The trail sidehills to the spine of the ridge before following a few waves of terrain to an opening. No distant views here, but the next opening offers fine views into the wilderness. Keep going.

Steep terrain sprawls below Twin Buttes.

After another short climb, the trail angles up along the north butte at 1.5 miles from the trail junction. You'll want to head up off-trail to the right and soak in the view from the top. But first, continue another few hundred yards to the precipitous view down into the canyon bowels from the first switchback as the trail begins its drop toward Butte Creek.

Go back a couple hundred yards and scramble a short way up to the butte. Don't miss it. The knob was so important to one family we encountered during research for this book that they scattered a parent's ashes on the summit.

EXTENDING YOUR TRIP

The trail down to Butte Creek makes for an 8-mile round-trip. Very fit hikers can hike 12 miles one-way all the way to a shuttle vehicle at the Godman trailhead on FR 46 about 5 miles north from the junction with FR 300.

119 Grizzly Bear Ridge

RATING/ DIFFICULTY	ROUND-TRIP	ELEV GAIN/ HIGH POINT	SEASON
***/3	8.2 miles	1350 feet/ 5400 feet	June–Nov

Maps: USGS Godman Spring, USGS Oregon Butte, USGS Elbow Creek, USFS Wenaha-Tucannon Wilderness map; **Contact:** Umatilla National Forest, Pomeroy Ranger District, (509) 843-1891, www.fs.fed.us/r6/uma/pomeroy; **Notes:** NW Forest Pass or federal equivalent required. Open to horses. Wilderness trail, mechanized equipment prohibited; **GPS:** N 46 01.696, W 117 46.676

  Although signs of elk are common, no grizzlies are found in the Wenaha-Tucannon Wilderness. If somebody gave Grizzly Bear Ridge its name

to help maintain the area's solitude, it worked. Trail No. 3103, open only to hikers and horses, is one of the gentlest and most interesting routes from the high country down into the heart of the 177,465-acre wilderness. This trip takes on just the upper portion of this 8-mile trail before it plunges to the Wenaha River.

GETTING THERE

From US Highway 12 about 4 miles west of Pomeroy (or 8 miles east of the junction with State Route 127), turn south near milepost 399 on Tatman Mountain Road. Follow the signs for Camp Wooten, joining the Tucannon River Road after 9 miles. (From points farther west, get on the Tucannon River Road at Dayton.) Turn south on Tucannon River Road. Pass Camp Wooten, drive about 2 miles, and turn right onto Forest Road 4620. Drive 4 miles and turn left on Kendall Skyline Road (FR 46). Go south on FR 46 for nearly 17 miles, passing the Godman Guard Station, and turn left onto rougher FR 300. Drive

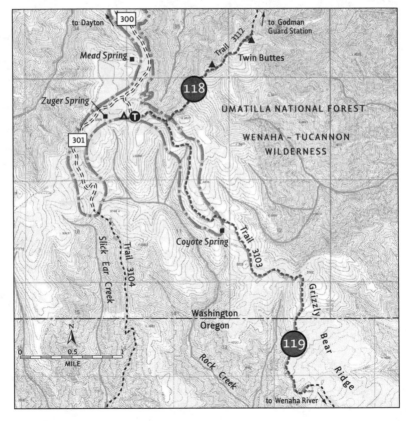

about 5 miles and bear left at a Y (may not be marked) to the trailhead and camping area at Twin Buttes Spring (elev. 5350 ft). Privy available.

ON THE TRAIL

Hike 0.3 mile on an old pre-wilderness roadbed to the junction with East Butte Creek Trail No. 3112 (Hike 118) and continue straight on Trail No. 3103 toward Grizzly Bear Ridge. Enjoy alternating through forest and big meadows sparse with grass as you gradually head down the ridge toward the heart of the Wenaha River canyon.

At 1.7 mile, cross a small drainage and a trickle of water called Coyote Spring before heading into an opening that becomes desertlike by late summer. The trail can fade here, but it's easy to find on the fall line of the ridge. Watch along the trail for shredded saplings, likely the late-summer and early fall work of bull elk as they polish their antlers and mark territory for the September mating season.

At the top of a startling 0.4-mile-long uphill grade in this generally downhill route, there's a grassy knob to explore off-trail to the left. It's prominent on maps at an elevation of 5162 feet.

Then continue down the trail along a semi-open slope and look for signs indicating the Washington-Oregon border. Some people will call this good—a nice place to picnic and turn back for a round-trip of 7 miles. But it's worthwhile to continue down the trail, watching the forest type change. More ponderosa pines are coming up, and there's a grove of western larch in the basin to the west. Soon the trail heads slightly uphill to daylight and open views on a knob before descending again. You've hiked 4.1 miles, just over halfway to the Wenaha River. This is a good spot to rest, take in the view over Rock Creek, and turn back.

Grizzly Bear Ridge crosses the Washington–Oregon border.

EXTENDING YOUR TRIP

Strong hikers can continue on trail another 4 miles to the Wenaha River for a total elevation drop of 2800 feet. Along the way you'll pass through rare old-growth ponderosa parklands. The trail drops more steeply in the last 3 miles down to the river. Backpackers can enjoy a two- or three-day 18-mile loop by heading upstream along the Wenaha and then climbing the steep Slick Ear Trail No. 3104 to a trailhead just 2 miles from the Twin Buttes Spring trailhead.

120 Oregon and West Buttes

RATING/ DIFFICULTY	ROUND-TRIP	ELEV GAIN/ HIGH POINT	SEASON
****/2	6.1 miles	800 feet/ 6387 feet	June–Nov

Map: USFS Wenaha-Tucannon Wilderness map; **Contact:** Umatilla National Forest, Pomeroy Ranger District, (509) 843-1891, www.fs.usda.gov/umatilla; **Notes:** NW Forest Pass or federal equivalent required. Open to horses. Wilderness trail, mechanized equipment prohibited; **GPS:** N 46 07.104 W 117 42.914

 *An easy and highly scenic loop to the highest summit in Washington's Blues, this hike is suitable for folks of all ages and abilities. Stand upon open summits, taking in sweeping views of rugged high tableland ridges and deep forested canyons cut by pristine waterways. Visit a historic fire lookout, flower-speckled ridges, and cool evergreen groves. And in this corner of the state where human visitation is light, chances are always good for viewing wild critters.*

GETTING THERE

From Pomeroy, head 4.5 miles west on US Highway 12 and turn left (near milepost 399) onto Tatman Mountain Road, proceeding 9 miles to Tucannon River Road (follow signs for Camp Wooten: The main paved road becomes Linville Gulch Road after about 1.2 miles and at about 6.5 miles you bear right onto Blind Grade Road). Now turn left and continue 11 miles south on Tucannon River Road (which becomes Forest Road 47; the pavement ends at 9 miles), turning right onto Patrick Grade Road (FR 4620). Proceed 4.1 miles to a junction with Kendall Skyline Road (CR 1424). (From Dayton, head east on Patit Road for 14 miles, turning left onto Hartsock Grade and driving 3 miles to the Tucannon River Road. Turn right and continue 13 miles, turning right onto Patrick Grade Road/FR 4620. Proceed 4.1 miles to the junction with CR 1424. Or reach this point from Dayton via shorter routes involving longer gravel sections.) Continue south on CR 1424 (which becomes FR 46 for 11.6 miles), bearing left onto FR 4608 at Godman Guard Station. Follow FR 4608 for 5.8 miles to the road's end at Teepee Campground and the trailhead (elev. 5500 ft). Privy available.

ON THE TRAIL

Getting to the trailhead is the tough part. Now from a high starting point, enjoy a nice hike into a small section of the sprawling 177,465-acre Wenaha-Tucannon Wilderness spanning the Blues in both Washington and Oregon. Starting from the Teepee Campground, which is generally pretty quiet except for deer and elk season, enjoy good views south into the Butte Creek drainage. Locate the Mount Misery Trail and start hiking. This trail travels 13 miles across the rooftop of the Blues, allowing for more day-

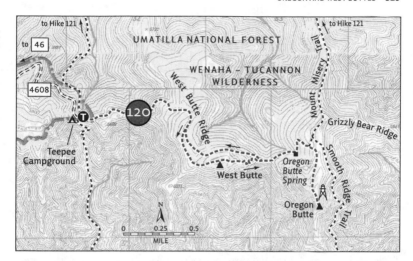

hiking options (see Hikes 121 and 123) as well as for some fine backpacking.

On good trail enter a mature forest of western larch. Thanks to these trees, the Blues turn gold come October. Reach a saddle after about 0.5 mile and then climb more steeply to an unsigned junction (elev. 6100 ft) at about 1.1 miles. The trail was recently rerouted left around West Butte. Head right on the old trail (returning later on the newer trail) to check out West Butte. After hopping over some downed trees the way is pretty easygoing. Soon enjoy good views to the south and southwest.

At 1.7 miles the trail skirts just below the summit of 6292-foot West Butte. From this summit, fourth-highest in the Washington Blues, take in excellent views of nearby Oregon Butte and the impressive Wallowa Mountains in Oregon. Locate the misspelled benchmark pointing to "Oreon Butte." It's another classic, like the "Ceder Butt" benchmark in the Snoqualmie Pass area.

The trail continues east, switchbacking

Oregon Butte's sun-kissed open grassy slopes

UNTRAMMELED EASTERN WASHINGTON

Large portions of the mountains and forests of northeastern and southeastern Washington lie within national forest land, but that doesn't necessarily mean they're protected. National forests are managed for "multiple use." While some uses (like hiking) are fairly compatible with land preservation, other uses (such as mining, logging, and off-road-vehicle use) usually aren't.

Recognizing that parts of our natural heritage should be altered as little as possible, Congress overwhelmingly passed the Wilderness Act in 1964 with bipartisan support (the House approved passage 373–1). One of the strongest and most important pieces of environmental legislation in our nation's history, the Wilderness Act afforded some of our most precious wild landscapes a reprieve from exploitation, development, roads, and harmful activities, such as motorized recreation. Even bicycles are banned from federal wilderness areas. Wilderness is "an area where the earth and community of life are untrammeled by man," states the act. "Where man himself is a visitor who does not remain."

While federal lands in northeastern and southeastern Washington had no shortage of areas qualified for inclusion in the wilderness system back in 1964, none were included. In 1978, with the passage of the Endangered American Wilderness Act, Eastern Washington received its first wilderness area (sharing it with Oregon): the 177,465 Wenaha-Tucannon Wilderness in the Blue Mountains. In 1984, a sweeping statewide wilderness bill was signed into law by President Reagan, creating the 7140-acre Juniper Dunes Wilderness on BLM lands and the 41,335-acre Salmo-Priest Wilderness in the Colville and Kaniksu National Forests.

While Washington ranks fourth among the states for total wilderness acres, nearly all of it is in the western half of the state. Only 3 percent of the Colville National Forest is protected as wilderness. Many conservationists feel that it's not enough. Large tracts of Eastern Washington national forest lands are under pressure to be developed or opened to more motorized recreation, especially the latter. While some of our public lands base should be designated for those uses, most of our last remaining roadless tracts of pristine wild country should be considered for their wilderness potential. The issue isn't about "locking up lands" for solitude. Water quality and wildlife security, for example, are major benefits of wilderness.

Areas in this book that some conservation groups have recommended for wilderness include Mount Bonaparte (Hikes 3 and 4); Thirteenmile (Hikes 17 and 18); Profanity, Twin Sisters, and Bald-Snow in the Kettles (Hikes 19-36); Abercrombie-Hooknose (Hikes 42 and 43); Grassy Top (Hikes 50 and 57); Upper Tucannon and Mill Creek in the Blues (Hike 122).   —C. R.

down to reach a junction with the Mount Misery Trail (elev. 6000 ft) at about 2.1 miles. Left returns to the trailhead—but, Oregon Butte awaits first. Head right and drop to a saddle (elev. 5940 ft) shaded with larches. Then start climbing again, passing reliable Oregon Butte Spring (elev. 6000 ft) and camps (just beyond) at 2.4 miles. Continue climbing via a few switchbacks to a junction (elev. 6160 ft) at 2.6 miles. Bear right, passing nice camps, and attain the northern shoulder of Oregon Butte. Traverse a grassy ridgeline and admire expanding views and windblown firs and whitebark pines.

At 3.1 miles, pass a hitching post and continue south 0.1 mile to the 6387-foot summit of Oregon Butte, graced with a lone fir and a 1931-built fire lookout that is still periodically staffed. The views from this point, highest summit in Washington's Blues, are wonderful. Stare south down the Crooked Creek drainage, over the mesas and tableland ridges that make up the Blue Mountains, and out to the lofty and rugged Wallowas. Look west across windswept ridges and east to Mount Misery and Diamond Peak, two more summits worth exploring

Once you've had enough time wallowing in the blues, return. Hike 0.6 mile back to the Mount Misery Trail and head west, reaching a familiar junction with the old trail at 1.1 miles. This time, however, bear right on the newer trail, traversing cool forest on West Butte's north side. At 1.8 miles, continue right at the west junction (elev. 6100 ft) of the West Butte Trail and descend, coming to the trailhead at 2.9 miles, for a total round-trip of 6.1 miles.

EXTENDING YOUR TRIP

Just west of the Oregon Butte summit spur-trail junction is the Smooth Ridge Trail junction. Follow this trail for about 1.9 miles to 5461-foot Danger Point for a unique perspective of the surrounding deeply cut canyons. Strong hikers can also travel 3.3 miles on the Mount Misery Trail along high and lonely ridges to Indian Corral (elev. 5700 ft), with its excellent campsites and reliable spring.

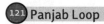
121 Panjab Loop

RATING/ DIFFICULTY	LOOP	ELEV GAIN/ HIGH POINT	SEASON
****/4	13.3 miles	3030 feet/ 5720 feet	June–Nov

Maps: USGS Panjab Creek, USFS Wenaha-Tucannon Wilderness map; **Contact:** Umatilla National Forest, Pomeroy Ranger District, (509) 843-1891, www.fs.fed.us/r6/uma/pomeroy; **Notes:** NW Forest Pass or federal equivalent required. Open to horses. Wilderness trail, mechanized equipment prohibited; **GPS:** N 46 12.332 W 117 42.435

  This challenging hike is a showcase of the Wenaha-Tucannon Wilderness. From easy-to-reach trailheads, you'll experience the sun-baked slopes, deep canyons, high plateaus, recovering burns and cool creeks of a very wild place.

GETTING THERE

From US Highway 12 between Dayton and Pomeroy, turn south toward Camp Wooten on Tucannon River Road (which becomes Forest Road 47). Drive 32 miles to Rattlesnake Trailhead on the left (elev. 3015 ft). Privy available. The trailhead is across from the entrance to the Washington Fish and Wildlife Department's Panjab South Campground (Discover Pass required) and just before the Umatilla National Forest's Panjab Campground (Northwest Forest Pass required). If you have another vehicle or bike, shuttle it up the road 2.3 miles to Panjab Trailhead, a popular staging area for equestrians.

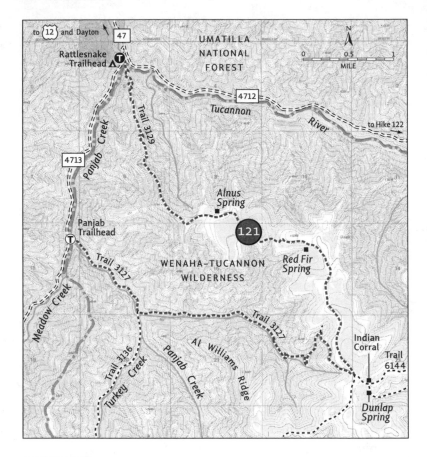

ON THE TRAIL

Rattlesnake Trail No. 3129 starts with a ford of Panjab Creek after a rambling start into the Panjab Campground. Bring sandals for the ford, which is behind campsite 1, or go farther up Panjab Creek and look for a fallen log to cross.

The trail immediately climbs from the creek (and the nearby Tucannon River) and begins switchbacking through the fireweed,

brush, and snags that recall the area's 2005 forest fires. An early start helps you cope with sun that beats down on this climb during summer mornings.

Climbing efforts are rewarded around 2.5 miles as the ridge trail gains the plateau. Rims that once loomed above in the distance are now your equals across the canyons. The plateau ranges from lush fireweed and plants revegetating the burns to wide-open

The Blue Mountains offer expansive meadows.

meadows—briefly green in the early season but soon turning desertlike in the coarse, dry soil.

At 3 miles, a sign marks Alnus Spring, which wets the greenery in the forest below the trail. The trail fades in some of these open stretches but is easy to pick up again. Soon you'll be cruising along forest edges in mostly open country. At 6 miles, watch for a four-way junction (shown as three-way on some maps) that's usually marked by a sign propped up with rocks in a starkly open slope near Indian Corral.

From this point, Rattlesnake Trail ends and continues ahead as Trail No. 6144 to Oregon Butte (Hike 120). Going left heads onto Trail No. 6144 eastward to Diamond Peak (Hike 123). (Nearby Dunlap Spring is developed for stock.) To continue on the loop trip, head down to the right (west) on a spur toward Panjab Creek. Drop into the woods and then descend a short steep shot to a junction as you enter the creek drainage.

Turn left and head down unsigned Panjab Trail No. 3127.

Suddenly you're in another world of greenery and water, crossing several creeks. In fact, the trail and an upper fork of Panjab Creek are one in the same for a short stretch. Enjoy the trail as it descends steadily along with the creek. At a junction with Turkey Creek Trail No. 3136, continue straight for the last mile to Panjab Trailhead for a hike of 11 miles.

If you didn't leave a bike or shuttle vehicle at this developed horse-staging area, you have an additional 2.3 miles of road walking downstream to Rattlesnake Trailhead.

EXTENDING YOUR TRIP

Explore Turkey Creek Trail No. 3136, which heads up along creeks 5 miles from Panjab Trailhead to Teepee Campground. Also in the area, just 1.5 miles south on FR 4713 from Panjab Trailhead, is Meadow Creek Trail No. 3123.

122 Tucannon River

RATING/ DIFFICULTY	ROUND-TRIP	ELEV GAIN/ HIGH POINT	SEASON
***/2	8 miles	500 feet/ 4050 feet	May–Nov

Map: USFS Wenaha-Tucannon Wilderness map; **Contact:** Umatilla National Forest, Pomeroy Ranger District, (509) 843-1891; www.fs.usda.gov/umatilla; **Note:** NW Forest Pass or federal equivalent required. Open to horses; **GPS:** N 46 11.315 W 117 37.519

   Enjoy this cool and shaded trail in a land of sun and hot temperatures. Hike up a deep canyon alongside the rippling Tucannon River through lush groves of old-growth fir, spruce, pine, and larch. A great hike in early season when the high country is still covered with snow, the Tucannon River Trail with its easy grade and inviting campsites also makes for a nice beginner's backpacking destination.

GETTING THERE

From Dayton, head east on Patit Road for 14 miles, turning left onto Hartsuck Grade and following it 4 miles to Tucannon River Road. (From Pomeroy, head 4.5 miles west on US Highway 12 turning left near milepost 399 onto Tatman Mountain Road and proceeding 9 miles to Tucannon River Road.) Continue 13.2 miles south on Tucannon River Road (which becomes Forest Road 47) to a Y-intersection. Bear left onto FR 4712 and follow this rough-at-times road 4.7 miles to its end and the trailhead (elev. 3550 ft). Privy available.

ON THE TRAIL

Start by crossing Sheep Creek on a sturdy bridge. The way follows a recently decommissioned road for about a 0.25 mile before transitioning to older roadbed. Traversing a bench above the Tucannon River, the trail skirts the Wenaha-Tucannon Wilderness before briefly passing through a small section of it. The 177,465-acre wilderness was created in 1978 to protect the habitat of one

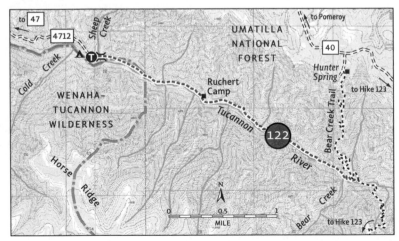

Majestic ponderosa pines—standing and fallen along the Tucannon River

of the largest herds of Rocky Mountain elk. They were introduced into the region in 1913. Hunters covet them, and during elk season this trail and many others in the region see quite a bit of human activity. Otherwise, it's pretty quiet in the backcountry of the Blues.

While most of this trail is outside the wilderness, the 12,600-acre Upper Tucannon River Roadless Area it traverses is as wild and pristine as any part of the adjacent wilderness area. The way passes through some recent burns, but plenty of towering trees survived the fires. The forest here is lush and cool, and where sunlight penetrates the canopy wildflowers grow in profusion. Pass through dark groves of spruce and open groves of pine. The river is always nearby, filling the forest with water songs.

At about 1.5 miles, come to Ruchert Camp (elev. 3675 ft). Just beyond, the river passes through a tighter stretch, where accompanying breezes funnel through and help keep the valley cool. Pass more riverside campsites and impressive groves of old trees.

At about 4 miles, just past where Bear Creek tumbles down the slopes to your south into the river, reach a junction with the Bear Creek Trail (elev. 4050 ft). To the left it climbs steeply out of the valley, and to the right it fords the Tucannon River (difficult in early season) before also climbing steeply out of the valley—making this a good spot to turn around.

EXTENDING YOUR TRIP

Follow the Bear Creek Trail in either direction for some lung-busting climbing with good views as your reward. The trail left melts out early, climbing more than 1500 feet in 2.5 miles up open slopes bursting with flowers (and ticks in early summer), reaching Hunter Spring and a trailhead accessed

from FR 40. The trail right steeply climbs 1800 feet, accessing a ridge that it then follows 4.2 miles to the Mount Misery Trail near Diamond Peak (Hike 123). Solitude is guaranteed.

123 Diamond Peak and Sheephead Corral

RATING/ DIFFICULTY	ROUND-TRIP	ELEV GAIN/ HIGH POINT	SEASON
****/3	5.8 miles	1300 feet/ 6379 feet	mid-June– Nov

Map: USFS Wenaha-Tucannon Wilderness map; **Contact:** Umatilla National Forest, Pomeroy Ranger District, (509) 843-1891, www.fs.usda.gov/umatilla; **Notes:** Open to horses. Wilderness trail, mechanized equipment prohibited. Last 2.7 miles of FR 4030 are rough, high-clearance recommended; **GPS:** N 46 07.096 W 117 31.806

Follow the Mount Misery Trail—a rather pleasant path actually—along the rooftop of Washington's Blues to stunning viewpoints and wild, rarely hiked country. Traverse meadows flush with wildflowers and mile-high ridges cloaked in larch, pine, and fir. Hike to Diamond Peak, second-highest summit in southeastern Washington, savoring breathtaking views of the deep canyons and cloud-piercing peaks south in Idaho and Oregon.

GETTING THERE

From Dayton, head 37 miles east on US Highway 12 to Pomeroy. (From Clarkston, travel 29 miles west on US 12 to Pomeroy.) Continue through town 0.5 mile past the historic courthouse, turning right onto 15th

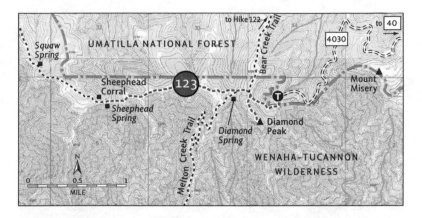

Street (signed for Umatilla National Forest and City Park), which eventually becomes Peola Road (and Mountain Road after that). At 15 miles, the pavement ends at the national forest and the road becomes Forest Road 40. After 7.8 miles, bear right at the junction with FR 42, continuing on FR 40. After 7.7 more miles, turn right onto FR 4030. Follow it for 4.5 miles (the last 2.7 miles may be rough for low-clearance vehicles) to the trailhead (elev. 5850 ft).

ON THE TRAIL

Start by leaving misery behind—that's Mount Misery, which looms over the trailhead to the east. For the stockmen who drove their cattle and sheep to the lofty hinterlands of southeastern Washington back in the early twentieth century, more than a few miserable moments often waited. To commemorate their efforts, or perhaps commiserate over them, they left the name "Misery" upon a spring and a prominent 6366-foot peak, third-highest summit (and an easy scramble from the trailhead) in Washington's Blues.

Following the Mount Misery Trail west, immediately enter the 177,465-acre Wenaha-Tucannon Wilderness, created in 1978 as part of the Endangered American Wilderness Act and spanning the Blues in both Washington and Oregon. Climbing at first on road and then bona fide trail, traverse slopes graced in blueberries and larches, which in fall add vibrant colors to this muted landscape. Pass through a gap that provides a preview of the sweeping views lying ahead, ranging from Hells Canyon to the high Wallowa Mountains of northeastern Oregon.

At 0.7 mile, emerge onto the first of several open, grassy, and flower-sporting "balds." Stay left at an unmarked junction (elev. 6275 ft) at 0.8 mile, unless you want to follow the Bear Creek Trail down into the Tucannon River valley (Hike 122). Follow the unmarked side trail that veers left for 0.4 mile to 6379-foot Diamond Peak, highest summit in Garfield County. Lying just outside of the wilderness boundary (hence the communications tower), this peak sports breathtaking views south, especially during sunrise and sunset. Scan the canyon country sprawled below, including the magnificent Grande Ronde Valley. Notice any mountain

Looking south across stark canyon country from Diamond Peak

mahogany on the peak? Washington's Blues are the northern limit for this tree—a species ubiquitous in the Great Basin.

The trip to Diamond Peak is short, so you may want to hike a little more. Return to the Mount Misery Trail and continue west, dropping into a forested saddle (elev. 6175 ft) where the Melton Creek Trail begins its long journey south to the Wenaha River valley. Your trail climbs steeply (albeit not for long), cresting a bald knob (elev. 6350 ft) with excellent views back to Diamond Peak.

Carry on, undulating between sage-scented meadows and fir and larch groves. There are plenty of good views along the way of waves upon waves of blue ridges lapping at the horizon. Check for animal tracks in the granite-pumice-till that blankets the ridges. See any cougar tracks? The big cats are abundant here. At 2.5 miles (from the trailhead), after a descent, come to the Sheephead Corral and spring (elev. 5975 ft)—a good place to rest, have lunch, camp, and call it a hike.

EXTENDING YOUR TRIP

If you want to push on a little farther, continue on the Mount Misery Trail another 0.5 mile climbing to a locally known knob called Sheephead (elev. 6125 feet) where there are excellent views out to Oregon Butte. The trail continues all the way to the Teepee Car Camp making it (with its numerous springs and camps) a great backpacking choice.

124 North Fork Asotin Creek

RATING/ DIFFICULTY	ROUND-TRIP	ELEV GAIN/ HIGH POINT	SEASON
***/2	20 miles	1750 feet/ 3080 feet	Mar–Dec

Maps: USGS Potter Hill, USGS Pinkham Butte, USGS Harlow Ridge, Umatilla National Forest map; **Contact:** Washington Department of Fish and Wildlife, Asotin Wildlife Area, Clarkston, (509) 758-3151, http://wdfw.wa.gov/lands/wildlife_areas /asotin, and Umatilla National Forest, Pomeroy Ranger District, (509) 843-1891, www.fs.fed.us/r6/uma/pomeroy;   **Notes:** Discover Pass required. Open to mountain bikes, horses. Motorcycles permitted after July 1. Watch for rattlesnakes, ticks; **GPS:** N 46 15.693 W 117 17.922

Late-winter and spring hikers in particular will appreciate the Asotin Wildlife Area's sanctuary from motorized traffic, which is prohibited part of the year to protect wintering Blue Mountains deer, elk, and bighorn sheep in the valley near the Snake River. The trail along North Fork Asotin Creek leads high into the Umatilla National Forest, creating options to please hikers of all levels. The creek has special status in wildlife circles: It's a spawning area for steelhead that swim hundreds of miles upstream from the ocean, a calving area for elk, a mountain quail recovery area, and a magnet for wintering swarms of ladybird beetles, better known as ladybugs.

Spring break along North Fork Asotin Creek

GETTING THERE
From Clarkston, follow Riverside Drive (State Route 129) south to Asotin. Just before crossing the bridge at Asotin, turn right on Bauermeister Drive (which becomes Asotin Creek Road). Drive 2.9 miles and turn right on County Road 1100. Go 11.2 miles and bear right at the fork onto South Fork Asotin Creek–Lick Creek Road (CR 181). Go 0.5 mile to an Asotin Wildlife Area gate, which is locked December 1–April 1. Drive or walk another 0.3 mile to the trailhead (elev. 1990 ft) on the left at the confluence of Lick Creek and North Fork Asotin Creek.

ON THE TRAIL
Immediately you must hop rocks across Lick Creek before starting on the trail that skirts a crop field planted for wildlife forage and

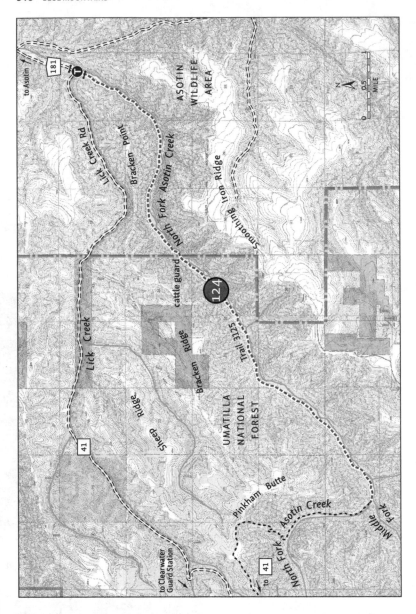

heads up North Fork Asotin Creek. Soon the rush of water will be a nearly constant companion. Hike this trail as long as you please before turning around, to get your desired mileage.

Spring hikers are likely to see signs of big game as well as wild turkeys. Grouse lurk in the thick streamside vegetation. Keep an ear open toward the steep open slope of basalt outcroppings for the chuckle of chukar partridges and the cascading call of canyon wrens. With so much prey concentrated here, it's no wonder that signs of black bears and cougars also can be found.

Hike nearly 4 miles on a pleasant cruising-speed trail that is wide enough for the ATVs the Asotin Wildlife Area managers use for maintaining the route. After crossing the cattle guard into national forest land, the trail eventually narrows into a single-track.

Understory vegetation includes elderberry, sumac, and Oregon grape. Potential hazards include the occasional rattlesnake, thorny blackberry vines, and scattered patches of poison ivy.

As the canyon begins to narrow, huge ponderosa pines shade the way. After 8 miles, a series of springs emerge from mossy basalt cliffs before you reach a small grassy meadow near the confluence of the Middle Branch of North Fork Asotin Creek. Check out this area, but tread lightly and don't linger. Thousands of ladybird beetles hibernate here in the matted grass and bark of dying trees.

This is a good turnaround point for a round trip of nearly 20 miles.

EXTENDING YOUR TRIP
The trail continues up the North Fork for about 1.5 miles. Then it switchbacks up a steep ridge to Pinkham Butte, where the views can be stunning. After the Lick Creek Road opens and snow melts, you can leave a car at the west trailhead on Lick Creek Road (11.5 miles west from the lower trailhead, near the junction of FR 41 and FR 4026) for an excellent 14-mile one-way trek in either direction. **Notes:** Trail No. 3125 upstream from the Middle Fork was scheduled for rerouting, possibly in 2013.

125 Puffer Butte

RATING/ DIFFICULTY	LOOP	ELEV GAIN/ HIGH POINT	SEASON
***/2	2.5 miles	600 feet/ 4500 feet	Apr–Nov

Maps: USGS Fields Spring, state park map online; **Contact:** Fields Spring State Park, (509) 256-3332, www.parks.wa.gov/parks; **Notes:** Discover Pass required. Dogs permitted on-leash; **GPS:** N 46 04.805 W 117 10.142

Wildlife abounds in this lightly visited region of high plateaus, deep canyons, and pine-forested hills. Washington's rugged and isolated southeastern corner consists of some of the most dramatic landscapes in the state. This short hike up Puffer Butte within Fields Spring State Park rewards you with stunning views that span east across the Snake River to Idaho and south to the lofty jagged Wallowa Mountains of Oregon. And while the views are grand, so are the wildflowers.

GETTING THERE
From Clarkston, drive 30.5 miles south on State Route 129 to Fields Spring State Park (the entrance is 4 miles past the tiny community of Anatone). Turn left into the park

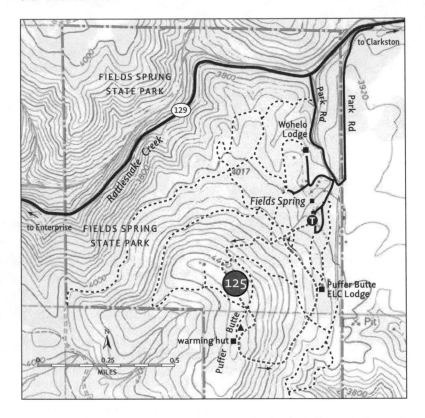

and come to a four-way junction in 0.4 mile. Continue straight for 0.1 mile to the large parking lot before the campground entrance. Locate the trailhead (elev. 4000 ft) on the south side of the lot.

ON THE TRAIL

Puffer Butte sits at the eastern edge of the Blue Mountains, teetering high above the sweltering Grande Ronde Valley. With its lofty elevation above 4000 feet, the butte is cloaked with cool pine, larch, and Douglas-fir forest. The butte's namesake

was a family—the Puffers—who frequently drove their cattle to the top of this butte when they observed Nez Perce peoples travel through the canyon below. The Nez Perce were forcibly removed from southeast Washington—once part of their traditional lands—in the 1870s.

The trail begins in mature conifer forest with a lush understory of maple. At 0.2 mile, just after crossing a closed-to-vehicles woods road (excellent for skiing in winter), reach a junction. Continue right—you'll be returning on the trail to your left. Soon after-

Grand views of the Grande Ronde Valley from Puffer Butte

ward, reach another junction. Bear left—the trail right leads to the Wohelo Lodge, one of two environmental learning centers within the 792-acre state park.

As you ascend gentle slopes, keep your senses tuned to the surroundings for wildlife. Elk and deer are profuse here, as are grouse and wild turkeys. There's little doubt that you'll be flushing these game birds out of the brush. At 0.8 mile, once again cross one of the park's service roads; then soon afterward, cross another one.

Now easily hiking along the broad butte, reach a junction at 1 mile with a short spur that bears right to Puffer's wooded, viewless 4500-foot summit. Visit if you like—then continue straight, reaching another junction at 1.2 miles at the edge of a sprawling meadow. Just to the right at timber's edge is the park's winter warming hut. If you haven't figured it out yet, Fields Spring State Park is a popular and excellent snowshoe and ski-touring center in the winter.

Your loop hike heads left across wide-open meadows of swaying grasses and dazzling wildflowers, including penstemon, daisies, desert parsley, scarlet gilia, sego lilies, and arrowleaf balsamroot. And outdoing the floral arrangement is the view—it's breathtaking! Stare south across the Grande Ronde Valley to the sky-piercing Wallowa Mountains; and east to the Craig Mountains of Idaho hovering above the massive Snake River Canyon.

The way then bends north, descending from the grassy slopes into pine forest. Continue losing elevation and after crossing a park road reach a junction at 1.9 miles. The trail right leads to primitive camping and more woods road—stay left, soon reaching the Puffer Butte Environmental Learning Center Lodge (elev. 4000 ft).

Locate the Spotted Bear Trail on the west side of the lodge and follow this short path 0.3 mile through pine forest, across a park road, and back to the main trail at a familiar junction (elev. 4100 ft). Turn right and return to the trailhead in 0.2 mile.

EXTENDING YOUR TRIP
Easily extend your hike by roaming the park's miles of old woods roads. Visit Fields Spring near the Wohelo Lodge and consider spending a peaceful night camping in the park under a cool canopy of pine and fir.

Conservation and Trail Organizations

GENERAL

Blue Mountain Land Trust
(509) 525-3136
http://bmlt.org

Chelan-Douglas Land Trust
(509) 667-9708
www.cdlandtrust.org

Conservation Northwest
(360) 671-9950
www.conservationnw.org

Ferry County Rail Trail Partners
www.ferrycountyrailtrail.com

Ferry County Trails Association
http://fctrails.com

Friends of Badger Mountain
www.friendsofbadger.org

Friends of Little Pend Oreille National Wildlife Refuge
http://refugefriends.com

Intermountain Alpine Club
www.imacnw.org

Kettle Range Conservation Group
www.kettlerange.org

Pacific Northwest Trail Association
(877) 854-7665
www.pnt.org

Tapteal Greenway Association
(509) 627-3621
www.tapteal.org

Washington Nature Conservancy
(206) 343-4345
www.nature.org/washington

Washington Trails Association
(206) 625-1367
www.wta.org

SPOKANE REGION

The Backpacking Club
(509) 467- 8099
www.backpackingclub.macwebsite
builder.com

Dishman Hills Conservancy
www.dhnaa.org

Friends of Mount Spokane State Park
www.mountspokane.org

Friends of the Spokane River Centennial Trail
(509) 624-7188
www.spokanecentennialtrail.org

Friends of Turnbull National Wildlife Refuge
www.fotnwr.org

Hobnailers
www.inlandnorthwesttrails.org/events
/Hobnailers.asp

Inland Northwest Hikers
www.meetup.com/Inland-Northwest
-Hikers

Inland Northwest Land Trust
(509) 328-2939
www.inlandnwlandtrust.org

Inland Northwest Trails Coalition
www.inlandnorthwesttrails.org

The Lands Council
(509) 838-4912
www.landscouncil.org

Palisades
www.palisadesnw.com

Riverside State Park Foundation
http://riversidestatepark.org

Spokane Mountaineers
(509) 838-4974
www.spokanemountaineers.org

INDEX

About the Authors

Rich Landers (left) and Craig Romano (Photo by Aaron Theisen)

Rich Landers, a native Montanan, has been the Outdoors editor for the *Spokesman-Review* in Spokane since 1977, covering hiking, conservation, hunting, fishing, climbing, bicycling, public lands, and other outdoor pursuits. He is a contributing writer for *Field and Stream* magazine and author of *100 Hikes in the Inland Northwest* and *Paddling Washington*.

Craig Romano grew up in rural New Hampshire, where he fell in love with the natural world. He has traveled from Alaska to Argentina, Sicily to South Korea, seeking wild and spectacular landscapes. He ranks Washington State among the most beautiful places on the planet, and he has hiked it from Cape Flattery to Puffer Butte. He is a columnist for *Northwest Runner* and *Outdoors NW* and author of nine books, among them *Day Hiking Olympic Peninsula*, *Day Hiking North Cascades*, *Day Hiking Columbia River Gorge*, *Backpacking Washington*, and *Columbia Highlands: Exploring Washington's Last Frontier*, which was recognized in 2010 as a Washington Reads book for its contribution to the state's cultural heritage. When not hiking and writing, he can be found napping with his wife, Heather, and cats, Giuseppe and Scruffy Gray, at his home in Skagit County. Visit him at http://CraigRomano.com and on Facebook at "Craig Romano Guidebook Author."

THE MOUNTAINEERS, founded in 1906, is a nonprofit outdoor activity and conservation organization whose mission is "to explore, study, preserve, and enjoy the natural beauty of the outdoors...." Based in Seattle, Washington, it is now one of the largest such organizations in the United States, with seven branches throughout Washington State.

The Mountaineers sponsors both classes and year-round outdoor activities in the Pacific Northwest, which include hiking, mountain climbing, ski-touring, snowshoeing, bicycling, camping, canoeing and kayaking, nature study, sailing, and adventure travel. The Mountaineers' conservation division supports environmental causes through educational activities, sponsoring legislation, and presenting informational programs.

All activities are led by skilled, experienced volunteers, who are dedicated to promoting safe and responsible enjoyment and preservation of the outdoors.

If you would like to participate in these organized outdoor activities or programs, consider a membership in The Mountaineers. For information and an application, write or call The Mountaineers Program Center, 7700 Sand Point Way NE, Seattle, WA 98115-3996; phone 206-521-6001; visit www.mountaineers.org; or email info@mountaineers.org.

The Mountaineers Books, an active, nonprofit publishing program of The Mountaineers, produces guidebooks, instructional texts, historical works, natural history guides, and works on environmental conservation. All books produced by The Mountaineers Books fulfill the mission of The Mountaineers. Visit www.mountaineersbooks.org to find details about all our titles and the latest author events, as well as videos, web clips, links, and more!

The Mountaineers Books
1001 SW Klickitat Way, Suite 201
Seattle, WA 98134
800-553-4453
mbooks@mountaineersbooks.org

The Mountaineers Books is proud to be a corporate sponsor of The Leave No Trace Center for Outdoor Ethics, whose mission is to promote and inspire responsible outdoor recreation through education, research, and partnerships. The Leave No Trace program is focused specifically on human-powered (non-motorized) recreation.

Leave No Trace strives to educate visitors about the nature of their recreational impacts and offers techniques to prevent and minimize such impacts. Leave No Trace is best understood as an educational and ethical program, not as a set of rules and regulations.

For more information, visit www.lnt.org, or call 800-332-4100.

OTHER TITLES YOU MIGHT ENJOY FROM THE MOUNTAINEERS BOOKS

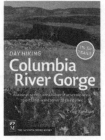

Day Hiking Columbia River Gorge
Romano
100+ fabulous hikes in and around the
Columbia River Gorge Scenic Area—
plus the Portland region

Day Hiking Central Cascades
Romano and Bauer
125 great hikes in the heart of
Washington State—including Lake Chelan

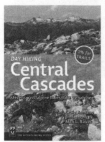

Day Hiking North Cascades
Romano
125 glorious hikes in the North Cascades…
and the San Juans too!

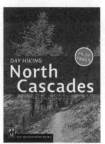

Backpacking Washington
Romano
70 overnight and multiday
routes throughout Washington State

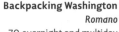

Day Hiking Snoqualmie Region
Nelson and Bauer
125 gorgeous hikes close to the Puget
Sound region—includes the Alpine Lakes

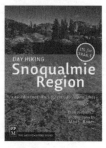

Day Hiking Olympic Peninsula
Romano
125 excellent hikes on the rugged, wild,
and beautiful Olympic Peninsula—
coast included!

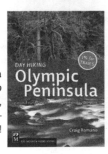

**The Mountaineers Books has more than
500 outdoor recreation titles in print.**
Visit www.mountaineersbooks.org for details.